D1222001

Social Control and
the State

Social Control and the State

Edited by
STANLEY COHEN and ANDREW SCULL

St. Martin's Press   New York

© Introduction Stanley Cohen and Andrew Scull, 1983
© Text Martin Robertson, 1983

All rights reserved. For information, write:
St. Martin's Press, Inc., 175 Fifth Avenue, New York, NY 10010
Printed in Great Britain
First published in the United States of America in 1983

ISBN 0–312–73167–1

Library of Congress Cataloging in Publication Data
Main entry under title:

Social control and the state.

   1. Social control—Addresses, essays, lectures.
2. State, The—Addresses, essays, lectures.   3. Social
control—History—Addresses, essays, lectures.
4. State, The—History—Addresses, essays, lectures.
I. Cohen, Stanley.   II. Scull, Andrew T.
HM73.S6254   1983   303.3'3   83-10960
ISBN 0–312–73167–1

Contents

303,33
So13C

Contents

PART II   CASE STUDIES

List of Contributors

JULIE VAIL BROWN is an Assistant Professor of Sociology at the University of North Carolina.

ROBERT CASTEL is Professor of Sociology at the University of Paris–viii.

STANLEY COHEN is a Professor in the Institute of Criminology, Hebrew University, Jerusalem.

PAUL HAAGEN is a Law Clerk for the Honorable Arlin Adams, US District Court, Philadelphia.

MICHAEL IGNATIEFF is a Fellow of King's College, Cambridge.

DAVID INGLEBY is at the Institute for Developmental Psychology, State University of Utrecht.

JOHN A. MAYER is an Assistant Professor of History at Oklahoma Baptist University.

DAVID PHILIPS is in the Department of History, University of Melbourne.

NICOLE HAHN RAFTER is an Associate Professor at the College of Criminal Justice, Northeastern University, Boston.

PAUL ROCK is Reader in Sociology at the London School of Economics and Political Science.

DAVID ROTHMAN is Professor of History at Columbia University, New York City.

ANDREW SCULL is an Associate Professor of Sociology at the University of California at San Diego.

STEVEN SPITZER is Chair of the Department of Sociology, Suffolk University, Boston.

GARETH STEDMAN JONES is a Lecturer in History and Fellow of Kings College, Cambridge.

Introduction: Social Control in History and Sociology

STANLEY COHEN and ANDREW SCULL

Specially written for this volume

The interrelationships between the modern state and its apparatus of social control have, in the past decade or so, become the focus for much innovative work in both history and sociology. There has, in fact, been a striking convergence of interests and cross-fertilization of ideas and methods between the two disciplines as they have approached this subject matter. Having long been considered topics of little intellectual moment, the history of crime and its punishment, of craziness and its treatment, of deviance and its control, of poverty and its containment have all become issues of major scholarly concern. The outcome has been a quantum leap in the quality and quantity of work being done in the field.

This volume is both a product of and a commentary upon this transformative period. The essays we have collected – dealing mainly with crime and madness – attempt to sort out and make sense of a diverse and rapidly expanding literature; to examine some of the (often fierce) debates that are so prominent a feature of this recent work on social control; to provide a sampling of empirical case studies indicative of the range of topics now being tackled; and to suggest some promising directions for future work on the subject. In an effort to present as broad and representative a survey as possible, we have made little attempt to secure an artificial unity of perspective from the contributors. To have done so would have been to impose an arbitrary and premature form of closure on a field very much characterized by sharp differences of emphasis and interpretations, differences that reflect the varying disciplinary backgrounds and intellectual and ideological presuppositions of those contributing to it.

'REVISIONISM' IN HISTORY?

Traditionally, changes in penal practices or transformations in characteristic societal responses to madness and the like have been at once

1

portrayed and explained as 'reform'. Within this quintessentially optimistic perspective, change is seen as inherently progressive. The direction of movement – from barbarism to enlightenment, from ignorance to expertly guided intervention, from cruelty and vindictiveness to scientific humanism – is viewed as clear and unambiguous. Granted, reality is frequently recalcitrant. Benevolent schemes at times end in failure, and control systems, like all human inventions, imperfectly and unevenly reflect the moral vision that creates and sustains them. But in time, further episodes of reform – better financed, better staffed, better understood – will doubtless ameliorate or eliminate the most serious problems. Even in the absence of such fine-tuning, the historical record of our society's approaches to the management of deviance is worthy of celebration rather than scepticism (McKelvey, 1977).

The adherents of this dominant model of progress, whether historical observers or current social policy practitioners, are the genuine heirs of the nineteenth-century reform tradition (Cohen, 1983). But reform, progress, humanitarianism, benevolence, doing good – these are precisely the taken-for-granted signifiers of this tradition now under attack. A 'revisionist' history – as Ignatieff and Philips explain, from somewhat different perspectives, in chapters 3 and 4 – has emerged with some shared points of departure: scepticism about the professed aims, beliefs and intentions of the reformers; concern with the analysis of power and its effects; curiosity about the relationship between intentions and consequences; determination to locate the reform enterprise in the social, economic and political contexts of the period. The problem of maintaining the social order – in the case of crime, so obvious; in the case of mental illness, less so, but still traceable (chapter 7) – becomes dominant.

This is not to say, though, that all those who depart from the reform vision of history constitute a unitary 'revisionist' school. The defenders of progressivism – for obvious reasons a more indignant defence for mental illness (see for example Quen, 1973, and Grob, 1978) than for crime – tend to play down the existence of competing and sometimes mutually incompatible explanations of major shifts in social control style and practice. One feature of all recent work – a self-conscious distancing from earlier conventional wisdom – is focused on, to the exclusion of all else. This gives a spurious ease to the counter-attack on 'revisionism'. But as Rothman and Scull (variously, participators and commentators in this debate) show in their current reviews which we include (chapters 5 and 6), the terrain is a lot more complicated. One side's revisionism is the other side's traditionalism. Sharp differences, for example, emerge on the question of *intentions*: are they to be taken simply at face value (and hence 'failure' explained in terms of faulty implementation), or seen as complex and potentially suspicious (with 'failure' the product of a permanent tension between 'conscience' and 'convenience'), or basically as ideological masks for more fundamental social changes (with 'failure' bearing no connection to professed purpose)?

Then – still staying within revisionist ranks – there is obviously a huge difference, in style and content, between the work of French post-structuralists, notably Foucault, and those working within the British historical materialist traditions, such as Thompson and Hay. Both bodies of work represent a clear advance over the amateurish and frequently self-serving accounts of the evolution of the social control apparatus previously offered.[1] But Foucault's work, part of which is appraised in David Ingleby's contribution on 'mental health and the social order' (chapter 7), is part of a grandiose project to produce an 'archaeology of the human sciences', even a 'history of the human soul'. While seeking to illuminate 'the genealogy of power', Foucault explicitly rejects any explanatory schema in which notions of central state power and the economic determination of action play any major role. Indeed, he presents neither a systematic discussion of politics nor a serious dissection of economic structures, part of the more general 'negative principle of avoiding Marxist formulations [that] runs through all his later work' (as Ingleby argues).

Moreover, despite his explicit concern with delineating major shifts in our responses to madness, criminality and sexuality, and despite his preoccupation with capturing the essence of the peculiarly distinctive 'power–knowledge spiral' that ushers in the modern world, he lacks the historian's commitment to the specifics of chronology (though the work is based on extensive if idiosyncratic archival research). He actually eschews any formal notion of historical causation. In all these respects, and also in his rejection of the notion of people as active historical subjects ('men making their own history'), his work is remarkably at variance with the more familiar Marxist themes in the histories produced by Thompson, Hay and their associates.[2] Ignatieff (chapter 4) pays particular attention to such concepts as 'agency' and historical determinism in comparing Foucault's work to the project of classical Marxism.

Central to Thompson's and Hay's concerns – summarized by Philips in chapter 3 – is a commitment, within an undogmatic Marxist framework, to examine legal repression as an instrument of state and, indirectly, of class power. Here we find a scrupulous regard for submitting the development of 'theory' to the discipline of empirical procedures and controls (as Thompson puts it, for him the alternative is 'a leap out of knowledge and into theology . . . a leap into the self-generation of "knowledge" according to [one's] own theoretical procedures' (Thompson, 1978,

p. 225); a delight, especially evident in *Whigs and Hunters* (Thompson, 1975), in the reconstruction of the particularities and peculiarities of person and place; and a reiterated emphasis on the active role that people play, individually and collectively, in the transformation of their social worlds. As Marxists, Thompson and his followers are committed to seeing the law and its enforcement as intimately bound up with class struggle as mediated through the activities of the state and the political apparatus. But they insistently return to the problem of the *legitimation* of coercion and domination, ultimately conceding the crucial and at least partially autonomous impact of ideological structures on the patterning of social control.

Whereas, as one would expect, conflict is seen as pervasive and ubiquitous in these products of English Marxist historiography, it makes only a token appearance in yet another variety of revisionist historical work on social control, a school of which David Rothman is perhaps the most representative figure. In his essentially functionalist and pluralist view (as Scull and Ingleby argue in chapters 6 and 7), social control does not operate in the defence of any particular social interests, but rather originates as a broadly based corrective to *generally* perceived threats of social disequilibrium and disorder. But (and it is here that Rothman does break with the conventional view of reform) society's response turns out to be *systematically* misguided; the programmes embarked upon are all but uniformly disastrous failures; their authors' goals are regularly and routinely undermined by pragmatic and managerial considerations; conscience inevitably proves no match for convenience (Rothman, 1971, 1980). Disillusioned and disenchanted with 'doing good', Rothman provides us with an ingenious and sophisticated argument for recognizing 'the limits of benevolence' (Gaylin *et al.*, 1978), buttressed by a wide-ranging assault on the deficiencies and blindnesses of the reform vision.

The traditions behind each of these three revisionist exemplars – Thompson, Foucault and Rothman – leave us with very different types of history, very different ways of showing that the motives and programmes of the reformers were 'more complicated than a simple revulsion at cruelty or impatience with administrative incompetence' (Ignatieff, chapter 4). But one side's complications are the other side's simplifications – and revisionism is now under attack for oversimplification, or reductionism.[3] All the contributions in Part I (note Ignatieff's description of himself as a 'former though unrepentant' member of the revisionist school) give us the flavour of current criticism, self-criticism and counter-attack.

AND IN SOCIOLOGY?

From the ranks of the historians and philosophers, then, we are offered a variety of interpretations which reflect deeply entrenched meta-theoretical differences about epistemology, materialist-versus-idealist versions of history, and the sources of social change. Each of the perspectives we have discussed has had a profound effect on sociologists' attempts to develop a theoretical understanding of the transformation of control structures. But if historical work on social control is evolving in these somewhat different directions, then sociological work itself can be said to be *re*-volving. In the classical nineteenth-century sociological tradition, the concept of social control was at the centre of the enterprise – both in relating sociology to political philosophy and in solving the emergent debates of macro-sociology (Janowitz, 1975). The unit of analysis was the whole society, and the question posed was how to achieve a degree of organization and regulation consistent with certain moral principles, but without an excessive degree of purely coercive control.

This was the great problem of 'social order' – posed most explicitly, of course, by Durkheim and his functionalist inheritors and understood in different ways by Weber and Marx. An examination of the continuities and discontinuities from this classical lineage is a rewarding exercise (see Janowitz, 1975). What largely happened in the twentieth-century development of sociology in America was that the concept of social control lost its original connections with the classic macro-sociological questions of order, authority, power and social organization. It was not that the concept became unimportant. Indeed, in the first indigenous American sociological tradition – the Chicago School of the 1920s – the concept of social control was much more central than is usually recognized. In Park and Burgess's famous text (1924, p. 785), 'All social problems turn out finally to be problems of social control.' Social control should be '. . . the central fact and the central problem of sociology' (p. 42).

But the way this sociological task was interpreted gave the clue to how the concept of social control was later to be used. Sociology was to be '. . . a point of view and method for investigating the processes by which individuals are inducted to and induced to co-operate in some sort of permanent corporate existence we call society' (Park and Burgess, 1924, p. 42). Whether functionalist or interactionist, this essentially social psychological perspective on social control was to remain dominant. The emphasis was on the *processes* of the individual's induction into society – that is, the problem of socialization.

Pick up now any sociological dictionary, encyclopaedia or first-year textbook – the sources of the discipline's folk wisdom – and this picture of social control still remains. Here is an example from a standard American introductory textbook: 'Sociologists use the term social control to describe all the means and processes whereby a group or society secures its members' conformity to expectations' (Horton and Hunt, 1980, p. 141). On the basis of such definitions, the standard method of interpreting the concept of social control is then to erect a typology of the 'means and processes' by which social conformity is achieved. Typically, the first and most basic process is seen as 'internalization' or socialization; then, second, there are the 'informal' means of social control such as social pressure, peer group opinion and so on; finally, there are the 'formal' methods of social control – those 'elaborated and specialized mechanisms', as Parsons blandly termed them, such as the police, the legal system and 'force'. Typically, little attempt is made to distinguish between the relative importance of these processes (conformity is achieved, according to the textbooks, 'in a number of ways whose relative importance is difficult to measure'; Horton and Hunt, 1980, p. 141), except to assume that socialization (teaching the individual to *want* to follow norms) is the most effective process. Only if it fails are rewards and punishments by external agencies brought into the picture.

This is not the place for general comment on the weakness of such formulations; they have been well exposed in the broader 'crisis' of sociology in the last two decades. This is social control without history and politics, a concept severed from its original organic connection in the project of classical sociology. Little wonder that, when historians came to look at such formulations, they found so much to criticize (see Mayer, chapter 1 and Stedman Jones, chapter 2 below).

Paradoxically, it took a number of related developments in the sociology of crime and deviance from the late 1960s onwards to re-connect the study of social control with its original connotations: paradoxically, because these were the most theoretically impoverished sub-fields of sociology. Not only were they identified fully with the simple-minded reform view of the history of control, but they carried to its extreme the separation of formal organized social control from the general question of conformity (a separation defensible perhaps only for definitional purposes – see Clark and Gibbs, 1965). Criminological positivism, as Matza so clearly showed, achieved the astonishing task of separating the study of crime from the study of the state (Matza, 1968). The reconnections came from many diverse sources. First, there was labelling theory, which – whatever its ultimate theoretical limitations – forced a reconsideration of social control not just as a reactive, reparative mechanism when other measures 'fail', but as the active force in shaping the very stuff of crime and deviance. As Lemert expressed it in his famous formula, 'Older sociology . . . tended to rest heavily upon the idea that deviance leads to social control. I have come to believe that the reverse idea (i.e. social control leads to deviance) is equally tenable and the potentially richer premise for studying deviance in modern society' (Lemert, 1967, p. ix).

This ironical world view of labelling theory was to find resonances from many other directions (Pearson, 1975). Such social movements as anti-psychiatry, radical social work, de-medicalization and de-schooling both fed from and contributed to an image of social control quite different from the bland textbook formulations. At its extreme, all state social policies began to be seen as forms of social control (Higgins, 1980), all ameliorative and progressive reforms as merely a subtle camouflage for further repression (Cohen, 1983).

But rhetorical extremes aside, the key theoretical development was to rebuild labelling theory's limited studies of social control 'culture' or control agencies on to a more politically and historically informed map. Ethnography gave way to history (see, for example, Scull, 1977). An emerging Marxist criminology and sociology of law returned the state to the centre of the drama. This was the point at which sociologists of crime and deviance 'rediscovered' history (Pearson, 1978) and where the diverse revisionist writings we mentioned earlier – those of Rothman, of E.P. Thompson's school, of Foucault and the French neo-structuralists – began having the type of influence that this volume records. What became recognized is that matters of crime, deviance, delinquency, illness and madness don't just every now and then touch on wider issues of politics, economics and power. They are intimately related – and, indeed, these very categories are politically defined.

SELECTING SOME ISSUES

Thus, both from history and sociology, there is an expanding literature on the relationships between social control systems and the societies of which they are a part and an essential support. Most such recent contributions are 'revisionist' in the sense that they seek to overturn conventional wisdom, or what has passed for wisdom; though in other respects, as we have suggested, they are strikingly different. The contributions, the strengths and the weaknesses of each approach need to be carefully distinguished and assessed, and it is something of this sort of intellectual stock-taking and critique that Part I of this volume is designed to provide. Each of the essays we have selected provides a separate viewing – sometimes enthusiastic, sometimes much less so – of a common set of themes. These include the uses of the concept of social control itself (Mayer, Stedman Jones and Rothman) and the competing claims of various current schools to have uncovered the history of the criminal law (Philips), psychiatry and mental hospitals (Scull and Ingleby) and the punitive institution in general (Ignatieff).

Because each of these contributions deals with a similar historical period, focuses on the same developments and engages with a common set of theoretical problems, a small degree of repetition is inevitable. But we have chosen to let our specially commissioned authors (Mayer, Philips and Ingleby) preserve the internal flow of their argument and also not to cut the reprinted pieces (Stedman Jones, Ignatieff, Rothman and Scull).

Part II, by contrast, consists of a series of separate empirical studies. These essays are not meant to cover the whole field but to provide a sampling of the kind of work that can be done within the new models. The four essays on various aspects of crime control (Haagen, Rafter, Rock and Spitzer) as well as the two essays on psychiatric control (Castel and Brown) all deal with various aspects of rationality and rationalization.

English criminal law in the eighteenth century was, until recently, widely reviewed as 'irrational' as well as barbaric. In making such judgements, historians were echoing the criticisms first made in the eighteenth century by such reformers as Beccaria and Bentham, a critique that culminated in the nineteenth-century reforms of Peel and Romilly. The absence and resistance to the establishment of a professional police; the consequent inefficiencies and uncertainties attached to the enforcement process; the compounding of these by the widespread and capricious use of pardons and the commuting of sentences; and the often disproportionate and savage character of the punishment visited upon those violators subjected to the full rigours of the law – all these were taken to be evidence of the backward and unenlightened character of England's rulers, their blind pig-headedness and lack of vision.[4]

The more recent work of Hay and his colleagues (reviewed by Philips in chapter 3)[5] has challenged this portrait. It suggests that, from the viewpoint of the English ruling class of the period, the system that Bentham and others attacked was instead quite 'rational' and well adapted to the maintenance of their hegemony.

Paul Haagen's essay (chapter 9) applies similar reasoning to an area of eighteenth-century law that conventionally has been seen as even more unambiguously senseless and counterproductive: the institution of imprisonment for debt. Until the legislation of the early nineteenth century instituted the new era of reformed prisons and penitentiaries, debtors formed one of the principal elements of the English prison population. Imprisonment for debt imposed massive social costs on English society, and appears at first sight to have been wholly without compensating social advantages. In fact, however, Haagen shows that, both instrumentally and ideologically, the law of debtor and creditor played a vital role in underpinning the power and privileged position of the English ruling class and in protecting property rights more generally. An apparently marginal element in the social control apparatus of eighteenth-century England, debt law turns out to be an important mechanism in protecting a social order that rested upon the exercise of discretionary, private power. And simultaneously it provides a subtle reflection and refraction of the fundamental logic of the social system it underwrites.

Stressing the essential weakness of the English state apparatus in the early eighteenth century, and the consequent uncertainties of legal domination, Rock's essay (chapter 8) provides a quite different perspective on the relationships that existed at this time between the peculiar geometry of the social order and the characteristic structures of social control. In constructing a fine-grained phenomenological description of this fragmented and highly decentralized system, he reminds us how remote from a modern 'policed' society early eighteenth-century England was, and how essentially 'unrationalized' its characteristic responses to crime yet remained.

The subsequent rationalization of the crime control apparatus under capitalism is explored on a larger and more varied canvas by Spitzer (chapter 13). He uses a comparative framework to analyse some connections between the changing forms assumed by the social control apparatus and the character of the larger social and political order. Foucault's history is one of the gradual development over the past several centuries of an ever more 'subtle, calculated technology of subjection', the steady refinements of disciplinary techniques that have made it possible to 'insert the power to punish more deeply into the social body' (Foucault, 1977).[6] But what is missing from this account is a systematic attempt to relate these developments to a recognizable portrait of either economic or political structures. While sharing Foucault's conception of punishment as 'a political tactic', and his scepticism about claims that the changing forms of penality can be equated in any simple sense with a process of humanization, Spitzer suggests a much more explicit set of linkages between the forms of crime control and changes in the underlying social and political ordering of people's lives. Similarly, he breaks with Foucault's over-simple equation of modernity and rationalization, seeing punishment, in Ignatieff's words (chapter 4) as 'the site of a recurring battle between rationalizing intentions and institutions, interests, and communities which resist, often with persistent success'.

Part of the interest and value of Spitzer's essay derives from his willingness to make use of materials drawn from non-Western societies to explore some of the complexities of accounting for changes in the crime control apparatus. Thus, the pao-chia system of Ch'ing China, the uses of the principle of vicarious liability in Tokugawa Japan and British colonial reliance on 'alien' tribal groups to police indigenous populations all serve to illustrate the dynamics and limitations of a variety of indirect and extensive control systems, and suggest some of the factors that lay behind the emergence of the more direct and intensive control systems characteristically found in modern industrial societies.[7]

In similar fashion, Brown's essay (chapter 11) on psychiatry in tsarist Russia provides a valuable comparative perspective on changing societal responses to madness. As the essays by Scull and Ingleby (chapters 6 and 7) reflect, most recent work on mental health and the social order has focused on developments in a handful of Western societies. Developments in Russia in some respects paralleled those in Western Europe, albeit at a somewhat later date: the growth of a state-sponsored network of asylums; the emergence for at least a brief period of a sense of optimism about the possibility of 'curing' lunatics; and the constitution of a body of 'professionals' laying claim to expertise in the diagnosis and treatment of insanity. But they came about, of course, in very different ways and in a strikingly different social setting: an authoritarian society wracked by internal tensions and divisions, an economically backward, semi-feudal social order in which the central government itself was the major force behind asylum reform. The resultant differences in the bureaucratic and professional apparatus of control are of considerable intrinsic interest, but they also suggest the socially contingent nature of the resolutions reached in the West. In Russia, for example, the asylum is an explicitly coercive institution, lacking even the thin disguise as a therapeutic institution it retained in Western Europe and North America and instead overtly forming part of the apparatus of repression. And the psychiatric 'profession' is denied even the precarious degree of autonomy and privileged status acquired by its European counterpart (see Scull, 1975, 1976).

As a result, while more directly and explicitly employed as agents of the state than their counterparts elsewhere, Russian psychiatrists are paradoxically much more sharply at odds with the political apparatus they allegedly serve. Whereas the 'free' and independent professionals of Western Europe and North America constitute an almost uniformly conservative group committed to the preservation of existing social arrangements, Russian psychiatrists in the late nineteenth century became radically disaffected and fiercely critical of the tsarist regime – an alienation that increased in proportion to their own failure to secure control over either the terms or the technical content of their work.

As this reminds us, social control in the modern era has been increasingly presided over by 'experts' in managing and manipulating an even more carefully differentiated population of deviants. Though largely unsuccessful in tsarist Russia, psychiatrists elsewhere secured at least a surface acceptance of their claims to be able, by reason of their superior knowledge, to identify, treat and rehabilitate their clientele. This psychiatric *savoir*, like that produced by other groups of controllers, has played a significant part in constituting and reconstituting the moral boundaries of the community, and accordingly demands critical scrutiny. Foucault's attempts to map modern discourses of madness and insanity and to see them as techniques of power, part of a 'common history of power relations and object relations' (Foucault, 1977, p. 24), are perhaps the most wide-ranging and ambitious assaults on this territory, but they are scarcely unique. In France, no less than in the English-speaking world, others have sought to refute, criticize, modify and extend his analyses, none more provocatively than Robert Castel, whose work has hitherto been largely ignored in England and North America (see Castel, 1976, 1979). In the light of the differences of both data and method, which, as Ingleby points out, separate French from English and American discussions of social control, the reader might profitably compare Castel's account of moral treatment – here (chapter 10) translated for the first time – with a recent discussion of its English variant (see Scull, 1981).

The differentiation of response to deviant populations proceeded, of course, on several fronts. Just as the mad were separated from the bad, then the mentally retarded from the mentally ill and the psychotic from the neurotic, so too did the various sorts of deviant come to be classified by age and by gender. For example, in the late nineteenth century juvenile delinquents began to be separated out for special treatment (Schlossman, 1977; Platt, 1969); Elaine Showalter has recently examined the development of elaborate accounts of and responses to women's special susceptibility to insanity (Showalter, 1981). In chapter 12, Rafter extends the analysis of differentiation by gender, examining the emergence of an entirely new type of penal institution, the women's reformatories that were constructed in the United States in the late nineteenth and early twentieth centuries. By focusing particular attention on one of these institutions, the Western House of Refuge in Albion, New York, she is able to exploit a rich store of archival material to survey both the reformatory's claims and the actual effects of its efforts to control and transform its inmates.

Gender remains – both in case studies and more particularly in general revisionist theories – a neglected concept compared with class and power. But few areas in the history and sociology of the 'normal' remain untouched by these stories about the social control of the abnormal, the deviant, the pathological. This, at least, is what we hope this collection shows.

NOTES

1. The most blatantly self-serving accounts being psychiatric histories written by psychiatrists – see Zilboorg and Henry (1973); Alexander and Selesnick (1967); Hunter and MacAlpine (1973).
2. Foucault's work, of course, falling squarely in the intellectual tradition that Thompson (1978) has recently subjected to such scathing criticism.
3. Note, for example, Sedgwick's sustained polemic against the conservative undercurrents of anti-psychiatry and similar attacks on the orthodox medical model of mental illness. His problem is to revise the revisionists without agreeing with the conservatives. Thus, with regard to Foucault's 'anti-history' of psychiatry: 'To reject Foucault's anti-psychiatric romanticism is not to endorse the liberal public-relations history of mental medicine' (Sedgwick, 1982, p. 147).
4. For the standard exposition of this view, see Radzinowicz (1948, 1956).
5. See also Spitzer and Scull (1977).
6. A speculative extension of this history into the present and future is to be found in Cohen (1979).
7. For an account of the influence of Western models in explaining and justifying the development of crime control models in the 'underdeveloped world', see Cohen (1982).

REFERENCES

Alexander, F.D. and Selesnick, S. (1967), *The History of Psychiatry*. London: Allen and Unwin.
Castel, R. (1976), *L'ordre psychiatrique: L'age d'or de l'alienisme*. Paris: Editions de Minuit.
Castel, R. (1979), *La Société psychiatrique avancée*. Paris: Editions Grisset.
Clark, A. and Gibbs, J.P. (1965), 'Social Control: A Reformulation', *Social Problems*, 12(4), 398–415.
Cohen, S. (1979), 'The Punitive City: Notes on the Future of Social Control', *Contemporary Crises*, 3(4), 339–63.
Cohen, S. (1982), 'Western Crime Control Models in the Third World: Benign or Malignant?', in R. Simon and S. Spitzer (eds), *Research in Law, Deviance and Social Control*, vol. 4. Greenwich, Conn.: JAI Press.
Cohen, S. (1983), 'Social Control Talk: Telling Stories about Correctional Change', in D. Garland and P. Young (eds), *The Power to Punish*. London: Heinemann.
Foucault, M. (1977), *Discipline and Punish*. London: Allen Lane; New York; Pantheon.
Gaylin, W. *et al.* (1978), *Doing Good: The Limits of Benevolence*. New York: Pantheon.

Grob, G. (1978), 'Public Policy-making and Social Policy', Paper delivered at Conference on the History of Public Policy, Harvard University, 4 November, 1978.

Hay, D. *et al.* (1975), *Albion's Fatal Tree: Crime and Society in Eighteenth-Century England*. London: Allen Lane.

Higgins, J. (1980), 'Social Control Theories of Social Policy', *Journal of Social Policy*, 9(1).

Horton, P.B. and Hunt, C.L. (1980), *Sociology*. New York: McGraw-Hill.

Hunter, R.A. and MacAlpine, I. (1973), *Psychiatry for the Poor*. London: Dawsons.

Janowitz, M. (1975), 'Sociological Theory and Social Control', *American Journal of Sociology*, 81(1), 82–108.

Lemert, E.M. (1967), *Human Deviance, Social Problems and Social Control*. Englewood Cliffs, New Jersey: Prentice-Hall.

Matza, D. (1968), *Becoming Deviant*. Englewood Cliffs, New Jersey: Prentice-Hall.

McKelvey, B. (1977), *American Prisons: A History of Good Intentions*. New York: Patterson-Smith.

Park, R.E. and Burgess, E.W. (1924), *Introduction to the Science of Sociology*. Chicago: University Press.

Pearson, G. (1975), *The Deviant Imagination*. London: Macmillan.

Pearson, G. (1978), 'Goths and Vandals: Crime in History', *Contemporary Crises*, 2(2), 119–39.

Platt, A. (1969), *The Child Savers*. Chicago: University Press.

Quen, J. (1973), Review of D. Rothman, *The Discovery of the Asylum,* in *Journal of Psychiatry and the Law*, 2, 105–20.

Radzinowicz, L. (1948, 1956), *A History of English Criminal Law and its Administration from 1750*, 2 vols. London: Stevens.

Rothman, D. (1971), *The Discovery of the Asylum: Social Order and Disorder in the New Republic*. Boston: Little, Brown.

Rothman, D. (1980), *Conscience and Convenience: The Asylum and its Alternatives in Progressive America*. Boston: Little, Brown.

Schlossman, S. (1977), *Love and the American Delinquent*. Chicago: University Press.

Scull, A. (1975), 'From Madness to Mental Illness: Medical Men as Moral Entrepreneurs', *European Journal of Sociology*, 16, 219–61.

Scull, A. (1976), 'Mad-doctors and Magistrates: English Psychiatry's Struggle for Professional Autonomy in the Nineteenth Century', *European Journal of Sociology*, 17, 279–305.

Scull, A. (1977), *Decarceration*, in *Community Treatment and Deviant*. Englewood Cliffs, New Jersey: Prentice-Hall.

Scull, A. (1981), 'Moral Treatment Reconsidered: Some Sociological Comments on an Episode in the History of British Psychiatry', chapter 4 in A. Scull (ed.), *Madhouses, Mad-doctors, and Madmen: The Social History of Psychiatry in the Victorian Era*. London: Athlone; Philadelphia: University of Pennsylvania Press.

Sedgwick, P. (1982), *Psychopolitics*. London: Pluto Press.

Showalter, E. (1981), 'Victorian Women and Insanity', chapter 12 in A. Scull (ed.), *Madhouses, Mad-doctors, and Madmen: The Social History of Psychiatry in the*

Victorian Era. London: Athlone; Philadelphia: University of Pennsylvania Press.

Spitzer, S. and Scull, A. (1977), 'Social Control in Historical Perspective: From Private to Public Responses to Crime', in D.F. Greenberg (ed.), *Corrections and Punishment*. Beverly Hills, California: Sage Publications.

Thompson, E.P. (1975), *Whigs and Hunters*. New York: Pantheon.

Thompson, E.P. (1978), *The Poverty of Theory*. London: Merlin Press.

Zilboorg, G. and Henry, G. (1973), *A History of Medical Psychology*. New York: W.W. Norton.

Part I

Reviews and Debates

1

Notes towards a Working Definition of Social Control in Historical Analysis

JOHN A. MAYER
Specially written for this volume

A number of historical interpretations of the nineteenth century, including many of those derived from the 'new social history', have followed a *gemeinschaft* to *gesellschaft* model in which a pre-modern or pre-industrial community is seen to have broken down under the processes of increasing market specialization and industrialization.[1] According to this schema, communal forms of organization no longer worked in a more specialized and functionally defined economic and social setting. Communal forms of socialization, control, work habits, time discipline and education became inadequate to the more complex society that emerged with industrialization and urbanization; yet many people, continually augmented by immigration from pre-modern cultures, persisted in older traditional sets of habits and beliefs.

According to this interpretation, the transitional stage of industrialism, with its breakdown of communal and deferential authority patterns, its economic and residential separation of classes, its disjunction between people's actual behaviours and the new behaviours needed for a modern industrial society, led to a sense of crisis among elites, generalized as a fear of the lower or dangerous classes.[2] To replace communal authority and pre-modern outlooks it became necessary to attempt to instil new habits of self-discipline upon the masses. Towards this end, members of the middle and upper classes who sensed this breakdown most acutely instituted a series of reform measures designed to impose social controls upon the lower classes; these reforms would control the behaviours of the lower classes towards the desired ends of self-discipline, industry, punctuality, thrift – in other words, towards what has come to be called middle-class morality.[3]

The widespread applicability of this modernizing synthesis has therefore led to a central importance for the concept of social control. The historical literature of social welfare and reform has come to be dominated by a social control interpretation which asserts that native-born upper and/or

17

middle classes used welfare agencies and institutions and various reform measures to control and direct the behaviour of the largely immigrant lower classes. The social control explanation has been widely applied to public and private relief agencies, to settlements, to juvenile reforms, to public schools and also to political reform movements; and these class-oriented social controls have been portrayed as having operated from the late eighteenth to the mid-twentieth century. The concept of social control has become the dominant paradigm for describing not simply reform movements, but inter-class relationships from the 1830s through the progressive era.[4]

In spite of this widespread applicability (or, more likely, because of it), social control interpreters have encountered a number of problems.[5] Scholars disagree on precisely who imposed the controls and what motivated them. One school argues that controllers were motivated by a nostalgia for a lost order, either as upper-class urban elites longing for a lost social authority and community,[6] or as middle-class migrants to the city longing for the community of their small-town origins.[7] Another focuses upon the exigencies of industrialism, whereby capitalists become the controlling group based on their needs for reliable modern workers, a stable and predictable social environment and the protection of their rights to ownership of the means of production.[8] A third school posits a rising professional middle class attempting to stake out areas of expertise and authority so that, while involved in addressing perceived social problems, they were also engaged in enhancing their own status, power and security.[9]

The 'nostalgia for a lost order' interpretation works best when applied to explicit attempts by reformers to re-establish a sense of community via increased inter-class contact – such as settlement houses and charity organization societies' friendly visiting programmes. But it works less well when applied to urban political reform, or to such social welfare measures as child labour laws; in the case of child labour laws and accompanying compulsory education laws, the reformers themselves saw their efforts as replacing older community methods in order to adjust to a new industrial order.[10]

Interpreters favouring the 'exigencies of capitalism' primarily argue the capitalist need for controlling workers in order to provide a stable, docile and productive labour force – hence the necessity to impose upon children and the working class the values of hard work and industriousness, thrift, temperance and so on. Depending on the rhetoric used, the argument is usually stated in functionalist terms. The functionalist argument emphasizes the new social functions needing to be performed during the transformation to a large-scale industrial economy; capitalists had more interests in seeing these functions performed because of their class economic interests.[11]

In some instances one senses a hidden agenda behind the 'exigencies of capitalism' argument: it poses a form of the standard question, why did socialism fail in America; or, less explicitly, why was there not more conflict, more protest and, finally, not a revolution, by workers and the poor? Alternatively, for those who do see conflict, why, out of all best possible worlds, did the United States emerge as an industrial capitalist society? The answer becomes that the poor and the workers were so controlled by the upper and middle classes that they could not effectively protest.[12]

A question rarely addressed, however, is whether the inculcation of middle-class values is an appropriate means to assure worker docility towards and acceptance of the industrial order. Would not public school education, with its emphasis on social mobility and knowledge as a tool of success, increase workers' expectations? Could not discipline better be achieved by placing children in factories than in schools? Would not teaching the poor to plan for success, to attempt to take control over their own futures by such measures as thrift, saving and personal discipline, sharply increase dissatisfaction and the likelihood of revolt during periods of hard times? If worker docility was the goal, would not a peasant outlook of docility towards one's condition and one's future as well as towards authority better serve the unskilled labour needs of industrialists than that of a psychologically modern outlook?[13]

The idea of a rising middle class staking out areas of expertise has received little attention from a social control perspective. Works on professionalization have emphasized the establishment of the profession rather than the particular programmatic activities that became the social control measures of the professionals.[14] Nevertheless, new professionals carried out many of the programmes studied by social control theorists. In charity and relief work, for example, social work experts emerged by the early 1900s. Were they themselves somehow controlled by the upper classes, as Gettelman and Piven and Cloward assert?[15] If so, then the mechanisms of upper-class control need to be demonstrated, not simply asserted. If not, how did their impulse towards professionalization lead to the particular programmatic activities they chose, and can those be related to a social control imperative inherent in professionalism?

In short, precisely who was doing the controlling, for what reasons, and by what means remain unclear issues.[16] Social control interpreters often do not address the further issue of whether the seemingly widespread social control measures were effective. Most social control studies concentrate upon the motivations of reformers, upon the resultant programmes such reformers set up, and then simply assert that the poor were controlled. They do not attempt to investigate rigorously whether behavioural changes were in fact imposed upon the poor.[17] For example, it has been argued that charity organization societies, through their systematic city-wide case study approach, attempted to control the working class by enforcing work, temperance, cleanliness, thrift and so on; but I know of no study that attempts to locate differences in working-class behaviours between cities that had and cities that did not have charity organization societies. Nor have I seen an argument showing evidence that the establishment of a charity organization society in any particular city produced marked differences in working-class behaviour and attitudes. The possibility of negative instances, or disproof of effectiveness, are simply not contained in the models used.

Indeed, a goodly number of social control studies, while patently presenting a functionalist analysis of institutions, utilize a rhetoric that suggests instead a primary concern to demonstrate the falseness of reformers' good intentions. Statements such as the following by Mohl and Betten abound in the literature of social control:

> Ostensibly created to aid the poor and provide for the needy, social welfare agencies and institutions have often served other and sometimes opposite purposes – inculcating or socializing children, Americanizing immigrants, serving up heavy doses of religion or morality, enforcing social order among the poor, and in general acting as instruments of social control.[18]

Such attempts to label reformers as essentially hypocritical and repressive agents of social control can occasionally lead to distortion of evidence. John Alexander, for example, in examining late eighteenth-century charity schools, argues that 'the poor were to be educated not so much for themselves as for society's needs.' For evidence he presents a statement by a supporter of the school who was 'thankful that children of the "poorer part of the community who would otherwise have been running through the streets habituating themselves to mischief, are rescued from vice and innured [sic] to habits of virtue and religion"'. Alexander then reiterates that 'These charities seem clearly designed not so much to elevate the poor as to keep them orderly.'[19] But his conclusions do not clearly follow from his evidence. Within the context of the times it could have been seriously and sincerely (and perhaps even realistically) believed that habits of virtue and religion would lead to success, or, at the least, would elevate one's life, whereas vice would in fact degrade it. Given such assumptions, these reformers would have had little trouble recognizing their own charitable motives – to elevate persons helped both them and society, as did saving them from degradation. The reformers would probably have had greater difficulty, in fact, in recognizing the motives Alexander ascribes to them from their own stated intentions.

Such essentially polemical labelling often produces interesting interpretive paradoxes. For example, Mohl and Betten's study of Gary, Indiana's settlements found that the settlements consciously attempted to destroy immigrant culture, imposed upon immigrants 'harsh demands for conformity and submission to American ways', and were derogatory, nativistic and paternalistic towards immigrants. Even Roman Catholic settlements 'represented imposition of American authority' (not defined in the article).[20] Given these statements, and given the fact that alternatives to these settlements existed (as Mohl and Betten point out), why would anyone subject themselves to such a barrage by going there? While the argument follows the logic of functionalism, the rhetoric used suggests that Mohl and Betten are interested primarily in demonstrating the bad faith (in an aggressive form of civil religion) of settlement workers; this being the case, they don't satisfactorily address this question.

Similarly, John Alexander argues that Philadelphia's relief system was a successful mechanism for controlling the poor: 'To be poor also meant the necessity to be deferential and of good character, for charity of all kinds required recommendations.' Yet, his description of the city's poor for the same period portrayed their behaviour as disorderly and even riotous, and he found their politics addressing their own interests rather than those of the rich.[21] The contradiction between his description of the poor and their supposed control by the upper classes is not explained.

The widespread attempt to label reform movements as social control efforts, and thus essentially conservative rather than liberal, while occasionally serving the purpose of polemics, often does little to help understand historical developments over time. Indeed, the very widespread usage of the concept of social control as a device to explain reform efforts produces a certain amount of confusion concerning the questions raised so far: who, why, how, and how well. It also confuses by clouding distinctions: if most social reform movements were simply class efforts to dominate workers, why was so much conflict engendered among the middle classes over a number of these reforms? What was the meaning of contemporary distinctions between liberal or reformer and the conservatives who opposed them? Were the various reforms all backed by the same groups whose overriding motives were to control the poor, or were there significant differences between various reformers and various reform movements? If the reformer's primary goal was social control, then for each reform one must ask, why this particular means of control rather than another?[22]

Thomas Bender, in looking at a number of discrete community studies, has found different authors asserting similar types of community breakdown; but these breakdowns stretch in time from the eighteenth to the twentieth centuries. He concludes that application of the *gemeinschaft* to *gesellschaft* model has led to ahistorical history.[23] A parallel problem exists with the concept of social control. Raymond Mohl argues that the search for order that Robert Wiebe discerned in the 1880s and 1890s actually emerged during the 1790s–1830s.[24] But if effective social control mechanisms were already in place by the 1830s, why did a sense of crisis and a new series of social control measures emerge a century later? Were antebellum social control efforts essentially responding similarly to similar problems as existed in the progressive era, as Mohl asserts?

The current social control approach, which in many cases attempts primarily to determine the 'real' and coercive motives behind particular reforms, and from such motives to infer function, cannot effectively deal with such questions. Part of the reason for this inability to make distinctions, as suggested above, may lie with historians' own motives. But the concept of social control being utilized presents a more serious reason. Its usage has been so broad as to render it more productive of confusion than of meaningful analysis. Social control has been applied to almost any upper- and/or middle-class effort to influence the behaviours of the working class. Such an attempt was initially useful for bringing the benefits of class analysis to reform efforts. But by working primarily to establish reformer motivation, and then to label reformers' efforts to influence behaviour as social control, distinctions between reforms have become blurred, and the meanings of particular reforms have been obscured; apples, oranges and peas have all been piled in the same basket.

Consequently, an analytic concept of social control that will provide clearer understandings of inter-class relations must be able to make distinctions among relationships different both in type and in context (place and time). In this sense, it must be able to become a narrower concept in order better to fit and explain particular situations. This would also help in analysing the actual functions performed by particular programmes.

At the same time, a broadening of the social control concept is needed. As currently utilized, historians have borrowed the sociological concept of social control as applied to the control of deviant behaviour;[25] thus the strong emphasis, in historical writing, on coercion. What social settlement workers saw as attempts to educate and uplift become, through the lens of deviance-derived social control theory, 'harsh demands to conform' and 'indoctrination'.[26] What is posited is the 'imposition' of controls, the 'enforcing' of work, the masses being 'terrorized'.[27] The social control concept as borrowed from the (often institutional) treatment of deviants is concerned with forcing individuals and groups to accept values and behaviours that are unwelcome (and sometimes alien) to them. With such a perspective, social control interpreters have tended to focus upon the systems and mechanisms set up by reformers to force change, and then to assume that social control occurred, that it was indeed imposed.

But in the nineteenth-century historical situation, the groups towards which controls were directed often were not deviants.[28] They were sub-cultural ethnic groups.[29] As such, they had great resources available with which to resist any attempts at control by the dominant culture. Their major resource, of course, was simply their membership in an ethnic culture; they possessed a systematic set of values, ways of perceiving, and group reinforcement of their beliefs, attitudes, mores and so on. Additionally, they had great institutional support. Every ethnic group developed its own institutional life – charities, mutual benefit societies, relief agencies, recreational groups, churches and cultural organizations. Such institutional completeness was perhaps most visible among the Jewish community; but it existed to a substantial degree in all ethnic groups. For example, Edward Kantowicz's study of Poles in Chicago found that 'the main theme of Polish-Catholic history in Chicago was the community building drive for institutional completeness'. And he believes they succeeded: 'The Polish ethnic groups supported such a wide range of institutions that they could perform nearly all the services their members required – religious, educational, political, recreational, economic – without recourse to the host society.'[30]

This immediately suggests at least two points: first, attempts by members of the dominant culture to control working-class ethnics through any single control system were limited in their effects. The existence of alternatives provided an element of choice, and the availability of choice severely strains the applicability of a deviancy model of social control measures.[31] Second, community building, the drive for institutional completeness and the desire for ethnic cohesiveness together suggest that ethnic leaders attempted to influence and guide the behaviours and attitudes of ethnic group members. So social control measures should not be seen simply as attempts by members of a dominant culture to control sub-cultures; each ethnic group also tried to control the behaviours of its own members. A broader definition of social control, related to its original meaning, would include these types of controls – a group's self-regulation of its own members.

Morris Janowitz has pointed out, in a different context, this need to return to a concept of social control broader than the deviancy model. Janowitz, in fact, defines social control as essentially the attempts by a social group or by a society to regulate its own members' behaviour without recourse to forcible coercion. Attempts to achieve such self-regulation imply either shared ideals, or attempts to find shared ideals which inform individuals' behaviour in such a way that coercion is unnecessary, yet society may function. He argues that the most prominent ideal within a free society is the preference for social control over coercion – citizens agree on the goal of limiting coercion to the greatest extent possible; but for society to continue functioning, and for coercion to remain limited, some forms of self-regulation are necessary. For Janowitz such social control efforts should be looked at in terms of the consequences of the failure of such self-regulation: increased legal coercion intruding into individuals' lives, or the loss of social order.[32]

The concept of social control as used by historians could therefore usefully be broken down into two broad categories: (1) coercive controls, which either use or imply force, legal or extra-legal, and (2) social controls, which consist of group self-regulation outside the boundaries of force, and which can be used on both a macro- and micro-sociological level. Together, these constitute a control system. This essentially broader concept of control better fits a pluralistic society such as the United States than a deviancy model, because it can better account for the fact that America has had numerous sub-cultures, each engaged in certain amounts of self-regulation. Similarly, numerous intergroup contacts frequently occurred whereby one or several groups tried to influence the others' behaviour, or, to put it differently, to negotiate concerning the limits and contents of shared ideals.[33] From a macro-sociological perspective, successful negotiations leading to accommodations between groups, often through politics, would represent successful self-regulation, or society-wide social control. The breakdown of these accommodations, as during the Red Scare, or in denials of the legitimacy of compromise, as with Prohibition, could represent a breakdown of social control. In other words, out-and-out legal or mob repression, widespread and massive disrespect for law as well as the concentration camp and genocide all represent either the failure or the rejection of social controls.[34]

From Janowitz's perspective, the ideal for social control, and the operational goal of social control endeavours, is the promotion of the greatest freedom for the individual or for the social group; through successful self-regulation, repression via police power is avoided. Social control still represents the attempts to influence or to change behaviours or attitudes, either of individuals or of sub-cultural groups, but the means to social control precludes the use of force. Thus persuasion, rhetoric, symbolism, operational rewards and (non-forceful) punishments provide a broad context of social control possibilities. But in precluding the use of force, the individual or group is left free to reject such regulatory efforts. For example, temperance advocates could attempt to persuade through tracts and speeches, and they could promise rewards and portray punishments to those who ignored them, but they could not force people to stop drinking. Prohibitionists, however, were unwilling to tolerate those who chose to drink, and the persuasion of social control was replaced by the coercive controls of Prohibition.

A concept of controls (both social and coercive) broader than one derived from the control of deviancy better serves as a tool for analysing both intra- and inter-group (and institutional) relationships. It can become a different angle of vision for perceiving the attempts of middle- and upper-class WASP culture to change the behaviours of the ethnic working class – ethnic working-class groups could resist, negotiate or, as often was the case, politically nullify such attempts. Similarly, while the deviancy model suggests that all controlling efforts were imposed, this broader definition includes the educational nature of certain controlling endeavours, and it recognizes that some attempts to influence or change behaviours would include as participants those voluntarily desiring to have their behaviour influenced or changed.

Precisely because this definition of controls is broader than the deviancy-derived model, it can more easily be broken down into different parts. Useful analysis requires the ability to distinguish the differences as well as to recognize the similarities of various controlling efforts; different types of controlling efforts imply different functional or motivational meanings. Consequently, a general factor for analysing differences among various controlling efforts is desired. One could attempt to distinguish by looking at the varying motives of the originating controllers (those who originally desire to set up a mechanism of control); but those motives would differ from person to person even on a single reform effort; and, more importantly, they would tell us little about the operational controlling process itself or its results. Another approach would be to differentiate according to the effectiveness of controlling efforts. This is a necessary and hitherto unattended task. But each reform effort needs a separate investigation of effectiveness. Since any single project, such as a movement to organize charitable activities, would differ greatly according to random and particular circumstances, such as leadership, population composition and point in time, effectiveness does not appear to be an adequate manner for deriving typological distinctions of controlling efforts.

A third possible means to find a way of talking about general differences in controlling efforts is suggested by focusing upon the word 'control' – how much control was actually exerted on participants? Put differently, how much choice was available to the participants or targets of controlling endeavours; how easily could they escape the attempt to influence or change their behaviour if they so desired? One can envision a continuum with unlimited freedom of choice (to choose whatever one wishes) at one end and one choice only – that which the controller wishes you to choose – at the other end. By comparing and contrasting particular control functions in terms of the amount of power exerted as regards choice allowed participants, useful distinctions between controlling efforts would be made.

Depending on the questions the historian desires to ask, such distinctions could be applied to the different analytic parts of a control system or of particular reform endeavours. One could look at the desires or intent of those who set up a control effort, and one could also analyse the operation of the control process itself. That there might be differences between these two requires making distinctions between them. A full analysis would also attempt to measure effectiveness: how many persons subjected to a particular controlling process behaved or expressed attitudes in conjunction with the ends or goals of the controlling effort? One must also consider regular behavioural changes resulting without regard to ends or goals, that is, unintentional consequences. Each of these three might differ from each other. The amount of power that originating reformers desired to exert might have differed significantly from the power that the eventual controlling process actually did exert; and the effectiveness of the controlling process might actually have been inversely related to the amount of power exerted.

Given this idea of differing amounts of power exerted leading to differing levels of choice allowed to participants, what types of distinctions can be made? One can envision a maximum exertion of power, allowing very limited choice, in a coercive control situation; a person, via force (usually the police power of the state), is placed into a controlling process from which there is no free withdrawal and in which behaviour is unavoidably subjected to material rewards and punishments. One obvious example of such coercive control is reformatory prisons. But it describes other situations also; certain categories of persons enmeshed in governmental welfare systems, persons on probation, certain sub-cultures of criminal society, peonage systems and perhaps many more situations. (An interesting parallel, of a primary rather than secondary controlling mechanism, is the situation of children within the family. They did not choose their place, they are dependent and subject to rewards and punishments, and they perceive either the applied or the implied (threatening) overwhelming power of the parents. Their exposure to their cultural milieu, through folk tales, nursery rhymes and myths, usually occurs within the context of this unequal power situation, and they cannot choose to withdraw from such exposure.)[35] Such coercive control is most easily conceptualized as applied to individuals, particularly deviants, but it could also be applied to groups, such as in the United States's past relationship with numerous native American tribes.

Distinctions between the above and seemingly similar programmes can be made on the basis of amount of choice. For example, one can envision programmes in which behavioural rewards and punishments are similar, and from which withdrawal is difficult, but which none the less are analytically different because of the participants' original choosing to participate in the control process. An example would be persons who freely commit themselves to mental institutions. Similar examples might include drug treatment centres, certain religious cults, homes for fallen women, the AFDC programme in numerous instances and so on. Such semi-coercive control would presumably have more explicitly reformatory ends than total coercive control; the desire to achieve conformity with particular socially (macro- or micro-) agreed-upon ends would become the explicit and sustaining purpose of the control processes. The boundaries between coercive and social controls would seem to meet at this point.

A yet fuller amount of choice would exist when persons consciously and freely associate themselves to a control process, that is, to an effort to shape or change behaviours and outlooks, from which they could easily withdraw at any point. The feature of continuous free association has led me to use the term 'associative social control' for such situations. Examples would include church membership, many social settlement programmes, Alcoholics Anonymous, most socialization to institutional behaviour (one's job or position in a corporation, political party, government bureaucracy, college and so on), taking a Dale Carnegie course, etc. The list of examples suggests the increased importance of psychological rewards and punishments in associative social control.

A further differentiation that can be made as regards choice suggests a further distinction. One may have the situation or opportunity to withdraw from attempts made to control oneself, but in order to choose, one must first be aware of the controlling attempt. Attempts to manipulate people without their becoming aware of it are pervasive in a society with modern media technology. Advertising and recent political campaign techniques are obvious examples; subtle psychological calculations for particular effects are often more important than the surface message. Similar examples include retail architectural and merchandising design. A person could easily reject or withdraw from such attempts at manipulation through exposure if aware of the attempt.[36]

Recognizing the several analytic parts of a controlling process – its origins, its actual operation and its effectiveness – combined with an awareness of differing types of control – social and coercive – each with different levels of imposed power or choice allowed, should enable historians to discuss controls with greater accuracy and complexity. It should also lead to an examination of the constituency towards which controls were directed, rather than just focusing upon the motivations and programme design of the controllers. This would compel the recognition that some controls may not have been effective; the constituency were often participants, not simply clay to be moulded, in the controlling process.[37]

The expansion of the concept of control into these categories, and particularly the inclusion of the category of associative social control, permits a more accurate reflection of a complex reality than a deviancy-derived social control model allows. For example, the category of associative social control more easily allows analysis of the social control efforts that occurred within ethnic groups. The community-building process that Kantowicz spoke of was often led by an elite who dominated ethnic associational organizations in the attempt to direct the activities of co-nationalists.[38] The associations, societies, churches and the like were thus important for their attempts to mould the behaviours of newly arrived immigrants as they adjusted to a new land. Did those elites, whom Barton sees as changing over time, themselves associate with parts of the larger Anglo-Saxon Protestant culture?[39] Did a two-tiered associational control process affect the cultural and social adjustment of immigrant communities? Questions such as these demonstrate a greater complexity than the more limited uni-directional perspective of social control currently in use. Interactions between elites and the larger culture, and between ethnic elites and the ethnic community, will have to be examined within this context for instances and modes of negotiation and accommodation as well as of attempted coercion and resistance to coercion.

This categorization also allows one to recognize that in any situation where numerous alternatives were available, any particular semi-coercive or associative control effort was not imposed but chosen. This holds true for both the constituency and the controllers. Thus the assumptions of Piven and Cloward that a relief system can control the behaviour of the working classes may work well in a society with only one major relief system. But if there were numerous sources of relief available, and if these sources varied in their expectations of aid-seekers, then the amount of choice available precludes the possibility of any one system from controlling a whole class or group of workers. If a person in need knew about the various choices available – ethnic agencies, missions, neighbourhood churches, Roman Catholic relief agencies, saloon-keepers and political bosses, in addition to various Protestant relief agencies – then that person would be able to choose where first to go for relief.[40]

Similarly, if there were alternatives available, why was any one control process chosen over another to reach particular ends? For example, why did Chicago build a temporary shelter for homeless men rather than resorting to a farm colony or simply mass arrests of vagrants, both of which were proposed? What does the choice of a less coercive measure suggest about the limitations of power among these particular controllers, or about their beliefs concerning the most effective means to achieve their ends? To what extent did the power of the constituency limit the power that controllers could apply in any particular process?[41]

The category of associative social control also allows recognizing, as the original social settlement workers did, the educative function of much of what has come to be called 'social control efforts'. The varieties of associative social control efforts probably increased any one person's choices about his own identity and behaviours; that is, they probably increased individual autonomy rather than decreased it. Take, for example, a newly arrived immigrant who wished to learn about the dominant culture of America; who wished to learn, in essence, in what kind of place (beyond the neighbourhood) he had landed. What better place than a social settlement's classes, clubs and lectures? Attendance did not force him to reject his own ethnic culture. But it did teach him about the dominant WASP culture, and it probably made him aware of a set of values and behaviours different from his own. Whether to accept a limited number of those values and behaviours as useful to himself, to attempt to become like a WASP, or to remain strictly within his own ethnic sub-culture remained his own choice.[42] One could argue that schools, which exposed one not only to the dominant culture but also, in many cases, to other ethnic cultures, had the same effect.[43]

Barton, Thernstrom and others have shown that different ethnic groups responded differently to their situation in America.[44] Some chose security, continuity and ethnic solidarity over social mobility. For example, Barton points out that Roumanians adopted more 'modern' behaviours such as small families and extended education that led to significant upward mobility. Slovaks emphasized the continuity of the ethnic community and stability more than upward mobility, and they continued to have large families and to leave school comparatively early. Consequently they developed a stable working-class life.[45] If a person within the Slovak community wished to escape this cultural conclusion, however, he could learn the appropriate middle-class behaviour patterns by associating himself with the associative social control mechanisms available – night schools, social settlement classes and so on.

In short, for persons who wished to become 'modern' or partly 'modern' – that is, to pursue individual social mobility – WASP associative social control efforts could provide the means to learn the appropriate modern behaviours – particularly future orientation as opposed to fatalism, as is evident in many such efforts' emphasis on the virtues of thrift, industriousness and various types of personal restraint. Whether one rejected one's own ethnic sub-culture, continued to associate with it or chose something in between still remained a matter of personal choice.

The ability to reject parts of one's cultural heritage could seem an immensely liberating activity from a personal perspective, particularly when one's role within a particular culture was a very repressed one. From a social control perspective, one would be rejecting one set of social controls (one's inherited local culture) for another (a different local culture, or some type of mainstream culture). The familiar and often autobiographical literary theme of leaving the confining village to seek liberty in the metropolis is an example of such autonomy; in a true peasant or tribal situation one rarely had such choices. A particularly striking example is found in the case of the heroine of *The Woman Warrior*.[46] A daughter of Chinese immigrants, she chose the mainstream white 'ghost' culture over her own by virtue of refusing a parentally arranged marriage and pursuing her higher education. The role of a woman in pre-Mao Chinese culture seemed severely limited to her in comparison with the possibilities available in the mainstream culture. Thus, her choice was a choice for greater personal autonomy. But, as I think the novel-memoir illustrates, the choice was not made without ambivalence.

The increased choices available in modern society not only increased individual autonomy, but they probably also increased personal ambivalence. The existence of alternatives made persons question the values and outlooks of their own cultural background, even if they remained attached to it, while those who chose to modify and change their beliefs and behaviours undoubtedly felt an ambivalence about abandoning their earlier beliefs and values. A sensitivity to the increased individual autonomy and consciousness in modern society and the sense of rootlessness and ambivalence that accompany it will allow a more accurate portrayal of the dilemma of modernity that is posed for individuals than the deviancy model, with its behaviourist assumptions, allows.[47] Hopefully, therefore, the model of controls presented in this essay will allow a more complex rendering of the society within which individuals pursued their private aims and purposes, as well as a more complex rendering of those individual pursuits and their meanings within the larger social setting.

An application of these categories to problems of interpretation raised earlier should indicate their usefulness to historical analysis. Mohl's contention that the search for order began in the late 1790s is based on his investigation of charitable reform movements typical to the antebellum period such as new charity schools, new relief agencies, tract societies and so on.[48] His analysis focused, however, upon the motivation of the originating reformers; he did indeed find them emitting expressions similar to those expressed later in the century. But a look at the programmes of the two eras suggests significant differences. The vast majority of antebellum reform efforts fell into the associative control category – people were not forced to participate in them and could refuse to. Progressive era reforms, by way of contrast, often employed the coercive power of the state – in efforts such as compulsory education laws, juvenile court systems, child labour laws and so on. As a result, a great many more persons were affected by progressive era control efforts than were affected by antebellum reform measures. And this difference of approach suggests very different perceptions for the two periods concerning both the causes and the remedies for social disorder.[49]

But even in the progressive era, not all efforts were coercive. One suspects as excessive the language Mohl and Betten used to describe settlements in Gary, Indiana, because settlement programmes also generally fell into the associative control category. How harsh could the 'harsh demands for conformity'[50] be when people could simply stop associating if they so desired? And if they had looked at the constituency, would they still have characterized settlements as 'enforcing order amongst the poor'[51]? Who are 'the poor', what percentage of 'the poor' actually associated with settlements, and how many actually allowed themselves to be indoctrinated? Utilization of the concepts of deviancy-derived social control, where one power has control over one defined group, appears to have distorted their description of past reality.

Finally, the disagreement concerning who originated controlling efforts to what end most likely results because there was not one single controlling effort occurring, but many thousands. The enlightenment liberalism in which the nation was born, combined with the nineteenth-century economic liberalism in which it was sustained, combined with the federal system of governance, led to an extremely limited role for central governmental authority in welfare and criminal concerns. With the federal and in many cases the state governments only peripherally involved in welfare matters, differing local elites usually had power to implement various control measures. Thus, in a town like Boston, Massachusetts, an old mercantile elite may very well have acted to restore a sense of lost authority, while in a newly industrializing town it might very well have been manufacturers who led the way.[52]

Not only did the elites involved vary, but local control systems also varied in their operation.[53] Consequently, one cannot speak easily of any national policy or even of a class policy in any very uniform way; local variations of class relations and of culture perceptions preclude it. Not until the US state governments, in the Progressive Era, and then the federal government in the New Deal, became increasingly involved in welfare matters did state and national policy emerge on matters such as juvenile crime, relief, compulsory education and so on. Even then, most states varied greatly one from another. The desire and push for uniformity (on a state-by-state basis) came from associations of welfare or criminal justice professionals. Their success in achieving such uniformity was often limited, however.[54]

Unlike a government with a single jurisdiction, as in Parliament, which established early its responsibility for welfare measures, the plurality of jurisdictions and the consequent plurality of welfare measures suggests the need for sensitivity to the complexity of control systems in the United States. The ability to make appropriate distinctions for accurately rendering this complexity of a pluralistic society is a necessary first step. Such sensitivity further suggests that to generalize from any single community study is hazardous; and that whatever synthesis finally emerges will not be theoretically unicausal but will make the attempt to integrate the various theoretical approaches and findings of a variety of local studies. As long as studies remain basically local, historical conflicts over the true nature of controllers and control systems are perhaps inevitable. But those studies might themselves be enhanced through an awareness of the complexity that a multitude of jurisdictions demands, and an awareness of the necessity to make appropriate distinctions.

NOTES AND REFERENCES

1. T. Bender, *Community and Social Change in America*, Rutgers University Press, New Brunswick, NJ, 1978, pp. 4–28, explicates the foundations of the *gemeinschaft* to *gesellschaft* model.
2. Bender, op. cit., pp. 45–8, points out the pervasiveness of this model in American historiography. See also S.B. Warner, *The Private City; Philadelphia in Three Periods of Its Growth*, University of Pennsylvania Press, Philadelphia, Pa, 1968; D. Rothman, *The Discovery of the Asylum: Social Order and Disorder in the New Republic*, Little, Brown, Boston, 1971; title essay in H.G. Gutman, *Work, Culture, and Society in Industrializing America; Essays in American Working Class and*

Social History, Vintage, New York, 1976, 1977, pp. 3–78. An interesting religious response to a sense of disorder is presented in P.E. Johnson, *A Shopkeeper's Millennium; Society and Revivals in Rochester, New York, 1815–1837*, Hill and Wang, New York, 1978.

3. A significant exception to the *gemeinschaft* to *gesellschaft* model is S. Blumin, *The Urban Threshold*, University of Chicago Press, 1976, pp. 148–66. Similarly, following the lead of Gutman, a number of new labour historians assert the formation of new worker communities rather than a simple community breakdown. See, for example, the introduction by M. Cantor (ed.), *American Working Class Culture; Explorations in American Labor and Social History*, Greenwood, Wesport, Conn., 1979, p. 6; J.T. Cumbler, *Working-Class Community in Industrial America; Work, Leisure, and Struggle in Two Industrial Cities, 1880–1930*, Greenwood, Westport, Conn., 1979, pp. 36–54.

4. Some of the more important social control interpretations have been: R. Mohl, *Poverty in New York 1783–1825*, Oxford University Press, New York, 1971; J.K. Alexander, 'Poverty, Fear, and Continuity: An Analysis of the Poor in Late 18th Century Philadelphia', in A. Davis and M. Haller (eds), *The Peoples of Philadelphia: A History of Ethnic Groups and Lower Class Life*, Temple University Press, Philadelphia, 1973, pp. 13–36; and C. Griffin, *Their Brother's Keepers; Moral Stewardship in the United States 1800–1865*, Rutgers University Press, New Brunswick, NJ, 1965. For juvenile reform, see J. Hawes, *Society Against Its Children: Juvenile Delinquency in Nineteenth Century America*, Oxford University Press, New York, 1971; A. Platt, *The Child Savers. The Invention of Delinquency*, University of Chicago Press, 1969; and S. Schlossman, *Love and the American Delinquent: The Theory and Practice of 'Progressive' Juvenile Justice 1825–1920*, University of Chicago Press, 1977. For schools, see M. Katz, *The Irony of Early School Reform; Educational Innovation in Mid-Nineteenth Century Massachusetts*, Harvard University Press, Cambridge, Mass., 1968; D. Tyack, *The One Best System: A History of American Urban Education*, Harvard University Press, Cambridge, Mass., 1974; and S. Schultz, *The Culture Factory: Boston Public Schools, 1789–1860*, Oxford University Press, New York, 1974. On sexual reform, see D. Pivar, *Purity Crusade: Sexual Morality and Social Control*, Greenwood, Westport, Conn., 1973. On settlements, see R. Mohl and N. Betten, 'Paternalism and Pluralism. Immigrants and Social Welfare in Gary, Indiana, 1906–1940', *American Studies*, 15, Spring 1974, pp. 5–30. For the strongest social control statement as applied to relief giving, see F.F. Piven and R. Cloward, *Regulating the Poor; The Functions of Public Welfare*, Pantheon, New York, 1971. Other works concentrating on social control through relief giving include: M. Gettelman, 'Charity and Social Class in the United States, 1874–1900', *American Journal of Economics and Sociology*, 22, April/July 1963, pp. 313–29, 417–26; and 'Philanthropy as Social Control in Late 19th Century America: Some Hypotheses and Data on the Rise of Social Work', *Societas*, 5, Winter 1975, pp. 41–59; Kenneth Kusmer, 'The Functions of Organized Charity in the Progressive Era: Chicago as a Case Study', *Journal of American History*, 60, December 1973, pp. 657–78; N. Huggins, *Protestants Against Poverty: Boston's Charities 1870–1900*, Greenwood, Westport, Conn., 1971; T. Naylor, 'Responding to the Fire: The Work of the Chicago Relief and Aid Society',

Science and Society, 39, Winter 1975–76, pp. 450–64; and W. Trattner, *From Poor Law to Welfare State: A History of Social Welfare in America*, Free Press, New York, 1974. This paper, in terms of examples and emphasis, will focus upon that with which I am most familiar, social welfare measures.

5. For critiques of the social control interpretation, see L. Banner, 'Religious Benevolence as Social Control: A Critique of an Interpretation', *Journal of American History*, 60, June 1973, pp. 23–41; C.S. Rosenberg, *Religion and the Rise of the American City; The New York City Mission Movement 1812–1870*, Cornell University Press, Ithaca, NY, 1971, pp. 243–73; W. Muraskin, 'The Social Control Theory in American History: A Critique', *Journal of Social History*, 9, June 1976, pp. 559–69; and Muraskin's review of Piven and Cloward in *Contemporary Sociology*, 4, November 1975, pp. 607–13; M.J. Wiener, review essay of A.P. Donajgrodski (ed.), *Social Control in Nineteenth Century Britain*, in *Journal of Social History*, Winter 1978, pp. 314–20; R. Luker, 'Religion and Social Control in the Nineteenth Century American City', *Journal of Urban History*, 2, May 1976, pp. 363–68; G.N. Grob, 'Reflections on the History of Social Policy in America', *Reviews in American History*, 7, September 1979, pp. 293–306.

6. R. Hofstadter, *The Age of Reform*, Vintage, New York, 1955, pp. 135–7; Huggins, op. cit., pp. 8, 11, 189–99.

7. Kusmer, op. cit., pp. 665–9; Platt, op. cit., p. 176. See also J. Quandt, *From Small Town to the Great Community: The Social Thought of Progressive Intellectuals*, Rutgers University Press, New Brunswick, NJ, 1970.

8. Gettelman, 'Charity', pp. 313–19, 326–9; 'Philanthropy', p. 50, Piven and Cloward, op. cit., pp. xv, 3, 7, 8; Gutman, op. cit., pp. 19–32.

9. B.J. Bledstein, *The Culture of Professionalism: The Middle Class and the Development of Higher Education in America*, W.W. Norton, New York, 1976; G.E. Markovitz and D.K. Rosner, 'Doctors in Crisis: A Study of the Use of Medical Education Reform to Establish Modern Professional Elitism in Medicine', *American Quarterly*, 25 March 1973; T. Haskell, *The Emergence of Professional Social Science: The American Social Science Association and the Nineteenth Century Crisis of Authority*, University of Illinois Press, Urbana, 1977.

10. See J. Addams, *The Spirit of Youth and the City Streets*, University of Illinois Press, Urbana, 1972 (originally 1909), pp. 107–62.

11. For examples, see Gettelman, 'Charity and Social Class'; Piven and Cloward, op. cit.; A. Dawley, *Class and Community; The Industrial Revolution in Lynn*, Harvard University Press, Cambridge, Mass., 1976; and P. Faler, 'Cultural Aspects of the Industrial Revolution: Lynn, Massachusetts, Shoemakers and Industrial Morality', in M. Cantor (ed.), *American Workingclass Culture; Explorations in American Labor and Social History*, Greenwood, Westport, Conn., 1979, pp. 121–48.

12. Piven and Cloward, op. cit., make this theme explicit. Naylor, op. cit., attempts to do so.

13. Some of these questions are derived from Wiener, op. cit. A cross-cultural comparison in worker attitudes would be most useful on this point. W. Manchester, *The Arms of Krupp 1587–1968*, Bantam, New York, 1968, pp. 170–3; R.P. Dore, *British Factory–Japanese Factory: The Origins of National Diversity in*

Employment Relations, University of California Press, Los Angeles, 1973.

14. Bledstein, op. cit., for example, emphasizes the self-disciplinary effects of professionalization; Haskell, op. cit., suggests that professionalization led to a withdrawal from wider activities. Robert Wiebe, *The Search for Order 1877–1930*, Hill and Wang, New York, 1968, pp. 111–64, is still a good general account of professionalization's connection to larger reformist endeavours, as is the more focused study by R. Lubove, *The Professional Altruist; the Emergence of Social Work as a Career, 1880–1920*, Harvard University Press, Cambridge, Mass., 1965.
15. Piven and Cloward, op. cit., pp. 39, 148–9, 250–62; Gettelman, 'Philanthropy', pp. 49–59.
16. A problem with a number of social-control-oriented works is the non-specificity of classes; although the terms 'upper' and 'middle class' are used, they are not defined, and changes in the class structure over time are not handled adequately.
17. See, for example, R. Mohl, 'Poverty, Pauperism, and Social Order in the Preindustrial American City, 1780–1840', *Social Science Quarterly*, 52, March 1972, pp. 934–48.
18. Mohl and Betten, op. cit., p. 5. See also Piven and Cloward, op. cit.
19. Alexander, op. cit., p. 21.
20. Mohl and Betten, op. cit., pp. 6, 10, 25.
21. Alexander, op. cit., pp. 19, 20, 22–5.
22. Some of these questions have been derived from Wiener, op. cit.
23. Bender, op. cit., pp. 48–60.
24. Mohl, op. cit., p. 934.
25. Social control as limited to deviance was seen in T. Parsons, *The Social System*, Free Press, Glencoe, Ill., 1951, pp. 249–320; such categorization as sociological orthodoxy can be seen in J.R. Pitts, 'Social Control. The Concept', in D. Sills (ed.), *International Encyclopedia of the Social Sciences*, vol. 14, New York, 1968, p. 383. For a history of the term, see M. Janowitz, 'Sociological Theory and Social Control', *American Journal of Sociology* 1, July 1975, pp. 83–108.
26. Mohl and Betten, op. cit., p. 6.
27. Ibid., p. 5; Piven and Cloward, op. cit., pp. 22, 33, 34.
28. Deviancy is in part a statistical concept; members of sub-cultural groups, while acting in ways that were not statistically average, nevertheless may have not been deviating from their own cultural group's behaviour. It is true, of course, as Rothman, op. cit., shows, that the attempt was made to extend categories of deviance (insanity, delinquency) to individual members of cultural subgroups; but the groups themselves, and the working classes as a whole, cannot be seen as deviant. For a look at the difficulties of defining deviance in past time, see K. Erickson, *Wayward Puritans, A Study in the Sociology of Deviance*, John Wiley, New York, 1966, pp. 5–6.
29. The functionalist–structuralist approach tends to assume that there is a society that is functioning or attempting to gain equilibrium. But if society is composed of numerous subgroups, each of whom pursues different ends and has different values, then disequilibrium would be the normal state of society,

as there would always be at least one group, and usually several, for whom society worked in a dysfunctional manner and who would actively be in pursuit of a different social equilibrium from that which other groups desired. Increasing work is being done to understand an indigenous working-class culture; since such work is currently unsynthesized, however, in this paper I will concentrate on ethnic groups.

30. E.R. Kantowicz, 'Polish Chicago: Survival Through Solidarity', in M. Holli and P. Jones, *The Ethnic Frontier; Essays in the History of Group Survival in Chicago and the Midwest*, W.B. Eerdmans, Grand Rapids, Michigan, 1977, pp. 183–92. For Chicago, for example, see C. Adler (ed.), *American Jewish Yearbook; 5561; September 24, 1900 to September 13, 1901*, Philadelphia, 1901, pp. 225–44; and I. Sonneborn (ed.), *Chicago Charities Directory*, Chicago, 1901.

31. J.A. Mayer, 'Relief Systems and Social Controls: The Case of Chicago, 1890–1910', *The Old Northwest*, 6, Fall 1980, 217–44.

32. Janowitz, op. cit., pp. 82–107. For a fuller treatment, see his *The Last Half-Century; Societal Change and Politics in America*, Chicago, 1978, pp. 3–52.

33. This paper concentrates on 'secondary' social controls – those consciously attempted by agencies, institutions, elite groups and so on; 'primary' social controls would be those imposed by one's primary relationships – family and peers. Several members of a NEH seminar who read an early draft of this paper suggested that intra-group social controls were significantly different from inter-group controls and so should have a different appellation: 'socialization'. I agree that this might clarify some distinctions between inter- and intra-group controls, but I have decided not to take their advice. I prefer to see socialization more narrowly as the assimilation of an individual to a particular institution, such as the family, a corporation or an association. The means to such assimilation consist of various controlling processes.

34. Janowitz, 'Sociological Theory', pp. 104–6.

35. See note 33. It perhaps becomes more clear at this point that I view socialization, as well as assimilation and acculturation, as subcategories of a broadly conceived control system: the controls are the means, the subcategories represent differing possible ends or results. It should be clear that the language, 'to influence behaviour', includes the goal of behavioural reinforcement.

36. E. Goffman, *Gender Advertisements*, Harvard University Press, New York, 1979, pp. 24–84; Daniel Boorstin, *The Americans; The Democratic Experience*, Random House, New York, 1974, pp. 113–17, 137–47, 434–47. A small or unified group in control of media, packaging, architectural, and other mass exposure devices raises the possibility that socially agreed upon ends, or the process of reaching socially agreed upon ends, could be subverted. Whether this has, in fact, happened, for the ends of selling consumer goods, is a question worthy of debate. See J. Mander, *Four Arguments for the Elimination of Television*, Morrow, New York, 1978.

37. Labour historians have generally recognized this fact which social welfare historians have at times neglected. (Particularly evident is the gap between the findings of social control theorists and historians of ethnic groups.)

Specialization within history results in limited outlooks, however, so that labour historians rarely look at the culture of *both* bosses and workers, nor do ethnic historians fully treat WASP attempts to act upon ethics. We see parts clearly, but rarely glimpse the whole.

38. Kantowicz, 'Polish Chicago', p. 192.
39. J. Barton, *Peasants and Strangers: Italians, Rumanians and Slovaks in an American City, 1890–1950,* Harvard University Press, Cambridge, Mass., 1975, pp. 70–90.
40. Mayer, op. cit., pp. 234–7.
41. See, for example, the problems of how to treat Chicago juveniles in *Cooperation,* 1, 2 February 1901, pp. 3–4; 23 February 1901, pp. 1–4; 16 March 1901, pp. 6–7; 11 May 1901, pp. 3–4; 2, 2 February 1902, p. 2; 3 March 1902 p. 5; 5, 3 June 1905, p. 171; 4 November 1905, p. 371; 9 December 1905, p. 415; 6, 16 June 1906, p. 139. The fact that several Chicago wards regularly turned out itinerants as voters for the Democratic Party undoubtedly helped to frustrate reformers' aims.
42. This structure parallels on the individual level the choices put forth by Bodnar for subcultural ethnic groups: John Bodnar, 'Immigration and Modernization: The Case of Slavic Peasants in Industrial America', *Journal of Social History,* 10, Fall 1976, pp. 44–71.
43. D. Tyack, *The One Best System: A History of American Urban Education,* Harvard University Press, Cambridge, Mass., 1974, pp. 251–4, suggests the differences among ethnic groups in their accommodation to education. See also Barton, op. cit., pp. 135–46. Compulsory attendance laws, and the motivation of some lobbyists/legislators, make school attendance seem to be a form of coercive control. But did the actual process (of attending school) operate in a coercive fashion? Parents who chose education for their children, who desired to send their children to school, were not being coerced, but rather felt themselves to be associating with and participating in society's educational ideals. The leaders of various ethnic communities often expressed the desirability of schooling, and the behaviours of certain ethnic groups suggest their valuing education. (The children themselves may have been coerced in such instances, but by the parents rather than the school system.) Such choosing clearly existed with parochial schools. Some parents were, on the other hand, forced to send their children to school against their wishes. So the extent to which compulsory attendance laws acted as a coercive process needs to be analysed in terms of the parents' differing perceptions of schooling – how many perceived it as an associative activity to participate in, and how many as a coerced and resented activity? No simple answer will emerge because different parents perceived schooling in different ways. Some parents, furthermore, were undoubtedly ambivalent – they desired schooling for their children but could not afford it. See John Modell, 'Patterns of Consumption, Acculturation, and Family Income Strategies in Late Nineteenth-Century America', in *Family and Population in Nineteenth-Century America,* Princeton University Press, 1978, pp. 206–40. What happened in school, as opposed to what got the children there, would require a similar analysis.

44. Barton, op. cit., pp. 117–46, 170–3; S. Thernstrom, *Poverty and Progress: Social Mobility in a Nineteenth Century City*, Atheneum, New York, 1969, pp. 80–191; T. Kessner, *The Golden Door: Italian and Jewish Immigrant Mobility in New York City 1880–1915*, Oxford University Press, New York, 1977.

45. Barton, op. cit., pp. 117–46, 170–3.

46. M.H. Kingston, *The Woman Warrior*, Random House, New York, 1976.

47. Historians using social control models have often posited a simple reward/punishment behaviouralist framework for assuming changing behaviours or attitudes as a result of reform programmes. Such a model would not work from an existentialist perspective whereby all creative choice would rest with the individual. For important insights into individual choice and consciousness, see F.M. Dostoevsky, *Notes From the Underground*, New American Library, New York, 1961; also A. Solzhenitzyn, *One Day in the Life of Ivan Denisovich*, Bantam Books, New York, 1963, and *The Gulag Archipelago 1918–1956, An Experiment in Literary Investigation III, IV*, Bantam Books, New York, 1975, pp. 597–617; A. Camus, *The Stranger*, Knopf, New York, 1946. Furthermore, usually a crude behaviouralism is employed. None of the historians mentioned above examines, for example, the importance of time delays in reward/punishment situations; nor do they consider differences between the effectiveness of rewards as opposed to punishments in attempts to direct behaviours.

48. Mohl, 'Poverty, Pauperism, and Social Order'.

49. For a good overview of these changing perceptions, see P. Boyer, *Urban Masses and Moral Order in America, 1820–1920*, Harvard University Press, Cambridge, 1978. See also R.H. Bremmer, *From The Depths; The Discovery of Poverty in the United States*, New York University Press, 1956; and T.L. Haskell, *The Emergence of Professional Social Science*, University of Illinois Press, Urbana, 1977.

50. Mohl and Betten, op. cit., p. 5.

51. Ibid.

52. N. Huggins, *Protestants Against Poverty: Boston's Charities 1870–1900*, Greenwood, Westport, Conn., 1971; Dawley, op. cit.; Johnson, op. cit; Faler, op. cit.

53. For an example of differing views concerning relief, see J.A. Mayer, 'Private Charities in Chicago From 1871 to 1915', PhD dissertation, University of Minnesota, 1978, pp. 69–117.

54. See, for example, C. Chambers, *Seedtime of Reform; American Social Service and Social Action 1918–1933*, University of Minnesota Press, Minneapolis, 1963, pp. 27–58.

2

Class Expression versus Social Control?
A Critique of Recent Trends in the Social
History of 'Leisure'

GARETH STEDMAN JONES*

For social historians, systematic interest in popular recreation and debate over the use of leisure is relatively recent. Pioneering research on the subject scarcely goes back beyond the end of the 1950s; and undoubtedly the growing attention which historians have paid to it has owed a lot to the increasing recourse to sociology and anthropology in the definition of problems worthy of historical research. The amount of work going on in this area is now on a sufficient scale to make it possible to step back and make at least some interim judgements on the ways in which the problem seems to have been conceived and to examine how far the conceptual instruments employed have been adequate either to posing the right questions or to resolving them.

But before examining the concepts employed, it is first necessary to stress that knowledge of this area still remains very uneven. Certain well defined themes have emerged, and this has encouraged research along a few oft-trodden routes, while leaving large parts of the landscape almost unmapped. Research has tended to concentrate upon the advance of a methodical capitalist rationality and the disappearance or decline of traditional forms of popular recreation in its wake. Problems which cannot be so comfortably contained within the terms of this juxtaposition have

Source: History Workshop, vol. 4, 1977, pp. 162–70.
* This article was a contribution to the conference, 'The Working Class and Leisure', organized by the Society for the Study of Labour History at the University of Sussex in Autumn 1975. Apart from minor stylistic changes to make the theme comprehensible to the general reader, the text remains unchanged. This text has been reproduced here because it was thought that discussion of the notion of 'social control' possessed wider historical relevance.

The research referred to in the text was a contribution to the conference at Sussex. A full collection of the conference papers is available from Sussex University through inter-library loan. In addition to these, two other works particularly relevant to this theme are R. W. Malcolmson, *Popular Recreations in English Society 1700–1850*, Cambridge, 1973; and Brian Harrison, 'Religion and Recreation in Nineteenth-Century England', *Past and Present*, no. 38, 1967.

tended to be neglected. There is no substantial study, for example, of how far changes in the sexual division of labour before, during and after industrialization produced changing sexually segregated patterns of leisure, or indeed of the pattern of segregation itself. We have a few tantalizing glimpses – if men spent St Monday drinking, women spent it washing – but it is a fair generalization to say that the relation between one-half of the working class and 'leisure' remains to be explored.

There are other areas, too, which, if not unknown, are certainly underplayed in the prevalent approach to the subject. Far more attention has been paid to the ways in which entrepreneurs or the propertied classes attempted to change popular uses of leisure time than to the ways in which craftsman, artisan or working-class activists attempted to organize their non-work time or sought to re-orientate the use of non-work time by others. Of course, something is known about the attitudes of Levellers, Jacobins, Owenites, Chartists, village radicals, non-conformist trade unionists and socialists towards popular culture. In some cases, extremely good work has been done. But it has not generally been integrated into the dominant approaches to popular and working-class recreation.

As a result of this unevenness of knowledge or emphasis, the cumulative picture conveyed by research into popular recreation and leisure is out of perspective. The sharply delineated foreground is occupied by Puritan, Methodist and Evangelical moral reformers, gentry deciding where to place their patronage, prescient magistrates, calculating employers, prurient municipal elites, entrepreneurial publicans and rationalizing merchants of leisure. Behind this obtrusive phalanx we can just make out the blurred and rather undifferentiated features of the rural and urban masses. Once or twice, their generally dim profiles are illuminated by 'a flashpoint of class conflict'. Forms of resistance may momentarily be discerned. But since, at this distance of time, evidence of their resistance can be found generally only in non-verbal activity – a burnt hayrick, for example, or a pitched street battle – it is then difficult to situate these 'flashpoints' in their surrounding terrain. It is as if the only records of the bourgeoisie came from the bankruptcy courts, the only evidence of marriage from divorce petitions. It is a major step forward to have opened up this vast area of social history – one, potentially, that will enable us to re-examine a lot of labour history in the light of a much broader knowledge of the ideologies of poor villagers, rural craftsmen, manufacturing artisans, factory and casual labourers – but it would be very dangerous to assume that our knowledge of these ideologies and the material situations which they articulated is still in anything but an extremely primitive state.

Some of the best studies have acknowledged this ignorance and conceded that, if the problem is to be posed adequately, then the case of the accused cannot satisfactorily be deduced from even the most discerning reading of testimonies bequeathed us by the case for the prosecution. But not all work has escaped the temptation to translate archival silence into historical passivity. Combined with the relative absence of studies examining active working-class attempts to determine the use of their non-work time, the composite picture presented of capitalist development, class relations and 'leisure' appears unduly slanted in one direction. It is as if class conflict in England has been a largely one-sided affair conducted by capitalism and its representatives; as if the rural and urban masses, like the newborn child in Locke's psychology, were simply a blank page upon which each successive stage of capitalism has successfully imposed its imprint. We have a picture in some ways uncannily similar to the grey, secularized, bureaucratized, rationalized landscape painted by Max Weber – a dismal progression from the poor commonwealth villager deprived of his village customs, through the Padstow miner forced to exchange his hobby horse for a Methodist hymnal, the poor Londoner constrained to abandon the spontaneity of the free-and-easy for the 'controlled' decorum of a Palace of Variety, the tea-drinking Whitsun rustic obediently enjoying his new forms of rational recreation under the benevolent gaze of parson and squire, the Edwardian artisan donning collar, tie and best suit to watch a football match, and so on to the interwar unskilled labourer exercising his last remaining freedom – the filling in of a pools coupon – and the postwar alienated proletarian diverting his class consciousness into the humble and vicarious partisanships offered by tele-Olympics and the 'match of the day'.

This picture is not simply the result of a scarcity of sources, nor is it simply a consequence of expecting too much from an early stage of research. The problem is primarily a conceptual one. Historians have made some real gains by being forced to address themselves to problems raised by sociologists and anthropologists. The result has been an immense broadening of the scope of history. But it is surely time that historians began to pay more critical attention to the concepts which sociology has placed at their disposal. Too often these concepts are passively accepted as if they were no more than harmless heuristic devices, without any consequence beyond the meaning conveyed by the words themselves.

In fact, this is usually not the case. A loose commonsense usage of a sociological term tends, on closer scrutiny, to be circular or strictly meaningless: a mere well-intentioned gesture in the direction of a non-existent rigour. On the other hand, any attempt at a systematic usage will entail a definite interpretive explanatory framework which cannot be manipulated at will. When historians on the lookout for some grander conceptual framework within which to situate their research move out from a narrow empiricism into a theoretical eclecticism, they may easily find themselves tumbling down all manner of slippery paths, which they had had no prior intention of descending.

One obvious example of this has been the frequent resort to notions of 'social control'. It is a phrase conveying an obvious and plausible meaning. It would appear to stand to reason that those with power and authority in society have an interest in imposing, maintaining or re-imposing 'social control', and it is in this loose commonsense form that many have used the idea of 'social control'. Sometimes it seems almost to be assumed that the concept is of Marxist provenance – social control being something which by definition a bourgeoisie continually administers, and in increasingly heavy doses, to an errant but gradually domesticated proletariat.

It is not difficult to demonstrate that a casual usage of 'social control' metaphors leads to non-explanation and incoherence. There is no political or ideological institution which could not in some way be interpreted as an agency of social control. There is no indication in the phrase of who the agents or instigators of social control may be: no indication of any common mechanism whereby social control is enforced: no constant criterion whereby we may judge whether social control has broken down – certainly not conflict, for this may ultimately, or even inherently, be a means of reinforcing conformity. Nor finally is there any fixed yardstick whereby we may know when social control has been reimposed. Since capitalism is still with us, we can with impunity suppose, if we wish to, that at any time in the last three hundred years the mechanisms of social control were operating effectively.

If a casual allusion to 'social control' turns out to be vacuous, it is equally clear that social control cannot merely be added on to a Marxist interpretation. The phrase 'social control' suggests a static metaphor of equilibrium, which might be disturbed and then reasserted on a new basis. It suggests therefore three successive states: a prior functioning, a period of breakdown, and a renewed state of functioning. Even stopping at this point, we can see a basic incompatibility with any Marxist interpretation. For if we seriously wish to adopt a Marxist explanation, it is impossible to operate this mechanical separation of periods of control and breakdown. A mode of production is irreducibly a contradictory unity of forces and relations of production. Just as, in order to survive, the relations of production must be continually reproduced, so is the contradiction embodied within those relations of production continually reproduced. Contradiction is not episodically, but continually present; the antagonism between the producers of the surplus and the owners and controllers of the means of production extracting the surplus is a structural and permanent feature. Thus, class conflict is a permanent feature, not a sign of breakdown, and the conditions in which class conflict may assume explosive or revolutionary forms bears only the emptiest of resemblances to a crude notion conveyed by the phrase 'breakdown of social control'.

Perhaps one simple illustration will indicate this difference. In some interpretations of the emergence and growth of rational recreation, the nineteenth-century railway network is presented unproblematically as an agent of material and moral improvement, transporting temperate workers to the seaside, arousing harmless wonder at the beauties of nature, lessening the temptations of drink and gambling and so on. If it is true, in other words, that reformers of manners progressed from coercion to a 'strategy of counter-attraction', then this success was the achievement of the entrepreneur whose pursuit of profit had resulted in the creation of a magnificent technology of moral improvement. But that is only one way of looking at the railways. For the building of stations and cutting of new lines by these same entrepreneurs involved the arbitrary demolition of vast tracts of poor housing and the peremptory eviction of tens of thousands. Thus, if the development of the railways was in one sense a reinforcement of new 'forms of social control', it was at the same moment an agent creating new problems of 'social control'.

More pertinent perhaps to the confusion caused by mixing Marxist concepts with notions of social control is the argument which runs: moral reformers, sabbatarians, Methodists, temperance enthusiasts and charity organizers in the end were not the real agents responsible for imposing the new forms of social control. For all their efforts, they remained the purveyors of minority causes, distasteful not only to workers but to the bulk of the middle class. The real instigator of new and more effective forms of social control was the capitalist of leisure. The domestication of the new industrial working class was the accomplishment not of Wesley, Wilberforce, Samuel Smiles or Octavia Hill, but of Charles Morton, Lord Northcliffe and Alfred Littlewood. Despite the avowedly anti-capitalist intention of this argument – the conviction that class harmony is an unnatural and undesirable state of affairs – it seems to me to resemble a revamped version of Adam Smith's 'unseen hand'. The greed and private vices of capitalists, unbeknown to them, create increasingly effective mechanisms of dousing, chanelling or diverting the class consciousness of workers, since the most effective agency of social control is the capitalization of the leisure market. What ever the status of this argument, it is certainly not Marxist; for, like Adam Smith, it restricts capitalism to the market place; and it assumes that ideologies prevalent within the working class will not, in any fundamental sense, be articulations of their productive relationships within capitalism, but the result of their position as consumers of leisure.

Before going any further in an analysis of the consequences of employing even a loose commonsense notion of social control in combination with other concepts finally incompatible with it, we should look at the systematic sociological uses of the term, for this should make us even more wary of the dangers of borrowing a term of whose credentials and genealogy and implications we are unaware.

The difficulties for the historian attempting to give some meaning merely to the phrase are more than confirmed by examining the theory. The concept was first popularized in American sociology by Edward A. Ross, who in 1901 produced a book called *Social Control. A Survey of the Foundations of Order*. Its inspiration was an attempt to sociologize Darwin in a social Darwinist direction. For the interaction between the organism and nature, Ross substituted one between the individual and society. What, in this theory, a society has to control is the animal nature of 'Man'. 'Man's' tendency to pursue his self-interest to the point of a war of all against all must be limited through learning or selection. The operation of Ross's concept was rather similar to that of Durkheim's *conscience collective*, which was also capable of constraining men's 'animal spirits' with a power directly proportional to the intensity of interaction around its specific forms. Family, marriage and religion were accorded this power at a primary level, while at the secondary level professional associations would act in a similar way to counteract the anomie endemic in economic life.

Ross's notion of social control – a constraining social element which held in check man's darker animal side – was taken up by Robert Park and the Chicago sociologists of the beginning of the twentieth century. The triadic state which, I have suggested, is implied by the word itself was indeed the way in which the concept was developed. There was first the state of 'natural order', defined by Ross as derived from the spontaneous meshing of men's personalities and sociability on the one hand and from their sense of justice and capacity for resentment on the other. This 'natural order' was similar to what another American sociologist, Charles Horton Cooley, described in 1909 as the 'primary group'. If this was stage one, stage two was breakdown, a state which, the Chicago sociologists believed, was brought about by urbanization, immigration, the breakdown of the small community into competing groups and a decline in the efficacy of natural selection (which, by the way, was held to have been accountable for the growing number of 'moral idiots or lunatics' – people who, according to Ross, 'can no more put themselves in the place of another than the beast can enter into the anguish of its prey'). Stage three, of course, is the re-creation of a moral rational order to replace the natural order rendered unviable by greater population density and heterogeneity: a process which Park saw as the shift from primary means of social control such as family, neighbourhood and community to secondary means of control such as police, political machine and courts.

If this first form of the concept of social control is not found very appealing, the second version popularized by Talcott Parsons is scarcely more attractive. His notion of social control is a derivation from a systematic theory of deviance. Here again there is a three-stage process, but this time of a psychological rather than biological kind. Stage one is the normal functioning of role expectations. Deviance (stage two) results not from 'animal spirits' but from learning derived from past interaction, specific personality factors or the pressures and opportunities of immediate interactional situations. When role expectations are frustrated, the motivation of the actor is likely to develop ambivalence which can lead to (a) loss of attachment to any object or pattern, (b) compulsive expression of only one side of the ambivalence, or, more usually, (c) a slightly schizoid state in which the acting out of both the conforming and alienated sides are segregated in time and·place.

Deviancy may be a danger to society, especially when deviants group together, but Parsons sees an ultimate source of social control in their ambivalence, and in the bridges that link Utopian or radical groups to the main value pattern. These bridges, according to Parsons, enable many members to sell out after a longer or shorter stay in a deviant organization. An alternative way back to stage three (normal functioning) is the allowal of partial deviance – the secondary institution like youth culture or organized gambling, which allows some deviance from the dominant value pattern, yet keeps the participants integrated within the dominant value pattern. By permitting the expression of some alienated feelings they may bring the 'actors' back to conformity.

This psychotherapeutic model can be applied to any process of social behaviour. Normally there will be structural arrangements for 'draining off' tensions which might trigger deviant behaviour. Primary groups like the family normally fulfil this role. Other modes include institutions of entertainment and play, through which the catharsis of antisocial desires can be secured. The party, the carnival or mass entertainment are cited in this sense. I will not carry on with an analysis of these sociological models of social control. Suffice it to say that both are functionalist models, whose primary reference remains the interaction between individuals and a social organism. The thought is not of an antagonistic class system based upon exploitation, but, for example, of an urban community and a working-class sub-culture. Contradiction is not the normal state of this system, since it is a *community*. Breakdown is analysed in terms of biologistic or psychologistic pathology. Hence it can be seen that an attempt to link the idea of social control with some Marxist or semi-Marxist theory of capitalist development will have unhappy results.

Few historians are committed functionalists, but it is not uncommon for social historians to fall unconsciously into the functionalist models I have described. This is partly the result of the technical problems of writing history. The historian's problem is generally that he or she knows a great deal about one period, which blurs into a relative ignorance of what came before and what came afterwards. Thus, there is a very strong temptation to begin with something called 'traditional society', as Malcolmson does in his very interesting book on popular leisure-time pursuits, or as Edward Thompson implied when he wrote about the moral economy of the eighteenth-century crowd. In this context, it is very useful to know from Keith Wrightson's research that many of the generally cited attributes of the eighteenth-century village were not traditional, but new creations of the century following 1640. But it makes one wonder how traditional the traditional customs which he describes as coming under attack from 1552 onwards really were. The legal historian, T. F. T. Plucknett, once showed that the medieval term, 'custom from time immemorial', need only mean 21 years. Clearly, the historian should refrain from calling the history he does not know 'traditional society'. This bad habit, it seems to me, has been one of the many unfortunate spin-offs from sociological theories of modernization. Historians are also at the mercy of their ignorance of what comes after their special period of expertise. Here again there is a spontaneous tendency to think in terms of a new equilibrium having been established, one which, again, it is tempting to consider to be the result of the successful imposition of social control.

Here, it seems to me, the terrain is even more dangerous than the notion of 'traditional society'. For what social control invites us to think of is a process of 'incorporation', 'accommodation', 'bourgeoisification' or, if one wishes to stress some revolutionary credential, one might call 'bourgeois hegemony', the re-establishment of 'false consciousness' or even 'repressive desublimation'. The point about these terms is that, although they may register some moral distance from the apologetic complacency of functionalist theory, they in no way break from its theoretical linkages. To say that a functional totality is based on alienation is only to add an epithet of moral or political disapproval. It does not change the causal relationship between terms within this functional totality. The plus signs are simply turned into minuses. We may think of sport, for example, as a healthy release for spontaneity and freedom, like the sociologist Eric Dunning; or we may think of it as a diversionary use of leisure time reinforcing the alienated consciousness engendered by the workplace. But there is no challenge here to the functionalist analysis of sport.

This overestimate of the operation of social control – by which is usually meant ideological control – is often accompanied by another commonly encountered strand in sociological thinking: the use of 'ideal types' derived from Weber, or, if again one wants to claim a Marxist ancestry, the approach to class consciousness associated with Lukacs. Just as Weber gives us idealized, not to say fantasized, pictures of the *rational* capitalist, so Lukacs provides us with a homologous idealization of the *revolutionary* proletarian. In the latter case, the result is a surreal model of revolutionary proletarian class consciousness, which has nowhere been observed to occur in real history. The problem for advocates of this model is to discover why history has deviated from it, and the answer is often the resort to the notion of hegemony, a concept which in some of its more recent usages works in a similar way to the functionalist notion of social control, but with a class terminology added. Gramsci's idea of hegemony is certainly useful in so far as it makes us look at the institutions through which the ruling ideology is transmitted. But it can give only a tautological answer to a false question if it is used to explain the absence of a revolutionary proletarian class consciousness in the sense envisaged by Lukacs. In Lukacs himself, the working class has either a revolutionary class consciousness or no consciousness at all (i.e., it inhabits the world of reification and possesses only 'false consciousness'). It is not therefore a large step for his latter-day sociological followers to translate this juxtaposition of terms into a historical process of transition in which originally revolutionary proletarians are 'incorporated' through the mechanisms of 'social control' or bourgeois hegemony.

In an analysis of leisure time the results of this sort of approach are particularly absurd: but for the effective maintenance of social control, the hegemony of the bourgeoisie, the capitalist confiscation of leisure time or whatever other ideological instrument is assigned this function by the analyst, we might expect workers to be singing revolutionary songs and preparing the uprising. The reason why they do not do so is because their putative class consciousness has been confiscated from them and diverted into some system-maintaining channel – chauvinism, sport or consumerism, for instance.

The question which we must pose to such theories is what they can actually explain. A long time ago, the historian Elie Halevy argued that a revolution in early nineteenth-century England had been prevented by the hold exercised by Methodism over the working class. Detailed examination of the evidence since this thesis was first put forward has shown that it explains neither the periodicity of revolutionary feeling, nor its geography. Halevy's thesis was by no means absurd, since Methodism was a very plausible candidate for the role he assigned it. But if Methodism can't be shown in any wholly convincing fashion to have prevented revolution, what are we to say about football? Interestingly enough, it emerges from John Hutchinson's research on football crowds before 1914 that Glasgow was one of the earliest centres of football as a mass spectator sport. We might, on the assumptions of the argument above, expect to find that its workers were particularly docile. But we certainly would not have expected to find that, a few years later, the city had become the most militant and even insurrectionary centre during the First World War.

It is very important to develop research into non-work time and the different ways in which workers have used it. But it would be a fundamental mistake to develop it into a subject in its own right. The greatest 'social control' – if one wants to use the words – available to capitalism is the wage relationship itself – the fact that, in order to live and reproduce, the worker must perpetually resell his or her labour power. The necessity to obtain work, to remain fit enough for work and to make ends meet is far more important than any packaged consumerist ideology which succeeds in intruding upon the worker's weekly or nightly period of rest and recuperation. Leisure time is clearly constricted by type and hours of work. To study leisure on its own is dangerous in two ways at least.

First, many of the struggles fought around leisure in the first half of the nineteenth century were no more than the epilogues of struggles being fought out in the course of the working week. The introduction of a new work process often changed the hours and intensity of work and its seasonality. If trade unionist or other forms of resistance failed, it is not surprising that the struggle to maintain an old pattern of leisure, built around a previous work process, quickly lost its point. It is interesting that most of the struggles over the transformation of popular recreation so far researched were one-off affairs. Even the fighting over street football in Derby in the early 1840s seems only to have lasted three or four years. Characteristically, while strikes are usually solid, struggles over popular recreation are divided. The very fact that so little verbal defence was made of traditional popular recreation is not merely because rational recreationists monopolized the means of communication; it was because workers themselves were very divided on whether traditional forms of recreation were worthy of defence. Generally, the most politically articulate sector of the local workforce did not come out strongly in its defence. Unless we think industrialization was a mistake, we need not find this attitude particularly surprising. Owenites and Chartists did not challenge the steam engine itself, but the capitalist's control over the steam engine and his use of it to systematically overwork his employees. The answer was to end the capitalist control of work, or to capture the state that sustained the capitalist. Traditional recreations not only occupied a subordinate place in this battle, but many political activists saw these traditional pastimes as positively counter-productive in the formation of a working class capable of fighting this struggle. Some must have seen these traditional pursuits in the way that Black Power militants regarded often celebrated aspects of traditional black culture in the 1960s as features injurious to the dignity of black people, as part of the syndrome symbolized by 'Uncle Tom'.

The second danger of studying leisure on its own is again related to the primacy of work, and the social relations within which it is carried on, in the determination of class position and in the articulation of class attitudes. To study leisure and popular recreation as a distinct subject – particularly if we try to think of it in terms of a polarity between 'class expression and social control' – leads to a real danger of over-politicizing leisure as an arena of struggle. Leisure institutions which remained essential to workers – pubs, for example – were strongly defended. But others were given up with little resistance, because they had ceased to have a point. It is really dangerous to interpret the disappearance of pre-industrial recreations simply as a huge defeat. Some historians have drawn parallels between strikes and struggles over popular recreation. Their fundamental dissimilarity must also be stressed. The struggle in the factory is a struggle inherent in the relations of production. Any argument about incorporation finds itself on weak ground here. Struggles over leisure time do not have this inherent antagonism built into them. The primary point of a holiday is not political. It is to enjoy yourself, for tomorrow you must work. To write into recreations a symbolic form of class conflict – or its reverse, a channelling or diversion of class consciousness – leads precisely to the inrush of theories of incorporation to explain why workers have appeared to accept the capitalization of leisure with apparent passivity. Of course, carnivals, fairs or football matches may become the occasion of major social struggles. They have in fact often been so. But in nearly all instances we would find that they acted as the occasion or the catalyst of the events they triggered and not as the cause. Lastly, we should find that, the further we pursued those causes, the further we should find ourselves from the tempting but tautological couplet: class expression/social control.

3

'A Just Measure of Crime, Authority, Hunters and Blue Locusts': The 'Revisionist' Social History of Crime and the Law in Britain, 1780–1850

DAVID PHILIPS

Specially written for this volume

The last decade has seen a fundamental change in the writing of serious historical studies of crime and the workings of the criminal law, law enforcement and punishment. This can be seen in studies dealing with a number of countries, including France and the USA, but is perhaps most notable in the work done in British history. From having been a 'non-subject' for serious historians, 'crime' (comprehending studies of criminals and criminal acts, courts, law-enforcement bodies and the apparatus of punishment) has now become an area of serious and steady growth in social history writing. This interest has extended back through a number of centuries, to the seventeenth century and earlier[1]; but it would be fair to say that the greatest amount of interest has centred on the period from the late eighteenth to the mid-nineteenth century, when the whole apparatus of the state dealing with the criminal law, police and punishment underwent a revolution as substantial as the Industrial Revolution that Britain was experiencing at the same time. This change was most marked in Britain, but similar changes in law, punishment and police in the same period can also be seen in the USA, France and other advanced countries of Europe. This essay concentrates on the British experience and the recent historical explorations of that experience.

There is nothing new about the basic *account* of the changes that were implemented in Britain in the period *c.* 1780–1850. Historians have long made some mention of the reforms made in the criminal law in this period: the eighteenth-century 'Bloody Code' of capital punishment was replaced, in all cases except murder, with sentences of transportation or imprisonment; the campaigns of John Howard, Sir Samuel Romilly, Sir James Mackintosh, Sir Thomas Fowell Buxton, Elizabeth Fry and others, to reform the law and the state of the prisons, are often mentioned as illustrations of the movements of the time towards humanitarian reform

under the influence of evangelical Christianity and Benthamite
utilitarianism. Robert Peel's establishment of the Metropolitan Police
Force in 1829 gets two or three sentences in most histories, as a milestone in
Britain's move towards a modern, more humane and less barbarous and
dangerous society. But until very recently there was little attempt to
analyse these developments intensively, and examine why things happened
as they did. Few historians bothered to examine the issues in any detail,
and, for those who did, teleology tended to be the order of the day. It was
assumed that events moved towards their 'proper' modern end: the
historians' task was simply to supply the narrative and explain why there
were so many culpable delays and hesitations in the coming of this
inevitable and desirable state of affairs. The inevitable end was the modern
type of uniformed professional police force, a state policy of encouraging
uniform and regular prosecution of discovered offences, restriction of
capital punishment to murder, and the use of imprisonment as the basic
punishment for most offenders.

When I first began working in this area in 1970, I came to it as a historian
interested in what a study of crime and law-enforcement would add to the
social history of English society; and I was surprised and disappointed to
find how little there was in the way of serious historical works that offered
useful frameworks of approach to these problems. Towering over the
whole field were Sir Leon Radzinowicz's four massive volumes
(Radzinowicz, 1948–68), published at intervals between 1948 and 1968 and
dealing with the transition from the eighteenth to the mid-nineteenth
century in England. No one who works in this area can afford to neglect
these volumes (amounting, in all, to over 2000 pages, with long scholarly
footnotes, appendices and substantial bibliographies), which represent a
triumph of industry and research in compiling the large amount of
information that they contain. But they are far more satisfactory as a
quarry for material than as a source of ideas for historical analysis.

Despite its title, the book is really about two themes, which run
unevenly throughout the four volumes – the campaign to reform the
criminal law and punishment (found mainly in vols 1 and 4), and the story
of the reform of the agencies of police (vols 2, 3 and 4). Radzinowicz wrote
these volumes essentially as a modern criminologist interested in how the
modern English legal, penal and police systems had developed. In
particular, he recounts how the campaigns of the reformers of the criminal
law (Cesare Beccaria, Jeremy Bentham, Romilly, Mackintosh, Buxton)
and the reformers of the police (Henry and John Fielding, Patrick
Colquhoun, Robert Peel, Edwin Chadwick) eventually came to successful
fruition; they did so after having had to struggle long and hard against an
opposition depicted as consisting of conservatives, vested interests and

people too short-sighted to realize that it was in their own best interests to adopt the 'modern' systems of criminal law (lesser penalties uniformly enforced instead of harsh ones enforced arbitrarily and capriciously) and police (uniformed, bureaucratic police forces instead of non-professional parish constables and *ad hoc* bodies of watchmen). Radzinowicz shows no interest in exploring the social history of the society he is dealing with, or of relating this to popular attitudes towards crime, the law and the police. He takes a simple linear view of reform as progress, and sets this out explicitly in his opening sentence: 'Lord Macaulay's generalisation that the history of England is the history of progress is as true of the criminal law of this country as of the other social institutions of which it is a part' (Radzinowicz, 1948–68, vol. 1, ix). There is no place in this explicitly 'Whig view of history' for any notion of reforms urged on the state and adopted by it as a means of improved social control; nor does this approach offer any analysis of how these moves by the state were seen and felt from below, by the people most affected by them.

Apart from the Radzinowicz volumes, serious historical material on this area was hard to find. On the topic of crime and criminals (apart from numerous popular and sensational works drawing heavily on Dickens, Mayhew and Jack the Ripper), the only work was Tobias's book (Tobias, 1967). This had begun life as a London University PhD, and was certainly a serious attempt to examine crime in nineteenth-century English society. But it lacked much in the way of a serious theoretical approach to the problem. Tobias's method was to read the material published by parliamentary inquiries, statistical society investigators, interested magistrates, prison chaplains, reformers and so on – of which there is a vast amount, since the topics of crime, the criminal law, police and punishment were issues of considerable fear and concern in the first half of the nineteenth century – and draw on this for his evidence. But he drew on it quite uncritically; there was no consideration of the fact that these documents were written *about* the lower orders by people from the middle and upper class who were used to making pronouncements about their social inferiors without necessarily knowing much about the realities of their lives. No allowance was made for the possibility that police reformers like Patrick Colquhoun and Edwin Chadwick had a vested interest in frightening their readers by painting as black a picture as possible of the dangers of the 'criminal class' or 'dangerous classes' in order to win acceptance for their schemes of reform; or for the idea that policemen and magistrates are always liable to put the blame for crime on a small group of worthless and dangerous professional criminals who are to be sharply distinguished from the rest of the 'honest poor'. Tobias accepted what these spokesmen said, virtually uncritically – the only check he imposed was to see if some other similar figure had said the same thing. Since he rejected any use of official criminal statistics for his study, and did not look at any of the records of actual court proceedings, this left the content of his book dependent on these published statements of opinion. There was no attempt to construct a theoretical apparatus, by which the considerable conceptual problems posed by a historical study of crime might be approached.

In the area of police, apart from Radzinowicz's work, there were few serious histories. What there was, was generally written from the administrative point of view – the problem of setting up and running efficiently a police force or forces – with little reference to the people with whom the police had to deal. Charles Reith had produced a whole string of police 'histories' (Reith, 1938, 1940, 1943, 1952, 1956), all based around the simple idea that the modern British police force was the best possible type of police, and that his job as historian was to chronicle the efforts of the noble reformers who struggled to get such a force established in the face of blind, pigheaded obstruction by selfish, lazy, short-sighted opponents, always acting (in Reith's view) in bad faith. One example conveys fully the flavour of Reith's level of historical analysis. The belief that the establishment of a police force would involve a sacrifice of public liberty

> . . . was the product of long-sustained, skilful propaganda by vested interests with heavy commitments in the freedom of crime from control by law. Behind these interests were ranged all who sought the fulfilment of political programmes by means of mob disorder, and, more unfortunately, the vast majority of sincere, progressive, political leaders, and most of the 'peaceably-disposed' patriotic citizens. [Reith, 1943, p. 28]

T.A. Critchley's history of the police (Critchley, 1967) was a more thorough and informed study, but it was still very much administrative history, written by a former Home Office civil servant.

Similarly, in the area of punishment, the standard available history remained that of the Webbs (Webb and Webb, 1922) – very sound on the details of the introduction and development of the penitentiary from the 1770s, on the reforms of John Howard, Sir George Onesiphorus Paul and Elizabeth Fry, and on the legislation of successive nineteenth-century governments; but offering no real ideas as to *why*, in that particular period, the system of punishment should have been changed so substantially and the penitentiary developed in its modern form. Nor did the Webbs really try to relate the changes in prison structure and administration to the social, economic and political changes of the period. An attempt to do this had been made in 1939 (Rusche and Kirchheimer, 1939), but unfortunately their analysis is weakest and thinnest at precisely the point where it is most needed: on offering a convincing relationship between the changes in the forms of punishment carried out between the 1770s and the 1860s, and the social and economic changes of the period.

A composite picture, drawn from these accounts, of what happened to the British legal and penal system from the late eighteenth into the mid-nineteenth century would go something like this. The eighteenth-century system was one of very severe penalties (the 'Bloody Code' of more than 200 capital offences, mainly property offences) but very weak and capricious enforcement machinery – there was no proper police force, prosecution was haphazard, and convicted people were often saved from the gallows by a pardon. Under the prodding of the reformers, the governments of the day were slowly brought to realize that this system was both inhumane and inefficient. So they abolished most of the capital offences and substituted instead prison terms, for which purpose new penitentiaries were built. And, being compelled to realize, belatedly, the need to enforce the laws uniformly, and the great dangers posed by the professional criminal class massed in the slums of the fast-growing towns, they introduced proper police forces piecemeal to the country, starting with the Metropolitan Force in 1829.

Generally, the history of crime, law, police and prisons remained peripheral history; those who wrote about it did not address themselves seriously to issues of power, political structure, analysis of reform and social change, or attempts to recover the views of the mass of the people affected by these changes. Serious historians could happily ignore these issues except where their own particular objects of interest happened to be involved in one of them (for example, Robert Peel as Home Secretary carried out some reforms of the criminal law and established the Metropolitan Police Force; accounts of Peel's political career had to note these achievements, however briefly).[2] As for sociologists or criminologists who might be interested in the historical aspects of their field, they were unlikely to find much to tempt them in the published historical works at this time. They would have found straight empirical narrative, informed by little or no analysis; even Radzinowicz's work, informed by his own criminological perspective, confronted the prospective reader with the need to plough through 2000 heavily footnoted pages in order to get his message, and few sociologists had the stomach for dealing with that much empirical history.

II

The most important influence in transforming this situation, as in transforming generally the social history written about this period, was that of Edward Thompson. *The Making of the English Working Class* first appeared in 1963. It reappeared, with a 'Postscript', in a large and widely read Pelican paperback in 1968, and it has exerted, and continues to exert, a seminal influence on the writing of modern British social history. Thompson's work inspired generations of students and historians with the idea of writing true social history – the history of the historically inarticulate lower classes of society – and of doing so (*pace* Trevelyan's definition of social history) *not* with 'the politics left out'; of exploring the popular culture of the masses via rituals, symbols, popular celebrations and popular disturbances; of rescuing various groups of workers, protesters and rebels from what Thompson called 'the enormous condescension of posterity'.[3] A similar influence stemmed from the earlier work of George Rudé (1959, 1962, 1964), who studied the activities of riotous crowds in the French Revolution and in late eighteenth- and early nineteenth-century England and France. Unlike Tobias or Reith, Rudé was not prepared to take at face value the expressed opinions of contemporaries that these riots were the work of 'mobs' of criminals, vagrants and the like. His patient work in reconstructing these events, making especial use of court records and newspaper accounts in order to do so, enabled him to rehabilitate the historical 'crowd', and to offer, in place of the picture of the anonymous, mindless mob, some glimpses of the 'faces in the crowd' (Rudé, 1964, p. 11) and of the ideas and rational aims of the riotous crowds. Similarly, Eric Hobsbawm (1959) offered the concept of the 'social bandit' as a useful framework within which to analyse the Robin Hood-type outlaw or bandit who is regarded as a popular hero and who can be found in most pre-industrial societies. In an essay in his *Labouring Men* (Hobsbawm, 1964), he offered an analysis of the Luddite machine-breaking which examined the activity in terms of the aims and aspirations of the machine-breakers and the long history of machine-breaking as a weapon in labour struggles, rather than simply dismissing the Luddites as backward, ignorant opponents of progress.

The effect of the Thompson–Hobsbawm–Rudé approach was to transform the writing of social history; and in doing so it opened up the social history of crime as an area of serious study. All three of these historians dealt with issues of violence and disorder in political struggles, and with the use of the law and the forces of authority to cope with them; and Thompson threw out some tantalizing references to crime and criminals, and to popular attitudes to the law, in *The Making of the English Working Class*.

Thompson continued to work in the area of the popular culture of eighteenth-century England, including crime; and he briefly gathered around him at Warwick University a group of graduate students working on crime and the law. In 1975 this group produced a collection of essays on crime and the law in eighteenth-century England (Hay, Linebaugh and Thompson, 1975); at the same time, Thompson published his study of the making and implementation of the 'Black Act' of 1723 (Thompson, 1975), which, while aimed initially at acts of defiance of the forest laws committed by groups of 'Blacks', effectively created more than 50 new capital offences – including taking deer, poaching fish, breaking down the head of a fishpond, cutting down trees, sending anonymous letters and appearing in groups armed and/or with faces blacked.

Easily the outstanding piece in *Albion's Fatal Tree* is Douglas Hay's first essay (Hay, 1975a); this gained rapid and deserved acclaim, and now stands as a model and challenge to anyone wanting to write serious historical studies of crime and the law. Hay combines a theoretical approach, which one might call roughly 'Thompsonian–Marxist', with a thorough grasp of the available evidence and its possibilities. He offers a credible picture of the workings, in late eighteenth-century England, not just of the legal system, but of the whole political and social system. He asserts boldly that the law and its mystique served an integral purpose in that society; and he shows, very convincingly, that those aspects that Radzinowicz (following Bentham, Romilly and the utilitarian reformers) castigated as irrational and inefficient in the legal and penal system made good sense to the men who actually ran the system as part of their structure of political power. Hay's other essay in that volume (Hay, 1975b) is a model of how best to study the incidence of a particular type of offence; in this case, he uses a range of sources well beyond the purely legal (especially the papers of the influential large local landowners) to set his study of poaching on Cannock Chase within a convincing local social and political context. Not only is this an impressive local study in its own right, but it also contributes valuable support, in terms of both evidence and analysis, to his general picture of the workings of the criminal law in the second half of the eighteenth century.

Thompson (1975) gives an analysis of the making of the Black Act, and relates it to the new money-hungry and property-protecting ruling class that was establishing itself under the rule of Walpole and his Whigs in the early decades of the eighteenth century. But the book offers more than just a reconstruction of the story of some men (the 'Blacks') who resisted the encroachment by the Whig 'new men' on their traditional forest rights and were ultimately hanged under the new law passed by the Whigs to deal with them. Thompson adds a short, but very effective, section at the end of the book (pp. 258–69), in which he takes up the question of the historical analysis of the Rule of Law – a piece that nicely complements Hay's essay (1975a). Here he warns not just against the conservative historian's tendency to assume that the law is neutral and above politics, but also against what he sees as a simplistic 'highly schematic Marxism' (that is, Althusserianism), which states that 'the rule of law is only another mask for the rule of a class'. Historical investigation shows that it is never so simple, says Thompson; the ruling class of eighteenth-century England certainly made use of the law to further their own interests, but they could never turn it purely into their own creature because the legitimacy of the law and of their whole political system depended upon people believing that the law was just and universal. So

> the rulers were, in serious senses, whether willingly or unwillingly, the prisoners of their own rhetoric; they played the games of power according to rules which suited them, but they could not break those rules or the whole game would be thrown away. And, finally, so far from the ruled shrugging off this rhetoric as a hypocrisy, some part of it at least was taken over as part of the rhetoric of the plebeian crowd, of the 'free-born Englishman' with his inviolable privacy, his *habeas corpus*, his equality before the law. [Thompson, 1975, 259, 263–4]

Here Thompson brings out the complexity involved in serious study of the law, and suggests some of its importance for understanding political, social and labour history.[4] Anyone who has worked on historical sources on crime and the criminal law (and presumably anyone working on the modern legal and criminal justice system) knows how tempting it is to come up with a simple all-embracing dichotomy, whether it be: 'good policeman/bad criminal' or 'good social protester stigmatized and punished as criminal/bad repressive authorities'. But such simple dichotomies, however tempting, are false. In the same legal system at the same time, one is likely to find all four of these types and a number of others besides; and it is no service to understanding to try to reduce this complexity to an easily manageable but crude stereotype. In early nineteenth-century England, for instance, one can find evidence of working people who felt their rights to be infringed by the establishment and activities of the 'New Police' and by their employers' strict legal enforcement of property rights; and they resented and resisted these aspects of the law. But they also valued their own small property rights and were prepared to go to law to protect them – to prosecute other working people in the courts for theft, if necessary (Philips, 1977, pp. 74–87, 123–9, 285–6). Thompson makes a similar point when he says: 'What was often at issue was not property, supported by law, against no-property; it was alternative definitions of property rights: for the landowner, enclosure; for the cottager, common rights; for the forest officialdom, "preserved grounds" for the deer; for the forester, the right to take turfs' (Thompson 1975, p. 261).

Thompson has been sharply criticized by some historians, lawyers and sociologists on the Left for this last section of *Whigs and Hunters*, and for his subsequent all-out attack on the influence of Althusserianism on historical writing (Thompson, 1978b). He has been accused of abandoning any attempt at a rigorous Marxist framework of explanation, of taking refuge in an ultimately conservative historian's empiricism, and of taking too much at face value the idea of the value of the Rule of Law (see for example Merritt, 1980). There is no doubt that Thompson's work from 1975 onwards *does* show an increasingly visible streak of radical-conservatism or Tory-radicalism; in his recent assertions of the rights of the 'freeborn Englishman' (first expounded in Thompson, 1963) and of the English jury system as a bulwark of liberty against the encroachments of an over-mighty executive, he can sound like a late eighteenth-century backwoods Tory squire thundering against the dangers of a too-powerful central government (Thompson, 1978a, 1978b, 1980). But none of Thompson's critics from the Left has yet come up with a convincing alternative analysis of the eighteenth-century issues that he raises and deals with. He may have forfeited his claim to be a good Marxist, in the eyes of many; but he remains a profoundly fruitful and suggestive historian of these areas.

Another, rather different, input into the historiography of crime and the law in the 1970s came from the sociologists of deviance and the 'New Criminology' (Becker, 1963, 1964; Cicourel and Kitsuse, 1963; Cicourel, 1968; Erikson, 1966; Lemert, 1967; Matza, 1964; Cohen, 1971). Historians who had found standard criminology useless as an aid to historical analysis found that labelling theory and various forms of analysis of 'deviance', 'moral entrepreneurs' and 'moral panics' offered fruitful insights with which to approach historical issues of crime and law (Philips, 1977, 1980; Davis, 1980). By stressing the wider aspects of 'deviance', and by focusing on the interaction between the law-breakers and the law-makers, this approach enabled one to get away from the arid rigidities of orthodox criminology; it stressed that 'crime' was not a given and constant phenomenon, the same in all societies and at all times, but rather something defined by those who made and enforced the law; it offered salutary scepticism about the meanings and uses of official definitions and statistics, and made the makers and enforcers of the law proper objects of study along with the breakers of the law (Philips, 1977).

However, for most historians in this area, labelling theory was more useful for the criticisms that it offered of conventional criminology than for anything positive that it could offer in its place. The actual studies seemed to concentrate disproportionately on marginal deviant groups (drug-takers, homosexual prostitutes and so on), and to avoid the central offences against property and person – such as burglary, robbery, larceny and aggravated assaults – with which historians of crime find themselves mostly concerned. There were even those deviancy sociologists who went so far as to suggest that crime was entirely the product of official reactions (Ditton, 1980). And no grand theory or model of approach that historians could usefully adopt has yet emerged from this work.[5]

The concept of 'social control' – despite its conservative origins in Durkheim's writings – has been freely employed by many sociologists of deviance critical of authority and the way in which its legitimacy is enforced. Historians have generally been reluctant to employ the term; and those who have used it in recent years have often done so in a sloppy and careless way, in which it becomes little more than a convenient catch-all term used to explain why one group is able to retain power – the old crude conspiracy theory clothed in new sociological terminology. Gareth Stedman Jones in particular (chapter 2 above) has strongly attacked historians' use of the concept in this way, and he has argued that historians of the Left, in particular, should avoid the use of such concepts. However, a recent book of essays on nineteenth-century themes (Donajgrodzki, 1977) has tried to use the concept as a focal point, with greater success. Its strength lies in directing historians' attention away from formal institutions to informal means of enforcing power and maintaining authority – via education, control of leisure, distribution of poor relief, etc. Critics such as Stedman Jones have not yet come up with a satisfactory alternative that can be used to convey this sort of informal authority, while avoiding the actual phrase 'social control' – Stedman Jones's own suggested alternative of 'class expression' certainly fails to do this – and some useful works on areas of nineteenth-century authority have come from historians taking a broad 'social control' approach.[6]

Of the historical work on crime and law that has appeared since 1975, none could be said to follow directly a Thompson–Hay line, nor a pure labelling theory or 'sociology of deviance' approach. As always with historical work, eclecticism and the demands of empirical research play a large part (perhaps too large a part for many sociologists' liking) in the work produced. Yet collectively, we can construct from these works a 'revisionist' picture – to set against the traditional picture outlined earlier – of what took place (and why) in the English legal and penal system between 1780 and 1850.

The area of punishment has seen some very innovative advances.

Rothman's account (1971) of the development of institutionalized asylums
– penitentiary, insane asylum, almshouse, reformatory, orphanage, school
– in America from the late eighteenth to the mid-nineteenth century
mounted a serious critique of the motives of the reformers who sponsored
these reforms, arguing that their motive was not simple humanitarianism
but a concern to re-establish a sense of discipline, obedience and hard work
in a society perceived as in danger of falling apart. Michel Foucault (1977)
took much further Rothman's argument that the replacement, in France,
England and the USA, of physical punishments by confinement in
penitentiaries from the end of the eighteenth century did not simply result
from greater humanity and a more squeamish civilization: this move, said
Foucault, substituted for the old punishment of the body a new one, more
subtle and far-reaching, attacking the mind and soul: 'The expiation that
once rained down upon the body must be replaced by a punishment that
acts in depth on the heart, the thoughts, the will, the inclinations'
(Foucault, 1977, p. 16).

The adequacy of both Rothman's and Foucault's books as historical
accounts has been sharply criticized;[7] but their general approach and
insights have been applied in a carefully documented historical study of the
development of the penitentiary in England (Ignatieff, 1978). Michael
Ignatieff focuses attention on the extent to which the reformers (Howard,
Bentham, Paul, Fry) pressed for their reforms of punishment and prison
conditions not simply in order to do away with barbarous hangings and
whippings, but also as a means of re-establishing discipline among the
lower orders and turning the 'unhappy wretches' being hanged in the
eighteenth century into 'useful members of society' via the penitentiary
and its reformatory regime. His comments on Elizabeth Fry's reforming
activities express one of the chief messages of the book:

> Philanthropy is not simply a vocation, a moral choice; it is also an act
> of authority that creates a linkage of dependency and obligation
> between rich and poor. Of necessity, therefore, it is a political act,
> embarked upon not merely to fulfil personal needs, but also to address
> the needs of those who rule, and those who are ruled. [Ignatieff, 1978,
> p. 153]

Ignatieff stresses that the penitentiary – the idea of prisons as places of
long-term confinement for the punishment and reformation of prisoners,
rather than simply as places of detention of debtors and of prisoners
awaiting trial and execution of sentence – was something new at the end of
the eighteenth century. Pentonville's 'model prison', opened in 1842,
became the model for numerous penitentiary prisons built throughout

Britain in the 1840s and 1850s. These became entrenched as the basis of the modern prison system, despite the manifest failure of the penitentiary regimes to solve the problems of crime. Ignatieff argues that the penitentiary prison became just one of the nineteenth-century array of 'total institutions' – along with the workhouse, lunatic asylum, monitorial school and factory – which were used to discipline deviant members of the working class.[8]

Ignatieff has subsequently (see chapter 4 below) withdrawn from some of the stronger assertions made in his book, and has admitted the validity of some of his critics' charges (for example De Lacy, 1980) that he and Foucault oversimplified the nature of the transformation and exaggerated the extent to which the governments of the time were able to implement the new penitential 'carceral regime'. But he would still affirm the basic validity of his account of the nature of the reforms and the motives of the reformers who sponsored them. A similar analysis has been made of those reformers concerned with juvenile delinquency who secured the institution of reformatory schools for juvenile delinquents in mid-nineteenth-century England (Eade, 1976).[9] These reformers (Mary Carpenter, Thomas Barwick Lloyd Baker, Matthew Davenport Hill and others) were motivated not just by humanitarian pity for the children they 'saved', but also by a desire to bring these children under the necessary religious and moral discipline, and to re-socialize them to become true (that is, middle-class; respectable) children again:

> [The delinquent] will be gradually restored to the true position of childhood. He must be brought to a sense of dependence by reawakening in him new and healthy desires which he cannot himself satisfy, and by finding that there is a power far greater than his own to which he is indebted for the gratification of these desires. [Mary Carpenter, *Juvenile Delinquents, Their Condition and Treatment*, London, 1853, p. 298; quoted in Eade, 1976, p. 105]

One can note a considerable similarity between the aims of these moral entrepreneurs of the reformatory movement, trying to turn the dangerously independent slum child into something approaching their idea of a respectable, dependent child, and those of their contemporaries who were trying to reform the way working-class people spent their leisure time, for fear of what might happen if those leisure activities continued unsupervised (Storch, 1977).

Recent work done on the establishment and functioning of the early police forces has added greatly to our knowledge of this area of change, and, it is to be hoped, has destroyed for ever the idea of a simple, linear progression from 'bad' old parish constables and watchmen to 'good' new, uniformed police forces.[10] As early as 1967, Allan Silver had written a very suggestive article, in which he discussed briefly the implications of the coming of what he called 'the policed society' with a 'bureaucratization of police functions'; and he linked this to the need perceived by the urban propertied classes in the early nineteenth century to introduce a force to protect themselves against riot and potential revolution (Silver, 1967). Silver's article was too brief to be able to examine the historical evidence in any detail, but he threw up a suggestive and challenging thesis, accompanied by enough evidence to make it plausible.

Similar ideas were taken up and examined, with some supporting local evidence, in two articles by Robert Storch (1975, 1976), examining the impact of the new police forces on working-class communities in the industrial North of England. Storch produced evidence of considerable popular hostility towards the police, who were seen as an agency that subjected working-class life to a considerable degree of surveillance and actively intervened, to try to change working-class patterns of behaviour and to stamp our or modify existing working-class sports and recreations. A similar finding was shown for the West Midlands industrial area of the Black Country (Philips, 1977); the newly established county police force devoted considerable effort to, and incurred a considerable amount of popular hostility from, attempts to suppress popular 'rough' sports. That same study showed that there was no sharp break between the 'old' parish constable regime and the 'New Police'. The New Police, in their early years, were not very efficient or numerous, they had a high turnover of manpower, and they concentrated much of their effort on the suppression of disorders; conversely, the parish constables were considerably more effective and adequate in dealing with offences and small disorders within the local community than historians had normally been prepared to give them credit for (Philips, 1977, chapter 3; see also Styles (forthcoming)).

A more recent study (Philips, 1980) has traced the development of the campaign to establish a professional police force for London, and the opposition to it, from the late eighteenth century through to the 1830s. It was in the period 1780–1850 that the key changes were made to the old eighteenth-century system of law: a professional police force was finally appointed for London, and, in the next three decades, for the other parts of the country; stipendiary magistrates were appointed for London to replace the unpaid gentlemen-Justices of the Peace, and their use was extended to other urban and industrial areas; the government took an active role in encouraging prosecution of offenders, making it easier by extending the scope of reimbursement of prosecutors' expenses and widening the range of offences triable by summary jurisdiction (Vagrancy Act 1824, Malicious

Trespass Act 1826, Larceny Act 1826, Metropolitan Police Acts 1829 and 1839);[11] and, of course, the criminal law and punishments were reformed in the manner already mentioned.

Resistance to these changes, especially to a new police force, came *not* just from short-sighted people or selfish vested interests. There was considerable resistance to the idea of a police force from the organized working class and from libertarian elements of the Whigs and Radicals; but most important for its political effectiveness in Parliament was the opposition by backbench Tory country gentlemen, who saw a new police for London as the thin end of a wedge which would ultimately undermine the whole of their eighteenth-century system (as analysed in Hay, 1975a). Their resistance was eventually overcome only by the pressure of urban middle-class propertied interests – seeking a police force to protect their property and persons against what seemed to be an inexorably growing tide of urban crime, and against the threat of revolution by the growing urban masses. These views were forcefully propagated by advocates of a new police, such as Bentham, Colquhoun and Chadwick; finally, Robert Peel was able to use them to achieve success when he managed to steer the Metropolitan Police Act through the House of Commons in 1829, after a number of other such attempts had failed in the previous 50 years.

We now have studies of the early years of operation of the Metropolitan Force (Miller, 1977; Jones, 1982), of some of the provincial and borough forces (Pilling, 1975; Weinberger, 1981; Field, 1981), and of the situation before the coming of the New Police (Styles, forthcoming). All of these take us further away from the pious teleology of Reith and towards a history in which the institution and operation of the agencies of police are subjected to the same sort of sceptical scrutiny that has long been given to most other administrative reforms.

In the area of studies of crime and criminals, we have some other works to put in place of Tobias's. Gatrell and Hadden (1972) showed that Tobias had been wrong to discard entirely the national criminal statistics as a source of historical evidence. Used carefully and patiently, the statistics can show fluctuations and trends in particular types of offence, and can be analysed in relation to the economic indicators, such as the trade cycle, the state of employment, the price of bread, etc. A local study of the Black Country based upon the court records of the local Quarter Sessions and Assizes (Philips, 1977), which enables one to examine the people who actually appeared in court and the offences for which they were tried, shows that the dramatic picture of crime accepted uncritically by Tobias from contemporaries' accounts, is misleading; most offences were 'prosaic and undramatic, involving small amounts being stolen, squalid robberies, burglaries and assaults, in which roughness was common, but not fatal violence, and in which the items taken were usually small amounts of coal, metal, clothing, food, money or personal possessions' (Philips, 1977, p. 287).

Recent similar local studies (such as Jones, 1982, chapters 3, 4 and 5) suggest similar pictures for other parts of early industrial Britain. This raises the question of why, if the picture was essentially as undramatic as this, so much concern and alarm should have been expressed about the issues of crime and law enforcement in the first half of the nineteenth century. The answer lies in the fact that most commentators on this subject tended to couple crime with disorder as the threat to be feared. It was the problem of coping with the new urban masses, seen, in the wake of the French and Industrial Revolutions, as posing a constant threat of riot and potential revolution, that fuelled the vigorous debate on the dangerous and criminal classes and the best strategies for maintaining law and order.[12] As Patrick Colquhoun said, in calling for the establishment of a national police agency,

> A new era in the world seems to have commenced, which imperiously calls for the adoption of such [police surveillance] measures; not only in this country, but all over Europe. The evil propensities incident to human nature appear no longer restrained by the force of religion, or the influence of the moral principle. On these barriers powerful attacks have been made, which have hitherto operated as curbs to the unruly passions peculiar to vulgar life: they must therefore be strengthened by supports more immediately applicable to the object of preserving peace and good order.

He assured his readers that it was

> A fact well-established, that it was principally through the medium, and by the assistance, of many of the twenty thousand miscreants who were registered, previous to the anarchy of France, on the books of the Lieutenant of Police, that the contending Factions in that distracted country were enabled to perpetrate those horrid massacres and acts of atrocity.

And now (1800), he warned his readers, the danger existed that the

> several thousand miscreants of the same description which now infest London. . . upon any fatal emergency (which God forbid!) would be equally ready as their brethren in iniquity were, in Paris, to repeat the same atrocities if any opportunity offered. [Colquhoun, 1800, pp. 562, 532–3].[13]

III

We can now try to draw conclusions about the overall picture that emerges from these 'revisionist' writings on what was happening to law and punishment in the period 1780–1850, and we can contrast it to the old account that could be gleaned from Reith, Tobias, Radzinowicz and others. Drawing on the insights and information of these recent studies, we can see the changes that were implemented in police, punishment and the substance and administration of the criminal law as part of the wider process in which the governing class of Britain adjusted to the changes and problems presented by the Industrial Revolution period. There is ample evidence that many of the country gentry would have liked to continue the eighteenth-century system of administration and enforcement of the law, which, as Hay has shown, suited their purposes well; and they put up a fierce rearguard resistance to the new changes in police and punishment (Hay, 1975a; Philips, 1980). But the eighteenth-century system had depended on the exercise of informal powers by landed JPs over their own small, semi-autonomous, local areas. The rapid growth of large towns and cities – above all, London, but also, from the 1780s, such industrial and commercial towns as Manchester, Birmingham, Glasgow, Liverpool, Leeds – with their large concentrations of working-class populations removed from face-to-face contact with squire and parson, posed problems for the maintenance of social order that could not be solved by the old methods of control. The development of the new factory system, in Lancashire and Yorkshire, with large numbers of workers massed under one roof and having to be disciplined into the new work rhythms demanded by the machinery and the factory management (Thompson, 1967; Pollard, 1968) similarly raised new and frightening problems of control. Added to this was the fear of revolution, which was never absent from the minds of the governing classes of Britain from the time of the French Revolution and through the events of the 1790s, Luddism, Peterloo, the Reform Bill agitation and Chartism in the late 1830s and 1840s. Not until the collapse of large-scale Chartism in 1848 could the British upper and middle classes breathe freely on this score.

To cope with these problems, the governing class had to take up, however reluctantly, the types of solution proposed by Jeremy Bentham and his utilitarian disciples; these involved moving towards a more bureaucratic and professional structure for the new urban industrial society. In the area of law and order, this move meant: in place of parish constables, police forces; in place of lay Justices, stipendiary magistrates; in place of local gaols and houses of correction, a system of penitentiary prisons, ultimately under national Home Office control. Bentham had called, from the late eighteenth century, for reforms to the criminal law to reduce capital punishment (following Beccaria), and for a police force to enforce the law uniformly; and in 1791 he had unveiled his plans for the Panopticon penitentiary, with its Orwellian vision of a system in which the prisoner could never hide from the all-seeing eye of the jailer. Similarly, he outlined plans for the reform of the Poor Laws, plans that were largely followed when his disciple Edwin Chadwick devised the structure of the New Poor Law of 1834. The Poor Law reform, too, moved from a highly localized, informal, diverse system towards a more centralized, bureaucratized, uniform structure.

Together with these moves towards greater bureaucratic uniformity in administration went an attempt to 'individualize' the masses being dealt with, in keeping with the new individualistic ethos of early industrial capitalism: the individual pauper was to be deterred by 'less eligible' treatment in the workhouse from applying for relief, just as the individual criminal was to be reformed and made penitent by solitary confinement in a penitentiary. The old eighteenth-century principle of treating the lower orders *en masse* – hang one offender in ten in the hope of deterring the other nine, and never mind if those nine are never formally punished; give out poor relief generally in times of hardship to prevent disturbances – gives way to an emphasis on the individual being dealt with under a bureaucratic system: arrest, prosecute and imprison *every* offender and reform each one through solitary confinement; force *each* able-bodied pauper to seek work rather than relief, by imposing the mechanical workhouse test and 'less eligibility'. Bentham's actual proposals were not necessarily the direct source of the reforms finally implemented, but his writings (and the writings and activities of his disciples Colquhoun, Romilly and Chadwick) offer an effective symbol of the impulses that led to the establishment of our modern bureaucratic agencies to control urban industrial society.[14]

The growth of towns and industries in the Industrial Revolution meant that the old face-to-face paternalist methods of keeping order would no longer serve. New methods of control were needed – in factory discipline and mass education, as well as in the distribution of poor relief and the administration of law, order and punishment. The prison, the workhouse, the factory and the school stand out in nineteenth-century Britain as concrete symbols of the attempts to instil a new sort of discipline and control in the masses of early industrial society. One must not, however, imagine that any of these changes were implemented neatly and perfectly, or that they were being carried out easily by all-powerful authorities in a political vacuum – they were always the subject of struggle and what amounted to bargaining by means of the use or threat of force. Throughout this period, there was resistance to these changes, especially from the working class as the group most affected: resistance to the New Police; resistance to the new penitentiaries; massive organized resistance to the implementation of the New Poor Law; resistance to the imposition of the new work rhythms and factory discipline. And the reformers were not usually able to get their projected reforms implemented in full by government, Parliament and embryo civil service; administrative inertia, political expediency and an unwillingness to incur large new expenditure imposed limitations on what was done. The authorities were generally forced to some sort of compromise in the final form taken by the reformed agency – some relaxation of the strict workhouse test in the implementation of the New Poor Law; relatively weak, decentralized, unarmed police forces instead of an armed, national body; legislation for a ten-hour day and protection of women and children workers in factories; modifications of the initial penitentiary regime.

It is within this broad framework of social change, social reform and class conflict that one must try to understand the changes in police, law and punishments. Both the social historian, interested in British society in this period, and the sociologist, interested in the development of modern forms of punishment and control, can only benefit from the historical study of crime, law and punishments being brought in from its peripheral position and given its rightful place in social history as part of the study of class conflict, popular culture, social change, social reform and the like. We can see that the reforms in law, police and prisons are of the same order as the contemporaneous reforms implemented to deal with poor relief, factory conditions, free trade, education, public health, urban sanitary conditions and so on and should be subject to the same analyses in terms of political power, political strategies and the aims and ideas of the reformers.[15]

This area, of historical studies of crime, law and punishment, having been strongly begun, still seems to be a field of thriving growth; and work is proceeding in the areas of eighteenth-century (Brewer and Styles, 1980; Styles, forthcoming; to be published; Innes, 1980; King, forthcoming; to be published) and late nineteenth- and early twentieth-century (Gatrell, 1980), as well as nineteenth-century, issues (Bailey, 1981; Jones, 1982). However, it would seem fair to comment that most of this work, both published and in progress, is much stronger on uncovering new sources of empirical material for the historian to use than on suggesting larger overviews, theoretical models or methods of approach to these sorts of problems in general. The model implicit in Hay's article (1975a) – brief and incomplete as it is – remains the most fruitful so far developed.

It is also true that not all historians working in the field would accept all the findings of what one can group together as the new 'revisionist' account of these events. Something of a 'counter-revisionist' school is developing. However, the only attempt so far to set out a self-consciously 'counter-revisionist' account (Bailey, 1981) has proved distinctly disappointing. Rather than offer alternative theoretical approaches to those of the 'revisionists', most of the contributors to that volume simply take refuge in a detailed but sterile empiricism, as if this somehow refuted larger theoretical overviews. They quote details, gleaned from the sources, to show that events and personalities were more complex than can be easily accommodated within the large 'revisionist' patterns. But this is simply to abdicate the historian's true function. More than two centuries ago, Voltaire rebuked historians of this sort, saying: 'If you have nothing to tell us except that one barbarian succeeded another on the banks of the Oxus and Jaxartes, what is that to us?' (Voltaire, in his article on history in the Encyclopaedia – quoted in Carr, 1961, p. 82).

Note here, Ignatieff's challenge to the counter-revisionist position (p. 77 below): the need to find a genuine model of historical explanation.

Future impressive advances in this field are not going to come from people who keep their noses buried in dusty files in the Public Record Office – or County Record Offices or libraries – and lift them only to tell us that they find the detailed process of interaction between the various individuals involved too complex to yield any overall patterns. To explain events as simply the product of a series of autonomous individual actions, and as 'one damned thing after another', is unsatisfactory history at any time. It would turn the history of crime and the law into a sort of antiquarianism, peering – pruriently or sedately – at the doings of criminals, police, judiciary and legislators. What is needed are some more broad concepts and approaches on which those working in the field can generally agree – about how one best defines and deals with 'crime', 'law', 'police', 'punishment', or aspects of them. Positivist criminology has been clearly shown to be inadequate as a tool, but neither labelling theory nor a Marxist approach has yet yielded much concrete history; the historians working in the field are going to have to develop and test their own tools for the job, without being able to rely on the sociologists or others to supply them with ready-made theories.[16]

NOTES

1. See, for example, the articles in Hay, Linebaugh and Thompson (1975); Cockburn (1977); Brewer and Styles (1980); and Beattie (1974, 1975).
2. See for example Gash (1961, chapters 9 and 14).
3. See for example Thompson (1967, 1971); Pearson (1978).
4. For a development of Thompson's views in regard to eighteenth-century society, see Thompson (1974, 1978a).

5. Taylor, Walton and Young (1973, 1975) are distinctly disappointing, in this respect, for those who hoped that a fruitful new Marxist criminology might emerge from one section of the 'deviancy' theorists. See Ignatieff, chapter 4 below.

6. See for example Donajgrodzki (1977, Introduction; chapters 2 and 5); Johnson (1970); Bailey (1981). Hay (1975a) explicitly eschews the use of the term 'social control', but the essay is all about demonstrating what others have called 'social control' being successfully applied by those who governed late eighteenth-century England.

7. See Ignatieff, chapter 4 below, for a good synthetic account of important criticisms that have been made of these, and his own book (Ignatieff, 1978). For a critique of some of Foucault's historical inaccuracies in relation to the nineteenth-century French prison scene, see Perrot (1980).

8. For a similar argument, in relation to lunatic asylums, see Scull (1979).

9. This thesis was written under her married name of Susan Eade; since then she has reverted to her maiden name; the one article she has so far drawn from the thesis is published under the name Magarey (1978).

10. See Hart (1978) – which, however, contains no reference to anything published later than 1973, and thus omits most of the recent relevant works.

11. See also Jones (1982), Miller (1977), Magarey (1978).

12. Stevenson (1979) gives a useful account of the disturbances, and fears of the authorities, throughout this crucial period; he draws effectively on recent work on riots, crime, law and order to provide this synthesis.

13. See also Alison (1844); and the similar examples and analysis in Palmer (1976).

14. Foucault (1977) calls one of his chapters (part Three, chapter 3) 'Panopticism', and uses Bentham's Panopticon effectively as a symbol of the new all-pervasive techniques of surveillance and discipline introduced in the early nineteenth century. Bentham himself pointed out that his Panopticon design could be used not only for penitentiaries but also for workhouses, factories, schools, asylums or any other place in which 'a number of persons are meant to be kept under inspection'. What Bentham called his 'simple idea in architecture', Foucault notes, enables a small number of people to control and keep under surveillance a large mass of people; and it breaks up that mass into many discrete individuals, each affected continually in his behaviour by the knowledge that he may be under observation at any hour of the day or night, whatever he is doing. The Panopticon also serves well the needs of a new bureaucratic system since its machinery can be worked by anyone; it 'automatizes and disindividualizes power . . . it does not matter who exercises power. . . . The Panopticon . . . produces homogeneous effects of power' (Foucault, 1977, p. 202).

15. See the attempt by Henriques (1979) to bring together an examination of the reforms in the Poor Law, factory legislation, public health, prisons and elementary education.

16. See Raphael Samuel and Gareth Stedman Jones, 'Sociology and History', *History Workshop Journal*, no. 1, 1976, pp. 6–8.

REFERENCES

[Alison, Archibald] (1844), 'Causes of the Increase of Crime', *Blackwood's Edinburgh Magazine*, 56, 1–14.

Bailey, Victor (1980), 'Crime, Criminal Justice and Authority in England: a Bibliographical Essay', *Bulletin of the Society for the Study of Labour History*, Spring 1980, 36–46.

Bailey, Victor (ed.) (1981), *Policing and Punishment in 19th Century Britain*. London; Croom Helm.

Beattie, J.M. (1974), 'The Pattern of Crime in England, 1660–1800', *Past & Present*, 62, 47–95.

Beattie, J.M. (1975), 'The Criminality of Women in Eighteenth-Century England', *Journal of Social History*, 8(4), 80–116.

Becker, H. (1963), *Outsiders: Studies in the Sociology of Deviance*. New York; Free Press.

Becker, H. (ed.) (1964), *The Other Side: Perspectives on Deviance*. New York; Free Press.

Bentham, Jeremy (1791), *Panopticon: Or the Inspection House*, vol. IV, in *The Works of Jeremy Bentham*, ed. J. Bowring. London, 1843.

Brewer, John, and Styles, John (eds) (1980), *An Ungovernable People: The English and their Law in the 17th and 18th Centuries*. London; Hutchinson.

Cain, Maureen (1974), 'The Main Themes of Marx' and Engels' Sociology of Law', *British Journal of Law and Society*, 1(2), 136–48.

Carr, E.H. (1961), *What is History?* London; Macmillan.

Cicourel, A.V. (1968), *The Social Organisation of Juvenile Justice*. New York; John Wiley.

Cicourel, A.V. and Kitsuse, J.I. (1963), 'A Note on the Uses of Official Statistics', *Social Problems*, 11, 131–9.

Cockburn, J.S. (ed.) (1977), *Crime in England 1550–1800*. London; Methuen:

Cohen, S. (ed.) (1971), *Images of Deviance*. Harmondsworth; Pelican.

Critchley, T.A. (1967), *A History of Police in England and Wales 900–1966*. London; Constable.

Davis, Jennifer (1980), 'The London Garrotting Panic of 1862: A Moral Panic and the Creation of a Criminal Class in Mid-Victorian England', in Gatrell, Parker and Lenman (1980), 190–213.

De Lacy, Margaret (1980), 'Grinding Men Good? Lancashire's Prisons at Mid-Century', in Bailey (1981), 182–216.

Ditton, Jason (1979), *Contrology: Beyond the New Criminology*. London; Macmillan.

Donajgrodzki, A.P. (ed.) (1977), *Social Control in Nineteenth Century Britain*. London; Croom Helm.

Eade, Susan (1976), 'The Reclaimers: A Study of the Reformatory Movement in England and Wales, 1846–1893'. PhD thesis, Australian National University.

Erikson, Kai T. (1966), *Wayward Puritans: A Study in the Sociology of Deviance*. New York; John Wiley.

Field, John (1981), 'Police, Power and Community in a Provincial English Town: Portsmouth 1815–75', in Bailey (1981), 42–64.

Foucault, Michel (1977), *Discipline and Punish: The Birth of the Prison*. London; Allen Lane.

Gash, N. (1961), *Mr. Secretary Peel*. London; Longmans.

Gatrell, V.A.C. (1980), 'The Decline of Theft and Violence in Victorian and Edwardian England', in Gatrell, Parker and Lenman (eds) (1980), 238–370.

Gatrell, V.A.C. and Hadden, T.B. (1972), 'Criminal Statistics and their Interpretation', in E.A. Wrigley (ed.), *Nineteenth Century Society: Essays in the Use of Quantitative Methods for the Study of Social Data*. Cambridge; University Press, 336–96.

Gatrell, V.A.C. Parker, G. and Lenman, B. (eds) (1980), *Crime and the Law: The Social History of Crime in Western Europe since 1500*. London; Europa.

Hart, Jenifer (1978), 'Police', in W.R. Cornish, Jenifer Hart, A.H. Manchester and J. Stevenson, *Crime and Law in Nineteenth Century Britain*. Dublin; Irish University Press, 177–209.

Hay, D. (1975a), 'Property, Authority and the Criminal Law', in Hay, Linebaugh and Thompson (1975).

Hay, D. (1975b), 'Poaching and the Game Laws on Cannock Chase', in Hay, Linebaugh and Thompson (1975).

Hay, D. (1980), 'Crime and Justice in Eighteenth- and Nineteenth-Century England', in Norval Morris and Michael Tonry (eds), *Crime and Justice: an Annual Review of Research*, vol. 2, University of Chicago Press, pp. 45–84.

Hay, D., Linebaugh, P. and Thompson, E.P. (eds) (1975), *Albion's Fatal Tree: Crime and Society in Eighteenth-Century England*. London; Allen Lane.

Henriques, U. (1979), *Before the Welfare State: Social Administration in Early Industrial Britain*. London; Longmans.

Hobsbawm, E.J. (1959), *Primitive Rebels: Studies in Archaic Forms of Social Movement in the 19th and 20th Centuries*. Manchester; University Press.

Hobsbawn, E.J. (1964), *Labouring Men*. London; Weidenfeld and Nicolson.

Ignatieff, M. (1978), *A Just Measure of Pain: The Penitentiary in the Industrial Revolution, 1750–1850*. London; Macmillan.

Innes, Joanna (1980), 'The King's Bench Prison in the Later Eighteenth Century: Law, Authority and Order in a London Debtor's Prison', in Brewer and Styles (1980).

Johnson, Richard (1970), 'Educational Policy and Social Control in Early Victorian England', *Past & Present*, 49, 97–119.

Jones, David (1982), *Crime, Protest, Community and Police in 19th Century Britain*. London; Routledge & Kegan Paul.

King, P.J.R. (to be published), 'Decision-makers and Decision-making in the 18th Century Criminal Law: The Social Groups Involved in the Punishment of Property Offenders and the Criteria on which their Decisions were Based'. Unpublished paper.

Lane, Roger (1974), 'Crime and the Industrial Revolution: British and American Views', *Journal of Social History*, 7(3), 287–303.

Lane, Roger (1980), 'Urban Police and Crime in Nineteenth-Century America', in Norval Morris and Michael Tonry (eds), *Crime and Justice: an Annual Review of Research*, 1–43.

Lemert, E.M. (1967), *Human Deviance, Social Problems and Social Control*. Englewood Cliffs, New Jersey; Prentice-Hall.

Magarey, Susan (1978), 'The Invention of Juvenile Delinquency in Early Nineteenth Century England', *Labour History* (Canberra), 34, 11–27.

Matza, D. (1964), *Delinquency and Drift*. New York; John Wiley.

Merritt, Adrian (1980), 'The Nature and Function of Law: A Criticism of E.P. Thompson's "Whigs and Hunters"', *British Journal of Law and Society*, 7(2), 194–214.

Miller, Wilbur R. (1977), *Cops and Bobbies: Police Authority in New York and London, 1830–1870*. Chicago; University Press.

Palmer, Jeremy N.J. (1976), 'Evils Merely Prohibited: Conceptions of Property and Conceptions of Criminality in the Criminal Law Reform of the English Industrial Revolution', *British Journal of Law and Society*, 3(1), 1–16.

Pearson, Geoffrey (1978), 'Goths and Vandals – Crime in History', *Contemporary Crises*, 2, 119–39.

Perrot, Michelle (ed.) (1980), *L'impossible Prison: recherches sur le système penitentiaire au XIXe siècle*. Paris; Seuil.

Philips, David (1977), *Crime and Authority in Victorian England: The Black Country 1835–60*. London; Croom Helm.

Philips, David (1980), '"A New Engine of Power and Authority": The Institutionalisation of Law-enforcement in England 1780–1830', in Gatrell, Parker and Lenman (1980), 155–89.

Pilling, Carolyn K. (1975), 'The Police in the English Local Community 1856–80'. MLitt. thesis, Cambridge University.

Pollard, S. (1968), *The Genesis of Modern Management*. Harmondsworth; Pelican.

Radzinowicz, L. (1948–68), *A History of English Criminal Law and its Administration from 1750*, 4 vols. London; Stevens.

Reith, Charles (1938), *The Police Idea*. London; Oxford University Press.

Reith, Charles (1940), *Police Principles and the Problem of War*. London; Oxford University Press.

Reith, Charles (1943), *British Police and the Democratic Ideal*. London; Oxford University Press.

Reith, Charles (1952), *The Blind Eye of History*. London; Faber & Faber.

Reith, Charles (1956), *A New Study of Police History*. Edinburgh; Oliver & Boyd.

Rothman, David (1971), *The Discovery of the Asylum: Social Order and Disorder in the New Republic*. Boston; Little, Brown.

Rudé, G. (1959), *The Crowd in the French Revolution*. Oxford; Clarendon Press.

Rudé, G. (1962), *Wilkes and Liberty*. Oxford; Clarendon Press.

Rudé, G. (1964), *The Crowd in History: A Study of Popular Disturbances in France and England 1730–1848*. New York; John Wiley.

Rusche, G. and Kirchheimer, O. (1939), *Punishment and Social Structure*. New York; Columbia University Press.

Scull, Andrew T. (1979), *Museums of Madness: The Social Organization of Insanity in Nineteenth-Century England*. London, Allen Lane, 1979.

Silver, Allan (1967), 'The Demand for Order in Civil Society: A Review of Some Themes in the History of Urban Crime, Police, and Riot', in D. Bordua (ed.), *The Police: Six Sociological Essays*. New York; John Wiley 1–24.

Stevenson, John (1979), *Popular Disturbances in England 1700–1870*. London; Longmans.

Storch, R. (1975), 'The Plague of the Blue Locusts: Police Reform and Popular Resistance in Northern England, 1840–57', *International Review of Social History*, 20, 61–90.

Storch, R. (1976), 'The Policeman as Domestic Missionary: Urban Discipline and Popular Culture in Northern England 1850–1880', *Journal of Social History*, 9(4), 481–509.

Storch, R. (1977), 'The Problem of Working-Class Leisure. Some Roots of Middle-Class Moral Reform in the Industrial North 1825–50', in Donajgrodzki (1977).

Styles, John (forthcoming), 'Sir John Fielding and the Problem of Criminal Investigation in 18th Century England', *Transactions of the Royal Historical Society*, 00, 000–00.

Styles, John (to be published), 'Embezzlement, Industry and the Law in England, 1500–1800'. Unpublished paper.

Taylor, Ian, Walton, Paul and Young, Jock (1973), *The New Criminology: For a Social Theory of Deviance*. London: Routledge & Kegan Paul.

Taylor, Ian, Walton, Paul and Young, Jock (eds.) (1975), *Critical Criminology*, London; Routledge & Kegan Paul.

Thompson, E.P. (1963), *The Making of the English Working Class*. London; Gollancz, (Harmondsworth; Pelican, 1968).

Thompson, E.P. (1967), 'Time, Work-discipline and Industrial Capitalism', *Past & Present*, 38, 56–97.

Thompson, E.P. (1971), 'The Moral Economy of the English Crowd in the Eighteenth Century', *Past & Present*, 50, 76–136.

Thompson, E.P. (1974), 'Patrician Society: Plebeian Culture', *Journal of Social History*, Vol. 7, pp. 382–405.

Thompson, E.P. (1975), *Whigs and Hunters: The Origins of the Black Act*. London; Allen Lane.

Thompson, E.P. (1978a), 'Eighteenth-Century England: Class Society without Class', *Social History*, Vol. 2, pp. 133–66.

Thompson, E.P. (1978b), *The Poverty of Theory and Other Essays*. London; Merlin Press.

Thompson, E.P. (1980), *Writing By Candlelight*. London: Merlin Press.

Tobias, J.J. (1967), *Crime and Industrial Society in the Nineteenth Century*. London: Batsford.

Webb, S. and Webb, B. (1922), *English Prisons Under Local Government*. London; Longman, Green.

Weinberger, Barbara (1981). 'The Police and the Public in Mid-Nineteenth-Century Warwickshire', in Bailey (1981), 65–93.

4

State, Civil Society and Total Institutions: A Critique of Recent Social Histories of Punishment

MICHAEL IGNATIEFF

Until recently, the history of prisons in most countries was written as a narrative of reform. According to this story, a band of philanthropic reformers in the second half of the eighteenth century, secular Enlightenment theorists like Beccaria and Bentham and religious men and women of conscience like the Evangelicals and the Quakers, set out to convince the political leadership of their societies that public punishments of the body like hanging, branding, whipping and even, in some European countries, torture were arbitrary, cruel and illegitimate, and that a new range of penalties, chiefly imprisonment at hard labour, could be at once humane, reformative and punitive. This campaign in Europe and America was powered by revulsion at physical cruelty, by a new conception of social obligation to the confined, and by impatience with the administrative inefficiency manifested in the squalid neglect of prisoners. The Enlightenment critique of legal arbitrariness and the vernacular of religious humanitarianism gradually created a moral consensus for reform which, after many delays and reversals, culminated by 1850 in the curtailment of hanging, the abolition of branding and the stocks, and the widespread adoption of the penitentiary as the punishment of first resort for major crime (Whiting, 1975; Cooper, 1976; Condon, 1962; Stockdale, 1977; O. Lewis, 1967; Teeters, 1935; D. Lewis, 1965).

All of these accounts emphasized conscience as the motor of institutional change and assumed that the reformative practice of punishment proposed by the reformers was, both in intention and in result, more humane than the retributive practices of the eighteenth century. A third common feature of these accounts was their administrative and institutional focus on change within the walls and within the political system which ratified or resisted these changes. With the exception of Rusche and Kirchheimer's

Source: Crime and Justice: An Annual Review of Research, vol. 3, edited by Michael Tonry and Norval Morris. University of Chicago Press, 1981, pp. 153–91.

work (1939) on the relation between prison routines and emerging patterns of labour market discipline after 1550, few studies of imprisonment ventured beyond the walls of the prison itself.

The history of prisons therefore was written as a sub-branch of the institutional history of the modern welfare state. As such it has had an implicitly teleological bias, treating the history as a progress from cruelty to enlightenment. In the early 1960s, historians in a number of fields, not just in the history of prisons but also in the history of mental health, public welfare, juvenile care, hospitals and medicine, began to point up the political implications of this history of reform. To interpret contemporary institutions as the culmination of a story of progress was to justify them at least in relation to the past, and to suggest that they could be improved by the same incremental process of philanthropic activism in the future. A reformist historiography thus served a liberalism of good intentions, which in turn seemed to legitimize dubious new initiatives – psychosurgery, chemotherapy and behaviour modification – as legitimate descendants of the reforming tradition. It was in part to question the legitimacy of these 'reforms' in the present that a new group of revisionist historians set out to study the reforms of the past. Another broader motive was perhaps at work too – the libertarian, populist politics of the 1960s revised historians' attitudes toward the size and intrusiveness of the modern state; the history of the prison, the school, the hospital, the asylum seemed more easily understood as a history of Leviathan than a history of reform.

Some, if not all, of the new historiography was avowedly political. Moreover, it saw itself offering intellectual support for the welfare rights, mental patients' rights and prisoners' rights campaigns of the time. These motives inspired an outpouring of new revisionist history on the modern urban school (Katz, 1968; Lazerson, 1971), the welfare system (Piven and Cloward, 1971), the asylum (Scull, 1979), the juvenile court (Platt, 1969) and the prison. Three works best embody the revisionist current as far as prisons were concerned. The first was David Rothman's *The Discovery of the Asylum* (1971), an ambitious and justly well-received attempt to relate the emergence of the penitentiary, the mental institution, the juvenile reformatory and the urban school to the transformation of American society from the late colonial to the Jacksonian period. The second major work, dealing with France, was Michel Foucault's *Discipline and Punish* (1978), which followed his studies of the origins of the mental institution (*Madness and Civilization*, 1967) and the origins of the hospital (*Birth of the Clinic*, 1973) and his work on the evolution of the social and natural sciences in the eighteenth and nineteenth centuries (*The Order of Things*, 1970). *Discipline and Punish* was not only about imprisonment but about the disciplinary ideology at work in education and in the army, and in the new psychology and criminology which claimed to offer a scientific analysis of criminal behaviour and intention. The third major work of the revisionist current was my own *A Just Measure of Pain: The Penitentiary in the Industrial Revolution* (Ignatieff, 1978). Narrower in scope than the others, it concentrates only on the penitentiary's emergence in England in the period from 1770 to 1840.

Despite these differences of scope and intention, all three agreed that the motives and programme of reform were more complicated than a simple revulsion at cruelty or impatience with administrative incompetence – the reformers' critique of eighteenth-century punishment flowed from a more, not less, ambitious conception of power, aiming for the first time at altering the criminal personality. This strategy of power could not be understood unless the history of the prison was incorporated into a history of the philosophy of authority and the exercise of class power in general. The prison was thus studied not for itself but for what its rituals of humiliation could reveal about a society's ruling conceptions of power, social obligation and human malleability.

Within the last two or three years, however, as the wider political climate has changed, these revisionist accounts have come under increasing attack for over-schematizing a complex story, and for reducing the intentions behind the new institution to conspiratorial class strategies of divide and rule. The critique has put into question the viability of both Marxist and structural–functionalist social theory and historical explanation, not only in the area of prisons, but by extension in other areas of historical research. These larger implications make the revisionist/anti-revisionist debate of interest to readers beyond the historians' parish.

What this review of the debate hopes to show is that revisionist arguments, my own included, contained three basic misconceptions: that the state enjoys a monopoly over punitive regulation of behaviour in society, that its moral authority and practical power are the binding sources of social order, and that all social relations can be described in the language of subordination. This does not, by implication, make the counter-revisionist position correct. In so far as it is a position at all, it merely maintains that historical reality is more complex than the revisionists assumed, that reformers were more humanitarian than revisionists have made them out to be, and that there are no such things as classes. This position abdicates from the task of historical explanation altogether. The real challenge is to find a model of historical explanation which accounts for institutional change without imputing conspiratorial rationality to a ruling class, without reducing institutional development to a formless *ad hoc* adjustment to contingent crisis, and without assuming a hyper-idealist, all-triumphant humanitarian crusade. These are the pitfalls; the problem is to develop a model that avoids these while actually providing explanation. This paper is a step towards such a model, but only a step. Since I am a former, though unrepentant, member of the revisionist school, this exercise is necessarily an exercise in self-criticism.

The focus on three books, and on a narrow if crucial period, is necessary because this is where debate has been most pointed and most useful. With the exception of David Rothman's *Conscience and Convenience* (1980), Steven Schlossman's *Love and the American Delinquent* (1977), James Jacobs's *Stateville* (1977) and Anthony Platt's *The Child Savers* (1969), the revisionist and counter-revisionist debate has not extended itself into the terrain of the twentieth century. We are still awaiting a new historiography on the disintegration of the nineteenth-century penitentiary routines of lockstep and silence; the rise of probation, parole and juvenile court; the ascendancy of the psychiatrist, social worker and doctor, and the decline of the chaplain within the penal system; the history of drug use as therapeutic and control devices; the impact of electric and TV surveillance systems on the nineteenth-century institutional inheritance; the unionization of custodial personnel; the impact of rising standards of living upon levels of institutional amenity and inmate expectation; the long-term pattern of sentencing and the changing styles of judicial and administrative discretion; the history of ethnic and race relations within the walls; the social and institutional origins of the waves of prison rioting in the 1950s and late 1960s. This is the work that needs to be done if historians are to explain the contemporary crisis in prison order epitomized at Attica and more recently at Santa Fe (Wicker, 1975; Silberman, 1978; for England, see Fitzgerald, 1977). The classics of prison sociology in the 1940s and 1950s described prisons as communities, guaranteeing a measure of order and security through a division of power between captors and captives (Sykes, 1958; Clemmer, 1940). Why has this division of power broken down so often in the 1960s and 1970s? Thus far, only Jacobs's exemplary study of Stateville Penitentiary in Illinois has offered a truly historical answer, integrating changes in institutional governance, inmate composition and expectation, and the racial politics of the outside world into a working explanation. His conclusions, that prisoners were often surer of their physical safety under the tighter and more self-confident authoritarian regimes of the 1940s than they were under the well-meaning but confused reformist regimes of the 1960s, might appear to suggest that a return to authoritarianism is the best way to guarantee prisoners' and guards' physical security, if nothing else. Unionized guards and the militant prisoners of today will not permit a return to the prisons of the 1940s. But if we cannot and ought not repeat history, we can at least learn from history where we went wrong. In the market place of good ideas – decarceration, inmate self-management, due process grievance procedures, institutional redesign, token economies, behaviour modification – history offers a reliable guide to consumer choice and its invariable lesson in *caveat emptor*. Criminal justice activists may be disappointed by the literature I will review here because no answers are offered to the question, What is to be done? I do hope there is use, however, in learning some of the subtler errors which good intentions can entrain.

WHAT HAPPENED: THE REVISIONIST ACCOUNT

Let me begin by describing the revolution in punishment between 1780 and 1850. Rothman, Foucault, and my own work may differ about explanation, but we do agree about what happened. In each society the key developments seem to have been:

(1) *The decline of punishments involving the public infliction of physical pain to the body.* Beccaria's campaign against the death penalty in the 1760s, the Pennsylvania statute of 1786, the reformed codes of the 'enlightened despots', the French revolutionary decrees against the capital penalty, and Romilly and MacIntosh's capital statutes campaign in England culminated by the 1850s in the restriction of the death penalty to first-degree murder and treason. The form of execution was also changed – in France the guillotine was adopted in 1792 as a scientific instrument of death, sparing the victim the possible incompetence of the hangman; the traditional Tyburn processional of the condemned through the streets of London was abolished in 1783 in order to curtail the public symbolism of the death spectacle (Foucault, 1978; Linebaugh, 1975, pp. 65–119; Linebaugh, 1977, pp. 246–70); public executions in England ended in the 1860s, and hanging henceforth took place behind prison walls (D. Cooper, 1974). The lesser physical penalties were also curtailed or abolished (abolition of branding in England, 1779; of pillory, 1837; of whipping of women, 1819; see also Perrot, 1980, pp. 59–60, for France). By 1860 the public ritual of physical punishment had been successfully redefined as a cruel and politically illegitimate means of inflicting pain.

(2) *The emergence of imprisonment as the pre-eminent penalty for most serious offences.* Imprisonment had been used as punishment on a selective but insubstantial scale prior to 1770. Places of confinement were generally used as waystations for persons awaiting trial, for convicted felons awaiting execution or transportation, and crucially for debtors. Nearly 60 per cent of the institutional population in Howard's census of 1777 were debtors (Ignatieff, 1978, p. 28; Pugh, 1968; Sheehan, 1977). Vagrants and disobedient servants convicted for a range of minor, work-related

property offences punishable at summary jurisdiction were confined at hard labour in houses of correction (Innes, 1980b; DeLacy, 1980, chapter 1; Beattie, 1974, 1977). This use of imprisonment increased in the eighteenth century, for reasons we do not yet understand. In England it was not until the suspension of transportation in 1776 that English JPs and assize judges began to substitute sentences of imprisonment for sentences of transportation (Webb and Webb, 1963; Ignatieff, 1978, chapter 4). At first, criminal law reformers like Beccaria showed no particular enthusiasm for imprisonment itself, preferring to replace hanging with penalties ranging from hard labour in public to fines. It was only after 1776 in America and after 1789 in France that imprisonment began to replace hanging as *the* penalty appropriate to modern, enlightened republics (Foucault, 1978, p. 115; Rothman, 1971, p. 59).

(3) *The penitentiary came to be the bearer of reformers' hopes for a punishment capable of reconciling deterrence and reform, terror and humanity*. In England between 1780 and 1812, half a dozen counties built small penitentiaries mostly for the control of minor delinquency. The first national penitentiary, Millbank, was opened in 1816. An enormous warren of passages and cells built in the style of a turreted medieval fortress near the Houses of Parliament, it soon was condemned as a costly failure – the prisoners were in revolt against the discipline more or less continuously in the 1820s; a violent outbreak of scurvy closed the prison for a year in 1824; but the lessons of failure were learned at Pentonville, opened in 1842. Its penitential regime of solitude, hard labour and religious indoctrination became the model for all national penal servitude prisons and most county prisons besides. In America the key developments of the penitentiary regime occurred between 1820 and 1830 – Auburn, 1819–23; Ossining, 1825; Pittsburgh, 1826; Philadelphia, 1829 (Rothman, 1971, pp. 80–1), and in France, La Petite Rocquette, 1836, and the juvenile reformatory at Mettray, 1844 (Perrot, 1980, pp. 60–1).

(4) *As systems of authority, the new prisons substituted the pains of intention for the pains of neglect* (Ignatieff, 1978, p. 113). Reformers like Howard were appalled that the squalor in neglected institutions was justified for its deterrent value. Accordingly, regular diets replaced the fitful provision of food in eighteenth-century institutions; uniforms replaced rags and personal clothing; prisoners received regular medical attention, and new hygienic rituals (head shaving, entrance examination and bath) did away with the typhus epidemics which were an intermittent feature of eighteenth-century European prison life. These hygienic rituals in turn became a means of stripping inmates of their personal identity. This indicates the ambivalence of 'humanitarian' reform: the same measures

that protected prisoners' health were explicitly justified as a salutary mortification of the spirit (Ignatieff, 1978, p. 100).

(5) *The new prisons substituted the rule of rules for the rule of custom and put an end to the old division of power between the inmate community and the keepers.* All accounts of eighteenth-century prisons stress the autonomy and self-government of prisoner communities. Since common law forbade the imposition of coercive routines on prisoners awaiting trial and debtors, they were able to take over the internal government of their wards, allocating cells, establishing their own rules, grievance procedures and punishments (Innes, 1980a, 1980b; Sheehan, 1977, p. 233; De Lacy, 1980, chapter 2). The implied authority model of the colonial American and British prison was the household. The keeper and his family often resided in the institution and the prisoners were called a 'family'. They did not wear uniforms, they were not kept to routines, and they defended an oral and common law tradition of rights, privileges and immunities (Rothman, 1971, p. 55). By the 1840s in all three societies, a silent routine had been imposed to stamp out the association of the confined and to wipe out a subculture which was held to corrupt the novice and foster criminal behaviour. Under the silent associated system of discipline, prisoners were allowed to congregate in workshops but were strictly forbidden to communicate. In the separate system at Pentonville and Philadelphia, prisoners were kept in complete cellular isolation and were forbidden any form of communication or association (Rothman, 1971, p. 81; Ignatieff, 1978, chapter 1; Henriques, 1972). While advocates of both systems argued fiercely over their respective merits, they both agreed in principle on the necessity of suppressing the prison subculture and ending the tacit division of authority between captors and captives which had prevailed in the *ancien régime*. From a positive point of view, solitude exposed the individual prisoner to the obedience training of routine and the religious exhortation of the chaplain. The chaplain, not the doctor or the governor, became the chief ideologist of the penitentiary, justifying its deprivations in the language of belief.

(6) *The new institutions enforced a markedly greater social distance between the confined and the outside world.* High walls, sharply restricted visiting privileges, constant searches and patrols ended the mingling of outside and inside in the unreformed prison. Before reform, visitors enjoyed the run of the yards, women commonly brought their husbands meals, and debtors and outsiders drank together in the prison taproom. The aim of reform was to withdraw the prisoner from the corrupting influence of his former milieu and, at the same time, to inflict the pains of emotional and sexual isolation. Once again the mixture of humane and coercive motivations becomes apparent. As an unintended consequence, however, the check to

the power of institutional personel offered by constant visitors was reduced. The new institutions, therefore, did not resolve the old question, Who guards the guards? Instead, they posed the question in a new and thus far more intractable way (Ignatieff, 1978, Conclusion; DeLacy, 1980, Conclusion).

All three versions agree that the emergence of the modern prison cannot be understood apart from the parallel history of the other total institutions created in this period – the lunatic asylum, the union workhouse, the juvenile reformatory and industrial school, and the monitorial school. Besides being the work of the same constituency of philanthropic and administrative reformers, these institutions enforced a similar economy of time and the same order of surveillance and control. They also expressed a common belief in the reformative powers of enforced asceticism, hard labour, religious instruction and routine.

The preceding paragraphs provide a schematic summary of the revolution in discipline as the revisionist account would have it. Before considering the explanations offered for this revolution, we ought to pause to consider the objections that have been raised to the revisionist account as valid description. A number of theses and monographs completed within the last couple of years have insisted that the descriptive picture is more complex, contradictory and inchoate than Foucault, Rothman or I have suggested.

Margaret DeLacy's excellent Princeton dissertation (1980) on county prison administration in Lancashire, 1690–1850, argues that even a relatively dynamic county administration like Lancashire lacked the resources to impose the highly rationalized Pentonville model on all the county institutions. Many of these remained much the same as they had been in the eighteenth century. Eighteenth-century historians, particularly Joanna Innes, have argued that the pre-reform prison was neither as squalid nor as incompetently administered as the reformers made it out to be (Innes, 1980b). By implication, therefore, the revisionist account may have been taken in by the reformers' sources. It is less clear, therefore, that the history of the institution between 1780 and 1840 can be described as a passage from squalid neglect to hygienic order.

Michelle Perrot and Jacques Leonard have made the same case for France, arguing that the highly rationalized institutions like La Rocquette and La Mettray cannot be taken as typical of the mass of local lockups, jails and hulks in mid-nineteenth-century France. In these institutions, the persistence of disease and the continued use of whipping and chains would appear to suggest a melancholy continuity with the worst features of the *ancien régime* (Perrot, 1980).

It appears, then, that the revolution in punishment was not the generalized triumph of Weberian rationalization which the revisionist account suggested. Foucault's work (and my own as well) remained captive of that Weberian equation of the *ancien régime* with the customary, the traditional and the particularistic, and of the modern with the rational, the disciplined, the impersonal and the bureaucratic. The gulf between the reformers' rationalizing intentions and the institutionalized results of their work ought to make us rethink this equation of modernity and rationalization, or at least to give greater room for the idea that modernity is the site of a recurring battle between rationalizing intention and institutions, interests and communities which resist, often with persistent success.

Yet even if we admit that Pentonville and the Panopticon (Bentham, 1791), Auburn and La Rocquette were 'ideal types' rather than exemplary realities of their time, we still have to explain why it became possible between 1780 and 1840 and not before to conceive and construct them. However much else remained unchanged in the passage from the *ancien régime* to the industrial world of the nineteenth century the penitentiary was something new and unprecedented and was understood as such by the great observers of the age, Alexis de Tocqueville, Charles Dickens and Thomas Carlyle. A counter-revisionist account that considers only the local institutions, which went on much the same as before, will miss what contemporaries knew had to be explained about their own age.

JACKSONIAN AMERICA: THE EMERGENCE OF THE ASYLUM

Let us turn to this business of explanation and let us begin with the American case, with the work of David Rothman. In Rothman's account, the new total institutions of the Jacksonian period emerged in an overwhelmingly rural and agricultural society, growing beyond the boundaries of the colonial past yet still a generation away from the factory system, industrialism, European immigration and the big city. It is a fundamental mistake, he argues, to interpret the total institution as an 'automatic and inevitable response of an industrial and urban society to crime and poverty' (Rothman, 1971, p. xvi). Americans were anxious about the passage of colonial society and the emergence of a restless, socially mobile population moving beyond the controls of family, farm and town meeting, but there was nothing in this process which itself required the emergence of the new asylums and prisons. The catalyst for institutionalized instruction was not social change itself but the way it was organized into an alarmist interpretation of disorder and dislocation by

philanthropic reformers. Crime was read for the first time not as the
wickedness of individuals but as an indictment of a disordered society. This
explains the emergence of new institutions aiming at the reformation and
discipline of the deviant, disorderly and deranged.

For a society which interpreted crime as the sign of the passing of the
colonial order, the penitentiary symbolized an attempt to re-create the
godly superintendence and moral discipline of the past within a modern
setting. Rothman demonstrates brilliantly that the language developed in a
society to explain disorder and deviance also defines the solutions it
develops for these problems. An environmentalist theory of crime and
faith in the reformative effects of isolation from the environment were
linked together in a system of ideas, each legitimizing the other.

Rothman is better at re-creating the reformers' systems of belief than in
locating these beliefs in a believable social and economic context. We need
to know something about actual trends in crime during 1780–1820 if we are
to understand the changing fit between reform and rhetoric and their
social context. In the absence of such data, crime becomes a static and
empty category in Rothman's analysis, and the reformers' alarmist
discourse drifts away from any point of reference.

Why, we need to know, were the Jacksonians so specially anxious about
change and disorder, and why did they look back with such nostalgia to
colonial society? Rothman simply accepts the Jacksonian reformers'
picture of the stable pre-revolutionary society they were leaving behind,
but surely this was a questionable historical fable. Many eighteenth-
century Europeans regarded colonial America as a restless, rootless,
dynamic and explosive society. Tom Paine's Philadelphia was no
deferential idyll (Foner, 1976). Yet Rothman never questions the
Jacksonians' rosy image of their own past, never asks how their account of
it should have been so out of joint with what we know of colonial society.

One would also have liked Rothman to explore the relationship between
the rise of the total institution and the theory and practice of Jacksonian
democracy. This was after all the period of the extension of universal
manhood suffrage in the United States. Tocqueville himself thought the
relation was one of contradiction: 'While society in the United States gives
the example of the most extended liberty, the prisons of the same country
offer the spectacle of the most complete despotism' (Beaumont and
Tocqueville, 1964, p. 79). As Tocqueville (1969) suggested in the 'tyranny
of the majority' sections of *Democracy in America*, democratic republics
which represent law and order as the embodied will of all the people treat
disobedient minorities more severely than monarchical societies which
have no ideological commitment to the consensual attachment of their
citizens. Rothman suggests but leaves unexplored the possibility of a

connection between Jacksonian popular sovereignty, an environmentalist theory of crime as being the responsibility of society, and an interventionist social therapy taking the form of the 'total institution'.

If we turn to Foucault, we find that the relation between forms of sovereignty outside the walls and carceral regimes inside constitutes the main axis of his interpretation. Public executions, which the reformers of the Enlightenment condemned as a carnal and irrational indulgence, can be read, Foucault argues, as symbolic displays of the highly personalized sovereignty of the king and of his alternatively vengeful, merciful relation towards his wicked subjects.

The execution suited a philosophy of order that ignored minor delinquency to concentrate instead on the ritualized dispatch of selected miscreants. This exercise of sovereignty in turn implied a loosely articulated political nation in which

> each of the different social strata had its margin of tolerated illegality; the non-application of the rule, the non-observance of the innumerable edicts or ordinances were a condition of the political and economic functioning of society . . . the least favoured strata of the population did not have in principle any privileges, but they benefited within the margins of what was imposed on them by law or custom, from a space of tolerance, gained by force or obstinacy. [Foucault, 1978, pp. 84–5]

The illegalities of the poor, like the tax exemptions of the rich, were tolerated because of the persistent weakness of an underfinanced, chronically indebted state, the tenacious survival of regional and local immunities, and the persistent countervailing power of the *parlements* (see Montesquieu, *The Spirit of the Laws*, 1748), the judiciary and the nobility. Above all, the margin of illegality enjoyed by the poor reflected a ruling conception of national power as the sovereign's will rather than the operation of a bureaucratic machine. The state, moreover, shared the punitive function with civil society, in the double sense that its public rituals (execution, pillory, whipping and branding) required completion by the opprobrium of the crowd if they were to have full symbolic effect, and in the sense that household heads, masters and employers punished directly without invoking the state's power.

Independently of Foucault, Edward Thompson and Douglas Hay seem to have reached a similar dèscription of the exercise of sovereign power in eighteenth-century England. They put the same emphasis on the symbolic centrality of the public hanging in reproducing awe and deference before the sovereign's mighty but merciful power, and they describe a philosophy of order essentially similar in its permissive approach to the small fish.

Permissive, however, is too nostalgic or sentimental a word for a tactics of order uneasily poised between an obvious and sometimes brutal concern to defend property rights and an equal distaste, moral, libertarian and economic, for the apparatus of state police (Hay, 1975, pp. 17–65; Thompson, 1975, Conclusion). The Revolution Settlement and the common law tradition imposed limits on the discretionary power of eighteenth-century magistrates, and the common people themselves were quite capable of forcibly reminding magistrates of 'the rights of free-born Englishmen' and of the protocol of customs guaranteeing free assembly (Thompson, 1971). It is possible that there was no corresponding corpus of rights in common law available to the French poor, but it is hard to believe that they did not hold to some customary beliefs and traditions about the proper bounds of monarchical 'police'.

Hay's and Thompson's works show up Foucault's tacit assumption that the only limits on public order policy were the mental assumptions of the authorities themselves and the structural weaknesses of the state apparatus. What is missing in his work is the idea that public order strategies were defined within limits marked out not only by the holders of power but also by those they were trying, often vainly, to persuade, subdue, cajole or repress. Foucault's account consistently portrays authority as having a clear field, able to carry out its strategies without let or hindrance from its own legal principles or from popular opposition. Power is always seen as a strategy, as an instrumentality, never as a social relation between contending social forces. We need to know much more about the social process by which the margin of illegality enjoyed by the poor in the *ancien régime* was established before we conclude with Foucault that it owed its existence to the toleration of the authorities.

CLASS CONFLICT AND THE PRISON

However we interpret the margin of popular illegality under the *ancien régime*, Foucault and I agree that the penitentiary formed part of a new strategy of power aiming at its circumscription between 1780 and 1850. This new strategy was the work of Burke's 'sophisters, economists, and calculators' – the monarchical administrators like Turgot and Le Trosne, and gentry men of letters like Beccaria. In England, the new ideology found expression in Henry Fielding's proposals for reform of London police in the 1760s, in Howard's penitentiary scheme of the 1770s and in the hospital and asylum reforms led by the provincial non-conformist professional classes in the 1790s (Ignatieff, 1978, chapter 3). In the 1780s, too, Bentham and Romilly began their campaigns for the codification of law and for the curtailment of public executions.

The ideal of reforming through punishment and of apportioning just measures of pain to crimes previously tolerated or ignored was compatible with the democratic ideals of the French Revolution – equal rights, equal citizenship, equal punishment – but it proved no less compatible with Napoleonic centralism and the Bourbon Restoration. Beneath the whole surface play of debate about political rights and regimes between the 1770s and 1840s, Foucault argues, a new 'carceral archipelago' of asylums, prisons, workhouses and reformatories slipped into place. The political divisions over regimes and rights hid a deeper, unstated consensus among the ruling orders on the exercise of power over the criminal, the insane and the pauper. This ideology forged in the 1760s by the Enlightenment reformers and opponents of the *ancien régime* was transmitted and reproduced by social interests in the Restoration and the July Monarchy, often deeply hostile to the rationalist or egalitarian spirit of the philosophers themselves.

In England, the first bearers of the new disciplinary ideology were the reforming county magistrates and the Dissenting professional classes of the provinces – reformist in politics, scientific in mental outlook, rational and improving in their management of labour, county finance and personal estates. The new asylums, prisons, workhouses and schools which they built appealed to their residual religious asceticism, to their scientific and rationalist outlook, and to their impatience with the administrative incompetence and political corruption of the *ancien régime*. In the crisis years of early industrialization after 1815, the disciplinary ideology was taken up by the evangelized professional, mercantile and industrial classes seeking to cope with the dissolution of a society of ranks and orders and the emergence of a society of strangers. The philanthropic campaigns to reform old institutions and to build new asylums, workhouses, prisons and hospitals gave expression to a new strategy of class relations. In return for the humanity of minimal institutional provision, the disobedient poor were drawn into a circle of asceticism, industriousness and obedience. They would return to society convinced of the moral legitimacy of their rulers. The persistent ideal of prison reform was a kind of punishment at once so humane and so just that it would convince the offender of the moral legitimacy of the law and its custodians. The penitentiary was designed to embody this reconciliation of the imperatives of discipline with the imperatives of humanity.

My own account places more stress than Foucault's on the religious and philanthropic impulses behind institutional reform. His version of the disciplinary ideology retains the secular rationalist tone of its initial Enlightenment formulation, while mine stresses the fusion of the secular rationalism embodied in Benthamism with the Quaker and Evangelical language of conscience epitomized by Elizabeth Fry. The penitentiary in England had at its core the religious discourse of the chaplain, just as the new Evangelical language of class relations had at its core the idea of rich and poor bound together in the common experience of sin and the common salvation of faith and industry.

My own account also places more stress than Foucault's upon the reformers' concern to defend and explain institutional routines to the confined. As a consequence I have put more emphasis on the humanitarian intentions of the reformers. They were genuinely repelled by the chains, squalor and neglect they discovered in existing institutions, especially because these compromised the moral legitimacy of the social system in the eyes of the confined. In their theory of the reform of character, the crucial task was to persuade the poor to accept the benevolent intention behind institutional deprivations. Once convinced of the benevolence of the system, reformers argued, prisoners would be unable to take refuge from their own guilt in attacking their confiners. Personal reformation thus meant succumbing to the benevolent logic of their captors. In Foucault's account, on the other hand, reformers were not centrally concerned to legitimize new penal measures as humane. Reformers, in his account, simply took the humanity of their measures for granted and looked to the discipline to routinize the habits of the poor. My model of the reform of character is one of symbolic persuasion; Foucault's is of disciplinary routinization.

We both agree, however, on the relation between this new strategy of power and the social crisis of the post-1815 period, exemplified in recurrent surges of distress-related crime, pauperism and collective pauper unrest. Foucault is sketchy in the extreme about the causation of this social crisis, but it is clearly implied as the backdrop of the institutional revolution in France. My account likewise does not purport to be a social history of crime and pauperism in the 1815–48 period, but it does locate three major sites of crisis. The first was the breakdown of social relations in the agricultural counties of the south-east between 1815 and 1831 as a result of the casualization of the agricultural proletariat. Rising rates of vagrancy, pauperism and petty crime through the 1820s and the explosion of the Swing Riots in 1831 are the symptoms of this crisis in rural social relations. The second site of crisis was in London, where the Anti-Corn Law Riots of 1815, the Spa Field disturbances of 1816 and the riots attendant upon Queen Caroline's trial proved that the existing parish constabulary was hopelessly outdated in coping with urban crowd control while the soldiery brought in upon these occasions was a clumsy, brutal, and therefore alienating instrument of order (Silver, 1967). In addition there was growing anxiety among magistrates and philanthropists about the rising incidence of juvenile crime in the metropolis after 1815. Masterless apprentices, orphans, underemployed youths, child prostitutes – all seemed to symbolize a breakdown in the order of the family, the parish and the workshop. The third site of crisis lay in the new northern industrial towns, where regional labour markets tied to single industries like cotton proved extremely vulnerable to cycles of demand in the international economy. Mass unemployment in 'bad years' like 1826 threw up the spectre of recurrent breakdown in labour market disciplines (Ignatieff, 1978, chapter 6).

There cannot be much doubt that the new strategy of mass imprisonment, the creation of the Metropolitan Police in 1829 and the diffusion of paid constabularies through the agricultural counties and the industrial towns in the 1830s, 1840s and 1850s must be seen as a 'response' to this crisis of public order (Storch, 1975). The creation of permanent police courts, the expansion of the scope of the vagrancy and trespass statutes and the formation of the union workhouse system in 1834 represented additional attempts to 'grapple for control', to cope with a social order problem the size and magnitude of which clearly grew faster than any of the authorities anticipated (Silver, 1967; Hart, 1955, 1965; Radzinowicz, 1968, vol. 5; DeLacy, 1980; Philips, 1977).

Yet there are dangers of social reductionism in this explanation. Institutional reformers did not justify their programme as a response to the labour discipline needs of employers. Indeed, the reform discourse antedates the labour discipline crisis. Howard's penitentiary schemes, the police theory of the late Enlightenment, the hospital and asylum campaigns of the 1790s – all anticipated the post-1815 crisis. Moreover, as Rothman pointed out in the American case, the fact of crisis itself would not explain why authorities chose the particular remedies they did, why they put such faith in institutional confinement when greater resort to hanging or to convict gang labour in public might have been equally eligible responses to the perceived breakdown of social controls.

Divide and Rule

Foucault's argument and mine none the less is that the massive investment in institutional solutions would have been inconceivable unless the authorities had believed that they were faced with the breakdown of a society of stable ranks and the emergence of a society of hostile classes. This diagnosis of the malaise of their times in turn suggested an institutional solution. Mass imprisonment offered a new strategic possibility – isolating a criminal class from the working class, incarcerating the one so that it would not corrupt the industriousness of the other. The workhouse likewise would quarantine pauperism from honest poverty (Foucault, 1978, pp. 276–8). Beneath the surface debate over whether these institutions were capable of reforming or deterring their target populations, Foucault argues, lay a deeper consensus among the ruling orders about using institutionalization to manufacture and reproduce social divisions within the working classes between working and criminal, rough and respectable, poor and pauperized. Foucault claims that this strategy of division actually worked – that the institutional quarantine of the criminal did create a criminal class separate from the working-class community. In this lay the secret 'success' of prison, beneath all its apparent failures as an institution of reform and deterrence.

The divide-and-rule argument works best in respect to the workhouse, where the creation of the Bastilles of 1834 (see Babington, 1971) does appear to have succeeded in making pauperism disgraceful to the poor. Before the Bastilles, the poor conceived of relief as a right and did not look upon it as a disgrace; afterwards, while many continued to insist on their rights, working-class respectability came to insist on avoiding the degradation of appealing for relief and ending one's days in the public ward. The Bastilles do seem to have dug the gulf deeper between pauperism and poverty within the value system and the social behaviour of the poor themselves.

As regards imprisonment, however, the divide-and-rule argument seems to me now to have fallen prey unwittingly to the problem inherent in what criminologists call 'labelling theory'. The notorious difficulty with this approach is that it makes the state's sanctions the exclusive source of the boundary between the deviant and the respectable. This would seem to ignore the degree to which, in the nineteenth as in the twentieth century, the moral sanctions condemning murder, rape and sexual and personal assault were prior to and independent of the punitive sanction, commanding assent across class lines. In punishing these offences, the state simply ratified a line of demarcation already indigenous to the poor. Even in the case of petty property crime, it is not clear that the criminal sanction was labelling acts which the poor excused as an inevitable response to distress or which they justified in the vernacular of natural justice. The poor, no less than the rich, were victims of property crime, and any study of London police courts in the nineteenth century shows they were prepared to go to law to punish members of their own class (Davis, 1980; Philips, 1977). If a constant process of demarcation was under way between criminals and the working classes, it was a process in which the working classes themselves played a prominent part, both in their resort to law and in the informal sanctioning behaviour which enforced their own codes of respectability. Doubtless there was sympathy for the first-time offenders and juveniles convicted for minor property offences during hard times; doubtless there were offenders whom working people felt were unjustly convicted. Certainly, repeated imprisonment did isolate the criminal from his own class. But it is a serious overestimation of the role of the state to assume that its sanctioning powers were the exclusive source of the social division between criminal and respectable. The strategy of mass imprisonment is better understood in class terms as an attempt by the authorities to lend symbolic reinforcement to values of personal honour which they themselves knew were indigenous to the poor.

The behaviour of the politicized sections of the working classes leaves no doubt that they drew a very strict demarcation between themselves and the criminal. Michelle Perrot's study of French prisons in 1848 shows that the revolutionary crowds who stormed the prisons reserved liberation for prostitutes, political offenders and conscripts, not for ordinary criminal offenders (Perrot, 1980, p. 241). In England, while political radicals often cited the criminal statistics as proof of the grinding pressure of distress on the poor, they never questioned the ultimate legitimacy of their convictions (Ignatieff, 1978, chapter 4; DeLacy, 1980).

Class Fear

Thus, if fears by the ruling orders of a potential union of interest and action between the criminal and working classes are to be regarded as having had some influence in generating public support for mass imprisonment, it must be recognized that these fears were without actual sociological foundation. We are dealing with a form of social fantasy detached from observable reality. Moreover, it is not clear how general these fantasies of revolution were, or even how influential they were in galvanizing public opinion in support of the total institution. The difficulty with arguments from class fear is that they are simply too vague, too global, to account for the specific timing of institutional or legislative change. Class fear among educated public opinion in the 1820s and 1830s may have contributed something to the consensus that public order was too parlous and insecure to go on with the haphazard punishment and police strategies of the eighteenth century. But class fear cannot account for the specific idiosyncrasies of the institutional solution – the faith in silence, solitude, religious indoctrination and hard labour.

If we return to what reformers said they were doing, it becomes clearer to me now than it was when I wrote *A Just Measure of Pain* that the adoption of the penitentiary in particular and the institutional solution in general cannot be explained in terms of their supposed utility in manufacturing social divisions within the working class. This is because at bottom reformers, like most of their own class, understood deviance in irreducibly individual rather than collective terms; not ultimately as collective social disobedience, however much distress and collective alienation influenced individuals, but as a highly personal descent into sin and error. Given this individualist reading of deviance, the appeal of institutional solutions lay in the drama of guilt which they forced each offender to play out – the drama of suffering, repentance, reflection and amendment, watched over by the tutelary eye of the chaplain. Foucault's neglect of the religious vernacular of reform argument obscures the deep hold which this symbolic drama of guilt and repentance held for the Victorian imagination. To be sure, this hypothetical drama bore little if any relation to what actually happened in prisons, asylums and workhouses, and many Victorians, Charles Dickens among them, knew this full well. But nevertheless, even sceptics like Dickens and Mayhew were not immune to the appeal of a symbolic system of associations in which the reform of the guilty criminal was held to reveal the triumph of good over evil, conscience over desire, in all men and women. If there was a social message in the ideal of reform through institutional discipline, it was that the institutional salvation of the deviant acted out the salvation of all men and women, rich and poor alike.

WHO DIRECTED THE CARCERAL ARCHIPELAGO?

Where does all this leave the problem of agency? Whose interests did the new institutions serve? In whose name were the reformers speaking?

Foucault and the Disciplinary 'Savoir'

On these questions of agency, Foucault's answers are notoriously cloudy. At some points, he refers to the 'bourgeoisie', though this is hardly an adequate categorization of the shifting alignment of class fragments, aristocrats, financiers, professionals and industrialists who competed for power in France between 1815 and 1848. At other points, Foucault slips into a use of the passive voice, which makes it impossible to identify who, if anyone, was the historical agent of the tactics and strategies he describes.

Yet before we condemn him out of hand, it is worth noting that Foucault is trying to work free of what he regards as the vulgar Marxist conception of agency according to which the prison is a tool of a definable class with a clear-sighted conception of its strategic requirements. He also rejects the functionalist model according to which the prison is the designated punitive instrument within a social division of labour. In place of these accounts, he argues that punitive power is dispersed throughout the social system: it is literally everywhere, in the sense that the disciplinary ideology, the *savoir* which directs and legitimizes power, permeates all social groups (with the exception of the marginal and deviant), ordering the self-repression of the repressors themselves. The prison is only the most extreme site for an exercise of power that extends along the whole continuum of social relations from the family to the market, to the workplace and to citizenship. If prisons and factories came to resemble each other in their rituals of time and discipline, therefore, it was not because the state acted in response to the labour discipline strategies initiated by employers, but because both public order authorities and employers shared the same universe of assumptions about the regulation of the body and the ordering of institutional time.

Given that all social relations were inscribed within relations of domination and subordination, ordered, so Foucault says, by a continuous disciplinary discourse, it is impossible to identify the privileged sites or actors that controlled all the others. The disciplinary ideology of modern society *can* be identified as the work of specific social actors, but once such an ideology was institutionalized, once its rationality came to be taken for granted, a fully exterior challenge to its logic became impossible. The institutional system took on a life of its own. One cannot say, Foucault argues, that the political apparatus of modern states actually controls the prison system. There is a formal chain of delegation and responsibility from the legislature to the bureaucracy, from the bureaucracy to the warden, and from the warden to guards and prisoners, but this does not take into account the way institutional systems develop their own inertial logic which each 'actor' feels powerless to change (even those at its very summit).

Since the appearance of *Discipline and Punish*, Foucault has reformulated this problem of agency as one of historical causation, putting a new stress on the way in which the new institutions emerged as the unintended consequence of levels of change, which in themselves were independent of each other – the new discourse on discipline in the Enlightenment, the search by the propertied for stricter legal and social protection, and the crisis in public order. The new discourse emerged prior to the social revolution of the nineteenth century and prior to the labour discipline needs of employers, but once in play ideologically, it provided the programme around which constituencies assembled their response to social turbulence and labour indiscipline. Once the disciplinary discourse's independence of its social grounding is granted, it becomes possible to work free of the various traps which the problem of agency has caused for historians – the conspiratorial all-seeing ruling classes of the Marxist account; the low rationality model of *ad hoc* responses to social crisis, and the hyper-idealist version of reform as a humanitarian crusade (see Foucault's interview in Perrot, 1980).

The Middle Class as a Ruling Class

But where does this leave the concept of a ruling class as the historical actor behind the making of the penitentiary? My own work has been criticized for using 'middle class' as a synonym for 'ruling class' in a period in which it would be more accurate to speak of a bewilderingly complex competition for political power and social influence by different class factions, professionals, industrialists, and merchants, aristocratic magnates, and small gentry farmers. While it is a convention of Marxist argument that such division of interest and jockeying for power were stilled whenever 'the class as a whole' felt threatened from below, my own work on the intense debates about social order policy suggests that choral unanimity was rare even in moments of universally recognized crisis. Unquestionably justices, members of Parliament and philanthropists recognized each other as the rich and regarded vagrants, pickpockets and the clamouring political mob as the lower orders, but their sense of 'we' versus 'they' was not enough to make the ruling class into a collective social actor. One can speak of a ruling class in the sense that access to strategic levers of power was systematically restricted according to wealth and inheritance, but one cannot speak of its acting or thinking as a collective historical subject. One can only ascribe historical effectivity to identifiable social constituencies of individuals who managed to secure political approval for penal change through a process of debate and argument in the society's sites of power. It would be wrong to think of these constituencies of institutional reformers as acting for their class or expressing the logic of its strategic imperatives. This would make them into ventriloquists for a clairvoyant and unanimous social consensus. In fact, they managed to secure only the most grudging and limited kind of approval for their programme. The penitentiary continued to be criticized from multiple and contradictory points of view: it was inhumanly severe; it was too lenient; it was too expensive; it could not reconcile deterrence and reform; the reformation of criminals was a sentimental delusion; and so on.

In his most recent reflections, Foucault himself admits that the new carceral system was not the work of an overarching strategic consensus by a ruling class, but instead fell into place as a result of a conjuncture between transformations in the phenomena of social order, new policing needs by the propertied, and a new discourse on the exercise of power.

Yet for all his disclaimers, Foucault's conception of the disciplinary world view, the *savoir* as he calls it, effectively forecloses on the possibility that the *savoir* itself was a site of contradiction, argument and conflict. In England at least, for example, a pre-existing legal tradition of rights imposed specific limits to the elaboration of new powers of arrest, new summary jurisdiction procedures, just as *habeas corpus* limited carceral practice towards the unconvicted. At every point, new proposals for police, prisons and new statutory powers raised the question of how to balance the changing conceptions of security against pre-existing conceptions of the liberty of the subject. Foucault makes no mention of these legal limits.

There is more than a touch of Marxist reductionism in Foucault's treatment of law as a pliable instrument of the ruling class. Recent Marxist legal theory describes the autonomy of law as a historical sedimentation of the outcome of earlier struggles over the competing rights of subjects which as such imposes rules not only on subjects but on rulers themselves. The jury system, the legal criteria of evidence and proof, and the legal ideology of the 'rights of free-born Englishmen' constituted a court of appeal in England against plans or projects for tightening the law's grip (Pashukanis, 1978; Renner, 1949; Fine *et al.* 1979, pp. 22–4; Thompson, 1975, Conclusion). Penal practice, far from representing the unfolding of an all-embracing disciplinary *savoir*, should be seen as embodying the compromise outcomes of often heated political and legal debates. Foucault seems to ignore the possibility of conflict between the claims of private wealth and the requirements of public order. Compromise was also required between the desire to punish minor delinquency more strictly and the desire to avoid criminalizing normally law-abiding members of the popular classes through mass imprisonment. The conflict between these two imperatives frequently pitted policemen against magistrates and magistrates against employers (Ignatieff, 1978, pp. 186–7). The erratic line of policy traced out by these conflicts could be said to have been functional to the reproduction of a ruling class only in the relatively trivial sense that the existing distribution of social relations was not overthrown by revolution; but once the elaboration of carceral policy is seen as the unplanned outcome of compromise and conflict, it seems rationalist and conspiratorial to call it an unfolding strategy of a carceral *savoir*.

'SOCIAL CONTROL' AS HISTORICAL EXPLANATION

These questions about the ruling class as a historical actor ought to be connected to earlier questions raised about the role of prisons in disciplining the working class. Given the frequency with which the popular classes themselves sought to invoke the penal sanction against members of their own social group, it would be difficult to maintain that they were simple objects of the punitive sanction. While the majority of punished offenders undoubtedly came from the popular classes, it would not follow from this that the function of imprisonment was to control those classes as such. Foucault's and my own work, I think, confused statements about the social fears motivating the construction of institutions with statements about their actual function.

The 'social control' model of the prison's function which informed my own work assumed that capitalist society was systematically incapable of reproducing itself without the constant interposition of state agencies of control and repression. This model essentially appropriated the social control models of American Progressivist sociology according to which society was a functional equilibrium of institutional mechanisms in the family, the workplace and marketplace working together to ensure the cooperation of individuals in the interests of social order (Stedman Jones, this volume, chapter 2; Rothman, this volume, chapter 5; Muraskin, 1976). As Stedman Jones has pointed out, the Marxist version of this idea, and the structuralist version of it reproduced in Foucault, carries on the assumption of society as a functionally efficient totality of institutions. When applied to prison history, this model implies that institutions 'work', whereas the prison is perhaps *the* classic example of an institution which works badly and which none the less survives in the face of recurrent scepticism as to its deterrent or reformative capacity. Instead of looking for some hidden function which prisons actually succeed in discharging, we ought to work free of such functionalist assumptions altogether and begin to think of society in much more dynamic and historical terms, as being ordered by institutions like the prisons which fail their constituencies and which limp along because no alternative can be found or because conflict over alternatives is too great to be mediated into compromise.

The second assumption in Marxist social control theory is that the use of the state penal sanction is essential to the reproduction of the unequal and exploitative social relations of the capitalist system. Marx himself qualified the centrality of state coercion, arguing that, while the hangman and the house of correction were central in the 'primitive accumulation' process, that is, in the forcible establishment of wage relations, once such wage relations were in place, 'the silent compulsions of economic relations' 'set the seal on the domination of the capitalist over the worker'. The extra-economic coercion of the state penal sanction was then invoked only in 'exceptional' cases (Marx, 1976, p. 899). My own work on the expansion of vagrancy, trespass and petty larceny statutes in the 1820s and 1830s suggested that state penal sanctions were required by employers, especially in the agricultural counties, to prevent their chronically underemployed casual labour force from passing out of the wage system into theft and vagrancy (Ignatieff, 1978, pp. 180–3; also Linebaugh, forthcoming).

Important as the penal sanction may have been in sustaining discipline in pauperized labour markets, or in constituting wage discipline itself in the face of worker resistance, we ought not to take these instances as typical of the role of state force once the wage bargain has been broadly accepted. We ought not to assume that exploitative social relations are impossible to reproduce without threat of force. Even in objectively exploitative, underpaid and unhealthy conditions of labour, one can conceive of men and women voluntarily coming to work not in the sense that they are free to choose wage labour, but in the specific sense that they derive intrinsic satisfaction from the sociability of labour, from the activity itself, from the skill they manage to acquire, and from the pride they take in their work. Marxist theories of labour discipline consistently ignore these aspects of submission to the wage bargain and consequently overstate the centrality of penal force in reproducing those relations. The fact that workers do submit to the wage bargain need not imply that they accept the terms of their subordination as legitimate; it is a cliché of labour history that those whose wage levels, skill and pride in craftsmanship gave them the most reasons for satisfaction with industrial labour were often the most militant in their political and moral challenge to it as a system. The point is simply that the punitive sanction of the state need not be regarded as decisive in the reproduction of exploitative and unequal social relations.

Going still further, it could be asked whether force itself, apart from its specific embodiment in state apparatuses of coercion, is decisive to the maintenance of social order. The tacit social theory of Foucault's *Discipline and Punish* describes all social relations in the language of power, domination and subordination. This would imply that individuals are naturally unsocial or asocial, requiring discipline and domination before they will submit to social rules. Not surprisingly, therefore, Foucault sees the family as an authority system, linked to the carceral system of the state outside:

We should show how intra-familial relations, essentially in the parent-children cell, have become 'disciplined', absorbing since the

classical age external schemata first educational and military, then
medical, psychiatric, psychological, which have made the family the
privileged locus of emergence for the disciplinary question of the
normal and the abnormal. [Foucault 1978, p. 215]

Can fathers' or mothers' social relations towards their children really be
defined only in terms of Foucault's disciplinary question? Foucault would
seem to be taking to the limits of parody a fashionable current of thought,
nourishing itself in the Freudian analysis of Oedipal conflict and in the
feminist critique of patriarchal domination, which has, to my way of
thinking, 'over-politicized' family social relations, neglecting the
collaborative and sacrifical elements of family attachment and over-
emphasizing the power aspects of family interaction. This makes it easy to
locate the family as an institution of domination on a continuum with the
prison, enforcing the same overarching disciplinary rationality; but it does
so by ignoring obvious distinctions between the basis of our obligations as
family members and our obligations as citizens to the law. It also neglects
the extent to which loyalty to one's family or the desire to maintain one's
authority as a family head can constitute the basis for rejection of state
authority, for example, in resistance by families to the introduction of
compulsory school attendance.

By describing all social relations as relations of domination, Foucault
neglects the large aspects of human sociability, in the family and in civil
society generally, which are conducted by the norms of cooperation,
reciprocity and the 'gift relationship'. He neglects that human capacity
which Adam Smith called 'sympathy', by which we voluntarily adjust our
behaviour to norms of propriety in order to stand well in the eyes of our
fellows (Smith, 1759). In Smith's social theory the order of civil society was
reproduced, without state direction or class design, by an uncoordinated
molecular process of individual self-regulation. Our obedience to legal
norms could be understood both in terms of this largely subconscious
order-seeking behaviour and as an expression of conscious belief in the
utility and the justice of such rules in themselves. In Smith's theory, threat
of penal sanction was not necessary to the reproduction of normal patterns
of obedience. Punishment did not constitute the order of civil society;
rather, it gave ritual and symbolic expression, in retributive form, to the
moral value attached by individuals to rule-obedient behaviour (Smith,
1763).

Smith's theory of social order may underestimate human beings' mutual
malignity, and it is justly criticized by Marxists for writing the facts of
power, domination and subordination out of its account of the social
process. But precisely because it tried to think of social order in terms that

go beyond the language of power, it offers a more persuasive account of those social activities which we do experience as uncoerced subjects than one which conceives of order as the grid imposed by a carceral archipelago.

My point here is not to argue the virtues of Smithian social theory as against Foucault's structural functionalism or Marxist social control, but rather to use Smith to point to hidden features of both: their state-centred conception of social order and their tendency to reduce all social relations to relations of domination.

How then are we to think through a theory of the reproduction of social life which would give relative weights to the compelled and the consensual, the bound and the free, the chosen and the determined dimensions of human action in given historical societies? Contemporary social theory is increasingly aware that it has been ill-served by the grand theoretical tradition in its approach to these questions – a Parsonian functionalism which restricts human action to the discharge of prescribed roles and the internalization of values; a Marxism which in its hostility to the idealist account of human subjectivity went a long way towards making the active human subject the determined object of ideological system and social formation; and a structuralism which likewise seems to make individual intellectual creativity and moral choice the determined result of cultural and discursive structure (Giddens, 1976). Work-a-day historians and sociologists of criminal justice may well ask at this point what this high-flown theoretical debate has to do with them, or what they could possibly contribute to it. Its relevance is that any theory or history of punishment must make some ultimate judgement about what weight to attach to the state's penal sanction in the reproduction of obedient behaviour. What weight you give depends ultimately on how much importance you attach to the consensual and voluntary aspects of human behaviour. The social control theory of the 1920s, as Rothman points out in an excellent review of that literature, placed so much stress on the consensual that it neglected the coercive; the social control literature of the 1970s exaggerated the coercive at the expense of the consensual (this volume, chapter 5). The first step back to a balance between these perspectives will require us to ask how crucial the state has been historically in the reproduction of the order of civil society. My suspicion is that the new social history of law and punishment in the 1970s exaggerated the centrality of the state, the police, the prison, the workhouse and the asylum.

If we are going to get beyond our present almost exclusive focus on the state as the constitutive element of order, we will have to begin to reconstitute the whole complex of informal rituals and processes within civil society for the adjudication of grievances, the settling of disputes and the compensation of injury. Historians have only just begun to study dispute and grievance procedures within civil society in the same way as these are studied in the anthropology of law (Diamond, 1974; Roberts, 1980). Among such studies are Edward Thompson's discussion of the 'rough justice' rituals of sixteenth- and seventeenth-century English villages, by means of which wife-beaters, scolds and couples who married out of their age cohort were subjected to public scorn and humiliation by their neighbours (see also Davis, 1975; Thompson, 1972; Thomas, 1971). Because studies of such grievance procedures exist only for the early modern period, it would be easy to conclude that the state expropriated such functions in its courts and prisons in the course of consolidating its monopoly over the means of legitimate violence (Weber, 1947, pp. 324–37).

But the idea that the state enjoys a monopoly over legitimate means of violence is long overdue for challenge. The crimes which it visits with punishment ought to be interpreted as the tip of an iceberg, as a small part of those disputes, conflicts, thefts, assaults too damaging, too threatening, too morally outrageous to be handled within the family, the work unit, the neighbourhood, the street. It would be wrong, I think, to conclude that early modern English villages were the only communities capable of exercising these *de facto* judicial powers. Until recently, social histories of the working-class family and the working-class neighbourhood were too confined within their subdisciplines to include discussion of the anthropology of dispute settlement and the social history of relations with the police, the courts and the prisons. But what is now opening up as an area of study is the social process by which crime was identified within these units of civil society, and how decisions were taken to channel certain acts or disputes for adjudication or punishment by the state. The correlative process, from the state side, is how agents like the police worked out a tacit agreement with the local enforcers of norms, determining which offences were theirs to control, and which were to be left to the family, the employer or the neighbourhood (Fine *et al.*, 1979, pp. 118–37). Such research would indicate, I think, that powers of moral and punitive enforcement are distributed throughout civil society, and that the function of prison can only be understood once its position within a whole invisible framework of sanctioning and dispute regulation procedure in civil society has been determined. We have always known that prisons and the courts handled only a tiny fraction of delinquency known to the police. Now we must begin, if we can, to uncover the network which handled the 'dark figure', which recovered stolen goods, visited retribution on known villains, demarcated the respectable, hid the innocent, and delivered up the guilty.

This new area of research will not open up by itself. Empirical fields of this sort become visible only if theory guides historians to new questions. This essay amounts to a plea to historians, criminologists and sociologists to involve themselves seriously with texts they have been apt to dismiss as abstract and ahistorical – the classical social theory tradition of Smith, Marx, Durkheim and Weber. The involvement ought to take the form of self-criticism; for, if I have argued correctly, these texts are the hidden source of some basic misconceptions – that the state enjoys a monopoly of the punitive sanction, that its moral authority and practical power are *the* binding sources of social order, and that all social relations can be described in the language of power and domination. If we could at least subject these ideas to practical empirical examination, a new social history of order, authority, law and punishment would begin to emerge.

REFERENCES

Babington, Anthony (1971), *The English Bastille*. New York: St. Martin's Press.

Bailey, Victor (1975), 'The Dangerous Classes in Late Victorian England'. PhD dissertation, Warwick University.

Beattie, J. M. (1974), 'The Pattern of Crime in England, 1660–1800', *Past and Present*, 62, 47–95.

Beattie, J. M. (1977), 'Crime and the Courts in Surrey, 1736–53'. In *Crime in England, 1550–1800*, ed. J. S. Cockburn. London: Methuen.

Beaumont, Gustave de, and de Tocqueville, Alexis (1964), *On the Penitentiary System of the United States*. Reprint. Carbondale: Southern Illinois University Press. Originally published 1835.

Bellamy, John (1973), *Crime and Public Order in England in the Later Middle Ages*. London: Routledge and Kegan Paul.

Bentham, Jeremy (1791), *Panopticon; or the Inspection House*. London: T. Payne.

Branch, Johnson W. (1970), *The English Prison Hulks*. Chichester: Phillimore.

Chill, Emmanuel (1962), 'Religion and Mendicity in Seventeenth Century France', *International Review of Social History*, 7, 400–25.

Clemmer, Donald (1940), *The Prison Community*. New York: Holt, Rinehart and Winston.

Cockburn, J. S. (ed.) (1977), *Crime in England, 1550–1800*. London: Methuen.

Condon, R. (1962), 'The Reform of English Prisons, 1773–1816'. PhD dissertation, Brown University.

Cooper, David D. (1974), *The Lesson of the Scaffold: The Public Execution Controversy in Victorian England*. London: Allen Lane.

Cooper, Robert Alan (1976), 'Ideas and Their Execution: English Prison Reform'. *Eighteenth Century Studies*, 10, 73–93.

Davis, Jennifer (1980), 'The London Garroting Panic of 1862: A Moral Panic and the Creation of a Criminal Class in Mid-Victorian England'. In *Crime and Law in Western Societies: Historical Essays*, ed. V. A. C. Gatrell, B. Lenman, and G. Parker. London: Europa.

Davis, Natalie (1975), 'The Reasons of Misrule'. In her *Society and Culture in Early Modern France*. Stanford, Calif.: Stanford University Press.

DeLacy, Margaret Eisenstein (1980), 'County Prison Administration in Lancashire, 1690–1850'. PhD dissertation, Princeton University.

Diamond, Stanley (1974), 'The Rule of Law versus the Order of Custom'. In his *In Search of the Primitive: A Critique of Civilization*. New Brunswick, NJ: Transaction Books.

Donajgrodzki, A. P. (ed.) (1977), *Social Control in Nineteenth Century Britain*. London: Croom Helm.

Evans, Robin (1975), 'A Rational Plan for Softening the Mind: Prison Design, 1750–1842'. PhD dissertation, University of Essex.

Fine, Bob, R. Lea, J. Kinsey, S. Picciotto and J. Young (eds) (1979), *Capitalism and the Rule of Law: From Deviancy Theory to Marxism*. Harmondsworth: Penguin.

Fitzgerald, Mike (1977), *Prisoners in Revolt*. Harmondsworth: Penguin.

Fitzgerald, Mike, and Joe Sim (1979), *British Prisons*. Oxford: Basil Blackwell.

Foner, Eric (1976), *Tom Paine and Revolutionary America*. London: Oxford University Press.

Foucault, Michel (1967), *Madness and Civilization*. Translated by Richard Howard. London: Tavistock.

Foucault, Michel (ed.) (1973), *Moi, Pierre Rivière . . . un cas de parricide au XIXe siècle*. Paris: Gallimard Julliard.

Foucault, Michel (1976), *La Volonté de savoir: histoire de la sexualité*. Paris: Gallimard.

Foucault, Michel (1978), *Discipline and Punish*. Translated by Alan Sheridan. New York: Pantheon.

Giddens, Anthony (1976), *New Rules of Sociological Method*. New York: Basic Books.

Goffman, Erving (1961), *Asylums*. Garden City, NJ: Doubleday/Anchor.

Gramsci, Antonio (1971), *Prison Notebooks*. London: Lawrence and Wishart.

Hart, Jennifer (1955), 'Reform of the Borough Police, 1835–1856', *English Historical Review*, 70, 411–27.

Hart, Jennifer (1965), 'Nineteenth-Century Social Reform: A Tory Interpretation of History', *Past and Present*, 31, 39–61.

Hay, Douglas (1975), 'Property, Authority and Criminal Law'. In *Albion's Fatal Tree*, ed. D. Hay, P. Linebaugh, J. Rule, E. P. Thompson, and C. Winslow. London: Allen Lane.

Henriques, Ursula (1972), 'The Rise and Decline of the Separate System of Prison Discipline', *Past and Present*, 54, 61–93.

Himmelfarb, Gertrude (1968), *Victorian Minds*. New York: Harper.

Ignatieff, Michael (1978), *A Just Measure of Pain: The Penitentiary in the Industrial Revolution, 1750–1850*. New York: Pantheon.

Innes, Joanna (1980a), 'The King's Bench Prison in the Later Eighteenth Century: Law, Authority and Order in a London Debtor's Prison'. In *An Ungovernable People: Englishmen and the Law in the 17th and 18th Centuries*, ed. John Brewer and John Styles. London: Hutchinson.

Innes, Joanna (1980b), 'English Prisons in the Eighteenth Century', PhD dissertation, Cambridge University.

Jacobs, James (1977), *Stateville: The Penitentiary in Mass Society*. Chicago: University of Chicago Press.

Katz, Michael (1968), *The Ironies of Early School Reform*. Cambridge, Mass.: Harvard University Press.

Labour History Society, Great Britain (1972), *Bulletin: Crime and Industrial Society Conference Report*.

Lasch, Christopher (1973), 'The Discovery of the Asylum'. In his *The World of Nations*. New York: Vintage.

Lazerson, Marvin (1971), *The Origins of the Urban School*. Cambridge, Mass.: Harvard University Press.

Leroy, Ladurie E. (1973), 'La Décroissance de crime au XVIIIe siècle: bilan d'historiens', *Contrepoint*, 9, 227–33.

Lewis, W. David (1965), *From Newgate to Dannemora: The Rise of the Penitentiary in New York, 1796–1848*. Ithaca, NY: Cornell University Press.

Lewis, Orlando F. (1967), *The Development of American Prisons and Prison Customs, 1776–1845*. Reprint. Montclair, NJ: Patterson Smith. Originally published 1922.

Linebaugh, Peter (1975), 'The Tyburn Riot against the Surgeons'. In *Albion's Fatal Tree*, ed. D. Hay, P. Linebaugh, J. Rule, E. P. Thompson, and C. Winslow. London: Allen Lane.

Linebaugh, Peter (1976), 'Karl Marx, the Theft of Wood and Working Class Composition: A Contribution to the Current Debate', *Crime and Social Justice*, 6, 5–16.

Linebaugh, Peter (1977), 'The Ordinary of Newgate and His Account'. In *Crime in England, 1550–1800*, ed. J. S. Cockburn. London: Methuen.

Linebaugh, Peter (forthcoming), *Crime and the Wage in the Eighteenth Century*.

McConville, Sean (1977), 'Penal Ideas and Prison Management in England, 1700–1850'. PhD dissertation, Cambridge University.

McKelvey, Blake (1977), *American Prisons*. Montclair, NJ: Patterson Smith.

Marx, K. (1976), *Capital*, vol. I. Harmondsworth: Penguin.

Muraskin, W. A. (1976), 'The Social Control Theory in American History: A Critique', *Journal of Social History*, 11, 559–68.

Pashukanis, B. (1978), *Law and Marxism: A General Theory*, 3rd ed. London: Ink Links.

Perrot, Michelle (1975), 'Delinquance et systèmes penitentiaire en France au XIXe siècle', *Annales: économies, sociétés, civilizations*, 30, 67–91.

Perrot, Michelle (ed.) (1980), *L'impossible prison: recherches sur le système penitentiaire au XIXe siècle*. Paris: Seuil.

Philips, David (1977), *Crime and Authority in Victorian England: The Black Country, 1835–60*. London: Croom Helm.

Piven, Francis F., and Richard Cloward (1971), *Regulating the Poor*. New York: Vintage.

Platt, Anthony M. (1969), *The Child Savers: The Invention of Delinquency*. Chicago: University of Chicago Press.

Playfair, Giles (1971), *The Punitive Obsession*. London: Victor Gollancz.

Pugh, R. B. (1968), *Imprisonment in Medieval England*. Cambridge: Cambridge University Press.

Radzinowicz, Sir Leon (1948–68), *A History of English Criminal Law*. vols. 1–6. London: Stevens.

Renner, Karl (1949), *The Institutions of Private Law and Their Social Functions*. London: Routledge and Kegan Paul.

Roberts, Simon (1980), 'Changing Modes of Dispute Settlement: An Anthropological Perspective'. Paper presented at the *Past and Present* Society Conference on Law and Human Relations, London, 2 July 1980.

Rothman, David J. (1971), *The Discovery of the Asylum*. Boston: Little, Brown.

Rothman, David J. (1980a), *Conscience and Convenience: The Asylum and Its Alternatives in Progressive America*. Boston: Little, Brown.

Rusche, George, and Otto Kirchheimer (1939), *Punishment and Social Structure*. New York: Columbia University Press.

Schlossman, Steven L. (1977), *Love and the American Delinquent: The Theory and Practice of 'Progressive' Juvenile Justice, 1825–1920*. Chicago: University of Chicago Press.

Scull, Andrew T. (1977), *Decarceration: Community Treatment and the Deviant – a Radical View*. Englewood Cliffs, NJ: Prentice-Hall.

Scull, Andrew T. (1979), *Museums of Madness*. London: Allen Lane.

Shaw, A. G. L. (1971), *Convicts and the Colonies*. London: Faber.

Sheehan, W. J. (1977), 'Finding Solace in 18th Century Newgate'. In *Crime in England, 1550–1800*, ed. J. S. Cockburn. London: Methuen.

Silberman, Charles E. (1978), *Criminal Violence, Criminal Justice*. New York: Random House.

Silver, Alan (1967), 'The Demand for Order in Civil Society: A Review of Some Themes in the History of Urban Crime, Police and Riot'. In *The Police: Six Sociological Essays*, ed. D. Bordua. New York: Wiley.

Smith, Adam (1976), *The Theory of Moral Sentiments*. Edited by D. D. Raphael. Oxford: Clarendon Press. Originally published 1759.

Smith, Adam (1978), *Lectures on Jurisprudence*. Edited by R. L. Meek, D. D. Raphael, and P. G. Stein. Oxford: Clarendon Press. Originally delivered 1763.

Stedman Jones, Gareth (1971), *Outcast London*. London: Penguin.

Stedman Jones, Gareth (1977), 'Class Expression versus Social Control?' *History Workshop Journal*, 4, 163–71.

Stockdale, Eric (1977), *A Study of Bedford Prison, 1660–1877*. London: Phillimore.

Stone, Lawrence (1979), *Family, Sex and Marriage in England, 1500–1800*. Harmondsworth: Penguin.

Storch, Robert D. (1975), 'The Plague of the Blue Locusts: Police Reform and Popular Resistance in Northern England, 1840–1857', *International Review of Social History*, 20, 61–90.

Sykes, Gresham (1958), *The Society of Captives*. Princeton: Princeton University Press.

Teeters, Negley D. (1935), *The Cradle of the Penitentiary: The Walnut Street Jail at Philadelphia, 1773–1835*. Philadelphia: Lippincott.

Thomas, K. (1971) *Religion and the Decline of Magic*, London, Weidenfeld and Nicolson.

Thompson, E. P. (1963), *The Making of the English Working Class*. New York: Pantheon.

Thompson, E. P. (1971), 'The Moral Economy of the English Crowd', *Past and Present*, 50, 76–136.

Thompson, E. P. (1972), 'Rough Music! le charivari anglais', *Annales: économies, sociétés, civilisations*, 27, 285–312.

Thompson, E. P. (1975), *Whigs and Hunters*. London: Allen Lane.

Thompson, E. P. (1980), *Writing by Candlelight*. London: Merlin.

Tobias, J. J. (1972), *Crime and Industrial Society in the Nineteenth Century*. New York: Schocken.

Tocqueville, Alexis de (1969), *Democracy in America*. Edited by J. P. Mayer. New York: Doubleday/Anchor.

Tomlinson, Margaret Heather (1975), 'Victorian Prisons: Administration and Architecture'. PhD dissertation, Bedford College, London University.

Trumbach, Randolph (1978), *The Rise of the Egalitarian Family: Aristocratic Kinship and Domestic Relations in 18th Century England*. London: Academic Press.

Webb, Beatrice and Webb, Sidney (1963), *English Prisons under Local Government*. London: Frank Cass. Originally published 1922.

Weber, Marx. (1947), *The Theory of Social and Economic Organization*. Edited by Talcott Parsons. Glencoe: Free Press.

Whiting, J. R. S. (1975), *Prison Reform in Gloucestershire, 1775–1820*. London: Phillimore.

Wicker, Tom (1975), *A Time to Die*. New York: Quadrangle.

5

Social Control: The Uses and Abuses of the Concept in the History of Incarceration

DAVID J. ROTHMAN

Over the past fifteen years, historians have set out a fundamental re-interpretation of American and European responses to the deviant and dependent. Although older accounts were not based on much substance, generally content to report rhetoric and ignore reality, still a distinctive view had predominated. Innovations were 'reforms' and the innovators were 'reformers', and all were worthy of celebration. In contrast, the new histories adopt a far more sceptical approach, so that reforms assume a dubious, really mischievous character and the reformers appear at best naive, and at worst duplicitous.

As with any such reversal of interpretation, overstatement and over-reaction are bound to occur. At times the revisionists are at fault, exaggerating their claims in order to distinguish themselves from their predecessors; and at times their readers are at fault, making judgments in black and white, ignoring all the grey in the texts. And, inevitably, some of those with historiographical bent, with an instinct to assign labels, fit the participants of the controversy into 'schools'. So it has become fashionable of late to talk of two camps: those who depicted the programmes and policies as reformist, humanitarian and progressive, against those who now present them as the triumph, in that key phrase, of 'social control'.

While it is hardly necessary to define the characteristics of a reformist tradition in history – more than enough has already been written about Whig historiography – it is important to define explicitly what is meant by *social control*. For as much as the term is currently used, so often is it abused, pasted on with little or no effort at clarification. A literary critic once remarked (in the 1950s) that *bourgeois* was a term children applied to their fathers in order to express their scorn politely. In this same spirit, *social control* seems to be a term that historians apply to express their scorn, perhaps not so politely. Hence it is vital to trace the roots of the concept, to

Source: Rice University Studies, vol. 67, 1981, pp. 9–20.

measure its strengths and weaknesses, and to evaluate its relevance to historical developments.

Those who think of social control as more or less synonymous with repression and coercion may be startled to discover that American sociologists first used the term to capture the very opposite quality, that of cooperation, of voluntary and harmonious cohesion. As ably traced by Morris Janowitz in *The Last Half-Century*, the history of the concept of social control begins with the effort of such sociologists as George Herbert Mead and E. A. Ross to promote a greater appreciation of the role of subjective and qualitative values in an understanding of society. Rather than assuming that the order of a society rested upon the regulatory power of the state, or even upon the regulatory power of narrow self-interest (as expressed, for example, in individual, self-interested economic decisions), Mead and Ross wished to broaden the analysis of the roots of social cohesion, or as Allan Silver recently suggested, to connect it more closely to sympathy than to fiat.

Two early definitions of social control provide the flavour of the argument. 'Social control', announced Mead, 'depends then upon the degree to which the individuals in society are able to assume the attitudes of others who are involved with them in common endeavors.' As Ross phrased it, social control stimulates an analysis of how men 'live closely together and associate their efforts with that degree of harmony we see about us'. For both of them, the critical concern was to understand the sources of empathy and harmony, how people associated together to perform common endeavours, how voluntaristic cooperation marked social activity.

To a historian, these phrases carry distinctly Progressive overtones. Indeed, the entire enterprise of Mead and Ross seems quintessentially Progressive. Despite a customary interpretation of the Progressive mind-set as especially sensitive to conflict, the Beardian kind of warfare between one economic interest and another, a second, and even stronger, ideological strain characterized Progressive thinkers – that is, a deep commitment to a notion of an ultimate harmony of interests. To Progressives, politics was not a zero–sum game; given the promise of American life, there was no need to think of trade-offs, of this interest winning at the expense of that one. To be sure, the voraciousness of some greedy speculators or businessmen would have to be curbed, and hence the state would have to correct imbalances of power. As Herbert Croly explained, Americans could no longer assume that expressions of individual economic self-interest would inevitably add up to the common weal. Nevertheless, these excesses aside, it was appropriate to anticipate harmony and cooperation to everyone benefiting from the American way.

If there was any single process that seemed absolutely irrelevant to this society, surely it was class warfare. To think of an inevitable and bitter conflict between labour and capital was mistaken, really absurd.

It is important to reckon with this feature of Progressive thought precisely because of its relevance to the sociologists who first advanced the concept of social control. What Mead and Ross were about was explicating how this fundamental harmony was being accomplished. They were, more often than not, being descriptive: here is how American society achieves cooperation without coercion or external discipline. Thus there was nothing ironic in Ross's intent to study how Americans reached the degree of harmony 'we see about us'. As a good Progressive, Ross did see harmony, and his sociology was intended to account for his observations.

Hence, at its birth, something very conservative clung to the notion of social control, both in its content and its orientation. Some later sociologists would deny this thrust, contending that the major element in the origins of the concept was the desire to introduce 'soft' considerations into a discipline that was, in a positivist tradition, hard. But the argument is weak. The idea of social control did place a premium on stability, collective order and cohesion. Those ready to explore the concept wished to understand the roots of order, not to examine the roots of change, and certainly not to foment change.

This orientation had profound intellectual implications. The interest in social control remained very strong through the 1920s and 1930s and gave a highly static quality to much of the research. Sociologists became increasingly adept at accounting for the forces that perpetuated an institution or practice, but their explanations were over-determined, making it difficult to understand how alterations in the system might occur. Everything seemed frozen in place. In essence, sociologists became so caught up with the sources of cohesion that they neglected to examine the sources of change. To offer one contemporary example of the results, Erving Goffman (who has much more in common with Ross and Mead than might be at first apparent), offered a brilliant examination of stigma in the early 1950s, drawing fascinating connections among the handicapped, the sick, the deviant and members of minorities. By the time Goffman concluded, it was apparent that the imposition of stigma and the management of stigma followed complex rules, so complex that it seemed impossible to think of violating or altering them. To be crippled or to be black was to be stigmatized, and no escape routes were open. Yet within a decade, black would become beautiful and the handicapped would mount successful campaigns to achieve their rights. Still, if one went back and reread Goffman, one found not a clue as to the causes of the change.

Let us place this argument into another context, making its relevance to social control still more apparent. When Ross and Mead explored the sources of harmony and cooperation, they were eager to investigate all aspects of society, from the role of religion and the marketplace to the family. Accordingly, they were prepared to label all of the institutions that came under their scrutiny institutions of social control, which were almost indistinguishable from institutions of socialization. Since the church made a vital contribution to fostering empathy, it was an institution of social control; since the family obviously fostered cooperation, it, too, was an institution of social control. In fact, given their concern for the sources of stability, it was almost impossible to draw the limits of the analysis, to know which institutions to omit from the list. The result of all this was that the term 'social control' became flabby, almost synonymous with the totality of the society. This development must be carefully noted, for it may well repeat itself, this time with historians. In all events, by the 1940s *social control* went out of style among sociologists. The textbooks might use the term, but serious researchers, with one or two exceptions, did not pursue the issue in the Ross–Mead tradition.

Had the history of the concept of social control stopped here, historians would not enter the story. In the pre-Second World War decades, historians seemed unaware of the Ross–Mead work, and social control did not enter the vocabulary. (For the record, it was the Chicago school of sociology, W. I. Thomas and Louis Wirth, that exerted the greatest inter-disciplinary influence, helping to make immigration history the first of the fields to draw on sociological theory.) But rather surprisingly, social control experienced a rebirth in the 1950s and 1960s, although rebirth does not quite capture the flavour of the development. In its new guise, the concept bore little relationship to the original use of the term. Social control in this new stage reversed its orientation, moving from cooperation to coercion, from harmony to conflict.

If Mead and Ross were essentially content with the promise of American life, those who revived the term *social control* were certainly not. Barrington Moore, Richard Cloward and Francis Piven, to name three of the major figures, were fierce critics of American capitalism, located well to the left on the political spectrum. From their perspective, social order and social cohesion, to the degree that it existed in American society, represented the outcome not of shared values but of manipulation and regulation. Cloward and Piven, for example, were convinced that social order was a good deal flimsier than others might recognize or concede. The problem was that symptoms of disorder were repressed, not merely on the streets but from the collective memory – and historians, of course, were in part to blame. When Cloward and Piven wrote about the 1930s, they focused on the incidents of class warfare, on the protests around WPA and relief restrictions. To most historians of the 1930s, the words that best characterize the popular response are depression (in a psychological sense), passivity, lack of violence and self-blame. To Cloward and Piven, however, the essence of the decade was protest, and then repression. Hence, when they rediscovered the term 'social control', they had in mind the various strategies that the ruling elite used to impose its will. The process of imposition, they recognized, was complicated, involving far more than the exercise of a direct police force. The elite had many more subtle instruments at hand. Thus, mechanisms of social control now referred to those less-than-obvious ways by which the ruling class foisted its will upon the lower class.

It was not caprice that brought Cloward and Piven to the use of the term 'social control'. Just as Mead and Ross had wished to take the analysis of social order beyond the use of force, to come closer to what we might think of as social psychology, so too Cloward and Piven, with their own special twist, shared this commitment. They were also convinced that a variety of manipulative strategies brought about conformity, that outright repression was not the sum of the story of how the poor were regulated. What Mead and Ross thought of as cooperation, they thought of as coercion – but all of them agreed that the value of a term like 'social control' was to sensitize researchers to the less-than-obvious ways by which stabilization (to use a neutral term) occurred.

It was this second definition of social control that came to the attention of historians, who for their own reasons were eager to adopt it. In the late 1960s, when the concept first entered historians' vocabulary, Progressive historiography had lost much of its appeal, certainly among the younger historians. The sources of their discontent were numerous. There may be an inevitable inclination of sons to rise up against fathers; the deep commitment of the outstanding teachers of history in the 1950s to New Deal, Rooseveltian, Progressive principles was likely to provoke a reaction. But more was at stake than adolescent rebellion. The historiography of the 1950s, crudely but not inappropriately labelled 'consensus' history, had backed itself into a corner; it was becoming increasingly difficult to match the assumptions of the historians with the realities of American life in the 1960s and 1970s. It is tempting to argue that post-Second World War historians were, unknowingly, at one with Ross and Mead in their search for the spirit of cooperation. The historians did not cite them and probably did not read them – but all of them were Progressives. All were committed to a notion that harmony and cooperation, with more or less qualifications, were at the core of the American experience. All celebrated that we were born free, that immigrants went through dark days but eventually made it, that blacks survived slavery to reap the rewards of *Brown v. Board of Education*, that the American political tradition was one of healthy pragmatism. No one political figure embodied this spirit more steadfastly than Martin Luther King. His Washington 'I Have a Dream' speech could just as easily have been titled 'the Promise of American Life'. King, on the eve of the black power movement, may well have represented the culmination of Progressivism in the United States.

The Progressive formulations had little appeal to a number of historians writing in the 1960s and 1970s. Did it really make sense to praise Roosevelt for his relief programme of the 1930s? Could anyone for a moment think that social security or unemployment insurance had done away with, or even chipped away at, the sources of poverty in this country? Yes, FDR may have saved capitalism in the United States – but the phrase now had a more ominous than heroic ring to it.

Generally, these historians became increasingly impatient with the word 'reform'. In the first instance, the term was stifling conceptually, a way of avoiding asking the difficult questions. To label a movement 'reform' was to suggest that its programme was logical and appropriate, the very sort that men and women of good heart would propose. So one did not have to ask why this programme rather than another came forward; precisely because it was a reform, its advantages were seemingly too obvious to demand investigation. No one need ponder why Americans in the 1830s wished to establish a common school, or a penitentiary, or a mental hospital system. All were obvious steps forward in the march of progress: it was better to educate the poor than to neglect them, to confine and rehabilitate offenders than to whip or hang them, to treat and cure the mentally ill than to lock them into attics or cellars. But such assertions assumed too much. Of all the possible ways to promote mobility or equality, why did Jacksonian Americans decide on schools? Of all possible ways to respond to deviance, why did Americans resolve on institutions? One searched the historical literature in vain for suggestions. No one, it seemed, had ever bothered to pose such fundamental questions.

The failure seemed all the more unfortunate because it was apparent and unmistakable that the reforms of one generation became the scandals of the next. Historians had explored their materials with a curious myopia. First they applauded the reformers who designed the system, then they applauded the reformers who exposed the system, and then they applauded the reformers who devised a new system – and the circle moved round on itself. So the founders of the insane asylums in the 1830s were heroes; those who crusaded against easy commitment laws in the 1880s were heroes; those who devised mental hygiene community programmes in the 1920s were heroes; and all those who exposed the horrors of the state hospitals were heroes. And on and on, historians wrote with a bewildering lack of discrimination. The formula seemed ever so easy: anyone who proclaimed to be acting in the name of the underdog warranted applause, no matter what the substance or the outcome of the programme. It was rhetoric that counted all the way.

Under such circumstances, a number of historians found the post-1950 definitions of a repressive social control a useful corrective, an antidote to Progressives' automatic championing of self-defined do-gooders. As we shall see, there was very little agreement among these historians as to precisely who was doing the controlling, for what ends, and with what degree of consciousness. But to put these considerations aside temporarily, the new concept of social control served historians quite well in a variety of ways. At the very least, it prompted them to read the rhetoric of reform with a more cold and calculating eye, to entertain the idea that a series of motives, not all benign, might well produce a seemingly humanitarian proposal. More, in this framework, historians began to devote far greater attention to the outcome of innovations, to become more concerned with reality than with rhetoric. To be sure, such an orientation does have its dangers. It is neither logical nor fair to judge a movement exclusively by its outcome. Authors are not responsible for translations. What a second generation does with a programme cannot be blamed on the first generation – and to analyse origins in light of subsequent developments may well distort the movement. Yet, that said, how necessary a corrective it was to begin examining the substance of the programmes. Heretofore, historians had been prone to deliver their applause at the end of act one, not bothering to stay around for act two, to ponder what happened when the first generation saw their programmes put into effect, let alone when the next generation took them over. At the least, the idea of social control moved social history from thought to actuality, a step that generated new information and new perspectives.

To be alert to the concept of social control was also to break out of the old morality play that Progressive historians were prone to present. In their world, well-meaning reformers were to one side, opponents to progress and humanitarianism (the selfish taxpayer who wondered why his dollars should support common schools or insane asylums) on the other. At times, the forces of evil triumphed over the forces of good, the nay-sayers won, and thus reform 'failed'. Indeed, it is barely stretching the point to claim that the failure of reform to achieve its goals became something akin to original sin, the fault of forces beyond anyone's ability to alter.

Against this tradition, it became far more interesting to ponder alliances, those made and not made, to analyse the constituency for innovation. Some of the results of this orientation have been to make reformers tools of the capitalist class, without much more evidence for the assertion than an ideological flourish. Nevertheless, at the least reformers have been brought back into society, moved off the pedestal and properly made part of the political process.

Even more important, can we now ask what is meant by success or by failure? Success for whom? Failure for whom? And soon complicated answers begin to emerge. A social control orientation does suggest that innovations were likely to confer benefits somewhere, and so the question becomes, where? If the prison did not serve the prisoner, then whom did it serve? If the asylum did not benefit the patient, then whom did it benefit? Indeed, if, countless exposés later, reformers continued to support the concept of incarceration, what does this tell us about the reformers themselves? One need not vouch for any one particular answer to see that the questions are good questions, worthy of analysis.

In sum, a coercive sense of social control became a very useful corrective to the concept of reform, prompting historians to offer a more complex analysis of innovations and to search more carefully in the reality of change. If some hear all this with a tone of bemusement and wonder why it took so long for some seemingly obvious considerations to surface, two reminders are in order. First, the strength of the reformist historiography must be fully appreciated, for it did block out these types of investigations. Second, much more than mere debunking is at stake here. The point at issue is not whether a particular reformer attacked prostitution and then went home and flagellated himself, or whether another reformer turned out to be advancing his own fortunes. Rather, innovations that in traditional terms represented the best of liberalism have been placed in a much harsher light, exposing much that heretofore had escaped notice.

To bring these general observations to the substance of the rise and perpetuation of prisons, mental hospitals, reformatories and almshouses, it is now apparent that no simple links connect these places of confinement to a spirit of humanitarianism. That all of their wards were filled with the lower classes, that proponents' rhetoric said more to society than 'do good', that within a few decades of their founding, they were invariably places of last resort (overcrowded, brutal and corrupt), that in origin they all adopted regimens of bell-ringing punctuality – these considerations remain beyond the explanatory powers of a concept of 'reform'.

By the same token, to attach a label of 'social control' to these institutions and to let the matter rest there hardly represents an advance. Taken by itself, the label is often redundant: what else are prisons if not institutions for control? Or it is too encompassing: is not every institution, from the family to the office place, an institution of social control, either an agent of socialization (in the Mead–Ross tradition) or an agency of coercion (in the Cloward–Piven tradition)? And social control by whom? For what purposes? And why in this form rather than in another? If once it was fashionable to think every process of social change could be explained by reference to 'status anxiety', one can detect signs of a new fashion, labelling every institution an institution of social control. It is as if sociology is a discipline filled with golden nuggets that can be easily carried over into history to advance the intellectual fortune of the purveyor.

On a more serious level, one of the most significant intellectual efforts to give meaning to the concept of social control has been to connect it to the growth of capitalism, or to a market economy, or to an industrial system. It is somewhat difficult to be precise here, because the authors are not. In fact, the first problem with such an approach is a remarkable vagueness about the characteristics of the economic system and how they connect, seemingly inevitably, to such institutions. To Michel Foucault, capitalism is a spirit that hovers over Western Civilization from the Enlightenment on, never changing, always promoting rationality, the rule of reason, surveillance and discipline. Taking this level of generalization down to the specifics of institutional history is well-nigh impossible. Everything is homogenized: the economy is the same in 1820 as in 1880 as in 1980, in England, in the United States and in France. And all practices within criminal justice, mental health, juvenile justice or social welfare are tied to this economy: the rise of the penitentiary in the early nineteenth century, the rise of parole, probation, psychiatric classification in the early twentieth century, the juvenile reformatory and the juvenile court, the almshouses and aid to dependent children. Everything gets pushed into this ideological bag, somehow or other.

Michael Ignatieff and Andrew Scull, one tracing the origins of English prisons, the other, English insane asylums, emphasize the impact of a market economy. But again, in their arguments, conception triumphs over data. Scull first argues that a new form of exclusion of the mentally ill was necessary once a market economy and an allegiance to a central political authority took hold in England. Then, apparently, a new conception of insanity itself occurred because of the factory system: industrial capitalism both demanded 'a reform of character' on the part of each labourer and taught society of the power of human interventions. Just as we can turn raw materials into manufactured ones, so we could and should turn the mad into the sane.

But several problems immediately appear. For one, national markets and national allegiance need not go hand in hand. The American experience was quite different: a political loyalty that transcended the boundary of the colonial town emerged in the 1790s, decades before anything approximating a national market appeared in the 1880s. This expanded loyalty did have profound consequences for punishment. Eighteenth-century towns had wherever possible banished offenders, uncaring if they left Andover to plague Northampton. In other words, alternatives to colonial warning out and banishment practices would have to be devised once state governments replaced colonial governments. Still, this process need not be related in any significant way to market considerations.

So, too, the idea of the potency of human interventions need not rest exclusively, or even primarily, upon the factory machine. Many considerations could, and did, promote such a view, from shifts in religious doctrine that abandoned Calvinistic notions of predestination and innate corruptibility, to changes in scientific knowledge that made the world appear more orderly and therefore more predictable. To single out and note only the effect of the machine upon thought may well fit with theories of economic determinism, but it leaves too much out of the story.

To propose some general guidelines for approaching the materials, let me suggest first that the substance of the developments will never be clarified without diligent attention to ideology, not as reflective of some machine discipline, but as vital in its own right. It is true that new ideas do not spring out of nowhere, but by the same token, they do not emerge from ready-made factories either. Whether one wishes to understand the rise of the asylum in the Jacksonian era, or the later invention of such procedures as probation, parole, outpatient care and the juvenile court in the Progressive Era, one should turn first to the rhetoric of the reformers – for it is here that one will find the strongest clues to the origins of the changes and the sources of their success, their legitimation, if you will.

If the rhetoric is analysed with an eye to more than the nobility of the writer, then both the fears and hopes of would-be reformers will emerge with clarity. Jacksonian prison reformers, looking at their society through the blinders of eighteenth-century notions of social order, were deeply uncertain as to whether a geographically mobile and open society – all that colonial communities were not – could perpetuate itself. And to ignore such fears, to insist doggedly that humanitarianism was the crucial point, or to focus exclusively on the novelty that was Lowell, is to miss the consideration that can best explain why prisons adopted their special architectural form and their internal routine, from the single cell and exercise yards of the Eastern State Penitentiary to the lock step at Sing-Sing. For their part, Progressive reformers, convinced of the promise of American life and confident that the deviant (exemplified by the immigrant from the ghetto) would turn law-abiding once he experienced the promise, eagerly expanded the discretionary authority of criminal justice administrators; they were ready to trust to the state, whether in the guise of judges or probation and parole officers, to treat the criminal, not the crime. Indeed, through the impact of this ideology, prisons assumed a new aspect; the organizing principle shifted from the model of a regimented, quasi-Utopian alternative to the society, to the model of the prison as a society. Henceforth, the prison was to approximate in so far as possible the outside community – and so striped uniforms, rules of silence and the lock step gave way to freedom of the yard, prison bands, prison teams, prison commissaries and the like.

Second, in reconstructing this history, the sources of the appeal of the rhetoric must be traced. In whose interest was it to translate such notions into practice, to build a system upon such a base? This is not a question to be answered *a priori*, but it must be the subject of investigation. Some of the immediate answers that suggest themselves may well be valid. It is probably true that asylum superintendents profited, and do profit, from the perpetuation of their buildings; that prison wardens were, and are, a force for keeping prisons in business. But the search must go further. For example, the Progressives' desire to enhance discretionary decision-making fits well with the needs of administrators in criminal justice, juvenile justice and mental health. Judges welcomed the freedom to give probation to whom they would and to be free of due process requirements in juvenile cases. Wardens delighted in their ability, under parole statutes, to influence decisions involving release time to inmates. District attorneys found such innovations useful as grease for the wheels of plea bargaining. Anyone who would try to write the history of Progressive reforms without attention to these considerations would be unable to explain their rapid passage or their longevity.

To come to the third and final point: without attention to these considerations, it is impossible to understand the outcome of these innovations, the inability of reformers to realize their goals. A Foucault-like analysis that focuses exclusively on the spirit of surveillance and discipline cannot explain the degeneration of the ideal. It is one thing to report on the ostensible power of psychiatrists, on the asylum keeper who peers everywhere, on the parole officer who regulates the life of his charges. But it is quite another to account for the fact that prisons never did appoint more than one psychiatrist for every 5000 inmates, that asylum keepers could never keep track of their thousands of patients, or that each parole officer had a case load of hundreds of ex-inmates. Those doggedly committed to notions of humanitarianism cannot do much better either. They may lament the corruption of the ideal and sigh at the fate of noble intentions, but moralizing is no substitute for analysis. Only by getting into the heart of the story – what made the ideal itself so susceptible to corruption, what sorts of alliances among reformers and administrators contributed to it, why reformers responded so passively to the perversion of their ideals – will the dynamics at work become clear.

In sum, the history of incarceration is too complicated to allow for 'either-or' approaches. It is not a question of reform *or* social control, ideology *or* reality, nobility on one hand *or* capitalism on the other. There is no quick fix available – not in public policy when it comes to trying to solve the problems of crime or mental illness or poverty – and not in history either. Put most succinctly, and without all the requisite qualifications, there remains a critical distinction between ideology and history, even if it takes a while to reach it.

BIBLIOGRAPHIC NOTE

The works most relevant to this essay include: Paul Boyer, *Urban Masses and Moral Order in America, 1820–1920* (Cambridge, Mass., 1978); Michel Foucault, *Discipline and Punish* (New York, 1978); Michael Ignatieff, *A Just Measure of Pain* (New York, 1978); Morris Janowitz, *The Last Half Century* (Chicago, 1978); George Herbert Mead, Francis F. Piven, and Richard Cloward, *Regulating the Poor* (New York, 1971); David J. Rothman, *The Discovery of the Asylum* (Boston, 1971), and *Conscience and Convenience* (Boston, 1980); Edward Ross, *Social Control* (New York, 1910); Andrew T. Scull, *Museums of Madness* (New York, 1979).

6

Humanitarianism or Control?
Some Observations on the Historiography
of Anglo-American Psychiatry

ANDREW SCULL

I

To judge by the increasingly strident tone of their mutual recriminations, historians of psychiatry have taken almost too much to heart J. H. Hexter's injunction that 'in an academic generation a little overaddicted to *politesse*, it may be worth saying that violent destruction is not necessarily of itself worthless and futile. Even though it leaves doubts about the right road for London, it helps if someone rips up, however violently, a "To London" sign on the Dover cliffs pointing south.'[1] At times, the protagonists in the debate on the meaning of lunacy reform have given the impression of attempting to destroy, not just each other's work, but each other. On the one side, there have been accusations of attempts to 'disguise contemporary social criticism and advocacy as history';[2] and of 'destructively misleading' research marked by 'errors, inconsistencies, unsupported assertions, and disparaging motivational assumptions' that, taken together, have produced 'work that must be embarrassing to the professional historian'.[3] And from the object of these assaults have come claims that their authors 'rely on platitudes of historiography and straw men'; and that the cries of villainy are a 'stratagem to give novelty to findings that are now no longer novel'.[4] Impelled by logic and evidence to swallow much of the revisionist case, it appears that even the opposition's 'leading voice' can do no better than resort to 'shrillness' in an effort 'to differentiate, in however marginal a fashion, his work from theirs. It is like putting a few touches of chrome on an automobile and saying that now a product differs from that of its competitors. Such a tactic may do well in the marketplace, but it has less relevance, one would hope, in the world of scholarship.'[5]

Clearly, whoever ventures into this fiercely contested territory takes his

Source: Rice University Studies, vol. 67, 1981, pp. 21–41.

life (or at least his scholarly reputation) into his hands. Matters take a decided turn for the worse when one enters the combat zone with the conviction that it is not simply that neither side possesses a monopoly of virtue, but rather that both are wrong; for one is now without allies and susceptible to attack from either front or rear. And when the foolhardy intruder is a trespasser from an alien discipline, the risk is high that (like the fate of one who intervenes in a quarrel between husband and wife) the outcome will be an assault from both forces simultaneously. Thus, like the proverbial liberal, I suppose the best I can look forward to is matching lumps on each side of my head.

II

I think it is only appropriate to begin by acknowledging that the debate on the interpretation of lunacy reform, and more especially the work of some of those in the revisionist camp,[6] has been the occasion for a significant advance in the historiography of psychiatry. As those who are acquainted with the work of Albert Deutsch on America or of Kathleen Jones on England will be aware, the picture of lunacy reform as on the whole relatively simple and straightforward progress towards enlightenment is far from being merely a straw man, erected solely to exaggerate the novelty and significance of a less simplistic alternative. Rereading even some of the best and most scholarly of more specialized accounts from this era (for example, Norman Dain's[7]) is sufficient to remind us vividly of how deeply embedded 'progressive' assumptions were in this period. And a glance at the treatment accorded lunacy reform in such more general surveys of Victorian social reform as David Roberts's *Victorian Origins of the British Welfare State* demonstrates how widespread their influence once was. For proponents of this viewpoint, the direction of the line of march and the sources of the impulse to march were essentially unproblematic:

> the obstacles to the improvement of asylums had been not vested interest but public ignorance and apathy. For centuries [sic] that apathy had remained unchallenged, but when nineteenth-century humanitarianism joined with a more scientific understanding of insanity it diminished. Yet neither humanitarianism nor science would have availed much had not government officials investigated the abuses and had not Commons [sic] placed asylums under the surveillance of government inspectors.[8]

Whatever the excesses and inadequacies of the various revisionist accounts of lunacy reform (to which I shall attend shortly), one must surely be grateful to them for liberating us from the narrowness and naïveté of a vision that reduced the whole process to a simplistic equation: humanitarianism + science + government inspection = the success of what David Roberts terms 'the great nineteenth century movement for a more humane and intelligent treatment of the insane'.[9]

We are now aware that such interpretations of social reform in general and lunacy reform in particular function more as intellectual straitjackets than as means to insight and understanding. In the present instance, the sources of the movement and the reasons for its success are infinitely more complex; the humanitarianism and the science indisputably more ambiguous; and the intelligence and humanity of the regimen in the public museums of the mad inescapably more dubious than any explanation of this sort allows.

In what follows, I shall begin by discussing in a little more detail the work of David Rothman and Gerald Grob. The former is clearly the best-known American exponent of the revisionist or social control approach to lunacy reform; the latter, the most tenacious and sophisticated defender of a modified form of the more traditional wisdom. I shall point to some of the serious reservations I have with the accounts offered by each of them; and I shall then attempt to sketch some elements of an alternative perspective on this example of nineteenth-century humanitarianism (though my account will have reference to England rather than the United States).

III

Despite their sharp and serious disagreements on both the sources of lunacy reform and their overall assessment of the movement, there is a curious formal symmetry in the work of Rothman and Grob. Both place major emphasis in their respective accounts upon the stated intentions and more or less acknowledged motivations of the lunacy reformers themselves. But strikingly and significantly, they employ the words of the asylum superintendents and their allies to reach almost diametrically opposed conclusions. As Johnson had earlier suggested was true of the history of schooling, it turns out that 'On the basis of this sort of evidence the enterprise may be represented as a quasi-coercive and essentially self-protective response or as the genuine outgrowth of humanitarian Christian consciences.'[10]

Out of the arguments of moral entrepreneurs like Horace Mann, Dorothea Dix and Samuel Gridley Howe, and the reports and other published writings of the less widely known medical superintendents and overseers of the earliest asylums, Rothman constructs an account of the discovery of the asylum that emphasizes its sudden eruption on to the nineteenth-century scene, and its uniquely American origins; and that locates the source of this transformation of social practices in an 'effort to insure the cohesion of the community in new and changing circumstances'.[11] The United States in the second quarter of the nineteenth century is portrayed as 'a society that has slipped, for reasons that remain unclear, into a temporary state of disequilibrium' and the drive to institutionalize the deviant is itself seen as 'a mysteriously diffuse movement toward equilibrium'.[12] As Rothman himself puts it, 'The response in the Jacksonian period to the deviant and the dependent was first and foremost a vigorous attempt to promote the stability of the society at a moment when traditional ideas and practices appeared outmoded, constricted, and ineffective. . . . The asylum was to fulfill a dual purpose for its innovators. It would rehabilitate inmates and then, by virtue of its success, set an example of right action for the larger society. . . . The well-ordered asylum would exemplify the proper principles of social organization and thus ensure the safety of the republic and promote its glory.'[13]

At the very outset of his analysis, Rothman rightly rejects a vulgar structural determinism that posits an automatic and inevitable linkage between urbanization and industrialization and the rise of the asylum. A few pages later, he insists that 'Institutions, whether social, political, or economic, cannot be understood apart from the society in which they flourished.'[14] Admirable sentiments; and yet in the body of his work, there is never any serious and sustained or clearly articulated attempt to link ideas and changing social practices with underlying structures. Worse, when his reliance upon the ideological level of analysis falters, Rothman tends to resort to the same quasi-magical incantations and invocations of demographic and economic developments that he had earlier stigmatized.[15] Throughout, there is a lack of perception of the fundamental divisions of American society, and of the shifting basis and nature of social conflict through time; a deficiency closely related to his failure 'to inquire into the group of class interests that institutionalization served . . .' and his inability to see social control as 'more in the interest of one social group than another'.[16] Instead, there is his constant resort to that curious explanatory variable, 'an imaginary homogeneous group labelled "the Americans"'.[17]

One might well argue that, given Rothman's characteristic analytic strategy, the larger social and political order *necessarily* remains opaque, since it is generally perceived only dimly and indirectly through the mediation of the perceptions of society's individual members. To the extent that people's ideas are used to demonstrate the existence of the underlying structures and that their *perceptions* of disorder are not kept analytically distinct from the reality of disorder (and Rothman is persistently inclined 'to use the reformers' claims of social upheaval as his primary evidence for the existence of disorder'[18]), any attempt to relate ideology and social structure threatens to dissolve into mere tautology. And at the level of the ideas themselves, there is a striking tendency to take the claims made at face value – a failure to perceive the degree to which the talk of looming disorder, the promotion of the institution's reformatory functions and so forth, were rhetoric (albeit significant rhetoric) designed by a particular social group for particular polemical purposes.

For example, this neglects the obvious question of 'whether it was in the professional self-interest of such reformers to exaggerate the extent of the upheaval in order to help loosen state legislators' purse strings'.[19] Was not the anxiety about the stability of the social order the anxiety of a specific class, the response of the bourgeois and professional classes to the corrosive effects of capitalism upon such traditional pre-capitalist social restraints as religion and the family? And does not Rothman's approach ignore the still precarious social status of the psychiatric profession, its members' strivings to build a strong institutional base for their profession, and their direct attempt to do so through 'the legitimation of the asylum and their own position in it'?[20]

An inadequate attempt to come to terms with the nature of the social and political order is something Rothman shares with that school of sociologists by whom he appears to have been most influenced and among whom he has certainly been most influential – those committed to the labelling or societal reaction theory of deviance. Once again, his work demonstrates how this narrowness of vision inevitably leads to an analysis that depicts social control as arbitrary. As Richard Fox has put it, 'The social control perspective flattens out . . . vital structural developments by positing an abstract conflict between a group of controllers and their victims, and then by moralistically upbraiding the controllers and their alleged inclination to dominate.'[21]

IV

It is, in part, the very weaknesses and excesses of the work of Rothman and other revisionists that have prompted the revival, albeit in a more sophisticated and seductive modern guise, of the traditional meliorist explanation. Gerald Grob, who has been the major figure in this movement, for the most part rests his critique of Rothman on quite other grounds than those I have just outlined. Yet, in the first instance, it is the implicit moral condemnation of the reformers and asylum superintendents that provokes some of his most severe strictures on Rothman's work. Like Jacques Quen, he seems most concerned to rescue the reformers' reputation for humanitarianism and benevolence.

Much of Rothman's animus against the reformers (so they allege) derives from his political stance *vis-à-vis* contemporary social policy in these areas, most notably a commitment to an explicitly anti-institutional position. There is, I think, a measure of truth to this claim (and certainly Rothman's nostalgic evocation of a pre-institutional Golden Age, the Paradise Lost with the advent of the asylum, has been eagerly embraced by the de-institutionalization ideologues). But there is a tendency here to refuse to see in their own eyes the motes they are so eager to point out in his. For their interpretations, and those of the other scholars in the field who receive their imprimatur,[22] are equally evidently grounded in a fundamental acceptance of a vision of history most congenial to (because supportive of) the powers that be; and in a largely uncritical adherence to orthodox liberal pieties.

Grob's own thesis is more deeply embedded in his materials than Rothman's, and thus less immediately apparent to the casual reader – as perhaps befits one who lays such stress upon 'understanding the past on its own terms'. After all, the more open one is about one's interpretive framework, the more vulnerable to the charge that one has allowed one's conclusions to shape one's selection of data, rather than the other way around. But this is not to say that in Grob's work the past in some mysterious way speaks for itself; or that no organizing intelligence intervenes here. To the contrary, Grob's vision of social process and his metahistorical assumptions continuously affect both his selection and presentation of materials. Theoretical models are not absent, merely underdeveloped and unselfconscious – and hence underscrutinized.

Grob is scornful of those who attribute the growth of the mental hospital to the attempt by dominant elites to restrain 'deviant groups or largely lower-class elements, thereby ensuring some measure of social control (if not hegemony)'.[23] As he sees it, 'A few saw reform as a conservative phenomenon in that it would diminish class rivalries and antagonisms and thereby preserve a fundamentally sound and moral social order. But many more were primarily concerned with uplifting the mass of suffering humanity and were not particularly aware of political or economic considerations.'[24] In arguing for the contrary position, the social control theorists have confused 'the by-product with the primary intention'.[25] And they have persuaded others of the correctness of their position primarily by illegitimately attributing motives on the basis of the consequences of the reformers' actions.

The danger in this, as Grob sees it, is clear:

It is, after all, extraordinarily difficult to infer motives from outcome without adopting a viewpoint that makes events the result of strictly rational, logical, or conscious behavior. Nor can we assume with any degree of confidence that undesirable consequences flowed from callous behavior or malevolent intentions, even though such elements were by no means absent.[26]

Yet even assuming that Grob has correctly judged which of these intentions were primary (and while the identification of human motivation is a peculiarly treacherous business, he presents no real arguments for this crucial assumption), and leaving aside the difficult issue of penetrating to unacknowledged but possibly powerful motives, he takes the content of their 'benevolence' all too much for granted. And behind this there looms a still larger issue, to which I shall recur: 'how far is it sufficient to comprehend [developments] in terms of the conscious purposes of contemporaries? Or should we not be concerned with the working out of unconscious function within some wider system of change?'[27]

If the origins of reform are here to be sought in benevolence (coupled with the pressures created by demographic change and the spread of new ideas about the treatment of mental disorder from France and England), what of its subsequent fate? Grob's answer is heavily conditioned by his view of nineteenth-century social policy as essentially incremental in character. Rather than being the result of conscious choices by legislators and officials, it represents the sum total of a series of unrelated decisions.[28] Further, the absence of effective means of collecting and analysing empirical data 'often led to the adoption of policies that in the long run had results which were quite at variance with the intentions of those involved in their formulation'.[29] (Again, he sees this as rescuing 'nineteenth-century legislators and administrators' from misplaced charges that they 'were deficient in intelligence or malevolent in character'.[30])

Within this overall framework, Grob then points to a number of more specific factors that he sees as linked to the collapse of the asylum's pretensions to cure.[31] The list is a long one: the growing size of the asylum; the influx of the lower classes, and particularly of the Irish and other ethnic groups; the consequent financial undernourishment of the system; the accumulation of chronic, incurable inmates; the difficulties associated with the 'routinization of charisma', as one generation of asylum superintendents succeeded another; and the transformation of the mental hospitals into 'strictly welfare institutions as far as their funding and reputation were concerned', thus solidifying 'their custodial character'.[32] All of these developments, we are informed, 'took place in several distinct stages and without any particular awareness of the eventual outcome'.[33] In this sense, he sees them as once more affirming one of his central theses, the accidental and 'non-malevolent' character of reform.

At this point, therefore, even Grob is driven to concede that, looked at without rose-tinted spectacles, Victorian lunatic asylums in many ways present a dismal and depressing picture. And yet, if the *results* can scarcely be applauded, or must be damned with faint praise, the benevolent *intentions* remain. Apparently, the history of lunacy reform records the efforts of a largely well-intentioned group of men (and the occasional woman) whose endeavours mysteriously always produced accidental and unintended unpleasant consequences. However unattractive, the institutions they founded were not 'inherently evil'. On the contrary, 'mental hospitals were not fundamentally dissimilar from most human institutions, the achievements of which usually fall far short of the hopes and aspirations of the individuals who founded and led them.'[34]

But this simply will not do. In the first place, conceptualizations that operate in terms of individuals' decisions or behaviour are simply incapable of adequately reflecting social reality, both because 'the policy or action of a collectivity . . . [is in many instances] not attributable to particular individuals' decisions', and because the form of the organization (or social system) may itself generate systemic effects. In particular, the bias of the system is not sustained simply by a series of individually chosen acts, but also, most importantly, by 'the socially structured and culturally patterned behaviour of groups, and practices of institutions, which may indeed be manifested by individuals' inaction'.[35]

With outcomes viewed as the product of benevolence combined with an endless series of incremental changes, no one of which was decisive, and each of which is entitled to virtually equal explanatory weight, even the most flagrant examples of misery and inhumanity can be portrayed as largely accidental, and in any event as in no way calling into question the fundamental goodness and legitimacy of the social system within which they occurred. A neat reconciliation is thus effected between apparently contradictory phenomena, in such a fashion that the myth of the social system's basic humaneness is further strengthened and supported. Hence, I take it, the shrillness with which Grob insists upon the primary, the virtually unqualified, hegemony of benevolent motives. For it is precisely the benevolence of the intentions that rescues the whole enterprise of 'reform' from the insinuations of the revisionists and other critics, leaving us to ponder the ironies of unintended consequences and historical accident – even while, as Ignatieff puts it, 'maintaining the state's reputation as a moral agent'.[36]

On any number of levels, therefore, the view of reform as the product of the 'accidental', malevolent distortions of a Manichean world represents a denial of, or a failure to come to terms with, the multiple ways in which structural factors constrain, prompt and channel human activities in particular directions. On a deeper level, consequences that appear unintended and 'accidental' considered from the viewpoint of the individual actor remain susceptible to investigation and explanation. Such explanation will always involve some abstraction from the complexities and particularities of individual events, and thus inevitably will do some violence to the richness of the historical record.[37] But, as Lawrence Stone has pointed out, if we are to explain anything at all, we must inevitably risk generalization and the use of analogy; indeed, without them we cannot so much as describe what we have found.[38] To denounce such attempts as producing 'oversimplification of complex social processes',[39] to insist too resolutely on seeing events as 'process'[40] or 'one damn thing after another', is virtually to guarantee explanatory impotence – to reduce explanation to a banal mixture of individual intentions (which in the present context are for Grob almost universally 'the best and most honorable of intentions'[41]), and inadvertent transformations (through a series of events, 'many of which were unanticipated and unpredictable'[42]) that lead society in spite of itself in morally unfortunate directions.[43]

V

In my own work on lunacy reform, which looks at this movement in Victorian England and not in the United States, I have attempted to demonstrate that the genesis and subsequent development of specialized segregative techniques for handling the mad was neither fortuitous, nor the product of the mere piling up of a series of incremental, *ad hoc* decisions bereft of any underlying dynamic or logic. The activities of the lunacy reformers, and the outcome of their endeavours, must be seen as intimately linked to a whole series of historically specific and closely interrelated changes in English society's political, economic and social structure; and to the associated shifts in the intellectual and cultural horizons of the English bourgeoisie. I shall not attempt to recapitulate the whole of that analysis here. Instead, I shall look at just two of the many issues that require discussion (albeit two rather important ones), and try to indicate the general directions in which I think we need to go if we are to resolve them.

Let us begin by considering the 'choice' of the asylum. Anyone claiming, as I would, that the adoption of the asylum as a response to madness was powerfully constrained by structural factors implies that the agents involved in the process could have acted otherwise only with extreme difficulty, if they could have done so at all. The assertion or denial of such an account thus rests upon a counterfactual claim that some specified agent or agents could or could not have acted (i.e., had or did not have the ability and opportunity to act) differently. Merely to state things in this form is to emphasize that, in all cases of this sort, empirical evidence must necessarily be indirect and lacking in certainty. But that the 'evidence must always be indirect and ultimately inconclusive'[44] is not to say that no empirical investigation is possible, or that we cannot reach a balanced judgement on these matters. Rothman is quite clear on this issue. Unfortunately, I think he is also quite wrong. As he puts it, 'There was nothing inevitable about the asylum form', and it was 'not the only possible reaction to social problems'.[45] On the most general level, much of the plausibility of these claims seems to derive from the essentially intentional account he offers of the origins of the asylum. Absent the fear of disorder and the sense that institutions to 'control abnormal behavior promised to be the first step in establishing a new system for stabilising the community, for binding citizens together',[46] the presumption must be that the asylum would not have been built. But if an explanation on this basis is defective (as I have argued it is) no such presumption exists.

At this point, Rothman could fall back on two related and more specific counter-arguments he presents to a structural account. First, there is his brief discussion and curt dismissal of the claim that the asylum was the 'automatic and inevitable response of an industrial and urban society' to deviance.[47] He appears, at first sight, to be on strong ground here, for not only is this 'explanation' implausibly crude and mechanistic, but it fails to meet even the simplest of factual tests. The economic and demographic developments to which it refers for the most part come *after* the birth of the asylum, in England[48] and still more unambiguously in America;[49] and the dissemination of the institutional approach bore no clear-cut relationship to whether a region was rural or urban.[50] But the support this rejection provides is illusory, for it rests upon the demonstrably false claim that the linkage to urbanization and industrialization is the only form a structural account of the origins of the asylum can take.

Rothman's second counter-argument is in a sense derived from the first and appears downright curious, if only because on its face it seems so unhistorical. It consists essentially in the assertion that, since, 'beginning about 1900, the asylum began to lose its centrality'[51] (a trend still more marked during the past two or three decades), its presence cannot have been structurally required in the nineteenth century. If the still more urbanized and industrialized twentieth century can abandon the institution, the nineteenth could have too, but for some failure of nerve, imagination or whatever. Perhaps; but this argument will not suffice to show it. For the notion that American (or English) society in the twentieth century is just like its nineteenth-century predecessor (only more so) strains credibility. And if the nature of the beast has changed, who can be surprised if those changes permit/require changes in the characteristic shapes and forms of the social control apparatus?[52]

Considerable familiarity with lunacy reform in England, and somewhat less extensive acquaintance with the American materials, suggest to me that the very issue with which we began may be something of a red herring. For the notion of making a choice implies the perception and weighing of alternatives; and what is most remarkable when one examines the sources is that most reformers seem to have assumed from the outset that any changes they might introduce would retain the asylum as their basis. Even in England, where the reform movement proceeded largely by exposing abuses in existing madhouses, the question posed was not whether or not to employ the asylum to treat lunatics (the answer to that was usually taken to be self-evident); but rather how the asylum model could be modified so as to overcome the defects that had just been exposed.

It would be misleading to suggest that there was no opposition to the asylum. To the contrary, the reformers on both sides of the Atlantic often met with considerable resistance, most generally on the grounds of cost, when they sought to build a network of public asylums, but also (and especially in England) because their schemes threatened to provide a precedent for increased central control over local administration. But opposition on these grounds was essentially negative. It was not linked to any alternative approach to the management of the mad, and hence its effect was to retard but not to deflect the movement to establish the asylum system.[53]

If one looks diligently enough, however, one can uncover a handful of figures whose opposition to the asylum rested on other, less limited grounds. In England in the years between 1810 and 1840, the crucial phase of the lunacy reform movement, there existed a small subterranean tradition that insistently criticized the asylum as a response to insanity. The critics we can identify were all medical men and their claims amounted to a fundamental assault on the very concept of institutionalization. In the words of George Nesse Hill, a provincial surgeon, 'asylums stand opposed to all rational plans of speedy and permanent cure of insanity, and from their very nature are the most unfavorable situations in which . . . lunatics . . . can be placed.'[54] The separation from the sane influences that surround the madman in the outside world exacerbated his problems, and the unfortunate inmates of asylums tended to feed off each other's delusions. The consequence, in the words of the well-known London medical writer, John Reid, was that 'many of the depots for the captivity of intellectual invalids may be regarded only as nurseries for and manufacturies of madness; magazines or reservoirs of lunacy, from which is issued, from time to time, a sufficient supply for perpetuating and extending this formidable disease.'[55]

In 1830, these ideas were revived and extended by John Conolly, previously the medical inspector of the madhouses in Warwickshire, then professor of medicine at the new University College, London, and later to become one of the most famous figures in nineteenth-century English psychiatry. While conceding that in some circumstances lunatic asylums were 'unavoidable evils', he insisted that they were pernicious places from which all but the distinct minority of the insane who could not otherwise be cared for ought to be kept. For two-thirds of the inmates, 'confinement is the very reverse of beneficial. It fixes and renders permanent what might have passed away . . . I have seen numerous examples . . . in which it was evident that . . . a continued residence in the asylum was gradually ruining body and mind.'[56] The sanest among us would find it difficult 'to resist the horrible influences of the place; – a place in which a thousand fantasies, that are swept away almost as soon as formed in the healthy atmosphere of a diversified society, would assume shapes more distinct; a place in which the intellectual operations could not but become, from mere want of exercise, more and more inert; and the domination of wayward feelings more and more powerful . . . [Patients] are subjected . . . to the very circumstances most likely to confuse or destroy the most rational and healthy mind.'[57] Indubitably, 'The presence of a company of lunatics, their incoherent talk, their cries, their moans, their indescribable utterances of all imaginable fancies, or their ungovernable frolics and tumult, can have no salutary effect.'[58] Quite the contrary, 'the effect of living constantly among mad men or mad women is a loss of all sensibility and self-respect or care; or, not infrequently, a perverse pleasure in adding to the confusion and diversifying the eccentricity of those about them . . . In both cases the disease grows inveterate.'[59]

Such arguments raised the claim, one not unfamiliar to our own ears, that the defects of the asylum were inherent in its very constitution, and hence ineradicable. In the words of an anonymous fellow-critic, the institution itself was always and necessarily 'an infected region' in which 'healthy impressions' could not possibly be received.[60] The force, relevance and importance of this critique are evident, even in my abbreviated presentation of it. Yet what is most striking is that, for all the impact these words had, they might as well have never been uttered. It is not just that they had no influence on social policy, or that they were met by counter-arguments that seemed plausible at the time. Rather, their fate was to be greeted by silence, to be consigned to oblivion.[61]

One can suggest a number of reasons for this general lack of impact: the critics' lack of numbers and organization; the conservatism induced by existing investments in the institutional approach; and the single-mindedness of the reformers, with their consequent lack of receptivity to alternatives to their chosen solution. But none of these seems sufficient, singly or in combination: a conclusion that is strengthened when one recalls that, during the 1870s and 1880s, bolstered by a half-century of evidence that made these claims seem prescient, they were revived on both sides of the Atlantic – in America by the newly emerging profession of neurology[62] and in England by such eminent medical psychologists as John Charles Bucknill, Lockhart Robertson and Henry Maudsley[63] – with comparable lack of effect.

There is, I think, a deeper reason for the failure of the anti-institutional position to secure a hearing, and one that emphasizes just how deeply embedded in the structures of nineteenth-century society the shift to the asylum was. The most fundamental source of the critics' difficulty lies in a simple question: it was all very well to suggest that the cure in this instance was worse than the disease, but what was the alternative? Few of those concerned with the plight of the insane . could contemplate with equanimity the prospect of leaving them in the sorts of conditions that commonly prevailed in the larger towns, where the squalor, disease and misery endured by the *sane* members of the lower classes were quite sufficient to provoke expressions of disgust and horror in those of their betters who came into contact with them. (Most, of course, took pains not to.)[64]

After all,

Millions of English men, women, and children were virtually living in shit. The immediate question seems to have been whether they weren't drowning in it . . . Large numbers of people lived in cellars, below the level of the street and below the water line. Thus generations of human beings, out of whose lives the wealth of England was produced, were compelled to live in wealth's symbolic counterpart. And that substance which suffused their lives was also a virtual objectification of their social condition, their place in society: that was what they were.[65]

In the circumstances, those who sought to improve the lot of the pauper insane but who were doubtful of the merits of the asylum confronted a painful dilemma. They could scarcely dispute MacGill's claim that 'The circumstances of the great body of mankind are of such a nature as to render every attempt at recovering insane persons in their own houses extremely difficult, and generally hopeless.'[66] And if they balked at the idea of keeping lunatics in such surroundings, it was hard to see how they could avoid concluding that the asylum was better than the other option available, the workhouse.

What stood in the way of ameliorating the environment of the insane still at large? To improve the living conditions of lunatics living in the community would have entailed the provision of relatively generous pension or welfare benefits to provide for their support, implying that the living standards of families with an insane member would have been raised above those of the working class generally. Moreover, under this system, the insane alone would have been beneficiaries of something approximating a modern social welfare system, while their sane brethren were subjected to the rigours of a Poor Law based on the principle of less eligibility. Quite apart from anything else, such an approach would clearly have been administratively unworkable, not least because of the labile nature of lunacy itself, and the consequent ever-present danger that, given sufficient incentive, or rather desperation, the poorer classes would resort to feigning insanity.

In any event, suggestions of this sort would have had no political appeal whatsoever to England's governing classes. Among the latter, 'there had developed by the 1830s a sense of precariousness about society. This was expressed in the form that there was a delicate balance between institutions and their operation, and the behaviour of the labouring classes. There was a feeling that any concession to idleness might bring about a rapid and cumulative deterioration in the labourer's attitude towards work. This produced a growing sensitivity towards the Poor Law';[67] and towards anything else that, by lessening the dependence of the labouring classes on market forces, might weaken the social fabric of Victorian society.

By now, an abhorrence of outdoor relief had been etched deeply into the bourgeois consciousness. In part this reflected the 'lessons' learned from the disastrous impact of Speenhamland. In part it reflected the ideological hegemony of classical liberalism. For the logical consequence of that doctrine's insistence on a man's freedom to pursue his self-interest and on his unique responsibility for his success or failure, when joined with its dogmatic certainty that intervention to alter market-derived outcomes could only be counter-productive, was to render the very notion of social protectionism anathema.

These obstacles, I suggest, presented a virtually insurmountable barrier to the development of a plausible, alternative, community-based response to the problem of insanity. Only the asylum plan offered the advantage of allowing scope for the exercise of humanitarian impulses while remaining consistent with the imperatives of the New Poor Law. Significantly, not only was none of the critics of the asylum ever able to suggest even the basis of an alternative programme (a *sine qua non* of their objections receiving serious consideration); but many of them ultimately conceded the futility of their opposition. Certain critics, while damning the asylum as 'a prison' in which 'the want of society, the absence of all amusement and employment, both of body and mind, must tend to *increase* rather than to relieve the morbid irritation of the brain',[68] had from the outset blithely declared that such a solution was perfectly satisfactory for paupers.[69] (In this vision, only the rich were to be spared the asylum's horrors. Perhaps only their sensibilities were sufficiently refined to notice them.) Others, possibly lacking the capacity to engage in such flagrantly jesuitical reasoning, responded by gradually widening the definition of those for whom the evils of the asylum were 'unavoidable' – till, in John Conolly's case, he became a leading and zealous advocate of county asylums for paupers.[70] In the last analysis, therefore, even its staunchest opponents were led to concede the asylum's inevitability.

VI

At the core of the reformers' approach to the asylum was a dual perception: positively, of the promise of cure; and negatively, of the revulsion against cruelty and inhumanity. The conjunction of these two elements was a source of the greater part of the moral energy and commitment that sustained the drawn-out campaign for reform. Throughout the asylum's history, one source of the drive to institutionalize the insane has been anxiety, fear of the threat the mad posed to life, property and the orderliness of social existence. In and of itself, however, fear provided only a weak argument for institutionalization; one that applied, at best, to a fraction of the insane. What was distinctive in many ways about the lunacy reform movement was its new-found conviction about the redemptive power of the institution, and its insistence upon extending the benefits of treatment to an ever-larger proportion of the mad. Certainly, in these connections we need to understand the relationship and appeal of lunacy reform to the Evangelicals, Quakers and Benthamites in England; and to the Quakers, New England Unitarians and those influenced by the Second Great Awakening in the United States. But we need to move beyond this to look for the broader sources of the profound shift in moral sensibilities that underlies and lends coherence to their activities – a humanitarian sensibility that finds expression in such diverse yet clearly related endeavours as controlling crime, relieving the poor and schooling the young, and that transformed slavery 'from a problematical, but readily defensible institution, into a self-evidently evil and abominable one'.[71]

This implies that we must take the 'humanitarianism' of the reformers very seriously indeed, and not dismiss it (as does Foucault) as 'so much incidental music'.[72] Of course, taking something seriously is not at all the same thing as taking it at face value or neglecting to subject it to further analysis. Reactions to traditional approaches to the management of the mad are sometimes taken to be self-evident. They were cruel and brutal on their face, so that mere knowledge of or exposure to the conditions under which lunatics were kept was 'naturally' sufficient to provoke horror and revulsion; and to prompt vigorous and sustained efforts on the part of those endowed with the requisite temperament, intestinal fortitude and religious sense of mission to rectify the treatment of the insane. In turn, once the general public were relieved of their ignorance and roused from their apathy by the activities of these men, reform straightforwardly followed.[73]

But, in the first instance, the claim of ignorance simply will not survive scrutiny. Broadsheets and other printed ephemera of the eighteenth century often took as their subject the horrors of the madhouse.[74] Hogarth and his many imitators likewise contributed to making the image of the madhouse a staple of the popular imagination in this period; as did a whole literature of asylum exposés, running from Defoe through Cruden down to the gothic novels of the early nineteenth century and the commitment scares later in the century.[75] That madmen were chained, whipped, menaced and half starved in asylums in the eighteenth century was well known at the time. Indeed, it could scarcely have been otherwise when, throughout the century, the inmates of Bethlem were exhibited before the impertinent curiosity of sightseers at a mere penny a time; and when every treatise on the management of the mad advocated such treatment. Even the king's mania prompted the use of intimidation, threats, shackles and blows,[76] a fact of which his subjects were scarcely unaware.

Such practices, then, were not something of which people became conscious only after the turn of the century. Yet it was only then that protests began to be heard that such treatment was cruel and inhumane. Only then did practices that had formerly seemed entirely appropriate and that had been advocated by the most eminent physicians and cultured men of their day[77] lose their appearance of self-evidence. And the process was a gradual and halting one. Even major figures in the reform movement did not succeed at a stroke in freeing themselves from the past. Sir George Onesiphorus Paul, for example, the prime mover behind the original County Asylums Act (1808), continued to believe that chains and the inculcation of fear were the best means of managing madness; he repeatedly expressed his approbation, based on close personal inspections, of the regime at the York Asylum.[78] Within less than a decade, other reformers excoriated 'the institution at York under the excellent management of Dr Hunter'[79] as the epitome of all that was wrong with previous approaches to the mad. Beyond the reformers' ranks, the old 'backward' attitudes persisted even longer, prompting not only some of the opposition to the reformers' schemes, but also episodes of blank mutual incomprehension, as conditions that one side viewed as unexceptionable were viewed by the other with shock and outrage.[80]

I think we must accept, therefore, that in this period an authentic shift in moral consciousness took place, whose outcome was the development of a new sensibility *vis-à-vis* the treatment of the insane. We can define, too, some of the central dimensions of this change. There is the movement away from a view of madness as 'the total suspension of every rational faculty',[81] and from an outlook that stressed the need to subjugate the madman, to employ external discipline and constraint to break his will; indeed, a sharp break with a conception of the lunatic as an animal, a brute stripped of all remnants of its humanity. There is, instead, a new emphasis on the susceptibility of the insane to many of the same emotions and inducements as the rest of us; an insistence that 'madmen are not . . . absolutely deprived of their reason';[82] and a belief that, through a suitable manipulation of inmate and environment, the qualities the lunatic lacks can and should be recreated or reawakened, so that he may once again be restored to the world, a sober, rational, 'self-determining' citizen. Fundamentally, to put it another way, there is an abandonment of external coercion (which could never do more than force the crudest and least stable forms of outward conformity) for an approach that promises to produce the internalization of the necessary moral standards, by inducing the mad to collaborate in their own recapture by the forces of reason.

There remains, of course, the extraordinarily difficult task of defining what were, in David Brion Davis's words, 'the material considerations which helped to shape the new moral consciousness and to define its historical effects'.[83] But that is too large an issue on which to trespass within the confines of this paper.[84] I suggest that an answer is not to be sought in some more or less crude reductionism, which seeks to unmask the material or economic interest that produces and shapes the 'humanitarian sensibility'. Though such elements are undeniably by no means absent, we need rather to seek a broader comprehension of how the ways men look at the world are conditioned by the nature of their activity in it; and, more specifically, of the manifold linkages between the changes in men's conceptions of insanity and larger changes in the conditions of social existence.

NOTES AND REFERENCES

1. J. H. Hexter, *Reappraisals in History*, 2nd ed. Chicago: University of Chicago Press, 1978, p. 138.
2. Gerald Grob, 'Treatment vs. Incarceration: The Mental Hospital in Historical Perspective'. Paper delivered at the Philadelphia College of Physicians, December 1976, p. 24.
3. Jacques Quen, 'Review of: David Rothman, *The Discovery of the Asylum*', *Journal of Psychiatry and the Law*, 2, 119–20. See also Gerald Grob, 'Welfare and Poverty in American History', *Reviews in American History*, 1 (1973), 43–52; and Grob, 'Public Policymaking and Social Policy', paper delivered at the Conference on the History of Public Policy, Cambridge, Mass., 3–4 November, 1978.
4. David Rothman, 'Review of: Gerald Grob, *Mental Institutions in America*', *Journal of Interdisciplinary History*, 7 (1976), 534.
5. Ibid., p. 536.
6. Particularly Rothman and Foucault. This may be the point to note that the labels *revisionist* and *anti-revisionist* obscure as well as reveal. There are important differences of tone, emphasis and sophistication between (say) Gerald Grob and those he himself identifies as his allies (Hale, Burnham, Dain, Rosenberg, *et al.*); and perhaps still greater divergences between Rothman and Foucault and the more historically and theoretically naive Thomas Szasz and Robert Perrucci.
7. Norman Dain, *Concepts of Insanity in the United States, 1789–1865*, New Brunswick, NJ: Rutgers University Press, 1964.
8. David Roberts, *Victorian Origins of the British Welfare State*. New Haven, Conn.: Yale University Press, 1960, p. 63.
9. Ibid., p. 62.
10. Richard Johnson, 'Educational Policy and Social Control in Early Victorian England', *Past and Present*, 49 (1970), 99.
11. David Rothman, *The Discovery of the Asylum: Social Order and Disorder in the New Republic*. Boston: Little, Brown, 1971, p. xviii.
12. Richard Fox, 'Beyond "Social Control": Institutions and Disorder in Bourgeois Society', *History of Education Quarterly*, 16 (1976), 203.
13. Rothman, *Discovery of the Asylum*, pp. xviii–xix. For a critique of the idea that the asylum was an American 'discovery' and a demonstration that the first critical stages of the American lunacy reform movement involved a heavy dependence upon ideas and examples borrowed from abroad, see Andrew Scull, 'The Discovery of the Asylum Revisited: Lunacy Reform in the New American Republic', in *Madhouses, Mad-doctors, and Madmen: The Social History of Psychiatry in the Victorian Era*, ed. A. Scull. Philadelphia: University of Pennsylvania Press, 1981.
14. Ibid., pp. xvi and xix.
15. E.g., ibid., pp. 13 and 57–8.
16. Fox, 'Beyond "Social Control"', pp. 204 and 203.

17. William Muraskin, 'The Social Control Theory in American History: A Critique', *Journal of Social History*, 9 (1976), 559.
18. Fox, 'Beyond "Social Control"', pp. 203–4.
19. Ibid., p. 204.
20. Nancy Jane Tomes, 'A Generous Confidence: Thomas Story Kirkbide's Philosophy of Asylum Construction and Management', in *Madhouses, Maddoctors, and Madmen*; Andrew Scull, 'From Madness to Mental Illness: Medical Men as Moral Entrepreneurs', *European Journal of Sociology*, 16 (1975), 219–61; Scull, *Museums of Madness: The Social Organization of Insanity in Nineteenth-Century England*, London and New York: Allen Lane and St. Martin's Press, 1979, pp. 90ff.
21. Richard Fox, *So Far Disordered in Mind*, Berkeley: University of California Press, 1978, p. 14.
22. Grob, 'Treatment vs. Incarceration', note 2.
23. At times like this, Grob speaks as though the social control thesis can be equated with an explanation in terms of class interest. But this, I think, is a mistake. David Rothman's analysis of the rise of the asylum is centrally based upon the notion of control – but not class interest. As we have seen, in his account the central factors are rather the fear of *Americans* about the stability of the social order and about the adequacy of existing institutions to meet the challenge of a fluid, mobile, expanding society, coupled with their sense that the asylum could restore the needed order and provide the very model of a new social equilibrium. This is in part a source of weakness rather than strength, since it leaves us with no coherent account of who is worried about what, and why. Grob, 'Public Policymaking', pp. 4–5.
24. Gerald Grob, *Mental Institutions in America: Social Policy to 1875*, New York: Free Press, 1973, p. 109.
25. Grob, 'Public Policymaking', p. 27.
26. Ibid., p. 30.
27. Johnson, 'Educational Policy and Social Control', p. 98.
28. Grob, 'Public Policymaking', p. 13.
29. Grob, *Mental Institutions*, p. 87. As Michael Katz points out, Grob's analysis at this point seems to embody the curious assumption 'that the acquisition of scientific knowledge automatically leads to rational, humanitarian solutions framed in the best interests of the people to which they were directed' (Katz, 'The Origins of the Institutional State', *Marxist Perspectives*, 1 (1978), 12–13).
30. Grob, *Mental Institutions*, pp. 86–7. I shall suggest below that malevolence, benevolence or lack of intelligence are not really the central issues that theories of massive social change ought to be addressing; and I shall indicate just how central I think they are as a metaphysical underpinning of Grob's work.
31. Rothman has seized on this portion of Grob's analysis to argue that, for all the bitterness of the latter's protests, he has been forced to swallow the revisionists' medicine; and accordingly, and with some surface modifications, to 'write a history of the mental hospital that is linked to the issue of order among the dangerous classes' (Rothman, 'Review of Gerald Grob', p. 535).

The claim is surely overstated, particularly if one looks at Grob's analysis in its entirety; but it is not without some limited merit, for at least on this more specific issue, his account falls uneasily between the 'progressive' and 'social control' traditions in the history of American psychiatry. However, Rothman's further claim that 'the central question, for Grob as for others writing in this field, is to explain the decline of mental hospitals into custodial warehouses' (ibid., p. 534) has a distinctly disingenuous ring to it. It was not the central question of Rothman's own work: 'The question this book addresses can be put very succinctly: why did Americans in the Jacksonian era suddenly begin to construct and support institutions for the deviant and dependent members of the community?' (Rothman, *Discovery of the Asylum*, p. xiii); and except for its being the issue on which the various contending parties are least deeply divided, there is little reason to accord it pride of place now.

32. Grob, *Mental Institutions*, p. 238.
33. Ibid., p. 259.
34. Ibid., p. 342.
35. Steven Lukes, *Power: A Radical View*, London: Macmillan, 1974, pp. 21–2.
36. Michael Ignatieff, *A Just Measure of Pain: The Penitentiary and the Industrial Revolution*, New York: Pantheon, 1978, p. 211.
37. The dangers involved here are something I am perhaps unusually sensitive to, because this is an offence of which sociologists are notoriously guilty and about which they are notoriously insensitive. (But then, prudently, sociologists customarily avoid exposing their accounts to the slings and arrows of an audience of historians.)
38. Lawrence Stone, *The Causes of the English Civil War*, New York: Harper and Row, 1969.
39. Grob, *Mental Institutions*, pp. 2–3.
40. Ibid., p. 176.
41. Ibid., p. 222.
42. Ibid., p. 176.
43. One possible objection to the position taken here that perhaps deserves some notice is the claim that the explanatory factors being adduced are not directly given to observation, and are thus in some sense metaphysical (for which read non-empirical, and not to be taken seriously). Notice, however, that while in one sense intentions, hopes, fears, etc., are 'surface' phenomena, with concrete empirical referents, in another sense they remain just as difficult and inaccessible to any but indirect observation as any more structural form of causality. In both areas, historical investigation provides us (and can only provide us) with data at the level of appearances. But we are all aware that there is an underlying reality that produces those 'appearances' and to which we must somehow penetrate if we are to explain anything satisfactorily.
44. Steven Lukes, *Essays in Social Theory*, New York: Columbia University Press, 1977, p. 29.
45. Rothman, *Discovery of the Asylum*, pp. xiv and 295.
46. Ibid., pp. 58–9.

47. Ibid., p. xvi.
48. See Scull, *Museums of Madness*, chapter 1.
49. Rothman, *Discovery of the Asylum*, p. xvi.
50. Scull, *Museums of Madness*, pp. 29–30; Rothman, *Discovery of the Asylum*, pp. xvi–xvii.
51. Rothman, *Discovery of the Asylum*, p. xvi.
52. For an analysis of these interconnections, see Andrew Scull, *Decarceration: Community Treatment and The Deviant: A Radical View*, Englewood Cliffs, NJ: Prentice-Hall, 1977.
53. Moreover, the opposition to increased centralization was under assault from a variety of directions and during the 1830s was confronted and dealt a decisive defeat over the issue of reform of the Poor Laws. Thereafter, resistance to similar measures aimed at the insane naturally came to be seen as less important, indeed futile.
54. G. N. Hill, *An Essay on the Prevention and Cure of Insanity*, London: Longman et al., 1814, p. 220.
55. John Reid, *Essays on Insanity, Hypochondriacal and Other Nervous Affections*, London: Longman et al., 1816, p. 205.
56. John Conolly, *An Inquiry Concerning the Indications of Insanity*, London: Taylor, 1830, pp. 17 and 20.
57. Ibid., pp. 22–3.
58. Ibid., p. 26.
59. Ibid., p. 22.
60. 'What', he asked his readers, 'would be the consequence, if we were to take a sane person, who had been accustomed to enjoy society, and . . . were to lock him up in a small house with a keeper for his only associate, and no place for exercise but a miserable garden? We should certainly not look for any improvement in his moral and intellectual condition. Can we then reasonably expect that *a treatment which would be injurious to a sane mind, should tend to restore a diseased one?*' Anonymous, *On the Present State of Lunatic Asylums, with Suggestions for their Improvement*, London: Drury, 1839, p. 39; emphasis in the original.
61. For very qualified exceptions to this general contemporary neglect, see 'Esquirol on the Treatment of the Insane', *Westminster Review*, 18 (1833), 129–38; Maximillian Jacobi, *On the Construction and Management of Hospitals for the Insane*, London: Churchill, 1841.
62. See Bonnie Blustein, 'The Conflict Between Neurologists and Psychiatrists in Nineteenth Century America', in A. Scull (ed.) *Madhouses, Mad-doctors, and Madmen*.
63. Scull, *Decarceration*, chapters 6 and 7.
64. Compare Chadwick's remark that 'The statements of the condition of considerable proportions of the labouring population . . . have been received with surprise by the wealthier classes living in the immediate vicinity, to whom the facts were as strange as if related to foreigners or the natives of an unknown country.' Edwin Chadwick, *Report on the Sanitary Conditions of the Labouring Population of Great Britain*, London, 1842. Or Disraeli's description of England as 'Two nations between which there is no intercourse and no sympathy: who are as ignorant of each other's habits, thoughts, and feelings as

if they were dwellers in different zones or inhabitants of different planets; who are formed by different breeding, are fed by a different food, are ordered by different manners, and are not governed by the same laws.' One is reminded of John Stuart Mill's acerbic comment that 'One of the effects of civilization (not to say one of the ingredients of it) is that the spectacle, and even the very idea of pain, is more and more kept out of the sight of those classes who enjoy in their fullness the benefits of civilization.'

65. Steven Marcus, *Engels, Manchester, and the Working Class*, New York: Vintage, 1974, pp. 184–5.
66. Stevenson MacGill, *On Lunatic Asylums*, Glasgow: For the Glasgow Asylum Committee, 1810, p. 4.
67. S. G. Checkland and E. O. A. Checkland (eds), 'Introduction', *The Poor Law Report of 1834*, London: Penguin, 1974, pp. 20–1.
68. Anonymous, *On the Present State of Lunatic Asylums*, pp. 16 and 41; emphasis in the original.
69. For a discussion of similar arguments by American neurologists in the Gilded Age, see Blustein, 'Conflict Between Neurologists and Psychiatrists'.
70. I plan to examine the remarkable convolutions of Conolly's life and thought in a subsequent paper. See John Conolly, *The Construction and Government of Lunatic Asylums and Hospitals for the Insane*, London: Churchill, 1847.
71. Thomas Haskell, 'Capitalism and the Origins of the Humanitarian Sensibility: An Alternative to the Social Control Thesis', paper delivered at the Institute for Advanced Study, Princeton, NJ, April 1979, p. 1.
72. Clifford Geertz, 'Stir Crazy', *New York Review of Books*, 26 January, 1978, p. 3.
73. Roberts, *Victorian Origins*, pp. 62–3.
74. A number of examples of these may be found in the Norman collection in the library of the Institute of Living, Hartford, Connecticut.
75. Daniel Defoe, *Augusta Triumphans*, London: Roberts, 1728; Alexander Cruden, *The London Citizen Exceedingly Injured, or, A British Inquisition Displayed*, London: Cooper and Dodd, 1739; Cruden, *The Adventures of Alexander the Corrector, with an Account of the Chelsea Academies, of the Private Places of Such as are Supposed to be Deprived of the Use of their Reason*, London: for the author, 1754; see Peter McCandless, 'Liberty and Lunacy: The Victorians and Wrongful Confinement', *Journal of Social History*, 10 (1976), 366–86.
76. I. MacAlpine and R. A. Hunter, *George III and the Mad Business*, London: Allen Lane, 1969.
77. E.g., William Cullen, *First Lines of the Practice of Physic*, Edinburgh: Bell and Bradfute, 1784.
78. Sir George Onesiphorus Paul, *Suggestions on the Subject of Criminal and Pauper Lunatics*, Gloucester, 1806; Paul, *Address to the Subscribers to the Gloucester Lunatic Asylum*, Gloucester, 1810; Paul, *Observations on the Subject of Lunatic Asylums*, Gloucester: Walker, 1812, especially pp. 28–37.
79. Paul, *Suggestions*, p. 8.
80. See Scull, *Museums of Madness*, pp. 65–6.
81. John Monro, *Remarks on Dr. Battie's Treatise on Madness*, London: Clarke, 1758.
82. G. De la Rive, *Lettre Addressée aux Rédacteurs de la Bibliothèque Britannique sur un*

nouvel Establissement pour la Guerison des Aliénés, Geneva, 1798.

83. Quoted in Haskell, 'Capitalism'.

84. I have attempted to sketch some elements of an answer to this question in my 'Moral Treatment Reconsidered: Some Sociological Comments on an Episode in the History of British Psychiatry', *Psychological Medicine*, 9 (1979), 421–8. For a related approach to these issues as they relate to slavery, see Thomas Haskell's 'Capitalism'. As Haskell argues in this paper, David Brion Davis's *The Problem of Slavery in the Age of Revolution* (Ithaca: Cornell University Press, 1975) can also be seen as moving in the direction advocated here.

7

Mental Health and Social Order

DAVID INGLEBY
Specially written for this volume

INTRODUCTION

In this chapter I shall review recent work on the role of the mental health professions in maintaining social order. In the public mind, this theme is perhaps most commonly associated with the libertarian politics of the late 1960s: the 'anti-psychiatry' of Laing, Cooper, Szasz, Goffman and others presented psychiatry as a bastion of the established order. Although this movement undoubtedly helped to popularize critical thinking about psychiatry, its very exuberance created a backlash in the ensuing decade: academics fled from its inarticulate romanticism, while the Left scorned its subjectivism and theoretical bankruptcy. The result of this was that, as the gloom of recession settled on the universities, this theme became distinctly unfashionable.

Recently, however, the tide appears to have been turning. Not that psychiatric topics have become a growth area within sociology: Barham,[1] for example, noted the dearth of sociological work on schizophrenia during the 1970s. Although Brown and Harris's[2] major study of depression has recently had a wide impact in Britain, the ambitions engendered for a social approach to psychiatry in America by the 'great society' programme of the 1960s withered along with the political impetus of that programme. Theorizing about the sociological significance of the psychiatric profession itself has been little engaged in since the work of the 'labelling theorists'. It is in the area of historical studies that the major developments have occurred: in France, the work that Foucault had begun in 1961 with *Histoire de la folie*[3] was continued in series of influential books, leading up to *La Volonté de savoir*[4] in 1976. A similar approach came to fruition in major works by Castel and others[5,6] and Donzelot;[7] the London-based journal *Ideology and Consciousness* (now renamed *I&C*) has vigorously championed this school (which, for want of a better word, I shall call 'post-structuralist'). In the USA, following Rothman's work[8] on the origins of the asylum in America, Scull[9] published a major study of psychiatry in nineteenth-century England. This historical work has been carried out in parallel with a re-examination of the penal system, for example by Foucault[10] and Ignatieff[11], and the two lines of enquiry have drawn considerable reinforcement from each other.

To call this research 'historical', however, is not to deny that its authors are concerned with the role of psychiatry today. Quite the reverse, in fact: Scull opens his book[12] with a sombre quotation from Marx, 'The tradition of all the dead generations weighs like a nightmare on the brain of the living', suggesting that the aim of his book is to help us to emerge from that nightmare by recalling it in the light of day. In a similar vein, Foucault[13] declares that the only history in which he is interested is 'the history of the present'. Perhaps, indeed, my contrast between sociology and history is a misleading one; what we are witnessing might more accurately be described as the development of a diachronic, rather than synchronic, perspective. But power is the stock-in-trade of historians, and if the work of the anti-psychiatrists and labelling theorists of the 1960s was vitiated by their feeble understanding of power relations, it is perhaps through an historical approach that a more adequate account of present-day psychiatric power will emerge.

What is the point of developing such an account? For most workers in this field, it is not simply a matter of intellectual curiosity or academic self-advancement, but of formulating a practical response to the problems posed by psychiatry: for them, the point is indeed to change the world rather than merely to understand it. Scull's concern with the contemporary situation is evident in his book on 'decarceration',[14] which amounts to a vigorous attack on contemporary mental health policy; while all the French authors mentioned above have risked personal involvement in psychiatric struggles (see Turkle[15] and Miller[16]). For anyone concerned with the well-being of the 'mentally ill', the task is to find alternatives to the ineffective and dehumanizing methods currently in use – methods whose inadequacies are likely to be vastly exacerbated by the cost-cutting policies of contemporary 'monetarist' governments. A coherent platform of policies needs to be developed in relation to mental health, in contrast to the evasive and ambivalent attitudes to psychiatry that have characterized Left politics in this decade. The development of a viable account of psychiatry's role in contemporary society is clearly the first requirement for these purposes.

Such an account will take issue with the received wisdom propagated by the profession itself on three main points. In the orthodox view, mental illness is a basic ingredient of the human condition, as natural as suffering itself. Second, those who deal with it are primarily motivated by the humanitarian concern to relieve suffering – recently, even, by the positive goal of increasing happiness. Third, the dominating role of the medical profession is seen as a rational one, justified because the skills that mental problems call for are precisely those that medicine as a profession happens to possess. According to this view, the nineteenth-century takeover of the field by medicine, and its consolidation in recent years, demonstrate the progressive spread in our society of principles of reason and humanity.

In contrast to this, what I shall call a 'critical' view argues that 'mental illness' is to a large extent socially caused, or even socially constructed; that the goal of treatment has to do with the maintenance of social order, rather than simply the relief of suffering; and that the domination of the medical profession is neither warranted nor desirable. This view by no means represents a homogeneous school of thought, but encompasses various formulations and shades of opinion – some of which were brought together in the book *Critical Psychiatry*.[17]

The orthodox reaction to such views is a predictable and often violently hostile one, as many writers in this field have found out to their cost. To implicate the form of modern society in the determination of mental illness is seen as childishly wishing away unpleasant facts of life; to question the motives behind treatment, as wilful obstruction of the relief of suffering, showing callous indifference to the plight of the mentally ill. And to challenge the powers of the medical profession is seen as irresponsible meddling with justified authority, inviting a return to eighteenth-century barbarism in the treatment of the insane. Such was the establishment's reaction to anti-psychiatry, which in some ways seemed to invite it; but more recent and scholarly critiques have fared little better.

The latest historical works, by showing how psychiatry came to be the way it is today, offer the promise of new insights into its nature as a social institution. In particular, they illuminate closely the way in which its power has been built up since the early nineteenth century, and directly challenge the picture of enlightened progress maintained by the profession itself. However, there are two major obstacles to the integration of this work within existing sociological perspectives, which this essay will attempt to confront.

One is the obvious fact that most of the historical work comes from three different sources: Britain, France and the USA. It is not possible to check accounts by seeking consensus between these sources, since the history of psychiatry may in fact have been different in each case. (In the 'Absolutist' states of Western Europe, for example, state power was more centralized and more ruthless than in Britain, so that certain relevant developments occurred sooner.) Furthermore (perhaps more seriously), these accounts embody very different theoretical frameworks;

consequently, they cannot be fitted together like the pieces of a jigsaw puzzle. Every historical account is shaped by the view of society and power that its author subscribes to. In this field, the sharpest conflict is perhaps between the broadly Marxist approach adopted by authors such as Scull, and the post-structuralist framework of the French school. (Even within the work of a single author, Michel Foucault, there are marked shifts of perspective.) Hence, in order to relate these works to each other and to existing sociology, it is necessary to go beyond the facts they record to the underlying contest of social theories. This I attempt with some trepidation.

The other obstacle is the fact that historical studies inevitably concentrate on goings-on in the profession and in the machinery of government, and say little about what went on in the asylums: conspicuously absent from the scene are the patients themselves, or indeed any of the lay public. It is, in fact, extremely difficult to reconstruct the nature of the individual cases that classical psychiatry dealt with, and this seems to have encouraged some authors to treat them almost as epiphenomena of psychiatry itself. Like the histories of colonial wars, these accounts tell us more about relations between the imperial powers than about the 'third world' of the mentally ill themselves. Yet however important a part psychiatry played in structuring the career of mental patients and the perception of their disorders, the fact remains that they existed: who they were, and what was up with them, makes a crucial difference to our interpretation of psychiatry's handling of them. The customary academic division of labour has led to a sharp separation between historical discussions of the profession and psychological discussions about mental illness itself: yet this gap must be bridged if we are to arrive at an adequate conception of either. My final section therefore will try to focus on questions about the nature of mental illness, as a precondition of establishing the social role of psychiatry.

The plan of this chapter, then, is first to review the recent historical literature on psychiatry and its allied professions, and then to discuss what it implies about the relation between mental health and social order. Out of this discussion will emerge several basic theoretical problems about social control in general, which will then be examined in relation to the concept of 'mental illness' itself. Finally, I shall try to bring the discussion down to a more concrete level, using the example of depression in working-class housewives and unemployed men to show how political considerations may influence the construction and treatment of these illnesses.

HISTORICAL STUDIES

In dealing with this field, the obvious organizing principle is chronological; two main periods suggest themselves, though the date dividing them is a matter of argument. In the first (the 'golden age' of psychiatry, as Castel[18] calls it), the central phenomena are the rise of the asylum as a remedial institution, and the capture of this domain by the medical profession: the period on which writers have focused is, roughly, the first half of the nineteenth century. The second period has no obvious starting date, having been entered at different times in different places. In it, we see the consolidation of medical gains; the broadening of the concept of 'mental illness', together with the addition of new functions of control and surveillance of the non-hospitalized population; and the development of new therapies and professional alliances, notably with psychology. With this – the 'modern age' – we arrive at the present, in which the medical model has begun to discard its traditional grounding in the practice of confinement. Within each period we have to distinguish British, French and American material, in terms both of its underlying data and of its methodological approach.

A note is perhaps in order to clarify the relation of this division between 'golden' and 'modern' ages to the conventional 'three psychiatric revolutions'. The first of these 'revolutions', in which reformers such as Tuke and Pinel are supposed to have laid the foundations of rational and humane treatment of the insane, corresponds to the beginning of the 'golden age'. The second – the invention of psychoanalysis – will be treated here as merely one example of the broadening of psychiatry's functions in the 'modern age'; while the third – the 'drug revolution' and the emptying-out of the mental hospital population – is not regarded by any of the authors reviewed here as involving a radical change in underlying strategy. For Scull,[19] as we shall see, there was no causal relation between the introduction of the major tranquillizers and the postwar decline in the mental hospital population; while for Castel[20] the legislation around 1960, which strengthened the medical profession's domination of psychiatry in Britain, France and the USA, was merely the finalization of a trend begun a hundred years earlier. As we shall see, each of these 'revolutions' was remarkable only for the way in which they transformed the *tactics* of psychiatry, without altering its strategy.

The 'Golden Age'

I shall begin with perhaps the most seminal work on the history of psychiatry, which – though it was written two decades ago and has since been repudiated in part by its author – laid the foundations for a critical

view of psychiatric history: Michel Foucault's *Histoire de la folie*.[21] As Alan
Sheridan points out in his penetrating study of Foucault's work,[22] this book
was merely the starting point for Foucault's project of relating knowledge
and power – but it was an especially felicitous choice of topic, since the
rationality of every age reveals its true character through the way it
handles madness.

In itself, Foucault's book merely sets the stage for the emergence of the
psychiatric profession, and leaves it to others to relate the subsequent
story. Psychiatry's fundamental preconditions were the social practice of
incarcerating the insane, and a firm belief in the 'otherness' of the mad.
Foucault shows how these preconditions were laid down in France by the
beginning of the nineteenth century. The adoption of this posture towards
insanity, according to him, marks the final breaking-off of a 'dialogue'
with madness – a dialogue that, he claims, had flourished in the Renaissance and before.

Foucault analyses this shift on two levels: first in terms of the policies
that regulated the treatment of the insane, and second in terms of the place
held by madness in popular and learned culture. Up to the mid-seventeenth
century, the mad had been allowed to remain in the open, either cared for
by their families or (when this was not possible) set loose to roam the
countryside. Although, like the lepers (to whom Foucault sees them as
cultural successors), these itinerant mad were excluded from the towns,
they were constantly encountered by the sane: repeatedly and ritually
excluded from the normal world, they comprised a floating population –
either wandering across the countryside in groups, or floating (literally)
down the waterways in the 'ship of fools'. In literature and art, the
'dialogue with madness' became an intense preoccupation: whereas the
preceding age had been haunted by death, the Renaissance imagination was
fascinated by madness and the secret lessons that it might unfold for reason
itself. Through drama, painting and texts such as Erasmus's *In Praise of
Folly*, this culture sought a familiarity with madness, and a mastery in
which reason could discover itself through its own negation.

In the 'classical age', however (from the middle of the seventeenth
century), madness becomes material for neither tragedy nor comedy, but
only for confinement. The signal event here for Foucault is the founding in
1657, by royal decree, of the first Hôpital Général in Paris, an institution in
which up to 6000 (or 1 per cent) of the city's population were to be confined
– not only the insane, but also all manner of disabled, poor and deviant,
whose common feature was their incapacity for productive work. This
institution represents the start of what Foucault calls 'the Great
Confinement', and is the seed of the hundreds of public asylums that were
to be established by the end of the nineteenth century.

However, the lineage is a distant one, and it was not for another two.

centuries that the establishment of public asylums became standard policy in most of the West. The *hôpitaux généraux* were not created as a response to madness, since the insane comprised only a small proportion of their inmates: they were primarily a way of dealing with poverty, in which the essential problem was seen as idleness and the essential remedy as hard work. Moreover, Foucault insists that the sudden creation of this institution was not merely a *response* to a pre-existing problem, but was the way in which the problem itself was constituted: he rejects any account of confinement in terms solely of its economic rationality (cf. the 'labour market' theory put forward by Scull, discussed below). The issues were not merely economic, but moral.

> Until the Renaissance, the sensibility to madness was linked to the presence of imaginary transcendences. In the classical age, for the first time, madness was perceived through a condemnation of idleness and in a social immanence guaranteed by the community of labour. This community acquired an ethical power of segregation, which permitted it to eject, as into another world, all forms of social uselessness.[23]

Foucault is thus not content with the idea that the confinement of the poor and the subsequent segregation of the insane was necessitated by the breakdown, in economic terms, of the system of domestic relief. (Indeed, he does not seem even to have considered such an explanation.) It was the classical age's intolerance of the 'immorality of unreason' that led it to banish the insane from public view.

That immorality was more than simply a matter of idleness; the classical concept of 'unreason' links sexual deviance (with its challenge to family stability and property relations), profanation of the sacred and *libertinage* such as Sade's (a mode of 'free thinking' in which reason sought to re-establish the dialogue with unreason, in the form of the passions). Thus it was the particular conception of sanity embraced by the 'age of reason' that constitutes, by opposition, the category of madness: the insane were simply *lacking* that faculty wherein (following Aristotle) our humanity lies, as 'animals possessing *logos*'. Therefore, on the one hand, there was nothing in madness with which reason could converse; and on the other, as virtual animals, there was no sense or even kindness in treating the insane in other than a 'brutal' fashion (cf. Scull,[24] discussed below). It was this view of the insane as a race apart that led to the practice of segregating them from the rest of the poor – not for their sake, but to spare the others from their offensive presence. 'The presence of the mad appears as an injustice: but *for others*.'[25]

The ideological nature of the classical age's concept of 'reason' comes across nowhere so clearly as in its descriptions of *unreason*. It is clear enough to us that this 'reason', which the eighteenth century took to be universal and sacrosanct, was a set of beliefs and norms of conduct specifically upholding the social order of that age. *Déraison* is a much broader category than *folie* (both are included in the original title of Foucault's book), and its elimination has obvious social control functions. Unreason manifests itself as a challenge to family, church and state, and its confinement is a police matter: 'Police, in the precise sense that the classical epoch gave to it – that is, the totality of measures which make work possible and necessary for all those who could not live without it.'[26] In definitions of unreason, no attempt is made to conceal the moral nature of the judgements involved: this did not happen until later, with the rise of 'objective', positivistic medicine. The doctor acted without embarrassment as an agent of social control (indeed, it is hard to see what was thought to be specifically medical about most of the judgements he was called upon to make). The *political* character of psychiatric decisions under this regime is not something imposed by sociologists of a later age; 'an astonishing synthesis of moral obligation and civil law is effected', says Foucault,[27] which explicitly embodies 'the great bourgeois, and soon republican, idea that virtue too is an affair of state, that decrees can be published to make it flourish, that an authority can be established to make sure that it is respected'.[28]

But this broadening of the category of madness – which went hand in hand, logically enough, with a vast increase in the numbers so detained – somewhat complicates Foucault's thesis of a shift in attitudes occurring between 1400 and 1800. For the conditions that excite such strong moral condemnation in the classical age do not seem to be the same ones that had fascinated the artists and writers of the late Middle Ages, as Foucault himself admits:

> If there is, in classical madness, something which refers elsewhere, and to *other things*, it is no longer because the madman comes from the world of the irrational and bears its stigmata; rather, it is because he crosses the frontiers of bourgeois order of his own accord, and alienates himself outside the sacred limits of its ethic.[29]

But is this the same madman? *Either* the transcendental folly celebrated in the earlier age had disappeared, and was replaced by the essentially moral aberrations of the classical age; *or* the two ages used the term 'madness' to refer to different things. Either way, we cannot simply say that a single, unchanging phenomenon – 'madness' – was dealt with in different ways in the two ages.

It is not even certain, from Foucault's account, that the treatment meted out *did* change in such a radical fashion. 'Banishment' is a word Foucault reserves for the classical age's response: yet to be publicly whipped and driven out of the city with quarterstaff blows[30] surely deserves no less strong a label. As for confinement, 'in the majority of the cities of Europe there existed throughout the Middle Ages and the Renaissance a place of detention reserved for the insane.'[31] Therefore, although the literary and artistic imagination of the late Middle Ages may have admitted madness to its counsels, it seems that the ordinary population did not.

Apart from these internal contradictions, several historians – notably Midelfort[32] – have challenged the factual accuracy of Foucault's account. Not surprisingly, the more the topic is studied, the more oversimplified his account seems to be. But such criticisms are often sterile, for two reasons. First, most critics rely on the English translation of *Histoire de la folie* – a version that omits about half the original text, and 80 per cent of the footnotes. Second, few critics confront Foucault's deeper argument about reason's dialogue with unreason, which represents the kind of metaphysical theme currently out of fashion with historians – and even, as it happens, with Foucault himself. For these reasons, *Histoire de la folie* is a work that is unlikely ever to be supplanted, however much it may be denounced.

The climax of the classical age – the moment at which the banishment of unreason by reason was made complete – is seen by Foucault, ironically, in that same act which for conventional historians of psychiatry represents the overthrow of the old order: Pinel's freeing of the inmates of the Bicêtre in 1794. In the orthodox view, this represents the triumph of humanitarianism and the re-admission of the insane to normal society. Foucault's reappraisal of this event is the most radical challenge that his book presents to conventional histories. For him, it was precisely because unreason had now been totally disarmed and negated, deprived of any positive value and significance, that it could be released from its chains and dungeons: only when this cognitive re-ordering was complete could the reformers embark on rationalizing the asylum system. The madman was readmitted to polite society only on condition that he assumed the identity of 'the perfect stranger': 'The city of reason welcomes him only with this qualification and at the price of this surrender to anonymity.'[33]

For the new *aliénistes* had anything but a tolerant, 'understanding' attitude to their charges. To be sure, they were opposed to the arbitrary cruelties of the eighteenth-century asylums: but only because these represented an affront to a well-organized society, and an unnecessary excess. A different view of human nature (which Scull, as we shall see, traces to the rise of the new economic order) led them to conclude that traditional methods were inappropriate; in their place, they instituted 'moral treatment', a comprehensive programme of re-socialization aimed at installing reason anew. There were no second thoughts, however, about the classical age's denunciation and abhorrence of madness itself.

With the reform movements of the early nineteenth century, and the setting-up of publicly financed and regulated asylums, the ground is laid for the 'golden age' of psychiatry and the capture of this territory by the medical profession. Before discussing further the nature of reform and the details of this capture, however, we should examine the account of the same period given by Scull.[34]

Scull, like Foucault, dismisses contemptuously the 'rhetoric of intentions' in which conventional histories deal. His account differs from Foucault's, however (as we have already indicated), in terms of both its underlying data and the explanatory approach adopted to them. First, his book is concerned with the English situation: developments here were not synchronous with those on the continent, a fact Scull attributes to the relative weakness of centralized state authority. No programme to match the scale of the *hôpitaux généraux* is found in the seventeenth century, because 'England possessed neither the incentive nor the means to use confinement as a means of disciplining the poor'.[35]

Second, for Scull the mainspring of social change is the economy: changes in the relations of production are seen as underlying the changing pattern of provision for the insane. This is not a reductive, deterministic materialism, for Scull sees change as mediated by the decisions of the ruling elite and legitimated by the ideas that they held at the time. However, the basic *épistème* of the Age of Reason, from which Foucault generated all the beliefs and practices of the period, plays relatively little part in Scull's account: no reference is made to the breaking-off of a 'dialogue with madness'.

Scull insists that the rise of psychiatry was part of a general change occurring in the societal response to deviance, in which we see the rise of centralized, highly organized state control, increasing segregation of deviants from the normal population, and ever more refined differentiation of varieties of deviance. He rejects, first of all, the explanation offered by Mechanic[36] and others for the phenomenon of confinement, in terms of the breakdown of earlier systems of poor law relief in the face of urban industrialization, and the huge problems of poverty and squalor that ensued. Close examination of the records shows that the pressure to build asylums was not associated, in time and place, with the growth of the cities: it largely preceded the latter, and was often strongest in rural counties.

The origins of confinement, according to Scull, lay rather in the relations of production – notably in the rise of wage-labour. First, a family dependent on wage earnings could not provide for its members in times of economic depression: large numbers of dependents were thus created by this system. (In 1803 one in nine of the population was receiving poor relief.) Second, the Elizabethan system of parochial relief was directly at odds with the market economy: 'to provide aid to the able-bodied threatened to undermine in a radical fashion and on many different levels the whole notion of a labour market.'[37] Wage-labour made the distinction between the able-bodied and non-able-bodied poor of vital importance, for 'parochial provision of relief to the able-bodied interfered with labour mobility.'[38] Segregating the poor in institutions had several practical advantages over domestic relief: it was efficient; it acted as a deterrent to the able-bodied malingerer; and it could actually create usable labour by instilling 'proper work habits' in the inmates.

The grounds given by Scull for the subsequent segregation of the insane into asylums are equally practical ones. The infirm in general interfered with the maintenance of workhouse discipline, by encouraging double standards: the insane in particular produced chaos and demoralization. However, to pay for acceptable standards of care for the insane in the community would have necessitated raising their standards above those of the majority, many of whom – quite literally – 'were living in shit'.[39] In this account we detect little of Foucault's emphasis on conceptions of morality or justice in relation to the insane – though no doubt such conceptions could easily have arisen as ideological justifications of a practical need.

The spearhead of the movement to provide public asylums for the insane were the reformers of the early nineteenth century, and on this group Scull's judgements are as harsh as Foucault's. Composed mainly of Evangelicals and Benthamites, they failed to offer a radical diagnosis of the evils of incarceration, still less of the system of wage-labour that led to it: in the end, their efforts only subordinated the needs of the insane still further to the demands of the economy. Scull offers a coldly unflattering account of their 'humanitarian' motives. Though they seem (in their own accounts) to be peculiarly brave and compassionate men, Scull argues that the moral contrast between them and the administrators whose 'abuses' they exposed was more apparent than real: '. . . what divided the reformers and their opponents was not the morality of one group and the immorality of the other, but rather the existence of two mutually incompatible paradigms of the essence of insanity.'[40]

According to the old paradigm, insanity removed its victim from the category of human to that of brute: thus, 'brutal' treatment was only natural, and anything else would have been as absurd as the provision of feather-beds for farm animals. According to the new paradigm, *all* nature – whether human or animal – was malleable: the insane could therefore be 'reprogrammed', as we would say, to function once again as productive members of society. We recognize in the latter the burgeoning ideology of capitalism, in which economic necessity dictates that the peasant should be transformable into a factory worker, and the housewife into a typist (and back again), as the need arises. In Scull's eyes the consequence of the reformers' efforts – however unintentional – was not to improve the lot of those already incarcerated, but to pave the way for a huge increase in their numbers. It was the market economy that required this remedy for insanity: so the reformers were natural allies of the bourgeois entrepreneurs and industrialists, and opponents of the gentry (with their vested interest in decentralized government). It was therefore no accident that the first bills to reform the asylum system came to grief in the House of Lords three times between 1816 and 1819.

The reformers' goal was the compulsory public provision and inspection of a nationwide asylum system: but the state of the existing asylums was one of the biggest obstacles to achieving this goal, so that a new concept of asylum care had to be promulgated. So keen were the reformers to achieve their goal that they failed – despite the eloquent arguments of such writers as Conolly[41] – to entertain the slightest suspicion that the asylum *itself* might contain severe inherent limitations: their concept of inhuman treatment was also, as Scull shows, a somewhat flexible one, which could readily be bent for the sake of preserving the essential working alliance with the asylum managers.

The insane asylum needed a new image; fortunately for the reformers, a highly suitable one was to hand, in the form of the 'moral treatment' pioneered by Samuel Tuke at the York Retreat since 1792. This regime had several powerful advantages.

First, it allowed the reformers to condemn vigorously the traditional methods of physical confinement, by providing an alternative technique of management based on *psychological* control: as elsewhere in capitalist society, the superior efficacy of *internalized* norms over external coercion was beginning to be appreciated. The chief instruments of control were the graded rewards and punishments of the 'ward system', still in use in Goffman's day,[42] and the relegation of the patient to the role of dependent child within a carefully constructed 'family' – a legacy of which psychoanalysis, with its stress on 'transference', still partakes. Shame and guilt were the chief agents of coercion in this familial 'total institution', as they are in the 'therapeutic community' of today.

Second, the new regime held out the promise of actual *cure*: patients were to be rehabilitated into 'something approaching the bourgeois ideal of the rational individual'.[43] Good work habits were an essential part of this ideal.

Third, by making it possible to claim that 'treatment, not punishment' was the aim of the regime, asylums were made more palatable to 'their true clients, the "patient's" family'.[44]

With its image thus refurbished, it was possible for the asylum to receive such universal acceptance as a rational response to insanity that in 1845 all the reformers' aims were translated into law. However, the fact that concern for the patients was only feebly enshrined in this legislation is shown by the ease with which the asylum system abandoned its ideals. In the latter part of his book, Scull shows that 'moral treatment' rapidly became a lost cause: for reasons of economy, asylums were built so large as to render it impossible, and neither the quality nor the quantity of staff provided approached the levels that its successful implementation demanded. The massive lower-class clientele of the new asylums was not to be pampered with such luxuries as Tuke had envisaged: as William Ellis wrote in 1840, 'to render them efficient assistance need cost very little more than to neglect them'.[45] It was in this way that, by the end of the century, the asylum system had become a vast network of 'museums of madness', and a living death to those it purported to serve.

The rise of the psychiatric profession.

The next question that Scull tackles is: How did medical men gain professional dominance over the asylum field? Whereas orthodox histories see the foundation of the psychiatric profession as a consolidation of the reformers' gains, Scull implicates it heavily in the betrayal of their early ideals.

Scull bases his account of the rise of psychiatry on the concept of professionalism put forward by Freidson.[46] Professional status involves effective monopoly control over a market for services: it depends on close supervision of training and qualifications, and on the possession of knowledge and skills publicly regarded as unique and efficacious. At the start of the nineteenth century, psychiatry did not constitute a 'profession' in this sense, but by 1850 it had become one. The key to this transformation, as the dates suggest, is the rise of the asylum system itself:

A dialectical process was at work, whereby the separation of the insane into madhouses and asylums helped to create the conditions for the emergence of an occupational group laying claim to expertise in their care and cure, and the nature and content of the restorative ideal which the latter fostered reinforced the commitment to the institutional approach.[47]

However, the success of medical men in dominating this occupational group was by no means as self-explanatory as the profession's own retrospective accounts make it seem. True, 'mad-doctors' had long shared responsibility for the insane, and had gained a measure of respectability in the late eighteenth century; but the ideas of the early reformers were not easy to reconcile with an increase in the power of this group. When the classical idea of the insane as subhuman creatures entirely devoid of *logos* was abandoned, its replacement by the notion of 'mental illness' was by no means inevitable; the view espoused by the reformers, in fact, saw madness as a loss of self-discipline, and its remedy as a matter of re-socialization. Medical men were challenged to show that their harsh methods of treatment had any therapeutic value, which they were conspicuously unable to do. In 'moral treatment', as practised by Tuke and Pinel, the physician's only role was to attend to the patients' bodily ailments; we would expect such a movement to have extinguished medical psychiatry altogether, rather than leading to its 'golden age'.

The fact that it did not was, according to Scull, entirely thanks to the ingenuity and political astuteness of the medical men. The initial reaction of this group to reform was hostile: their traditional methods were being harshly attacked, and the proposed alternative seemed to relegate them to auxiliary status. The proposals for statutory inspection of asylums by laymen were particularly threatening:

> If one follows Freidson in considering autonomy, the right to deny legitimacy to outside criticism of work and performance, as one of the core characteristics of any profession, such proposals to introduce lay control and evaluation of 'expert' performance must clearly be seen as of enormous strategic importance; and as likely to provoke intense opposition from those threatened by such control.[48]

Not surprisingly, therefore, the 'mad-doctors' initially allied themselves with the opponents of reform within the House of Lords.

When it became apparent that they had backed the losing side, however, the doctors had to devise a new strategy. Since they could not beat the reformers, they had to join them; thus, moral treatment ceased to be a threat to the doctors, and became instead the sphere in which they could most obviously and naturally excel. Emphasis was now placed on their long tradition of experience in administering asylums, while the difference between moral treatment and mere custodial care was played down. Tuke, in any case, had failed to provide an ideology on which a distinctive profession could have been securely based – he was a firm believer in amateurism, and made little effort to provide a 'scientific' rationale for his methods. The mad-doctors, on the other hand, had all the trappings of expertise: if challenged that they had never actually *cured* anyone, they could invoke the worse threat to the patients' interests that lay in leaving the field of treatment open to all comers. It did not greatly matter that the new ideology stressed social, not physical, causes and treatments; for (after all) the asylum doctors were administrators rather than physicians: indeed, links between psychiatry and the rest of medicine remained tenuous for many years.

By 1850, medical men had achieved a position of dominance in the asylum system at every level; in 1841 they founded their own Association, and journals devoted to enlarging and displaying their expertise were founded in 1848 and 1853. Their ability to demonstrate the power of cure had not improved during the half-century – but then, lacking the problem of attracting a clientele, this hardly weakened their position.

During this period, in fact, all the contradictions inherent in the medical profession's domination of the sphere of mental problems are clearly visible, and so too are the equivocations with which the profession has constantly defended its position. On the one hand, legitimacy is claimed via the argument that all mental disorders have a physical basis, which doctors alone are capable of understanding; but if it is necessary to concede that some disorders do not, nothing is lost, since doctors uniquely possess all the other skills that might be relevant as well. Those who challenge the profession, whether from law, psychology or social sciences, do not know what they are talking about, since the criteria for 'knowing what one is talking about' remain firmly with the psychiatrists themselves.

There is, indeed, a striking parallel between the takeover of moral treatment by the nineteenth-century mad-doctors, and the assimilation into modern medicine of the 'therapeutic community' movement (whose motives strongly resemble the former's – right down to its emphasis on the importance of 'the work habit'[49]). Both movements called for a practice sharply at variance with standard medical treatment – for example, the breaking-down of barriers between staff and patients, and an emphasis on the latter's responsibility. Both had to tailor their objectives to the constraints of the medical model, and in consequence lost much of their *raison d'être*. Consider also the case of psychoanalysis: despite Freud's own protestations,[50] this field is dominated in most countries by the medical profession, though nothing in the theory justifies this. However expedient it is for the profession to claim monopoly rights over such techniques as these, such domination actively hinders rather than helps their application.[51]

It has to be admitted, however, that, although Scull's account enables us to see clearly the longstanding historical roots of present contradictions, it does not add greatly to our understanding of the social control function of

psychiatry. *Professional* control, yes; the extent of psychiatric power over
the patient, and the fact that this is often exerted solely in the profession's
own interests, are both starkly portrayed. In essence, however, the sort of
power struggle he relates could have taken place over any other
handicapped group; there is a big gap between asserting that psychiatry is
not a rational and disinterestedly benevolent practice, and that it is an
instrument of social control. Scull's economic arguments explain the rise
of institutionalization as a solution to social problems, including insanity,
and his examination of professional power struggles shows how the
doctors came to take charge of the new asylum system. The extent to
which this solution contributed to the maintenance of social order, on the
other hand (as opposed to merely being socially *expedient*), cannot be
established without saying something about the way in which insanity was
defined: and Scull, unfortunately, takes the category of 'madness' for the
most part as given.

In Foucault's account, by contrast, the moral and political ingredients of
déraison are specified in detail. (There is evidence that the English mad, too,
were not all completely out of their minds. Conolly, for example, refers in
1830 to the fact that 'the crowd of most of our asylums is made up of odd
but harmless individuals, not much more absurd than the numbers who are
at large'.[52]) In the last two pages of his book, Scull moves towards the
position that psychiatry is 'pre-eminently a moral enterprise', and that the
application of the medical model to deviance has 'demonstrable utility to
those who benefit most from the social order'. However, because he has
little to tell us, from the materials at his disposal, about what precisely the
'mentally ill' were up to, he is not able to utilize this particular explanation
of the rise of the medical model. As we shall see below, there are powerful
arguments for imputing social control functions to the medical model, and
it may be that such arguments need to be invoked in order to explain fully
how doctors managed to persuade the authorities of their suitability for
running asylums. Scull, however, is precluded by the limitations of his
source material from using any such arguments.

Nevertheless, despite these limitations of Scull's account, it clears the
way for the analysis of social control functions, at least in the negative
sense of undermining the profession's own self-image – that of rationality
and disinterested benevolence. To critics who adduce these revelations
about the origin of psychiatry, defenders of the profession tend to reply
that psychiatry has long since rid itself of any undesirable legacy from the
nineteenth century: the critics, they say, are trying to visit the sins of the
fathers upon the children's generation. But this view fails to recognize the
fundamental continuity – despite three so-called 'revolutions' – in
psychiatry's role: it is not surprising that, as Scull shows, so many of the

arguments and tactics used by the profession to defend its position remain unchanged after a century and a half. To use another biblical metaphor, it is more a question of whether the leopard can change his spots.

For a comparison between the English and American systems we may turn to Rothman's *The Discovery of the Asylum*, published eight years before Scull's book. In the USA as in England, public insane asylums showed a remarkable increase in the first half of the nineteenth century: from 2 state asylums in 1824, we reach a total of 28 in 1860. Rothman's explanation of this trend is that concern about madness stemmed from a sense of social upheaval experienced during the period in question. Insanity was perceived as an ill-effect of this upheaval, and consequently the recommended cure was to withdraw the mad from society and create around them a 'model' environment.

Though Rothman sees the asylum as a uniquely American discovery, the lines of this 'moral treatment' are familiar from England and France. The rise of medical power, and the subsequent decline in standards of asylum care, also followed the same pattern as in Europe. However, as Scull has pointed out,[53] Rothman places so much faith in the accounts given by the protagonists of the asylum movement themselves that he fails to link this movement to the larger social and political order: his analysis therefore does not penetrate to the level at which developments in America, England and France can be related to each other. Though he sees psychiatry as an attempt to control social unrest and disorder, he does not see this control in the context of economic forces or class interests. Indeed, the very use of the term 'social control' tends to suggest a contradiction-free entity – 'society' – that does the controlling.

Returning now to the situation in France, Castel's *L'ordre psychiatrique* provides a sequel to Foucault's discussion of the classical age. Though, regrettably, no English translation of Castel's book has appeared, Miller[54] has provided a valuable commentary on it, from which the following account draws freely. Castel's analysis locates the rise of psychiatry in the specific context of the foundation of a new social order following the revolution of 1789, which makes it hard to generalize the elements of his account to Britain or America.

Castel observes that the new regime treated madness with a sense of urgency quite out of proportion to the numerical size of the problem. Under the *ancien régime*, internment was sanctioned by the *ordres du roi* or *lettres du cachet*, sought nine times out of ten by the family but on occasion by the local authorities. When the *lettres du cachet* were abolished in 1790, an alternative system of legitimation had to be found for such incarcerations, consistent with the notion of the contractual relationship between citizens that was supposed to replace the repressive authority of the monarch. But madness threatened the very basis of the 'contractual society', because it removed the personal responsibility which necessarily underlay contractual relationships: so incarceration could not be invoked as a *penalty*.

The solution was to make it a *treatment*; like others deemed lacking in responsibility, the insane were placed under a *rélation de tutelle*, which defined everything done to them as being in their own interests. Psychiatry became, in effect, a parallel apparatus to the legal system, with a sphere of intervention defined precisely in terms of the inapplicability of the latter. Though its powers were claimed strictly in the name of a benevolent paternalism, it nevertheless operated as a 'soft' apparatus of control, complementary to the 'hard' apparatus of the law.

What sets Castel apart from most English and American critics of psychiatry, however, is his explicit rejection of the notion of the state as the source of all social control: like the later Foucault, he sees power relations as generated within separate and specific 'instances', psychiatry being one such example. The important point is that psychiatry plays an important part not only in *policing* norms, but also in *creating* them. The doctor (like all other 'experts') is not merely an agent of the state, but has a domain of power all of his own. Such an approach neatly avoids the problem of mediation between state and professional power – of how the goals of the profession come to be allied to those of the state; but it achieves this, apparently, simply by refusing to recognize any such alliance.

Castel, then, explains the rise of psychiatry in terms of the downfall of the monarchy; medical expertise was required to replace one of the many functions of the sovereign, that of legitimating decisions about the insane. The task of the *aliénistes* was first and foremost to exercise authority: such authority did not need to be backed up by any recognized ability to cure patients.

Why should this authority have come to be vested in medical men? Castel's answer is in terms of the adoption of asylum care as the means of dealing with the insane. (In this respect his account is similar to Scull's, though he notably avoids referring to incarceration itself as a by-product of the system of wage-labour.)

The transfer of power to the doctors was not made immediately, but only after the judiciary, the family and the local administrators had all shown themselves incapable of assuming it. Initially, too, the asylum fell into disfavour as a means of dealing with insanity; in addition to public scepticism about its therapeutic value (such as we have already seen in England), it was burdened by the stigma of its association with the absolutist monarchy. Nevertheless, for the hard core of cases who could not be assimilated into the community, asylums had to exist: so a different *pratique asilaire* had to be devised, and along with this a new technology and a new group of experts to administer it – the *aliénistes*.

What led to the 'golden age' of psychiatry, according to Castel, was thus the coming-together of three elements: the practice of isolating the insane; the construction of a highly structured internal order, legitimated by medical knowledge, to replace the external one; and the strict subordination of the patients to the power of the doctor and his staff. We see now more precisely how the doctor assumed the power previously wielded by the sovereign, any suggestion of despotism being removed by the rationalization of the whole system within the framework of medical knowledge.

The particular form of *savoir* adopted was based on the already archaic eighteenth-century system of classification by external signs. Although this rendered the *aliénistes* outdated in relation to their colleagues in physical medicine, this was hardly a defect, Castel argues, because their fundamental preoccupation was in any case with questions of social order rather than pathology; the old system lent itself well to an environmentally oriented view of illness and treatment.

Thus the extension of the doctors' role to the area of social problems was achieved not by the reduction of the latter to malfunctions of the body, but by the creation of a new area of medical expertise, which translated moral problems into technical ones. This new area, of which 'moral treatment' was the paradigm, arose in parallel with other forms of hygienism and philanthropy, aimed at preventative intervention and operating outside the asylum. The field of expertise *par excellence* of the doctors was the recognition of those disturbances that could not appropriately be dealt with by legal sanctions, and their systematization into an orderly framework; it was thus inevitable that doctors and the judiciary should have been constantly treading on each others' toes, as disagreements multiplied over the boundaries of individual responsibility. (Cf. the now famous case of Pierre Riviere.[55] Roger Smith[56] has described in detail similar conflicts which arose in Victorian England.) Eventually, too, it was necessary for the experts to extend their systems of classification and methods of treatment beyond the limits of the asylum and its population – at which point we enter what I have termed the 'modern age' of psychiatry.

Though Castel prefers not to see social control experts as merely acting on behalf of the state, he nevertheless reveals an important confluence of interests between the *aliénistes* and the central political power. Both were threatened by the counter-revolutionary supporters of church and family, who opposed centralized forms of welfare and sought to maintain the private sector. The asylum movement in England met with opposition of a similar nature from the aristocracy, as we have seen; in France, the opposition seems to have been more successful, since the law of 1838 did not make the creation of asylums mandatory. Thus, in France, the 'golden age' of psychiatry never really existed: psychiatry never enjoyed the total monopoly over the care of the insane that it had sought.

In this admittedly sketchy and superficial précis, we begin to see the differences both of method and of data that separate Castel's account from Scull's (and the French writers in general from the American and English). Possibly the difference in subject matter is more apparent than real, since elements of the French bourgeoisie's 'contractual society' were also discernible in America, and (less so) in England. The methodological differences, however, are altogether more difficult to define and to reconcile.

Though Castel sees the rise of medical power over the insane rather as Scull does, as an instance of 'medical imperialism', he has a different view of its motives and effects. First, it does not so much capture a territory as create one: professions do not provide the solution to pre-existing 'social problems', but actively define 'the social' itself. Second, the immediate motive is not so much financial gain as power – though one could argue that the two are so closely allied as to be indistinguishable. Next, the knowledge that 'legitimates' this power does not do so from an absolute frame of reference: following Foucault,[57] the distinction between knowledge and power is eroded. 'Expert knowledge' is very largely the codification, rather than the rationalization, of professional practices; the acquisition of professional power is not achieved *through* the recognition of the validity of its knowledge-claims, but resides *in* that recognition. Finally, power is not delegated to professions from a central source, the state: it arises in separate 'instances' (medicine, the judiciary, education and so on) which interlock in complex ways with each other. The model of economic infrastructure 'determining' cultural superstructure is decisively rejected, since it ignores the determination of economic relations themselves by instances of power. Whether this paradigm shift resolves the problems of explaining the role of 'experts' like psychiatrists in maintaining social order, or merely adds to their obscurity, is a question we shall return to later.

The Modern Age

What I have called the 'modern age' has no precise or uniform starting date, but is defined by the following developments. First, the primacy of medical expertise in dealing with the insane is firmly established: asylum management, and decisions about who should be incarcerated, are formally entrusted to members of the medical profession. The concept of 'mental illness' is accepted as an appropriate formulation for all kinds of insanity. (In the USA and most of Europe, this is achieved by the mid-nineteenth century.)

Second, with the base of asylum practice securely established, medical authority is extended *beyond* the asylum population; 'mental illness' overlaps insanity, to cover deviations not severe enough to call for incarceration. New categories of pathology are devised, notably the concept of 'neurosis'. New sites of intervention are established in which psychiatry can attack pathology at its very roots – family life, industry and the school system – and new specialities are developed, some relatively autonomous from the medical profession, but all based on the medical model and most under the ultimate jurisdiction of the psychiatrist. Clinical and educational psychology, psychoanalysis, criminology and social work all participate in this expansion, which starts in earnest in the first two decades of the twentieth century.

Finally, to legitimate these interventions further and to maximize their efficiency, the 'human sciences' come into being – methods of surveillance and theories that extend into every nook and cranny of social life, employing techniques established as reputable within the realm of the natural sciences, and borrowing the latter's charisma and its air of superhuman neutrality. As all these developments reach their maturity, we reach what Kittrie[58] has termed 'the therapeutic state', in which a vast area of social and personal problems are subsumed under the category of illness and dealt with by 'treatment' – the whole operation being seen as apolitical, value-free, and nothing more than the application of technical expertise. Indeed, the medical model functions so effectively as a basis for exerting power that its original site of operation, the asylum, is now being quietly dismantled – with very little threat to the apparatus as a whole.

What precisely *is* the 'medical model'? Much abstract effort has been expended, both by psychiatry and its critics, in trying to define it in terms of a theory of mental disorder. One version (the 'faulty machine' model) confines it to the hypothesis of physical malfunction: such an interpretation is vigorously championed by certain psychiatrists, and is also the basis of Szasz's[59] criticisms. This interpretation, however, is too limited. In addition to 'organic' disorders, psychiatry also recognizes – indeed, mainly deals with – 'functional' ones: the notion of 'psychological' causes dates from the 'golden age' of psychiatry, and anticipates the rise of psychology as a separate profession.

We might pursue this attempt to define the medical model in terms of the conditions it treats, by listing family resemblances between 'mental' and 'physical' illness. The latter is marked by varying degrees of suffering and incapacity, and by a general (but culturally specific) agreement on its undesirability: so too is 'mental' illness, but this does not help us to define it with any degree of accuracy. The most we can say about the condition itself (as I have argued elsewhere[60]) is that it consists of experiences or behaviour deemed undesirable and incapable of being understood within the common-sense framework of accountability (that is, as the products of a responsible agent). Even this (given the difficulty of deciding what 'common sense' is) leaves us with a concept far too nebulous ever to have been the basis of such a massive social transformation.

Nor does it help much to interpret 'mental illness' as 'conditions to which psychiatric expertise is deemed relevant', since the nature of that expertise is equally nebulous. Even in the 'golden age', greater weight was placed on the asylum doctors' effectiveness as managers than on their physical skills. In the modern age, moreover, the medical model underlies practices that may be engaged in by experts far removed from the medical profession.

It is much more useful, as Foucault's works (in particular, *Naissance de la clinique*[61]) demonstrate, to define the medical model – and 'mental illness' – in terms of a particular set of practices and power relations. In these practices, first, authority is exerted not in the name of law or morality, but by virtue of the doctor's right to choose for the sick person what shall be in his own best interests. When this authority is coupled with *parens patriae* – the right of the state to manage the lives of persons deemed lacking in responsibility – the doctor's power is more formidable still; but even the private patient who voluntarily seeks treatment puts himself 'under the doctor', as the saying goes. The same imbalance of power characterizes other professional relationships using the medical model, even if the partners are labelled 'client' and 'therapist'. Medical practice has an 'infantilizing' effect, as Freidson[62] has shown, precisely because the powers it invokes are those of a parent. The fear of pain and death provides a powerful (if irrational) stimulus for the patient's trust in the doctor, while the Hippocratic oath serves as an essential reassurance that 'it's all for your own good'. The power thus established can even transcend the authority of an eighteenth-century monarch over his own subjects, as the hounding and harrassment of George III by his doctors vividly demonstrated.

When the patient's experience and behaviour are regarded as symptoms of physical illness, they are completely emptied out of moral significance: whereas in an earlier time they might have been ascribed to the agency of the devil, or a possessing spirit, they are now not seen as intelligible at all. Symptoms are neither 'good' nor 'bad', 'worthy' or 'base', but simply natural events without any human authorship – nobody's property, and hence disposable without debate.[63] This disappearance of the moral dimension is central to the medical model; as Roth puts it, 'The progress of science and of enlightenment can be traced as a development from a stage in which moralistic and transcendental attitudes were predominant to one in which rational and deterministic explanations of phenomena have come to be accepted.'[64] The great value of medical knowledge as a basis for maintaining social order is that it can be used to regulate morality without seeming to do anything of the sort.

At the same time, as Parsons,[65] Ewins[66] and Treacher and Baruch[67] have noted, the 'sick role' has wider social consequences for the patient:

> A sick person's status is conditionally legitimated when he willingly makes himself dependent on other people who are not sick – friends, family members, doctors, etc. – rather than on fellow sufferers. This creates real barriers to group formation among the sick, and little possibility of positive legitimation. The sick role thus not only isolates and insulates the sick person, but also exposes him to very powerful forces compelling him to become reintegrated into society as a fully participating member.[68]

The dependence of both sick and healthy people on the medical profession is further reinforced by its tendency to appropriate skills to itself – to 'disable' the lay population, as Illich[69] puts it, by withholding information (or formulating it in an esoteric dialect), and by discrediting the ordinary person's competence.

Finally, the medical model firmly locates the problem as residing *inside* the patients themselves: though the cause of their illness need not be viewed as a physical process, the illness itself can be treated separately from any environmental factors that may be seen as having led to it.

This set of practices grew up around the treatment of physical illness, but we can see clearly what a powerful means of maintaining order it becomes when transposed to the field of 'mental' disturbance. In diminishing the status of the patient, it functions of course as a 'professional ideology', enabling doctors to operate with a minimum of challenge: more importantly, though, the fact that doctors are allowed to function *at all* in the mental sphere was probably due in the first place to the ease with which they could impose authority, rather than to their therapeutic skills.

Moreover, hardly any other professional group has been able to achieve a comparable degree of extra-legal authority without invoking – however subliminally – the power of the doctor. Even Tuke, who had no use for medical men other than to cure physical ailments, was careful to retain the terminology of 'patients' and 'treatment'; psychologists and social workers, though they may prefer 'clients' to 'patients', nevertheless deal in 'diagnoses', 'treatment plans' and so on. The 'psy-professions' all achieved their present standing by exploiting the power inherent in the medical model: the power to eliminate moral considerations from their discourse, to make individual patients (rather than their situation in life) the focus of attention, and to subordinate them to their own authority.

It would be misleading, therefore, if we allowed Foucault's emphasis on the practical to persuade us that the medical model is merely a *codification* of power relations, in other words that it is entirely reducible to political terms. For the professional experts who manage the 'therapeutic state' enjoy not simply power, but authority: the medical model does not just define their practices, but supplies a framework that *legitimates* them. Without calling on this storehouse of public trust, it is doubtful if these experts could ever have gained their present position.

As the 'therapeutic state' gained momentum, it acquired increasing legitimation through the grounding of its practices in scientific knowledge. The knowledge-claims in which it sought justification for its practices became less narrowly based on *medical* methods of observation and theorizing, and conformed instead to the general paradigm of the natural sciences. As the most imposing of psychiatric textbooks put it, 'The foundations of psychiatry must be laid firmly on the ground of the natural sciences.'[70]

In his book on the prison system,[71] Foucault finds great symbolic value in Bentham's design of the 'panopticon' – an institution in which all the inmates, arranged like the radiating spokes of a wheel, are visible to the central authorities at the hub. This architectural image serves as an eloquent metaphor for the human sciences: a system of knowledge whose radii penetrate into every corner of life, and thus make possible swift and effective control.

Moreover, the positivist basis of this system provides a form of knowledge that lends itself peculiarly well to the task of rationalizing the maintenance of social order. As I have argued in detail elsewhere,[72] the presuppositions that enable natural–scientific methods to be transposed wholesale into the study of people are clearly ideological in nature. The ideal of 'objective' observation ignores the value judgements and tacit cultural knowledge involved in the description of people; both the rules of 'scientific' data collection and the insistence on causal (rather than interpretative) explanations eliminate from the outset the possible intelligibility and moral validity of the behaviour under scrutiny. In sum, positivism depoliticizes reality. An epistemology based on the principle of 'treating people like things' both supports and is supported by the mental health services' methods of organizing human material.

Professional diversification. As psychiatry leaned increasingly on its 'scientific' image as a source of legitimation, so it was enabled to extend its practice beyond the severely deranged asylum population that formed the traditional province of medicine. Simultaneously, a range of different professional disciplines grew up to compete with psychiatry for the new sites of intervention outside the asylum. Some, like industrial psychology, exploited territories in which psychiatry had little stake, and thus avoided conflict with it; others, like psychoanalysis or clinical psychology (which purported to give 'treatment'), entered into direct competition with medicine, and alternated between open conflict and conciliatory submission. Alongside all these disciplines stood the apparatus of the law, continually creating both boundary disputes and opportunities for partnership. Thus, the 'therapeutic state' consists of a complex web of related professions, and its development is a story of territorial conquests, symbiotic alliances, secessions, (professional) assassinations, bartering and bullying – very much like the history of Europe itself.

Psychiatry, as we have seen, owed its very existence to a genius for absorbing alien practices, and this 'eclecticism' continued to be the secret of its success in the modern age. Only when new approaches presented too radical a challenge to the mainstream (like Laing and Cooper's idea of schizophrenia as a 'voyage') were they driven from the fold: otherwise, an extraordinary range of theories and treatments (organic, dynamic, familial, behavioural, communal and so on) are encompassed within the profession. 'Psychiatry in Dissent', as Clare's book[73] is entitled, is therefore the normal state of affairs. The profession's most remarkable achievement was its recruitment of Freud. Though psychoanalysis was in many ways incompatible with the rest of psychiatry, it nevertheless answered the profession's need for an approach to the 'neuroses', and the resulting alliance proved so successful (in America, at least) as to earn itself the label of psychiatry's 'second revolution'. Today, however, with public regard for psychoanalysis on the wane, and with cost increasingly a barrier to its application, analysts are being gently eased back out of the fold (according to Reich[74] and Murray[75]).

The fixed centre of psychiatry, however, is the physical approach, which links the profession most visibly to the rest of medicine. Psychiatry's leaders have always been sensible enough to see that without this link the profession's power would be disastrously reduced: though non-physical approaches can be assimilated as long as they satisfy positivistic criteria, the link with medicine provides the essential lifeline of respectability and trust. (Those on the other end of the lifeline, however, have been noticeably less enthusiastic about maintaining it, and psychiatry's battle for equal status with other medical specialities has been hard-fought.)

Perhaps not surprisingly, in view of the concentration of resources the organic approach has enjoyed (substantially reinforced today by the drug companies), it has gained some notable successes in this century. The first of these was Wagner Jauregg's cure for general paresis of the insane in the 1920s. Insulin coma therapy, ECT and pre-frontal lobotomy followed soon after, all surrounded by controversies as to whether their effects were desirable or even ethical. But the main achievement was the development in the 1950s of the major tranquillizers for treatment of the psychoses, followed by similar break-throughs relating to anxiety and depression – psychiatry's 'third revolution'. Whether the effect of these treatments really proves the validity of the approaches underlying them is a question I have examined elsewhere;[76] but there is no doubt that it was perceived as proving it quite decisively by psychiatry itself, government departments, the media and many of the general public.

The 'drug revolution', in conjunction with increasing awareness of the harmful effects of institutionalization, is generally thought to be the main reason why psychiatry's original home base – the asylum – is currently being phased out in the long-term policy of most Western nations. Scull[77] has offered a powerful critique of this argument, demonstrating that (1) any correlation between the rates of decline of the hospitalized population and the rate of increase in drug use disappears when the statistics are examined in detail; (2) criticism of the asylum environment had been available for over a century, starting with such authors as Conolly;[78] and (3) it is arguable that the new drugs made it harder, not easier, for the majority of inmates to adapt to life outside the asylum.

Scull's explanation for the demise of the asylum solution to mental disorder is, quite simply, that the capitalist state can no longer afford it. Clearly this is an important factor, if not the chief one; but I do not think that the availability of new drugs was entirely coincidental. This technical development was important, though, not because it really 'cured' the patients, but because it put into psychiatrists' hands a form of treatment that did not depend on the asylum for its administration: drugs could be prescribed anywhere – the general hospital, the outpatient clinic, the private consulting room or the general practitioner's surgery. (With long-term injections, treatments could be several months apart.) These other places of work had been in increasing use ever since the profession had widened its interests to include non-psychotic disorders: the new drugs held out the promise that *all* patients would soon be treatable in these places alone. The main error in Scull's argument, therefore, was the assumption that a 'treatment' could have practical consequences only if it did all that was claimed for it.

Turning now to non-physical approaches, Armstrong[79] has provided a detailed account of how the concept of neurosis was exploited to encompass the disorders of the non-hospitalized population, and enabled psychiatrists to step over the boundaries of the asylum. When Freudian theory supplanted neurology in the explanation and treatment of neuroses, psychiatry was enabled to turn its attention to the vast area of adaptation to everyday life: as Kovel[80] describes, a highly successful alliance was set up with the 'mental hygiene' movements of the early years of the twentieth century.

Although psychiatry has succeeded in absorbing most of the non-physical approaches to 'mental health' and its maintenance, a significant entrepreneurial role in developing these has been played by the neighbouring profession of psychology – which, indeed, largely owes its existence to the exploitation of this field. Stone[81] charts the rise of the psychologist in America and Britain during the first 50 years of this century and examines the opportunism, entrepreneurship and negotiations involved in establishing psychology as a professional practice in the school, factory and subsequently the hospital. Both world wars are highly significant in his account, along with the important but neglected work of industrial psychologists during the interwar years. The First World War provided an opportunity for psychologists on both sides of the Atlantic to establish a professional practice in industry – in Britain through their fatigue study in the munitions factories, and in America through their intelligence- and aptitude-testing activities in the army medical and personnel departments.

Stone shows that fundamental problems arose in connection with an industrial strategy based on these techniques – techniques that had been developed in the laboratory and classroom and imported into industry. He subsequently examines a reconstruction of the role of the psychologist in industry and the emergence of a new strategy based on personality and temperament testing – techniques pioneered by industrial psychologists. During the Second World War psychologists who had previously been working in industry were employed by the army to use their techniques in the screening of army recruits for liability to battle fatigue, and were brought into a working relationship with psychiatry. This relationship provided the basis of the successful bid of psychologists to a place in the mental hospitals of the newly formed National Health Service following the war, and constituted their essential functioning role.

By and large, the territory that psychology has secured is the application of the concept of 'mental health' – construed as 'successful adaptation' or 'coping' – to areas where nobody is conspicuously sick. Thus child psychology, while leaving the treatment of problem cases largely in the hands of clinicians, has concentrated on a preventive role. Its energies have been directed towards perfecting an efficient technology of socialization, in family and school: psychologists have gained power as 'experts' in the public eye, advising the lay population about how to bring up their children. Enormous effort has been expended on discovering the preconditions of 'optimal' development – hardly anybody stopping to ask the question, 'optimal for what?'[82]

Although psychiatry and all the disciplines related to it claim 'scientific' backing for their practices, what is conspicuous in this whole field is the almost megalomanic air of competence and success displayed by the professions themselves, in contrast to the intellectual vulnerability of their theories and the uncertainty of their remedies. One reason for this discrepancy resides perhaps in the competitive relation that exists between practitioners in the mental health field. Since a discipline's legitimating *savoir* has to serve the function of boosting its image, it can be permitted only to a limited extent to provide the kind of critical feedback that is necessary for real progress to be made. No profession can afford to betray too serious signs of self-doubt, since its exaggerated claims are necessary in order to maintain a hold on a market already characterized by a general inflation of professional self-estimates. This in turn probably accounts for further characteristics of these disciplines.

First, since no discipline can afford to lose face by admitting that it might be drastically mistaken, much time often elapses before defects clearly visible to outside critics are taken seriously by the discipline itself. This rigidly defensive posture accounts both for the tendency for invective and railroading to replace debate within this field, and the slow pace at which progress, in any sense, is made.

Second, each discipline puts considerable energy into denigrating the efforts of its rivals – not usually a difficult task. As Kovel puts it, 'When primal therapy proclaims itself superior to gestalt, and bioenergetics to both, we are not witnessing anything fundamentally different from the competition obtaining between, say, Ford and Chrysler.'[83] But if all automobile manufacturers claim their rivals are untrustworthy, there is a risk that the public will opt for bicycles instead: so the 'eclecticism' of psychiatry creates a kind of cartel between certain core specialities – a gentlemen's agreement to respect (in public, at least) the usefulness of each other's approaches.

Third, the public have little opportunity to make realistic judgements about the success of each approach. This is because the nature of 'the problem' is to a large extent defined by the discipline that claims to be able to solve it, and only its practitioners are generally in a position to test its claims. As a result, fashionability becomes a major determinant of survival, and new approaches tend to have a short half-life – what Jacoby[84] wittily (but irrelevantly) calls 'the planned obsolescence of ideas'.

Approaches to the 'therapeutic state'. In American sociology, Zola[85] was among the first to focus concern on the growing exercise of medical power in the enforcement of moral norms, and to analyse the process of 'medicalization of deviance'. In the same tradition, Conrad and Schneider[86] describe the way in which psychiatry has constantly endeavoured to find new sites of intervention and new forms of deviance to bring under the rule of the medical model. Alcoholism, drug addiction, delinquency, child abuse, hyperactivity and homosexuality have all provided opportunities for the expansion of the medical empire, and this expansion has furthered the maintenance of social order. (In the next section we shall consider the limitations of the hypothesis of 'medical imperialism', and of this way of using it.)

The American writer whose work on the 'therapeutic state' has reached perhaps the largest audience is Christopher Lasch. His *Haven in a Heartless World*[87] parallels to an extraordinary extent the work of Foucault and Donzelot (see below) in focusing on the family as the object of social control – though so great were the divisions between French and American thinking in the 1970s that these writers seemed to have reached similar conclusions virtually independently. Lasch shows how numerous professional agencies, underpinned by sociology and psychology, have penetrated the family to the point where it can hardly be considered as the locus of any authority in its own right.

Another attempt to treat systematically the diversification of psychiatry's functions in the modern age is Castel, Castel and Lovell's *La Société psychiatrique avancéé*, which has been extensively reviewed by Peter Miller.[88] These authors distinguish two phases of diversification (corresponding to psychiatry's so-called second and third revolutions): first, the extension of the concept of psychopathology to the non-hospitalized population, which occurs with Freud; and second, the formal reorganization of the mental health services under the rubric of community care', undertaken during the 1960s. Concentrating on the USA, the account given is in terms of a professional re-negotiation of territories, rather than a centralized strategy of control; this approach is argued for on the basis of the 'liberal' character of American society, yet it evidently reflects also Castel's methodological preferences, as we saw above.

Another way of going about the study of this complex of disciplines is to focus on a single site of intervention. This is the approach adopted by Donzelot,[89] who considers one crucial site – the family – and documents the activities of the many agencies that sought to regulate its goings-on. Donzelot entitles his book *La Police des familles*, yet immediately makes it clear that 'Police' is to be understood not in the normal sense, but in that which the eighteenth century gave to it.[90] Such general activities of regulation may be carried on outside the framework of the law, and under the guise of a purely benevolent humanitarianism. Though 'the sanctity of the family' plays a central role in capitalist ideology (especially when the contrast is with communism), it is a family carefully monitored and controlled from the outside: while the human sciences exhaustively scrutinize its inner life, medicine, social work, the 'psy-professions' and the courts set firm limits to its autonomy.

In the modern state, parenthood – both the actual process of reproduction and the socialization of the offspring – has to be carefully supported, but at the same time closely regulated. Here women, in their capacity as childbearers and 'cultural missionaries', constitute an important locus of intervention. The key to this intervention is the family doctor; through a special alliance with the mother, he is able to promote forms of mental and physical health that, as it were, smuggle a whole regime of moral discipline into the family. In this way, the patriarchal and dynastic powers are tacitly undermined.

Another set of agencies – the 'tutelary complex' (educationists, social workers, psychologists and the juvenile courts) – takes charge of childhood. Though the courts, for example, are expected to back up parental authority, they in fact function to supplant it. Thus, the welfare state's benevolence towards the family is of a strictly pragmatic kind, rather like the aid that is nowadays given to developing countries.

Donzelot, however, is not concerned to give yet another account of how the family has been invaded and undermined by the state.[91] It is a question of balance: a balance 'between the necessity of imposing social norms of health and education, and that of maintaining the autonomy of individuals and the ambition of families as a principle of free enterprise'.[92] And it was Freud – whom Donzelot compares to Keynes in this respect – who hit upon such a principle, by devising a therapy that enhanced autonomy yet retained the family as 'the horizon of all individual paths'.[93]

Donzelot, as we have noted, rejects any Marxist ideas about the family or its attendant professions being 'ideological apparatuses of the state'. Like his colleagues Castel and Foucault, he is concerned to trace the 'genealogy' of power: as the latter puts it, genealogy is

a form of history which can account for the constitution of knowledges, discourses, domains of objects, etc., without having to make reference to a subject which is either transcendental in relation to the field of events or runs in its empty sameness throughout the course of history.[94]

So 'the social' is to a large extent the *creation* of these disciplines; it is not a case of a centralized political power handing out pre-existent social problems for professions to solve in a predetermined way. Whether the genealogical approach is capable of providing a coherent account of the professionalization of social problems, however, is a question we shall take up in the next section.

'Productive' power and psychoanalysis. There is a more important sense in which the post-structuralists see psychiatry and its related disciplines as exerting a 'productive' kind of power, and this is best illustrated by considering the case of psychoanalysis, in the light of Foucault's latest book, *La Volonté de savoir*.

This book is the first volume of a projected 'History of Sexuality', and in it Foucault explains the nature of the connection he intends to trace between power and sexuality. Foucault starts by discussing the evolution of power since the classical age. The power of the monarch was coercive, external and essentially repressive: the torture of criminals literally stamped this power, in a visible form, upon their bodies. The limit of sovereign power was the 'power over death', that is, the monarch's right to demand the life of a subject, either in recompense for his crimes or to further the monarch's own military aims.

As Foucault's *Surveiller et punir* argued, however, the modern state exercises its power in different ways. Its aim is a disciplined mind, rather than a subjugated body; norms are 'internalized', so that individuals cohere in a smoothly functioning whole. In itself this description of the changing nature of power is not at all novel, having been received as wisdom among sociologists since Weber. Foucault, however, claims that with this change a new area of power comes into being – 'power over life': a colonization of the most intimate biological forces. Contraception, abortion, sex education and efficient maternity services begin to be actively promoted, together with norms of psychosexual 'health': a person's 'private life' ceases to be his or her own business, but is documented and regulated by a host of agencies – in which psychoanalysis plays a central role.

Just as Donzelot showed that the 'privatization' of family life concealed increasing intervention by outside agencies, so Foucault claims that the reason we have not noticed the rise of this domain of power is because we have accepted the cliché that our ancestors banished sex from consciousness – that they never talked about it. Only the mighty Freud, so the legend goes, could tear aside the veil of prudery and hypocrisy and bring us back to sexual reality. On the contrary, says Foucault: nineteenth-century doctors, in particular, talked incessantly about sex – especially the sex lives of children; and it was precisely in this endless discussion of sex that its control resided.

Under the *ancien régime*, the ecclesiastical authorities had jurisdiction in sexual matters: confession became, in the Counter-Reformation, the main device through which sexuality was captured in the grip of language. In the nineteenth century, medical authorities took over this pedagogic function, and replaced moral distinctions with scientific ones: what now had to be maintained were not morals, but 'norms of development'. Freud's 'talking cure', then, is the literal successor to the confessional rite, in which the analyst is 'holy father' and judge: Foucault gives a new edge to the old saying that psychology begins where priests leave off. The important point, he claims, is that this endless discussion of sexuality, on and off the couch, does not in any way 'liberate' it: it only serves to organize it more effectively within the framework that the discourse enshrines.

Critical theory, too, has concerned itself with the expropriation of the 'inner life', and from within this tradition Kovel[95] echoes Foucault in his discussion of the role of psychiatry in organizing subjectivity. By alleviating (for a minority) the problems of scarcity and toil, Kovel argues, capitalism created the conditions for a liberation of personal energies that might have led to its own destruction: thus, at the beginning of this century, psychiatry was called on to provide a way of channelling these energies in a non-disruptive direction, via the organized pursuit of 'self-realization' and 'successful adaptation'. Whereas the theme of lowered productivity ('fatigue') was dominant in many early definitions of neurosis, mental health (for the middle class, at least) was not for long defined merely in terms of fitness for work.

The intensive disciplining of private life that Foucault and Donzelot document in the nineteenth century seems not to have been noticed by critical theorists, but the important point on which both they and the post-structuralists agree is that control of this domain is exerted not by an opposition of wills, but by more subtle means of colonization. Whereas the locked doors of the asylum, backed up by legal powers of incarceration, represented the old form of coercive power, its new embodiment (astonishingly prefigured by 'moral treatment') is psychotherapy – voluntarily sought and gratefully accepted. Thus, says Foucault, we should not imagine that talk about sexuality is what liberates it, or that 'repression', in the sense of banishment from public awareness, is what dominates it.

It should come as no surprise by now to find Foucault here attacking the most sacred tenets of 'progressive' left-wing thought. Such a view decisively rejects the received Freudo-Marxist wisdom that psycho-analysis, correctly interpreted, furnishes the necessary theoretical framework for understanding the psychic economy of capitalism, and for specifying the preconditions of its overthrow. It reopens all over again the question that has plagued intellectuals for half a century: what are the true political colours of psychoanalysis?

In addition to Foucault's *La Volonté de savoir* and Donzelot's *La Police des familles*, two other works buttress the post-structuralist condemnation of psychoanalysis: Deleuze and Guattari's *L'Anti-Oedipe*[96] and Castel's *Le Psychanalysme*.[97] Both argue that the idea of a 'true' Freudianism, waiting to be discovered in all its pristine radicalism beneath the mildew and tarnish of ideological 'distortions', is a chimera that has led the Left seriously astray. The focus of Deleuze and Guattari's critique is the insistent 'familialism' of psychoanalysis: far from liberating us from the tyranny of 'the papa–mama matrix', they say, it seeks to impose its rule even more thoroughly. If the patient doesn't have an Oedipus complex of his own, then – before going any further – the analyst will install one for him.

Castel focuses on the inequality of power in the relationship between patient and analyst: the autocracy of the latter is maintained inviolate by the banishment of certain topics from the discourse altogether. Any questions to do with the analyst's exercise of his powers are treated as material for interpretation only: they cannot be permitted to have a realistic referent. Thus, 'free association' is the perfect complement of the bourgeois ideal of 'free speech': anything may be said, on the understanding that none of it has to be acted on.

How are we to evaluate these criticisms? Even if they apply to most of what goes under the name of psychoanalysis, do they necessarily apply to all? Such a question is of increasing practical concern, especially to those who wish to use psychoanalytic therapy in the name of specific radical causes (such as feminism). There is no space to try and answer this question here, though I have tried to make a start elsewhere.[98] But whatever the political *potential* of psychoanalysis, the conclusion for this section is clear: psychoanalysis by no means represents the resumption of a 'dialogue with madness', as Conrad and Schneider,[99] along with many on the Left, optimistically suppose.

THEORETICAL PROBLEMS

It should be apparent by now that the recent historical studies of mental health professions have added considerable detail and depth to the sociological understanding of 'mental illness' and its relation to the wider social order. It will be equally clear, however, that large parts of this account remain incoherent and poorly formulated; many unstated assumptions are made, some of them questionable, and there is a lack of communication between different workers in the same field, which threatens to create a stale division of 'schools'. In order to examine some of these assumptions, and to open up an interchange between approaches, I shall consider in this section some of the basic theoretical problems.

All the writers discussed above ascribe effects to psychiatry and its related professions that go beyond simple relief of suffering and aid to the incapacitated, and are ignored or denied in the ideologies of the professions themselves. Apologists such as Grob,[100] discussing the appalling effects of the nineteenth-century asylum system, tend to dismiss these as 'unintended consequences' or accidental side-effects; the critics, however, seek to present them as central to the profession's social role or function. It is here that the first main theoretical problem arises: how does one show that an activity performs a 'social function' that is not avowed by its practitioners? In particular, what is the link between the 'social order' and the professions, such that the latter acts so as to stabilize the former?

In the literature discussed above we find several different ways of tackling this question, each associated with a particular social theory. First, writers who invoke 'social control' as a general explanatory process tend to hold a functionalist view of society. Society is regarded as an organic unity, stabilized by self-regulating processes: the social control of deviance, including that which is labelled 'mental illness', is merely one such process. 'Social order' is defined not in terms of a particular political arrangement (such as the feudal, bourgeois or communist 'order'), but as a property transcending all of these, rather like the physicist's concept of 'entropy'. (An exception to this is Szasz,[101] who holds to a kind of *laissez-faire* individualism also shared by some other 'anti-psychiatrists'; according to this, the 'order' that psychiatrists maintain is that of the bureaucratic, collectivist state, which seeks to suppress the natural free order of society. The mythology from which this view derives is obvious and all too familiar, as Sayers shows.[102])

Rothman,[103] who regards the nineteenth-century asylum as a response to 'social upheaval', appears to take this view, and so also (implicitly or explicitly) do most American sociologists of deviance, including 'labelling theorists'. It is a view that may fairly be characterized as 'metaphysical', since it does not seek to reduce social control processes to more directly intelligible activities, such as the defence of particular interests. Hence 'social control' appears as unmediated by any cognitive processes; it is a case of professionals unconsciously acting out a latent social tendency in favour of stability. (To be fair, Rothman *does* provide evidence that some of the American asylum reformers saw their role in terms of preserving social order; but such avowals form the exception rather than the rule.)

The hypothesis of 'medical imperialism' appears to have arisen partly in response to functionalism's failure to endow human agents with intelligible and plausible motives. This view sees professions in an entrepreneurial role, providing important economic advantages for their members by providing a 'labour market shelter' – in other words, a secure monopoly over those areas of work in which they are deemed to be the experts. How these privileges operate has been analysed in detail by Freidson,[104] and as we have seen Scull, in *Museums and Madness*, makes full use of the latter's approach in his account of the takeover of the asylum by the 'mad-doctors'. Conrad and Schneider,[105] too, use the same basic model in their account of the extension of medical activities into spheres not hitherto regarded as medical problems at all (such as classroom control).

We should not perhaps attach too much weight to the indignant protestations of the medical profession that such a model debases their lofty humanitarian motives to the level of pure greed. Disavowals of the profession's interest in gaining power and money for itself acquire an increasingly hollow ring, as the accuracy of Freidson's model becomes more apparent. Nevertheless, it may be wrong to assume that a profession's entrepreneurial role leads it to seek indefinite expansion of its activities, as the use of the term 'imperialism' implies. As Strong has pointed out,[106] doctors do not seize every opportunity to extend their activities; indeed, they actively resist some that are presented to them. Some types of work are deemed more congenial than others, and presumably this distinction has to do with the profession's image of its own competence.

A more important problem with the notion of 'medical imperialism' is that there is a fundamental mismatch between *explanans* and *explanandum*, if we are seeking to understand professions that keep socially disruptive elements in line. Certainly, the pursuit of professional self-interest distracts doctors from the relief of suffering; but it does not necessarily lead them into activities reinforcing the social order. In a free market, doctors should be just as inclined to promote deviance as to suppress it, as long as it's good for business: why not dignify with the name of 'therapy' the dispensing of psychotropic drugs to people who simply want to get high? This, as it happens, is exactly what dozens of 'stress clinics' that have recently sprung up in the USA set out to do;[107] but the organizational reaction to this event provides the answer to our question. There are certain constraints on the activities a profession is allowed to engage in, and sanctions are effected through agencies of licensing and regulation – in this case, via malpractice and drug offence suits.

However, the 'mandate' that professionals have is seldom reducible to an explicit direction from a central authority: it has more to do with a broad fit between the needs of those in power and the abilities of the profession. A good example of this is the mandate that the *aliénistes* acquired in the early nineteenth century: as Castel shows,[108] their job was primarily to constitute an authority to replace the defunct *ordres du roi*. It mattered little if they could neither cure anybody by the old physical methods of treatment, nor properly master the new psychological ones. This, however, puts us back in the realm of unstated ideologies and unavowed motives.

The same realm is unavoidably occupied by writers who approach the problem from a Marxist viewpoint. Here, the mental health professions are seen not as part of the mysterious mechanism by which 'society' controls its own members, but as agents of class domination: the interests constraining professional activities are not the profession's alone, but those of capital. Such analyses have to bridge two fundamental gaps. First, they have to show that professional interventions produce change in a direction that does indeed suit capital's interests; second, they have to demonstrate that this does not come about by accident, but in a systematically mediated way.

To bridge the first gap, it is necessary to show that 'mental illness' represents a threat not to order in general, but specifically to capitalist order. This entails looking at the illnesses themselves. Take, for instance, the neuroses; Stone[109] documents how these were defined initially as a problem of productivity ('brain fag'), and how psychologists saw their services as primarily useful to industrialists. Kovel[110] points out that, even though later conceptions of mental health stressed the fulfilment of personal goals rather than production quotas, this too can be seen as a recuperative device vital to the suppression of political idealism. The chief problem for any analysis that sets out to relate mental illness to capitalism is that psychiatry's chief territory is the area that Marxist theory traditionally has least to say about: emotional life, intimate relationships, the family – Donzelot's 'the social'. For example, crucial to the interpretation of women's 'mental illness' is the nature of the link between capitalism and patriarchy; yet no theoretical agreement has been reached on this issue within Marxism.

In general, Marxist commentators alternate between viewing mental illness either as a genuine affliction, caused by contradictions in the social order, or as 'deviant' behaviour, misconstrued and reified as illness. According to the first analysis, psychiatry helps to preserve the existing order because it covers up the problems that arise at the tension points within the system, defining them as *individual* disorders and masking their wider social dimensions. On the 'deviance' view, psychiatric diagnosis and treatment is a thinly disguised method of identifying and bringing into line those who fail to perform as their place in the system demands. I shall discuss these views in greater depth below.

The second problem, that of identifying the nerves and sinews of capital's 'hidden hand', is generally skimped. Kovel, for example, does not consider the problem of mediation between economic forces and professional ideologies: as in much critical theory, 'capitalism' becomes an intelligent organism with a life of its own (much like 'society' in functionalist analyses), which automatically senses its 'needs' and devises ingenious ways of meeting them. If only mental health professionals were overtly the lackeys of the capitalist ruling class, the problem would be easy to solve: in their own eyes, however, they are quite the opposite – the disinterested champions of happiness and fulfilment for the individual. On the whole, psychiatry is careful to preserve a 'non-ideological' stance;[111] as a branch of medical technology, it avoids overt commitment to any identifiable moral – still less, political – position. Its commitments can be discerned only through examination of its practice. The notion that human problems can be dealt with in an apolitical way is of course a powerful ideology in its own right; but the question of *how* psychiatry comes to act in harmony with the interests of capital is seldom tackled. Though piecemeal analyses exist – Scull's work being perhaps the best example considered here – they are generally undermined by the prevailing confusion of current Marxist theories of the state.

Turning to the post-structuralist school, we find an approach that has sought to resolve this confusion by escaping from Marxist presuppositions altogether. Foucault and his colleagues quite explicitly reject the notion of 'economic base' and central state power: Foucault frequently denies that he has a 'system' or a 'schema', but the negative principle of avoiding Marxist formulations runs through all his later work. Historically, this is bound up with the split arising after 1968 between the intellectual avant-garde and the French Communist Party: the former felt that the political causes that they had espoused were hindered rather than helped by the party's insistence on subordinating them to a unified schema of 'class struggle'.

Thus, what the post-structuralists primarily stress is the *diversity* of forms of power, and their lack of origin in a central source; no common cause need unify the struggle for colonial freedom, gay rights and prison reform. Poulantzas[112] has criticized this 'micro-politics' and its shortcomings are evident in the field examined here.

As we have seen above, Foucault, Castel and Donzelot seek a 'genealogy' of power (cf. Nietzsche's 'genealogy of morals'). In this approach, 'power' takes on a life of its own: thus, the emergence of the *aliénistes*, and the subsequent proliferation of mental health professions, is seen as a more or less autonomous process, not called into being by any central or 'infra-structural' forces. The main value of this approach lies in its readiness to recognize the untidiness and unpredictability of this process. However, the antithesis between this view and the monolithic economic determinism that is its shadowy rival is a false one. A model in which the wider social order imposes *no* constraints suffers from the same defects as 'medical imperialism': it ignores the fact that professions are not their own masters, but operate by virtue of a mandate, and have to tailor their activities accordingly. The undertones of the word 'genealogy' are misleading, since professions are not dynasties and do not acquire their power by inheritance; they have to earn it.

Nor is a Marxist approach inherently incapable of recognizing the complexity of professional power. Though the mental health professions have, to some extent, created the spaces in which they operate, their activities are not arbitrary or solely constrained by those of their neighbours: there is a consistency about the value that they enforce and promote. Indeed, despite the obligatory denials of its existence, one suspects that a fairly classical Marxist set of expectations about what a historian should look for informs the enquiries of the post-structuralists. This is evident in the earlier quotation from Donzelot;[113] though it is 'the nineteenth century' rather than 'capitalism' that is portrayed as seeking a balance in its dealings with the family, it is the demands of 'free enterprise' that are specified as one pole of this balance.

That professions *do* need a mandate to operate is a fact that this school consistently plays down; indeed, we can detect the urge to do away with the whole notion of 'legitimation', as used by Weber and the critical theorists. Foucault is often represented, by his followers and his critics alike, as achieving a sort of Nietzschean reduction of truth to power. But whereas one can readily concur with the rejection of an absolutist conception of 'rationality' such as underlies the writings of Habermas, it is not clear that Foucault *does* dispense with the notion of legitimation, or that he could afford to do so. For to regard the *savoir* of a profession as merely an encoding of its practices would ignore the fact that the *savoir* is used, day by day, to *justify* the practices; a diagnosis cannot be reduced to a prescription for treatment, however closely the two may be bound up. The writings of this school have clearly demonstrated the futility of trying to understand theories in the 'human sciences' in isolation from the practices they inform: but they have not succeeded – if indeed they ever set out to do so – in showing that the notion of 'ideology' is dispensable.

The same applies to the concept of 'repression'. It is worth quoting

Foucault's views on this at length, since they make clear how his own work has evolved:

> When I wrote *Madness and Civilisation* . . . I think indeed that I was positing the existence of a sort of living, voluble and anxious madness which the mechanisms of power and psychiatry were supposed to have come to repress and reduce to silence. But it seems to me now that the notion of repression is quite inadequate for capturing what is precisely the productive aspect of power. In defining the effects of power as repression, one adopts a purely juridical conception of such power, one identifies power with a law which says no, power is taken above all as carrying the force of prohibition. Now I believe that this is a wholly negative, narrow, skeletal conception of power, one that has been curiously widespread. If power were never anything but repressive, if it never did anything but to say no, do you think one would be brought to obey it? What makes power hold good, what makes it accepted, is simply the fact that it doesn't only weigh on us as a force that says no, but that it traverses and produces things, it induces pleasure, forms knowledge, produces discourse.[114]

This passage is a splendid corrective to the search for a simple opposition between subjects in every instance of power. But again, neither Marxism nor psychoanalysis is necessarily tied to such a narrow view of power: it is an elementary, though widespread, mistake to equate Freud's concept of repression with an opposition of wills, and much of Marxist theory since the 1920s is taken up with the problem of finding subtler concepts of domination than simple 'coercion'. 'Defence mechanisms' in Freudian theory do indeed 'induce pleasure, form knowledge, and produce discourse', and so do the apparatuses of ideology in much Marxist theory. Nevertheless, to reduce power *entirely* to its 'productive' functions would be to leave out a vital ingredient: though conflicts may be subtle ones, a power involving no contradiction whatsoever would be merely a kind of social grammar that does not deserve the name.

The Nature of Mental Illness

The second outstanding theoretical problem lies in the assumptions made by writers of these various schools about the nature of the 'disorders' that the mental health professions deal with. It should be pretty obvious that it is impossible to characterize properly the activities of the latter without specifying in some detail the former; but, as I stated in my Introduction, this task tends to be neglected, partly because historical data about 'patients' is scarce, and partly because it seems to raise too many 'psychological' problems. Most writers have worked along the same lines as Foucault: 'Rather than asking *what*, in a given period, is regarded as sanity or insanity, as mental illness or normal behaviour, I wanted to ask *how* these divisions are operated.'[115] (In fact, as we saw above, Foucault says rather more about the former question than most.)

One crucial, and extremely vulnerable, assumption underlying nearly all the work we have considered is that 'mental illness' is in reality a moral matter – a form of deviance. That assumption now needs to be examined in detail. It is clearly not self-evidently true: hardly any psychiatrists would accept it, and most laymen ('patients' included) would probably deny it too. Thus, to support the claim that mental illness is really deviance it is necessary not only to show that it is, but to account for the near-universal failure to recognize it as such.

For psychiatry to make any positive contribution to social order, it is necessary that 'mental illness' should in some way *threaten* that order. It is not enough merely to say that the boundaries of mental illness categories, like those of physical illness, are culturally determined: this is easy to demonstrate, but it is not necessarily a political matter (unless one devalues the very concept by making *all* reality 'political'). Again, we might – like the ethnomethodologist Jeff Coulter – adopt the view that the moral norms enshrined by the concept of 'mental health' are simply 'propositions not intelligibly subject to doubt',[116] basic conventions of thought and conduct that have to be observed by members of a given culture in order for their actions to be recognizable at all. It is indeed true historically that the concept of 'mental illness' has evolved antithetically to that of 'intelligible conduct'; but this entirely begs the question as to whether behaviour *deemed* meaningless might in fact have some purpose or point.[117]

It is possible to construct a limited notion of the political significance of psychiatry without departing from the official definition of mental illness in terms of suffering or incapacity – just as some authors have done for physical illness. This is the approach adopted by Sedgwick,[118] and favoured by those on the Left who see it as the only alternative to 'anti-psychiatry'. Without claiming that psychiatry in any sense 'keeps people in line', its activities can nevertheless be seen as political, in that they reinforce existing class divisions in the unequal distribution of treatment resources: moreover, to the extent that the organic bias of psychiatry leads it to neglect the role of social conditions in generating mental illness, it can be seen as helping these conditions to go unchallenged. Such views, however, seldom lead to any proposals more radical than an increase in public spending on treatment and research.

Most of the writers we have examined, however, do see psychiatry as 'keeping people in line', and this view is generally associated with a simple reduction of mental illness to deviance. To do this is to adopt what I have called a 'normalizing' approach to mental illness[119] – that is, to see its so-called symptoms as intelligible, readily yielding up their meaning to those who are willing to side with the deviant. That this meaning may be denied, even by the 'patient', is seen merely as part of the strategy of control: what more powerful way to suppress an unwanted reaction or perception than to call it a symptom of illness? Rosenhan's celebrated experiment,[120] in which eight perfectly sane volunteers, once having gained admission to a mental hospital, were unable to convince the staff of their sanity, demonstrates how firmly the 'illness' label sticks.

As I have argued, the 'normalizing' approach has scored some notable successes – for example, the demonstration by Goffman[121] and Laing and Esterson[122] that so-called 'psychotic' behaviour may be seen as an intelligible reaction to the intolerable situation a patient occupies within hospital or family, if only we are prepared to look closely at that situation. Where a patient has been diagnosed ill despite his or her own denials, and where treatment has consisted in suppression of his or her activities by physical or chemical restraint, the 'deviance' model is in its element. However, the majority of symptoms that psychiatrists treat today do not so easily divulge their moral (still less, *political*) significance.

All this is perhaps envisaged in Foucault's notion of the shift from 'repressive' to 'productive' power, but it creates a major problem for theories of control. It is hard to accept that the person who does not understand why he or she is acting or feeling in a certain way, and voluntarily seeks 'treatment' in order to stop it, is in any useful sense a 'deviant'; merely to call this deviance 'residual', as Scheff[123] does, simply bypasses the problem. It is not that the 'rules' the mental patient breaks are unstated ones; rather, as Coulter pointed out,[124] he or she is not really 'breaking' a rule at all.

There seems little point in holding out against the strong pressures to call such a person 'ill', especially since that is often the label the person is asking for. Yet it is still possible, I would maintain, to ascribe to such a condition a political significance that transcends any that a physical illness could possess. That is to say, these conditions are 'socially constructed': psychiatry, in its 'productive' capacity, has devised categories and practices for handling them that are linked intimately to political assumptions about each person's place in the social order.

We may start by noting that such conditions can often be seen as a negative emotional reaction to structural features of a person's environment. They are not, however (as the 'deviance' view implies) straightforward protests against that environment, or complaints about 'problems of living'. A person who can still protest and complain is not mentally ill; as psychoanalysis has amply demonstrated, it is when distress cannot be formulated and expressed that it becomes translated into 'symptoms'.

For Freud, the reason why certain experiences could not be handled by the ego in a 'healthy' way was that they threatened the ego's defences, and thus had to be repressed; the view put forward here departs from Freud only in that the ego and its defences are seen as *socially* structured, however much their dynamics may be intra-psychic. A person's capacity to confront his or her own experiences consciously, without becoming mentally ill, will depend at least in part on the adequacy of the shared world of interpretations that makes up his or her 'ego'. To the extent that this world is dominated by ideology, that is, by mystifications and collective delusions that foster the *status quo*, it will inevitably be harder for a person to come to terms with his or her own reality. Thus, people experiencing stressful emotions will seek to interpret these emotions in a way consistent with their general view of the world; the ideology that they share, however, may deter them from perceiving the true significance of the emotions – indeed, from perceiving them at all.

Since such individuals cannot accept what they are really feeling, they have to interpret it as something else; and since the emotions in question are unpleasant ones, it will almost certainly be experienced as 'illness'. In other words, persons' social situation may lead to distress; but their conventional beliefs about that situation may make it impossible for them to acknowledge the connection between it and their distress. This failure to connect may receive powerful encouragement from the availability of a psychiatric 'syndrome', which provides a handy alternative interpretation. I shall illustrate this view by discussing 'depression' as it arises in the unemployed, and in mothers of young children.

First, much evidence – the most recent being Fagin's study[125] – shows that the loss of a job is commonly followed by general feelings of ill-health, and by a psychological syndrome that contains the elements of grief, anger and guilt, but is experienced as 'depression'. From a certain political viewpoint, grief and anger are perfectly intelligible reactions to the situation; those feelings are not available to the 'ill' person as such, however. Why not? Basically, I would argue, because the ideology of labour renders them inappropriate: since the wage-labourer 'only works for the money', loss of a job should not cause pain as long as reasonably adequate welfare payments are available. As the Duke of Edinburgh recently observed, one should rather rejoice at the new-found availability of leisure. Hence, to accept one's feelings as *real* (that is, warranted), grief and anger would involve a complete overturning of the conventional ideology of work and why people perform it.

Guilt, and a sense of worthlessness, arise from the equally ideological conviction that those who lose a job do so because of their own shortcomings; strictly speaking, ideology creates rather than represses this feeling, but we can assume that it will conflict with other, more rational, perceptions of the situation. All in all, then, the person who loses a job can experience his or her emotional reaction to this event only at the price of overturning his or her political philosophy. Consequently, we should expect to find that those who are most ready to do so will suffer less from the transformation of their emotions into feelings of 'illness'.

Turning to the second case, Brown and Harris[126] have documented an alarming incidence of 'clinical depression' among mothers of young children with no job. (There are other predisposing factors, but we need not consider all of these.) Again, the affective ingredients of the condition are anger, despair and apathy: and again, these are experienced as worrying signs of illness rather than true feelings. In this case, the ideology of womanhood blocks any such perception: resentment cannot be fastened on one's children and the task of looking after them, since as a mother one's instinct must be to love them. Moreover, as a woman, anger ought not to be part of one's make-up. To argue for the reasonableness of one's despair and apathy would be to blaspheme against sacred ideals of marriage and parenthood. Again, those who have less invested in these ideals are probably less inclined to experience their reactions as 'illness', and thus better able to deal with them; Bem[127] found that women with the least 'feminine' attitudes were the ones who coped best with motherhood.

Though these illustrations are undeniably crude and sketchy, it is obvious how the general pattern of explanation can be generalized to other situations (such as the 'hyperactive' schoolchild, or the 'confused and depressed' elderly person). Such an explanation does not deny the real incapacitation that this sort of condition entails; but at the same time it shows how inadequate it is to say that it is merely 'caused' by the social situation. Rather, it is socially *constructed*: the ideology of work and motherhood, coupled with widespread acceptance of the concept of 'depression', combines with the real stress of the situation to produce a clinical outcome instead of (in Freud's phrase) 'ordinary unhappiness'. The 'productive' power of the mental health professions thus lies in the generation of schemas of self-misinterpretation.

We should not imagine, however, that mere political 'consciousness-raising' will suffice to cure or prevent such reactions. Ideologies are matters not of intellectual assent, but of deep emotional commitment: in the case of motherhood, for example, it is likely that one's attachment to the conventional stereotype is closely bound up with one's relationship in fantasy to one's own mother.[128] Such an explanation, therefore, does not deny that intensive personal help may be required to overcome even a 'socially constructed' illness.

It is not claimed, of course, that such an account is generalizable to all other illnesses and situations. It is extremely unlikely that any one model will fit all 'mental illnesses'; each of the ones we have considered above may well have its own sphere of applicability. What I have attempted to demonstrate is simply that an understanding of psychiatry's social role cannot evade detailed analytic work at a psychological level; perhaps the time has come to turn the spotlight away from professional history, and back on to 'illness' itself.

NOTES AND REFERENCES

1. P. Barham, 'Schizophrenia, Science and Sociology', *Sociology*, 13 (1979), 503–30.
2. G.W. Brown and T. Harris, *Social Origins of Depression*. London: Tavistock, 1978.
3. M. Foucault, *Folie et déraison, Histoire de la folie a l'âge classique*. Paris: Plon, 1961. English trans., *Madness and Civilization*. New York: Pantheon, 1965; London: Tavistock, 1967.
4. M. Foucault, *La Volonté de savoir*. Paris: Gallimard, 1976. English trans., *The History of Sexuality*. Vol. 1: *An Introduction*. New York: Pantheon, 1978; London, Allen Lane, 1979.
5. R. Castel, *L'ordre psychiatrique: L'âge d'or de l'aliénisme*. Paris: Editions de Minuit, 1976.
6. F. Castel, R. Castel and A. Lovell, *La Société psychiatrique avancée*. Paris: Editions Grasset, 1979. English trans., *The Psychiatric Society*. New York: Columbia University Press, 1982.
7. J. Donzelot, *La Police des familles*. Paris: Editions de Minuit, 1977. English trans., *The Policing of Families*. New York: Pantheon, 1979; London: Hutchinson, 1980.
8. D. Rothman, *The Discovery of the Asylum*. Boston: Little, Brown, 1971.
9. A.T. Scull, *Museums of Madness: The Social Organisation of Insanity in Nineteenth-Century England*. London: Allen Lane, 1979.
10. M. Foucault, *Surveiller et punir*. Paris: Gallimard, 1975. English trans., *Discipline and Punish*. New York: Pantheon, 1978; London: Allen Lane, 1978.
11. M. Ignatieff, *A Just Measure of Pain: The Penitentiary in the Industrial Revolution, 1750–1850*. London: Macmillan, 1978.
12. Scull, *Museums of Madness*, p. 13.
13. Foucault, *Discipline and Punish*, p. 31. (British edn.).
14. A.T. Scull, *Decarceration: Community Treatment and the Deviant – A Radical View*. Englewood Cliffs, NJ: Prentice-Hall, 1977.
15. S. Turkle, 'French anti-psychiatry', in *Critical Psychiatry: The Politics of Mental*

Health, ed. D. Ingleby. New York: Pantheon, 1980; Harmondsworth: Penguin, 1981.

16. P. Miller, 'The territory of the psychiatrist', *Ideology and Consciousness*, 7 (1980), 63–106.
17. D. Ingleby (ed.), *Critical Psychiatry: The Politics of Mental Health*. New York: Pantheon, 1980; Harmondsworth: Penguin, 1981.
18. Castel, *L'ordre psychiatrique*.
19. Scull, *Decarceration*.
20. Castel *et al.*, *La Société psychiatrique avancée*.
21. Foucault, *Folie et déraison, Histoire de la folie*.
22. A. Sheridan, *Michel Foucault: The Will to Truth*. London: Tavistock, 1980.
23. Foucault, *Madness and Civilization*, p. 58.(British edn.).
24. Scull, *Museums of Madness*, p. 64.
25. Foucault, *Madness and Civilization*, p. 228.
26. Ibid., p. 46.
27. Ibid., p. 60.
28. Ibid., p. 61.
29. Ibid., p. 58.
30. Ibid., p. 10.
31. Ibid., p. 9.
32. E. Midelfort, 'Madness and Civilization in Early Modern Europe: A Reappraisal of Michel Foucault', in *After the Reformation: Essays in Honour of J.H. Hexter*, ed. B.C. Malament. Philadelphia: 1980.
33. Foucault, *Madness and Civilization*, p. 250.
34. Scull, *Museums of Madness*.
35. Ibid., p. 21.
36. D. Mechanic, *Mental Health and Social Policy*. Englewood Cliffs, NJ: Prentice-Hall, 1969, p. 54.
37. Scull, *Museums of Madness*, p. 37.
38. Ibid.
39. Ibid., p. 100.
40. Ibid, p. 65.
41. John Conolly, *An Inquiry Concerning the Indications of Insanity*. London: Taylor, 1830.
42. Scull, *Museums of Madness*, p. 120.
43. Ibid., p. 69.
44. Ibid., p. 95.
45. William Ellis, cited in Scull, *Museums of Madness*, p. 115.
46. E. Freidson, *Profession of Medicine*. New York: Dodds, Mead, 1970; *Professional Dominance*. New York: Atherton, 1970.
47. Scull, *Museums of Madness*, p. 44.
48. Ibid., p. 145.
49. Maxwell Jones, *Social Psychiatry*. London: Tavistock, 1952.
50. S. Freud, 'The Question of Lay Analysis' (1926), in his *Standard Edition*, vol. XX. London: Hogarth, 1960.

51. G. Baruch and A. Treacher, *Psychiatry Observed*. London: Routledge & Kegan Paul, 1978.
52. Conolly, *Inquiry Concerning the Indications of Insanity*, cited in Scull, *Museums of Madness*, p. 96.
53. A. Scull, 'Humanitarianism or Control? Some Observations on the Historiography of Anglo-American Psychiatry' (chapter 6 above).
54. Miller, 'The Territory of the Psychiatrist'.
55. Foucault (ed.), *Moi, Pierre Rivière.* . . . Paris: Gallimard/Juillard, 1973. English trans., *I, Pierre Rivière*. New York: Pantheon, 1975; London: Peregrine, 1978.
56. Roger Smith, *Trial by Medicine: Insanity and Responsibility in Victorian England*. Edinburgh: University Press, 1981.
57. M. Foucault, 'Truth and Power', in *Power/Knowledge: Selected Interviews and Other Writings 1972-1977*. Hassocks: Harvester Press, 1980; New York: Pantheon, 1980, pp. 116 and 133. Originally published as 'Verité et Pouvoir', *L'Arc*, 70 (1977).
58. N. Kittrie, *The Right to be Different*. Baltimore: Johns Hopkins University Press, 1971.
59. T. Szasz, *The Myth of Mental Illness*. New York: Harper and Row, 1961.
60. D. Ingleby, 'The Social Construction of Mental Illness', in *The Problem of Medical Knowledge: Towards a Social Constructivist View of Medicine*, ed. A. Treacher and P. Wright. Edinburgh: University Press, 1982.
61. M. Foucault, *Naissance de la clinique*. Paris: PUF 1963. English trans., *The Birth of the Clinic*. New York: Pantheon, 1973; London: Tavistock, 1973.
62. Freidson, *Professional Dominance*, pp. 119–21.
63. D. Ingleby, 'Ideology and the Human Sciences', *The Human Context*, 2 (1970), 159–87: reprinted in *Counter Course*, ed. T. Pateman. Harmondsworth: Penguin, 1972.
64. M. Roth, 'Psychiatry and its Critics', *British Journal of Psychiatry*, 122 (1973), p. 374.
65. T. Parsons, *The Social System*. New York: Free Press, 1951.
66. D. Ewins, 'The Origins of the Compulsory Treatment Provisions of the Mental Health Act'. Unpublished MA thesis, University of Sheffield, 1974.
67. A. Treacher and G. Baruch, 'Towards a Critical History of the Psychiatric Profession', in Ingleby, *Critical Psychiatry*.
68. Ibid., p. 139.
69. I. Illich, *Disabling Professions*. London: Marion Boyars, 1977.
70. W. Mayer-Gross, E. Slater and M. Roth, *Clinical Psychiatry*. London: Cassell, 1960.
71. Foucault, *Surveiller et punir*.
72. D. Ingleby, 'Understanding "Mental Illness"', in Ingleby, *Critical Psychiatry*.
73. A. Clare, *Psychiatry in Dissent*. London: Tavistock, 1976.
74. W. Reich, 'Psychiatry's Second Coming', *Encounter*, 57 (1981), 66–72.
75. R.M. Murray, 'A Reappraisal of American Psychiatry', *The Lancet*, 3 February 1979, 255–8.
76. Ingleby, 'Understanding "Mental Illness"', p. 38.
77. Scull, *Museums of Madness*, p. 13.

78. J. Conolly, *An Inquiry into the Indications of Insanity.*
79. D. Armstrong, 'Madness and Coping', *Sociology of Health and Illness*, 2 (1980), 293–316.
80. J. Kovel, 'The American Mental Health Industry', in Ingleby, *Critical Psychiatry.*
81. M. Stone, 'The Origins of Clinical Psychology: Psychologists in Industry in the 1920s and 1930s'. Unpublished paper, London School of Economics.
82. D. Ingleby, 'The Psychology of Child Psychology', *The Human Context*, 5, (1973), 557–68: reprinted in *The Integration of a Child into a Social World*, ed. M.P.M. Richards. London: Cambridge University Press, 1974.
83. Kovel, 'The American Mental Health Industry', p. 98.
84. R. Jacoby, *Social Amnesia: A Critique of Conformist Psychology from Adler to Laing.* Boston: Beacon Press, 1975.
85. I.K. Zola, 'In the Name of Health and Illness: On Some Socio-political Consequences of Medical Influence', *Social Science and Medicine*, 9 (1975), 83–7.
86. P. Conrad and J.W. Schneider, *Deviance and Medicalization: From Badness to Sickness.* St Louis: Mosby, 1980.
87. C. Lasch, *Haven in a Heartless World: The Family Besieged.* New York: Basic Books, 1977.
88. P. Miller, 'Psychiatry – the Renegotiation of a Territory', *I&C*, 8 (1981), 97–121.
89. Donzelot, *La Police des familles.*
90. Foucault, *Madness and Civilization*, p. 46.
91. cf. Lasch, *Haven in a Heartless World.*
92. Donzelot, *La Police des familles*, p. 232.
93. Ibid.
94. Foucault, 'Truth and Power', p. 117.
95. Kovel, 'The American Mental Health Industry', p. 75.
96. G. Deleuze and F. Guattari, *L'Anti-Oedipe: capitalisme et schizophrenie.* Paris: Editions de Minuit, 1972. English trans., *Anti-Oedipus: Capitalism and Schizophrenia.* New York: Viking Press, 1977.
97. R. Castel, *Le Psychanalysme: L'ordre psychanalytique et le pouvoir.* Paris: Maspero, 1972.
98. D. Ingleby, 'Psychoanalysis and Ideology', in *Towards a Critical Psychology of Development*, ed. J.M. Broughton. New York: Plenum, (forthcoming).
99. Conrad and Schneider, *Deviance and Medicalization.*
100. Gerald Grob, *Mental Institutions in America: Social Policy to 1875.* New York: Free Press, 1973.
101. Szasz, *The Myth of Mental Illness.*
102. S. Sayers, Review of *Ideology and Insanity*, by Thomas Szasz, *The Human Context*, 7 (1975), 356–9.
103. Rothman, *Discovery of the Asylum.*
104. Freidson, *Professional Dominance.*
105. Conrad and Schneider, *Deviance and Medicalization.*
106. P.M. Strong, 'Sociological Imperialism and the Profession of Medicine: A Critical Examination of the Hypothesis of Medical Imperialism', *Social Science and Medicine*, 13A (1979), 199–216.

107. 'The Quaalude Scam', *Newsweek*, 28 September 1981, p. 47.
108. Castel, *L'ordre psychiatrique*.
109. Stone, 'The Origin of Clinical Psychology'.
110. Kovel, 'The American Mental Health Industry'.
111. cf. Clare, *Psychiatry in Dissent*.
112. N. Poulantzas, *State, Power, Socialism*. London: New Left Books, 1978.
113. Donzelot, *La Police des familles*, p. 232.
114. Foucault, 'Truth and Power', p. 119.
115. Foucault, 'Questions of Method: An Interview', *I&C*, 8 (1981), p. 4. (French version originally published in *L'impossible prison: Récherches sur le système penitentiaire au XIXe siècle*, ed. Michelle Perrot, Paris: Editions du Seuil, 1980.)
116. Jeff Coulter, *Approaches to Insanity*. London: Martin Robertson, 1973.
117. Ingleby, 'Social Construction of Mental Illness', p. 133.
118. P. Sedgwick, *Psycho Politics*. London: Pluto Press; New York, Harper and Row, 1982.
119. Ingleby, 'Understanding "Mental Illness"', p. 48.
120. D. Rosenhahn, 'On Being Sane in Insane Places', *Science*, 179 (1973), 250–8.
121. E. Goffman, *Asylums*. New York: Anchor, 1961; Harmondsworth: Penguin, 1968.
122. R.D. Laing and A. Esterson, *Sanity, Madness and the Family*. Volume 1: *Families of Schizophrenics*. London: Tavistock, 1964.
123. T. Scheff, *Being Mentally Ill: A Sociological Theory*. London: Weidenfeld and Nicolson, 1966.
124. J. Coulter, *The Social Construction of Mind*. London: Macmillan, 1979.
125. L. Fagin, *Unemployment and Health in Families*. London: Department of Health and Social Security, 1981.
126. Brown and Harris, *Social Origins of Depression*.
127. S. L. Bem, 'Sex Role Adaptability: One Consequence of Psychological Androgyny', *Journal of Personality and Social Psychology*, 42 (1975), 155–62.
128. cf. N. Chodorow, *The Reproduction of Mothering*. Berkeley: University of California Press, 1979.

Part II

Case Studies

8

Law, Order and Power in Late Seventeenth- and Early Eighteenth-century England

PAUL ROCK

Money . . . is the true Fuller's Earth for Reputations, there is not a Spot or a Stain but what it can take out. A rich Rogue now-a-days is fit Company for any Gentleman; and the World . . . hath not such a Contempt for Roguery as you imagine.

Peachum (Jonathan Wild), The Beggar's Opera, *Act 1, Scene IX.*

INTRODUCTION

This paper will offer a highly schematic and focused explanation of a few features of communal and organized crime at the beginning of the eighteenth century. It will largely concentrate on the negotiated character of criminal and social order. I intend my argument to illuminate the effects of rudimentary policing [1] and some special properties of moral status. That argument has been made possible by a deliberate arrangement of structural metaphors, an arrangement which can be justified only by principles of utility and parsimony. [2] It does not pretend to be comprehensive. Neither is it designed to capture any essential truths about criminal phenomena. Rather, it has knowingly neglected much that would prove interesting. For instance, there is no full discussion of the ordering of moral beliefs, although those beliefs furnished vitally important recipes for political action. There is no attempt at developmental analysis despite the enlightenment which would undoubtedly flow from an examination of the evolution of criminal processes. Mine will be a comparatively simple exercise in social statics, dwelling on the relationships between social distance, crime and the coercive capacity of the state. Such an exercise cannot assign logical or 'causal' primacy to the individual phenomena which it describes. It must merely insist on the analytic interdependence of its parts.

Source: International Annals of Criminology, Vol. 16, 1977.

DECENTRALIZATION AND FORMAL SOCIAL CONTROL

The quality of formal social control in England at the end of the seventeenth century stemmed chiefly from the peculiar geometry of its relations. The aggregations and concentrations of the English people gave rise to an irregular and uneven policing. They imposed and refracted markedly varying constraints on possibilities of central direction. Indeed, the very idea of *policing* is probably anachronistic, because there was then no counterpart to any contemporary agency. Certain areas were unpatrolled or unpatrollable, and they enjoyed an autonomy of state control. They developed about the external and internal frontiers of the country, transforming it into a landscape of regulated and deregulated regions. Some parts achieved a political consequence which translated the moral status of their inhabitants into a matter which demanded negotiation rather than simple control.

Gregory King's estimates suggested that England and Wales possessed a population of over 5 million which was spread most unevenly over their terrain.[3] While half a million people were congregated in London, 880,000 lived in the other cities and towns, and 4 million lived in villages and hamlets. Substantial tracts of England were an unpoliced wilderness without a system of established roads.[4] Such wild areas were inhabited by 'squatters' and 'heathers' who formed communities lying outside official management and constituting no recognized part of the political body.

Travel was hazardous, even inside London itself,[5] and roads were frequently impassable. There was no uniform or effective system of maintenance, and floods, ruts, quicksands, holes, subsidence and defective drainage so affected routes that they sometimes could not be used for long periods. In Sussex, for instance, travel was virtually abandoned during the winter months. Rogers states: 'in 1700 the roads [were] scarcely less dirty, dangerous and unreliable than they were in the Middle Ages.'[6] Riders could be thrown, carriages upset and heavy carts rendered useless. Journeys of even a few miles might take a considerable length of time and their success was always problematic. Places adjoining London were taken to be relatively inaccessible,[7] and Rogers describes Glasgow as having been 'unimaginably remote from southern England'.[8]

The social significance of distance and the practical reach of action were thus radically modified by the sheer physical difficulty of movement. Major relations were structured by the effort which was required to sustain them. But effective access was not only influenced by physical contingencies. It was also circumscribed by the illiteracy of many Englishmen.[9] In a society which was heavily dependent on oral communication and personal confrontation, the social world of most was confined and local.

It is therefore appropriate to portray England as a web of tenuously connected and necessarily self-supporting groupings. It was an array of separate areas which were distinguished by such marks of isolation as the possession of peculiar dialects and economic interests. So remote were some communities that local currencies had to be improvised when the central money supply failed.[10] Problems of central co-ordination were such that each county tended to display an appreciable political autonomy, an autonomy which was itself nurtured and defended by local elites.[11] The English counties were dominated by their own governments in miniature:

> the county was, not inappropriately, referred to as the 'country', for it was a microcosm of the nation, having its armed force, the militia; its judiciary, the justices in petty or quarter sessions; its local parliaments, such as the meetings of the lord lieutenant with the deputy lieutenants. . .[12]

At all levels, a fluid exchange of support and information between sectors of the country was obstructed. Not only was there an enforced immobility,[13] but there were few institutions devoted to the business of political co-ordination and the compilation of reports. For many practical purposes, a large number of communities were virtually self-policing. While the movement of groups regarded as deviant may have been hindered,[14] so also was that of agents of control. As Thompson observed, 'the provincial magistracy was often in extreme isolation. Troops, if they were sent for, might take two, three or more days to arrive, and the crowd knew this very well'.[15] Poor transport and communications reduced the radius of efficient military action,[16] and it was impossible for comparatively secluded populations to rely on useful relief from outside. Unless the members of a community armed themselves to form a surrogate militia, as the population of Goudhurst did to meet a group of smugglers,[17] the maintenance of a legally defined order could become most problematic. Throughout the late seventeenth and early eighteenth centuries, there were instances of areas being forcibly seized and held against control agencies. Thus, in 1670, the country about Kempsey was governed by a 'band of marauders',[18] and in 1692 a highwayman named Whitney offered to police the roads in exchange for a fee and a pardon. He claimed effective control over a sizeable portion of the country.[19]

THE COERCIVE INSTITUTIONS

The magnification of distances was probably less significant than the inability of the state to muster an appreciable institutional response to law-breaking. The state lacked the force to exact uniform compliance. Indeed, the Hammonds claimed that central government was in abeyance in the first decades of the eighteenth century.[20] The rudimentary formal control that did exist was exerted by four major organizations each offering a set of opportunities for the shaping of crime.

The Army

Any substantial congregation of vagrants, smugglers, poachers or robbers formed a grouping which could not be mastered by routine policing agencies. It constituted a mobilization of force which was overwhelming.[21] Henry Fielding remarked that constables were frequently reluctant to act, and 'they could not be blamed for not exposing themselves to sure destruction; for it is a melancholy truth that, at this very day, a rogue no sooner gives the alarm, within certain purlieus, than twenty or thirty armed villains are found ready to come to his assistance.'[22] Constables were, moreover, rooted to their own small policing districts and could not properly act outside them. Anyone who was mobile could fairly readily place himself outside the aegis of the constable's authority.[23] The constable's work was further complicated by his local links. He was nominally the occupant of an unpaid and voluntary position, returning to an unofficial place in the community after a period of duty. His implication in a network of relations inevitably constrained his ability to serve as an anonymous and authoritative agent of control. In consequence, 'the army was the only police force that stood between authority and anarchy, and the only preventive service that could enforce the revenue laws . . . It was impossible to put down even a formidable gang of poachers without the help of the military.'[24] The radical decentralization and enforced self-reliance of communal control thus made all but the most routine tasks onerous and uncertain. The army was the chief organization that could muster adequate force, numbers and institutional competence to manage particular problems of law enforcement. But it was an organization of last resort and was itself weak.

Partly because Britain lacked land frontiers, the role of a standing army became increasingly subordinated to that of the navy.[25] There was a steady decline in funds allotted for military purposes during the first decades of the eighteenth century,[26] and troops had to be scattered among small towns for their maintenance.[27] That shift in strategic emphasis was sponsored by those who resisted the establishment of a national, centralized army. Such a concentration of force could threaten local accumulations of power, accumulations which dispersed political control and strengthened oligarchy.[28] The bulk of defensive work became transferred to a militia which was under local rather than state supervision.[29] There was, in particular, a sustained opposition to the use of the army as a policing institution. The organizational base for a French system of *gendarmerie* was not only eroded, but there were gross political impediments to its emergence.[30] The Commonwealth had provided an earlier model of superintendence by an army acting as a police force, and it was a model that was effectively rejected by consequential groups.

The army could only be an instrument for the resolution of extraordinary crises. It was organizationally ill-equipped to perform work other than the suppression of riots, and even that work was held in disfavour by military authorities.[31] It was most generally summoned to handle specific episodes of social unrest, and its role was circumscribed functionally and temporally. The presence of troops appeared to generate friction,[32] and 'troops billeted in a town quickly became unpopular, even with those who had first called them in. With uncanny regularity requests for the aid of troops are followed . . . after an interval of five or six weeks, by petitions for their removal.'[33] The army could thus be a repressive implement, but it was incapable of engaging in the commonplace business of monitoring and detecting crime.[34] It represented a crude and insensitive solution to social problems, and individual or sporadic crimes were beyond its powers of management. Its control work can have had only the most oblique impact on the constitution of everyday criminality.

The Militia

The second major coercive institution was composed of the militia and trained bands. They were the armed forces of a decentralized and oligarchical authority, being locally recruited and based, and symbolizing opposition to a national system of social control.[35] But they, too, were ill-financed and often represented no more than a nominal force. Musters were infrequently held, armaments were defective, and there was no standardized supervision of their activity.[36] The militia proved an uncertain support for legal order. While it provided a rudimentary reserve against foreign invasion, it was held by some to be less sure in the settlement of domestic disputes.[37] On occasion, its embeddedness in local communities led it to become markedly partisan in its management of law-breaking. It was sometimes partial to those who attempted to resist the collection of taxes and revenues. It did little to restrain rioting in 1675, and troops had to be called in to replace its reluctant members.[38] Moreover, like the army, it was unable to undertake routine peace-keeping and detection work.[39] It was, again, employed chiefly as an agent of riot control, and it was inept at patrolling mundane criminal events. It formed one of the buttresses against political disorder, but its general influence seemed slight and it declined steadily throughout the eighteenth century.

The Constables

In the formal division of control work, the minute supervision of local populations was exercised by the constables and watch. They were required to regulate the activities of a community, enforcing an order upon all the detailed life of their social worlds. The crossing of parish boundaries was patrolled. In London, nightly checks were made on lodgers who had entered a district and watchmen were enjoined to arrest strangers. They were required to apprehend 'Nightwalkers, or any other persons whatsoever that are uncivil, or cannot give a good account of themselves, and the Reason for their being abroad. . . .'[40] The migrations of gipsies, labourers, fortune-tellers and peddlars were surveyed and directed. Those who wandered without a legitimate purpose could be handed from one constable to another across the parishes until they were returned to their last place of settlement. Within the boundaries, there was supposed to be a coerced hierarchy, decorum and order. Servants who had left employment without leave were controlled. Ale-houses were inspected, violations of the Sabbath suppressed, and gambling curtailed.[41] Constables could punish mothers bearing bastards, whip vagabonds, force the unwilling to work, uphold apprenticeship statutes, confine begging to the licensed, restrain lunatics and detain the suspicious. They also had to embark on fine detective and crime-control work. They were formally responsible for raising the hue and cry, apprehending criminals and housing them until they were charged.

The maintenance of control in local areas was often precarious. Constables were organized by procedures laid down by the Statute of Winchester, a statute that had been devised to manage a dispersed, settled and weak population.[42] They were based on a division of territory into policing districts that had been appropriate to medieval England. They fell under the supervision of numerous and competing authorities; were governed by diverse structures of rules; and could not engage in any concerted action.[43] They were able to exercise only the most limited powers of arrest and did not have to act outside their own, often Lilliputian, areas. In the City of London alone, for instance, there were 676 precincts.[44] They could not search or forcibly enter property. Their work had virtually no bureaucratic support, no system of records, and no effective mobilization of aid when they were confronted by numbers of antagonists. Generally serving for short terms, they achieved little professional competence and could not accumulate or transmit developed skills. So structurally orphaned were they that they were rendered no legal assistance for guidance or defence. If they were sued or tried, they were without institutional funds to pay fines or underwrite the costs of legal representation. They formed an amateur and often reluctant force. As largely unpaid officials, their commitment to the occupation tended to be slight.

The constabulary system was prone to break down whenever it confronted a substantial concentration of crime.[45] Although the constables may have been able to control the more visible activity of individuals or small groups, they could be defied by almost any organized or sizeable grouping.[46] Thus the mobile populations of vagrants represented a segment of society which fell outside effective management.[47] Again, the suppression of riots, as in Kendal in 1696 and in Coventry in 1705, was beyond the capacities of conventional policing.[48] There was therefore a token policing which appeared efficient only when the members of a community were geographically static, scattered and peaceable.

The Practical Diffusion of Violence

The weakness of public agencies was accompanied by a spread of corrective violence into private or semi-private control. England became transformed into a mosaic of petty organizations which grew up around the practical possibilities of aggression and defence. Force became a matter of opportunity rather than legal right. The distribution of private violence exerted a critical influence on the shaping of crime, the recruitment of victims and the experience of immunity. It rested on the power which flowed from wealth and social organization. Men were armed, and those who commanded resources could equip themselves with their own police forces.[49] Houses and estates were sometimes turned into fortified units that were designed to provide some security.[50]

Immunity in some areas could simply be grasped by force or organization. The boundaries between areas of private licence and public regulation were highly fluid during the late seventeenth and early eighteenth centuries. They were responsive to the application of violence, and the private area could be enlarged by those who possessed adequate coercive power.[51] Resistance enabled men to carve out regions of liberty for themselves.

In part, the capacity of groups to appropriate social space rested on a shift in the nature of violence that could be offered. In the middle of the sixteenth century were the beginnings of technical innovations in arms that subverted the basis of a feudal control scheme. The Statute of

Winchester had established a policing organization that depended on a special distribution of the means of violence. Authority and power could be decentralized because representatives of the state and sovereign possessed military skills and equipment which were denied the rest of the population. A combination of fortifications, the horse, armour and the stirrup were too formidable to be resisted by an ill-armed people fighting on foot.[52] Centrifugal political tendencies can emerge when groups are radically differentiated in their ability to procure weapons and training in combat.[53] Such superiority enables those charged with control work to be widely dispersed. It led to a style of devolution which continued to underpin police methods at the beginning of the eighteenth century.

Yet the spread and improvement of firearms had brought about a minor revolution in relations between state and populace. The development of cheap, efficient and portable guns threw the prevailing balance of power out of joint. In particular, the invention of the flintlock gave individuals a new range and a new power to intimidate.[54] First introduced in about 1635, it came into widespread use by the end of the century.[55] It led to a democratization of violence. In Europe, the appearance of such handguns was partially responsible for the growth of standing armies under the command of a central authority. It prepared the way for an implosion of power. Those armies could be put to the work of organizing domestic social control. But in England, as I have argued, the army played a much more modest part and was relatively incapable of counteracting the effects of the new distribution of violence. There arose a corresponding uncertainty in policing. Smugglers, poachers and footpads were more nearly equal to those charged with their suppression.[56] There were, moreover, new forms of crime attendant upon the dispersal of force. Thus it is possible that the evolution of the highwayman may be attributed to the spread of light arms.[57]

England was fissured to form an agglomerate of largely independent groupings which were capable of wielding impressive force in their own right. Their allegiance to royal and state institutions was occasionally problematic. The revolts of 1640, 1688, 1715 and 1745 illustrate how militarily and politically autonomous some significant segments could become. In 1715, for example, the outcome of the Jacobite rebellion hinged chiefly on the ability of oligarchs loyal to the Hanoverians to defeat those allied to the Pretender. One of the most critical phases of the rebellion was resolved by the capacity of the army of tenants mustered by the Earl of Sunderland to overwhelm the forces of the Earl of Seaforth and the Marquis of Huntley. In that encounter, they underscored the extent to which private groups could detach themselves and become the possessors of formidable power. Such groups could uphold a practical and *de facto* order which was only tangentially related to legally constituted government. The state held no monopoly over the exercise of violence:

> The power of the seventeenth-century gentry was sanctioned by violence: riding out against their enemies, ham-stringing their neighbour's dogs, beating their farmers' sons, or shooting down their riotous labourers. They played ducks and drakes with the law when it suited them, breaking with impunity what they were supposed to maintain.[58]

When the state could guarantee neither physical security nor legal control, effective government passed in large measure over to those who were independently powerful. Political order was mediated by webs and hierarchies which developed around local centres of influence. Those networks were structured by access to the Court and by the possibilities that were afforded by command over territory and people.[59] Patronage bestowed order on the otherwise rudimentary structures created by a weak government and a weak system of communal control. Relations with a patron knit the client into a fluid system of power which substantially replaced formal state government. Positions within that system were personally awarded and personally exploited. Offices, prerogatives and franchises became items of property that were practically removed from external supervision.[60]

Patronage, in turn, was crystallized by one of the most pervasive models of political organization, the transformation of society into a collection of domains managed by a small number of powerful families.[61] Membership of a central family, or its contractual equivalent in the form of a connection with a patrimonial bureaucracy, defined a person's substantial worth and privilege. It produced a population which possessed an effective immunity against the exercise of almost all legal regulation.[62] Significantly, the moral status of the patron or the well patronized could neutralize virtually every form of deviancy but treason, itself a fundamental attack on the moral basis of hierarchy. Thus, although a number of peers were tried for murder by the House of Lords between 1660 and 1702, no penalties were inflicted on them.[63] Such trials may have had some limited symbolic effect, but it appears that they were never intended to inflict significant stigma or pain. Indeed, Hay has argued 'the private manipulation of the law by the wealthy and powerful was in truth a ruling-class conspiracy, in the most exact meaning of the word'.[64] Similarly, Defoe observed 'the Gentry and Magistrates of the Kingdom, while they execute . . . Laws upon us the poor Commons, and themselves practising the same Crimes, in defiance of the Laws both of God and Man, go unpunish'd'.[65]

THE TRANSFORMATION OF COMMUNITY AND POPULATION

Officially, the practice of shedding responsibility forced communities to assume corporate liability for crime. A parish formed one of the few identifiable and permanent structures which could be administratively absorbed into the formal control system. It was required to pay indemnities to those who were robbed while travelling in its area, although that obligation was waived at night and on Sundays. It was also supposed to constitute itself into a collective police force, the hue and cry, and those who did not respond to a muster could be punished. Hue and cry transformed the community into a group of vigilantes, the *posse comitatus*, who were expected to hunt the criminal in periods of crisis. The poverty of formal patrolling and policing was ostensibly remedied by casting the entire adult male population into the role of constable.

In the eighteenth century, the hue and cry seemed to be principally successful against isolated and unarmed people who were conspicuous strangers. Its effectiveness depended, too, on a quarry being comparatively incapable of travelling with any speed to a refuge which might confer anonymity. Urbanization was tending to render the *posse* somewhat anachronistic. It might have countered one who fled on foot to unpopulated territory, but around London, for instance, it was difficult to single him out from anyone else. John Fielding argued:

> at a [great] distance from London . . . it would be absolutely impossible for any villain in the country to escape justice; but near London I apprehend [the hue and cry] would lose its affect, not only from the vast variety of passengers on the road, mounted and dressed alike; but if they should not succeed before the rogue reaches London, seeking him there, by means of the hue and cry, would be fruitless indeed.[66]

The hue and cry was not able to produce any substantial concerted activity or prolonged pursuit. It was a local response which was spatially confined because of the difficulties of movement. It was also cumbersome to organize, and the responsibility for its mobilization seemed undefined until quite late. Before 1735, it appears that its raising was supposed to proceed almost spontaneously.[67] Moreover, like the army and the militia, it did not form a skilled policing response, able to pursue regular detective or patrolling work. It presented no more than a sporadic and weak restraint in those areas where crime was at all common.

Partly as a remedy for defective policing,[68] and partly as its cause,[69] social control was formally delegated to the entire population. The inhabitants of England were turned policemen on themselves. Throughout the eighteenth century, the state depended on private self-interest as its cardinal means of exerting control.[70] People were methodically bribed, exhorted and coerced to transform themselves into agents of the state. The management of deviance was forced to become a matter of personal enterprise. Since 1691, legislation routinely offered considerable rewards for the successful prosecution of certain offences. The scope of crimes covered by such rewards was steadily enlarged until it embraced burglary, house-breaking, horse-stealing, highway robbery and the like. State rewards became systematically supplemented by other sums offered by insurance companies, the excise and voluntary associations. Neighbours, friends and associates of the victim might also contribute to particular rewards. It eventually became a matter of course for the victim himself to promise a reward, often by public advertisement. So commonplace did this practice become that a failure to follow it could be construed as a tacit condoning of an offence.[71] The business of crime control became entrepreneurial, an area to be exploited for gain by small organizations devoted to thieftaking.[72]

Coercion was supplied by a major strategy that was designed to make deviants accessible to enforcement work. In the absence of any official procedures for accomplishing the business of detection, criminals were sealed against much formal control. For some purposes, they had to be treated as the population of a virtually independent region. It is significant that the epithet 'thieves' republic' was to become common, indicating an appreciation of the independence of deviant worlds. When they could not be adequately surveyed from without, techniques had to be deployed to make them visible. Those techniques rested on the standard diplomatic devices of subversion and disruption.[73] An internal disunity was fostered to throw up information that could never have been otherwise obtained. As Winslow observed, 'the greatest threat to the individual smuggler . . . appears to have been neither the revenue officers nor the Army and Fleet, but rather the informer.'[74] People were encouraged to inform on others in order to gain their own pardon. In some cases, the statutes stipulated that the informer should not himself be in custody if he sought a pardon. In others, it was laid down in a utilitarian fashion that he must bring about the conviction of a certain number of offenders or a conviction for a crime that was more heinous than his own. Arrested suspects were urged to turn evidence in an effort to win their freedom.

Impeachment might have granted the informer a limited or major immunity against prosecution, and much legal process was designed to promote the defection of criminals. Such a systematic use of the pardon made possible the acquisition of what was tantamount to a licence to commit crime. For instance, under an Act of William and Mary, a person who was not in custody and who brought about the conviction of two or more persons guilty of highway robbery could earn a free pardon for all similar crimes which he may have committed before he had impeached his associates.[75]

Accomplices were enjoined to turn on one another. Thieves were set against receivers. It was intended to introduce a fundamentally divisive element into criminal organization, and that intention would seem to have been partially realized. The tactic of flourishing pardons engendered suspicion and disarray. For instance, one of the participants in a mail robbery revealed how the threat of competitive impeachments could undermine solidarity. That participant, Wilson, recalled how he had been shown a letter by a Post-Officer:

> 'Sir, I am one of the Persons who robbed the Mails, which I am sorry for; and to make Amends, I'll secure my two Companions as soon as may be: He whose Hand this shall appear to be, I hope will be entitled to the Reward and his pardon.' As soon as I read it, I knew it to be *Sympson's* Letter, so that without any more Words I made a Discovery and I am of Opinion that any Man in *England* would have done the same. That League of Friendship which was between us was certainly dissolved by this Design against me. As for those who talk of Solemn Oaths and Protestations, I can assure them never were any such amongst us; and if there had, no Oath is binding. . . .[76]

The fear of impeachment often led associates to scramble among themselves for the privileged status of informer. One arrest could produce long chains of prosecutions. The state came to rely progressively on such machinations. As Thompson observed, 'in the state papers we seem to meet a society of creeps and informers'.[77] Government accordingly was involved in the generation of two distinct planes of regulation. On one plane, law and policing agencies tried to manufacture a moral universe whose contours and consequences were clear. There was a lucid dramatization of the properties of social order. A great number of offences were made capital. Gallows confessions, sermons, legal statutes, jurisprudence and judicial pronouncements emphasized the magnitude of the divide which separated the wicked from the good. The criminal and the deviant were thrust out beyond the margins of propriety, and order was ritually affirmed. On the other plane, however, everyday control practices systematically made those margins ambiguous and murky. The consequences of law were eminently negotiable. Legal penalties and inducements combined to create an equivocal, malleable and complex scheme which could be exploited by the knowing. In the case of hanging, for instance, the death sentence was attached to numerous offences but comparatively few people were actually executed. Hall argued, 'in the early part of the eighteenth century the persons, lay and official, who administered the criminal law, invented and indulged in practices which almost nullified the capital penalty in most non-clergable offences'.[78] Law was open to ample bargaining and collusion. Deviant populations could not be immediately controlled, and command over information conferred a power which could affect most court proceedings. Justice came to resemble a market place in which an elaborate trading economy developed. The moral and the immoral, the regulated and the regulators, came to be utterly entangled in one another.

THE POSSIBILITIES OF AUTONOMY

I have argued that policing was most irregular. It was shaped by power and influence; it was distorted by geographical contingencies; it revolved around the distribution of population; and it made available different opportunities for negotiation and accommodation. Such variable control reflected and encouraged the emergence of multiple relations with the political centre. The country's communities and regions were presented with diverse possibilities of establishing a place within the legal and moral order. Some were wholly subordinate to the centre, some evolved modes of compromise with it, and others were relatively free of its influence. When central direction was precarious, the nature and significance of illegality were substantially defined by its social location. Indeed, even so small an area as London was popularly mapped out into districts which carried radically contrasting moral connotations. Rogers remarks that in The Dunciad, for example, 'a topographic identity becomes a moral equivalence'.[79]

A number of areas were virtually autonomous of formal social control. Powerful figures and communities became detached from the centre for the purpose of undertaking criminal enterprises. Social regions could become independent on occasion because those held responsible for administering justice were themselves implicated in law-breaking.[80] In a division of labour based on geographical segregation, entire communities could pursue wrecking, smuggling or poaching as collective projects. Just as the southern border towns of the United States are now sometimes given to wholesale participation in smuggling, so coastal towns in England had widely ramifying communal involvements in crime. Thus Romney in Kent was so taken up with smuggling that revenue officers were unable to safely consign those whom they had arrested to the town's gaol. Even the mayor supported smuggling. Similarly, in 1708 the magistrates of Wigtown were involved with the smugglers who attacked the revenue officers; 'Robert Walpole, a JP of Norfolk, had smugglers call regularly at his back door at Houghton and even used an Admiralty barge to run his wine up the Thames';[81] and a justice of the peace led a group of smugglers who assailed the salt-officer at Conway in 1712.[82] In the instance of wrecking, too, Rule observes 'it shows how strong was the local strength of tradition if such a form of criminal action could be persistently employed by the whole community'.[83]

As important was the preservation of urban areas which retained much of the character of the medieval sanctuaries. Some, like the liberties of the Fleet, Marshalsea and King's Bench Prisons, were protected by statute.[84] Within their bounds, prisoners could purchase an immunity from the enforcement of much legislation.[85] They represented rich farms to be managed by prison administrators for profit. Other areas held on to an immunity long after the formal abolition of their privileges. The sanctuaries had originally been districts which fell under a lay or ecclesiastical jurisdiction that was independent of royal control. One form was the temporary refuge offered by all churches and churchyards. Fugitives could enjoy a limited safety there if they submitted to a discipline and agreed to abjure the realm within forty days.[86] Such a practice was effectively banned by the middle of the sixteenth century, but another kind of sanctuary persisted in law and then in fact for several hundred years more. This more significant form, perpetual sanctuary, constituted an extreme instance of franchise.[87] Its legal status was tantamount to that of a foreign territory, not dissimilar to the contemporary embassy. Representing the domain of some powerful authority, it fell outside the reach of royal justice. Its inhabitants 'took a new oath of allegiance and obeyed a new sovereign and a new law, which could protect them against any other. . . .'[88]

The independence of the original perpetual sanctuaries was progressively eroded from the fifteenth century onwards. The early legislation of Henry VIII was supplemented by Acts of 1604, 1606, 1623, 1693, 1722 and 1727. Yet a few of the sanctuaries survived because the state lacked the power to eradicate them all. A marriage between geographical advantage and organizational strength allowed the Mint, the Savoy, Whitefriars, St Giles and other districts to retain their autonomy. Like the rural communities of smugglers and wreckers, the thieves' districts of London enjoyed considerable stability. As Pike remarks,

> Sanctuaries . . . were for many generations stronger than a medieval

police or ambitious law-givers. In the reign of William III not only were there sanctuaries in England, but they existed in places not even mentioned in the statute of Henry VIII. . . . In London and its neighbourhood they abounded.[89]

The sanctuaries were spaces appropriated from central and local government. They were held by law, by tradition or by force. They concentrated populations, established styles of collective life, and set up frontiers between centrally dominated and privately governed space. Growing up around an area of religious or lay power, a particularly stigmatized district (such as a leper hospital or an insane asylum) or a geographically propitious region, they became organized and relatively permanent. Those sanctuaries which could not claim a direct charter were often supported in their claims by forged documents.[90] Others simply formed places which were maintained against law enforcement agents, places that could not be easily gained or regained. In a sense, they were functionally and historically akin to the *seigneuries collectives* which the guilds of Europe had attempted to found. Such collective lordships were able to act as appreciable rivals to the barony and the king. They were endowed with privileges, the right to jurisdiction, and a region which was their own. In some instances, they offered protection to criminal fugitives.[91] The London guilds sometimes managed to acquire these lordships, either by open charter or by surreptitious means.[92] London in the fifteenth and sixteenth centuries contained a number of areas of semi-private jurisdiction.

It is plausible that the latterday bastard sanctuaries of the seventeenth and early eighteenth centuries preserved something of the nature of the districts once controlled by the *seigneuries collectives*. It is certainly the case that English professional crime took on many of the trappings of the fraternity or mystery, that it resembled the guild in its purpose and structure. First emerging at some time in the fourteenth century,[93] it revolved around a division of labour, an apprenticeship system, patterns of mutual support, the exclusion of outsiders, and the construction of a community of colleagues.[94] Central problems and practices were celebrated in a special language which often assumed an arcane and intricate form. For instance, the business of picking pockets or engaging in confidence games was lent structure by a highly developed vocabulary which described all the salient roles and procedures of the craft.[95] Such crime was typically the work of small, intimate groups who collaborated together over long stretches of time. Through apprenticeship and closure, the world of many professional criminals became stabilized and isolated. There are, for example, revealing continuities between the work styles and terminology of the sixteenth-century pickpocket and his heir in contemporary England and America.[96]

Unwin has argued that guilds and their unofficial surrogates, the adulterine guilds, represented the predominant organizational style of almost all groups at the time when professional crime acquired its initial form. The guild, in turn, hinged on the fraternity:

> there can be no manner of doubt that society in the 14th and 15th centuries was literally honeycombed with fraternities in every direction. . . . That of this great mass of social activity we should know so little is simply due to the secretive nature of the facts.[97]

Secrecy was grossly enhanced when the activity that was organized was itself unambiguously deviant. Yet, *a priori*, it seems reasonable to suppose that the fraternity served as a model for criminals and outlaws as well as for those following legal pursuits. In a society displaying a poverty of organizational metaphors, where the typical social unit was small and the craft monopolized occupational structures, the choices available to those managing problems of social co-operation were most restricted. Many pariah and dispossessed groups *did* adopt the fraternal form as a matter of course.[98] For example, the highly stigmatized occupation of coal-heaving was made up of men who, when some amelioration of their conditions was proposed, '*naturally* sought to organize themselves into a fraternity, such as that of the Billingsgate porters who were "free" of the city'.[99] Indeed, the fraternity suggested a most useful pattern for any clandestine group which affected secrecy and rested on solidarity. Contemporary descriptions of criminal groups may simply have borrowed from readily available simile. Yet there tended to be a routine dependence on the language of the craft or mystery. Vagrants, vagabonds, confidence tricksters, thieves, prostitutes and cheats were regularly portrayed as if they constituted some version of the adulterine guilds.

The sanctuaries may then be regarded as the domain of *de facto* collective lordships which seized regions and held them. They formed natural areas governed by a specific, illegitimate segment of society. The originating charters of the sanctuaries might have proved useful to those who sought immunity,[100] but, in practice, they had been superseded by claims based on force, special calling and custom. Just as there was a goldsmiths' or a bankers' quarter in a London that was occupationally segregated into different districts, so there were a number of criminal quarters under the dominion of those who practised illegal mysteries. One such area was described by Ward in 1709, and his account strongly conveys an impression of the sheer density of the deviant populations of certain districts:

We steer'd our course up *Salisbury-court* where every two or three steps we met some Old Figure or another, that look'd as if the *Devil* had Rob'd em of their *Natural Beauty*. . . . *Theft, Whoredom, Homicide* and *Blasphemy*, peep'd out at the very Windows of their *Soul; Lying Perjury, Fraud, Impudence,* and *Misery*, were the only *Graces* of their *Countenance*. . . . All this part, quite up to the Square, is a *Corporation of Whores, Coiners, Highway-Men Pick-Pockets,* and *House-Breakers*; who, like *Bats* and *Owls*, Sculk in Obscure Holes by Day-Light, but Wander in the Night in Search of Opportunities wherein to Exercise their Villainy.[101]

Indeed, despite its relatively small size, London was most heterogeneous.[102] The localism and decentralization of the country were reflected in microcosms in its capital city. London was divided up into diverse areas which were highly distinctive. Its growth had been so rapid and ill-planned that its various parts lacked cohesion and organization. Districts and villages had been absorbed and fused to become a collection of areas without a recognizable centre. The disparities between the parts were reinforced by the absence of a network of roads providing ready access from one area to another. What roads there were tended to be badly maintained and often dangerous,[103] and it was physically difficult to move about the metropolis. Such hindrances were further aggravated by the proliferation of 'dangerous districts' and unpatrolled spaces into which it was thought perilous to wander.[104] Travel at night was especially hazardous because of the unlit, narrow and pitted nature of the streets.

People usually lived in or near their workplace, grouped together with others who followed a similar trade.[105] Most areas were thus relatively homogeneous: distinguished by a separate mode of occupation; following a distinct timetable; differentiated from one another by the wealth of their inhabitants; and forming largely self-contained worlds which emphasized particular styles of life. The populations of neighbouring districts were often kept apart by a great social distance. London constituted a mosaic of discrete and bounded areas. Addison remarked, for example:

When I consider this great city in its several quarters and divisions, I look upon it as an aggregate of various nations, distinguished from each other by their respective customs and interests. . . . In short, the inhabitants of St James' notwithstanding they live under the same laws, and speak the same language, are a distinct people from those of Cheapside, who are likewise removed from those of the Temple on the one side, and those of Smithfield on the other, by several climates and degrees in their ways of thinking and conversing together.[106]

The congregations of criminals in the bastard sanctuaries not only reflected the radical diversity of London, and were not simply an ecological counterpart of the areas in which weavers or chandlers gathered: they also represented the internal marches of the city.[107] The policing, administration and jurisdiction of London were splintered and stratified in an extraordinarily complex fashion. The various parts that came to form the greater metropolis retained most of their original institutions of control, and the resulting whole contained abundant anomalies and conflicts. London was governed by a number of distinct and autonomous authorities who 'had little to do with each other and, as far as they were concerned, ruled the separate kingdoms'.[108] Burgesses' courts, manorial courts, magistrates' courts, the courts of the City Companies, sheriffs' courts and aldermanic courts vied with one another. Separate police agencies patrolled their several districts and precincts. Beadles, javelin men, constables, watchmen, sheriffs' officers, the train bands, City Marshals, magistrates' assistants and King's Messengers attempted to impose some order, but their work was not co-ordinated. It lacked central direction or even a precise demarcation of tasks. Different organizations maintained their own goals and prisons, and Defoe observed: 'There are in London . . . more public and private prisons, and houses of confinement, than any city in Europe, perhaps as many as in all the capital cities put together.'[109]

The city was thus carved up into a welter of sectors of control. The principal administrative regions fell under the Cities of London and Westminster and the counties of Surrey and Middlesex. Within these regions there was a mass of individual districts. Political and geographical areas did not necessarily coincide, and the divisions often appeared most arbitrary. The areas themselves were frequently characterized by jurisdictional uncertainty, particularly at their boundaries. Indeed, Rudé states that Westminster's government was 'for many years a jungle of rival jurisdictions'.[110]

Between and within such regions there were abundant zones that were marked by ambiguity. On the frontiers between different jurisdictions were to be discovered places that were not clearly regulated by any single authority or by any authority at all. 'The activities of constable and watchman were for the most part limited to his own parish, precinct or liberty, and where the authorities of city and county marched there was every opportunity for the development of little Alsatias.'[111] [112] Bastard sanctuaries were threaded along these borders. St Giles's, for example, was officially sited in neither Westminster nor the City but abutted on both.[113]

The strength of the sanctuaries was supported even further by their internal design.[114] Since 1580, there had been a series of attempts to prevent the physical growth of London. Coupled with restrictions aimed at controlling the spread of plague, these proscriptions made it illegal to erect buildings on new foundations. For about a century, any construction work had to take place covertly in areas that were already built up. New buildings became ever more dense because a substantial proportion of the rapidly increasing population were denied work in the City of London. Since few were freemen, they were debarred from pursuing trades there. More and more buildings were consequently piled into a belt fringing on the City's liberties. Effective authority to restrain development was at its weakest in that interstitial zone, the zone which formed the ring of debatable jurisdictions. Building regulations were systematically evaded by making new structures as unobtrusive as possible. Areas that conferred invisibility on construction were fully exploited. Behind walls and at a distance from public space, courts and yards were built up, alleys were narrowed, cellars extended and garrets put to use. There thus arose a great maze of intricate passages and huddled buildings that were compressed into the interstices of official power. One area was actually named the 'Caribee Islands' because of its topographical complexity. Deteriorated and adapted by the beginning of the eighteenth century, those mazes proved almost impossible for enforcement agents to penetrate.[115]

Ecology, stigma, organization and custom conspired together to preserve the sanctuaries. Some of their last legal privileges were lost in 1727, but they continued as if no law had been passed. For instance, mid-nineteenth-century descriptions of the Mint and St Giles's reveal little change in the areas.[116] Thus Binney discussed the Mint of the late 1840s as 'a well-known harbour of low-characters, [containing] knots of thieves at the corners of the different streets',[117] and Beames remarked that 'rookeries still survive by their very isolation, by their retention of past anomalies'.[118]

THE MEDIATIONS OF POWER

The criminal areas of the country and town are examples of structures which defied direct formal control. Their regulation had often to be mediated and tortuous, involving processes of suborning and the brokerage of power. Attempts to impose order were sometimes more redolent of conciliation and diplomatic manoeuvre than straightforward command. Those attempts illustrate how criminality was negotiated rather than awarded, entailing a practical recognition of political necessity.

Internally, English society was arranged into a series of groupings which enjoyed vastly discrepant privileges. The least powerful were in no position to barter for the significance of their actions or their selves. They were the objects of an uncomplicated repression, governing their movement, employment and behaviour. The meanings of that group were defined by a particular vision of the social order. It was a vision infused with organic imagery, an imagery which depicted the state as a corporate being with distinct outlines and an inner differentiation of unlike parts. The social organism excluded many. It was constituted by groups which performed fixed and identifiable functions. Those groups represented the only authentic components of society, the only members entitled to recognition as the morally substantial: 'The freeholder on the land and the freeman in the town were, each in his own sphere, the accredited elements in a society, in comparison with which other men appeared, not as rival classes, but as adjuncts or excrescences, or even social dangers.'[119] Indeed, in an organic language, the politically marginal were a disordering agent akin to disease, parasite or pathology. Much of the writing on crime alluded to the emergence of epidemics and disorders which plagued the body politic. The outsider was not a natural feature of social organization. Thus Nourse condemned the hiring of an excessive number of servants, arguing 'tho' they seem to be a Part of the Body, and to add to the Bulk, [they] do in Truth suck the best Juice to themselves, whilst the genuine Parts languish and decay'.[120]

Groups lying outside the approved contours of society were not awarded the same worth as those firmly embedded within them. They were taken to be less than fully human, a qualitatively different breed of men who required special treatment. All their actions were necessarily tinged with their twin qualities of dangerousness and devalued social status. When regulation rested on the maintenance of an uncertain correspondence between private interest and a special conception of the corporate good, those without a manifest commitment to the political order were alien and threatening. As strangers, they did not merit the same concern as those who were secure. The significance of what they did and who they were was thus quite different from that of the morally grounded population. Large segments of that penumbral group were expected to be hanged as a matter of course. The wandering and the rootless, the gipsy and the unpropertied, the follower of a disreputable trade were assumed to be preordained for execution.[121] It was the offender, not the offence, which fixed the meaning of law-breaking: 'The privileged might often commit great crimes with impunity; for petty offences the unprivileged were hanged.'[122]

By contrast, some groupings not only served as the principal dispensers of justice but were themselves too powerful to be wholly exposed to it. The holders of wealth and authority were able to translate their activities into areas free of almost all interference. Indeed, 'liberty' was defined as the right to an independence of external control. Those who enjoyed such liberty occupied a place which neutralized many of the more conventional connotations of their acts. Peers could do murder with considerable impunity, and Ogg states that their trials in the House of Lords 'usually had an element of farce'.[123] A systematic resort to patronage afforded some groups the opportunity to acquire an unofficial licence to break the law. Highwaymen, for example, were at one time heavily recruited from the ranks of the powerful,[124] and they were buttressed by protective associations which reduced their chances of being executed. Although pardon did not mechanically follow conviction, and many highwaymen were hanged, a substantial measure of immunity could be achieved by such men.[125]

That shaping of invulnerability and freedom was also to be discovered in the formal organization of the state. Offices in a patrimonial bureaucracy were generally held to be proper sources of private profit. Those who secured posts as governors, prison administrators, city marshals, government ministers and the like were led to treat their positions as something like personal property.[126] Many offices were purchased, sometimes in competitive auction. The expenses that were laid out had to be offset by the money that could be earned by the official.[127] Offices in agencies of social control were almost invariably bought, and their incumbents were tacitly allowed to reimburse themselves by means of bribery and extortion.[128] When some scandal occurred, the business of official extortion was usually defined as tolerable provided certain implicit limits had been respected. Thus the Earl of Macclesfield, while Lord Chancellor, was found guilty of embezzling some £100,000 of chancery funds. He defended himself by asserting that such appropriations had 'long been practiced without blame'; was fined £30,000; and received a promise from the king that the fine would be repaid to him from the privy purse.[129] The powerful were therefore occasionally encouraged to describe criminality as a normal and largely uncontrolled feature of their work. Offices represented protected areas of law-breaking even within the confines of law-enforcing bodies.

Legitimate concentrations of power accordingly constituted structures which were granted an impressive autonomy. They deflected most regulation. Concentrations of illegitimate power also presented obstacles to regulation. They had a political consequence in their own terrain which sometimes rivalled that of government. They could be managed either by subversion or by co-option. That policy of co-option, in turn, conferred some stability and *de facto* legitimacy on areas of criminal enterprise. An orderly institutionalization and incorporation of criminal sectors was one strategy of a weak government, and it rendered the very meaning of criminality uncertain. Piracy offers an important illustration of that form of translation of legality.

Until the end of the eighteenth century, the seas around Britain were never completely controlled by the navy. Although the volume of piracy fluctuated, the state was rarely able to suppress it.[130] Acts might have been passed to order its elimination, but there was no policing agency to implement them fully. Instead, the state was sometimes constrained to recruit pirates themselves to patrol the seas.[131] Pirates were co-opted to serve as privateers or, indeed, as adjuncts to the navy during wartime. In this fashion, the management of piracy turned as much on bribery and alliance as on simple conflict. Pirates could not be easily suppressed because they were the major possessors of force. Possessing the means of violence, they were useful as privateers; they could be supported by foreign states; or they could take virtual command over territories, a command which bestowed a tenuous legality on their activities. Madagascar and the West Indies formed such bases at one time. The governors of the American colonies, too, were quite frequently prepared to grant letters of marque to pirates. It appears that they were tacitly supposed to supplement their incomes with the profits of raids. Piracy was often an entrepreneurial exercise funded by the wealthy and the powerful. Some expeditions even gained royal patronage. The seas were thus politically and legally ambiguous areas which were open to complicated processes of compromise and exploitation. The status of pirates was quite indefinite:

> In international affairs . . . the distinction between enemy and criminal is a nice one . . . [the difference between pirate and privateer] relates more to power and to claims to legitimacy than to the actual activities of the pirates or their protectors.[132]

Those with influence in the criminal regions were sometimes of too great a moment to be treated with any stance but deference, a deference which might be generalized. One highwayman, for example, was able to become Attorney General.[133] Pirates could be knighted.[134] Indeed, there was some mobility between the legal and illegal centres of power. Just as pirates might become respectable, so the respectable could turn pirate or highwayman. There was an occasional equivalence of authority and command which eased a transition in the ambiguous area of the independently powerful. There were real structural affinities between the organizations which incorporated legitimate and illegitimate enterprises. Officers in patrimonial bureaucracy were prone to profiteering, blurring the moral character of their undertaking. Members of criminal corporations sometimes turned to apparently benevolent activity, blurring the immorality of their projects. Viewed naively, the difference between the acts of a City Marshal like Charles Hitchen and a receiver and thieftaker like Jonathan Wild is very slight. Each was able to accuse the other of criminality and corruption. Each claimed a public usefulness for his own role. While Hitchen was dismissed for corrupt practices and then reinstated, Wild believed himself entitled to petition for the honour of the freedom of the City of London. It was perhaps only a nominal distinction which fixed what and who were criminal. Indeed, Wild was to serve as a symbolic archetype for satires on Hanoverian government, the affinities being emphasized in criticisms of Walpole and his ministers.[135] Wild became Walpole and Walpole Wild. As Thompson argued,

> an examination of the practices of the administration in these years reveals the same use of informers and evidences, employment of blood-money, the same casual sacrifice of colleagues who had outlived their utility, and a similar parasitism upon the public. . . . The 'subculture' of the Hanoverian Whig and the 'subculture' of Jonathan Wild were mirror-images of one another.[136]

On a more modest scale, the contingencies of social control forced the state to recruit the deviant as its own agent. Diffusely, such recruitment took the guise of the specific and temporary contracts which marked the employment of the reward and pardon system. Accused men became temporary instruments of government. More particularly, that tendency to recruitment led official institutions to hire pirates as pirate-catchers, smugglers as revenue-officers,[137] thieves as thieftakers and poachers as gamekeepers. In France, one of the most celebrated of all policemen, Vidocq, was himself rescued from the world of deviants and sent back to control it.[138] Few but those personally schooled in deviant practices were able to acquire the expertise of a competent enforcement agent. Such men, in turn, often played equivocal roles, acting as the middlemen of crime.[139] Serving as factors, they mediated the operation of law. They defined the immunities and vulnerabilities of criminal and allegedly criminal populations.

The most significant development of that role of middleman was realized in the eighteenth-century thieftaker. Thieftakers were not original to that time, but they came to a special prominence in the economy of rewards and pardons created by the state.[140] Thieftakers could not borrow from any body of knowledge or practice produced by formal agencies of control. Theirs could also be a dangerous undertaking because it lacked effective support in a situation where violence was common. Since it was not eased by any considerable exchange of information and aid, it became practised by those who merged imperceptibly with the world which they were supposed to regulate. It became the special province of those who exercised some initial command in that world. Those who were best positioned structurally were the receivers, and receivers either became thieftakers or were displaced by them.[141] The thieftaker-receiver existed on the interface between the reputable and the disreputable. He was armed with the ability to impeach the older receiver and to control competition. He had some capacity to restrict the potential treachery of clients and informers. Further, his domination of routine policing enabled him to work outside official scrutiny. Enjoying a practical immunity, which was strengthened by the collusive aid of official enforcement agents, he could retain his organizational integrity at a time when other groups were in some disarray. He held one other major advantage. Because he was one of the few people who were properly and professionally engaged in trafficking between criminals and non-criminals, he was provided with a useful front. His dealings could be explained as part of a legitimate calling. His clients were dependent on him, but it was not necessarily a reciprocal dependence. Receivers have often informed, but their clients tend to protect them.[142]

The thieftakers relied on an intimate acquaintance with deviance, and, because their stake in it was principally financial, they often husbanded and encouraged crime in order to develop a flow of useful and manageable cases.[143] Thus Mandeville alluded to the 'Damage the Public sustains from the Trade that is drove by the Thiefcatchers, and the various ways now in vogue of compounding Felonies, by which the Safety as well as Maintenance of Thieves and Pilferers are industriously taken care of, and the Laws that enforce prosecution altogether eluded'.[144] Thieftakers might support thieves, afford them protection and ensure their immunity. In many instances, they monopolized police work and enjoyed total discretion over the selection of those who would be arraigned. Howson has remarked that the manipulation of rewards and pardons gave thieftakers 'virtual power of life and death over thieves'.[145] They appeared to engage in the business of wholesale crime farming, carefully reaping profits from cultivated areas of rule-breaking. Their mediating role led to elaborate patterns of co-option, collusion and conflict. As herdsmen of deviance, they culled as well as protected, delivering to the courts people who were refractory or strangers within their territories. They tended to penalize those who were incapable of offering much resistance or retaliation when arrested. There was thus a major process of discrimination against the marginal, the novice and the unorganized, the main structures of criminal activity being largely unaffected provided they submitted to a new discipline.[146] Despite their predatory and conservative role, they constituted the only active agency of control which was able to superintend the behaviour of criminals. They were the real predecessors of the contemporary police, being employed as a necessary albeit unfortunate model for the founding of the Bow Street Runners.[147]

The principal thieftaker of the eighteenth century, Jonathan Wild, established an almost total monopoly over thief-catching, receiving and thieving in southern England.[148] His subordinates stole on commission, and surrendered what they had taken to Wild who then returned the goods to their erstwhile owners. As a major broker in stolen goods, Wild was able to ascertain what thefts had taken place and was armed with material to control his dependants. He employed his power as thieftaker to suppress rivals and to maintain an internal discipline. His organization was consequently a political accomplishment, a significant instance of the brokerage of crime and power. He described himself as a 'factor' journeying between different worlds.[149] His command over criminal worlds represented an *imperium in imperio*, an accumulation of power which required at least temporary acknowledgement by the state. At his trial, Wild protested: 'I have brought many bold and daring malefactors to just punishment, even at the hazard of my own life. . . . I have done merit, because at the time the things were done, they were esteemed meritorious by the government. . . .'[150] Similarly, Hall observed: 'during Wild's career as a thieftaker he was rendering valuable services to the police for which he received the usual reward from these officials, a compensation still paid to criminals. He was not prosecuted, and he was permitted to operate.'[151] Wild managed to acquire the status of expert and consultant on matters of crime control. His advice was sought by the Privy Council in 1720,[152] and there were rumours of his assuming a clandestine role for the state.[153] Calling himself 'Thieftaker-General of Britain and Ireland', he surrounded himself with the trappings of authority. In short, Wild came near to assuming an official place as policeman and broker:

> [Governments] not only receive and accept of Informations of the worst of Crimes, from the worst of Criminals, and take Knowledge of the Offence from the Offenders themselves, but encourage such Criminals to come in and confess the Offence, and Discover their Accomplices, Promising as well Pardon for the Crimes, as a Reward for the Discovery, even to those who are Guilty. Now this willingness of the Government to detect Thieves, seem'd to be a kind of authority, for *Jonathan* in his vigorous persuit of those he thought fit to have Punish'd . . .[154]

It was that authority, recognized by magistrates and the government,[155] which lent force to the argument that criminality was negotiable and fluid. What distinguished Wild's organization in the first decades of the eighteenth century was also to characterize the Sicilian *mafiosi*:[156] the capacity to serve as an acknowledged and necessary intermediary between weak community and weak government. That capacity was sufficient to ensure, however briefly, the assumption of political stature and immune status.

CONCLUSION

I have argued in a somewhat simplistic fashion that legal domination in the late 1600s and early 1700s was uncertain. A forced communal self-sufficiency and relatively uninfluential enforcement agencies combined to permit the emergence of much variation in the subordination of different groups. Some groups were allowed to attain a comparative autonomy and were shielded against formal social control. In turn, those who were in effective command over those groups were able to negotiate the character of criminality and criminals. At its extreme, such variation had the consequence of confusing the borders between morality and immorality, between legality and illegality:

> Such were the blessings of that state;
> Their crimes conspir'd to make them great:
> And virtue, who from politics
> Has learn'd a thousand cunning tricks,
> Was, by their happy influence,
> Made friends with vice:
> And ever since,
> The worst of all the multitude
> Did something for the common good.[157]

NOTES AND REFERENCES

1. Radical criminologists have been urging a return to what are basically eighteenth-century forms of policing. It seems useful to examine some of the implications of such a system in its original guise. For one instance of that radical plea, see J. Young, 'Working Class Criminology', I. Taylor *et al.* (eds), *Critical Criminology*, London, Routledge and Kegan Paul, 1975.
2. I have tried to defend such an approach in 'Some Problems of Interpretative Historiography', *British Journal of Sociology*, September 1976.

3. Quoted in D. Ogg, *England in the Reigns of James II and William III*, Oxford, Clarendon Press, 1955, p. 30.
4. Cf. J. Parkes *Travel in England in the Seventeenth Century*, London, Oxford University Press, 1925, p. 1.
5. ibid., pp. 18-20
6. P. Rogers, Introduction to D. Defoe, *A Tour Through the Whole Island of Great Britain*, Harmondsworth, Penguin, 1971, p. 24.
7. Cf. P. Rogers, *Grub Street*, London, Methuen, 1972, p. 4.
8. Rogers, Introduction to Defoe, *A Tour Through the Whole Island of Great Britain*, p. 24
9. Cf. P. Laslett, *The World We Have Lost*, London, Methuen, 1965, pp. 19, 66.
10. Cf. Parkes, *Travel in England in the Seventeenth Century*, p. 283.
11. Cf. J. Scott, *Comparative Political Corruption*, Englewood Cliffs, NJ, Prentice-Hall, 1972, p. 38.
12. Ogg, *England in the Reigns of James II and William III*, p. 122.
13. Cf. M. R. Zirker, *Fielding's Social Pamphlets*, Berkeley, University California Press, 1966, p. 17.
14. Cf. M. Beloff, *Public Order and Popular Disturbances*, London, Oxford University Press, 1938, pp. 22-3.
15. E. Thompson, 'The Moral Economy of the English Crowd in the Eighteenth Century', *Past and Present*, February 1971, no. 50, pp. 120-1.
16. Cf. S. Andreski, *Military Organization and Society*, London, Routledge and Kegan Paul, 1954, p. 79.
17. Cf. P. Pringle, *Honest Thieves*, London, Robert Hale, 1938, p. 35.
18. Cf. Beloff, *Public Order and Popular Disturbances*, p. 23.
19. Cf. G. Clark, *The Later Stuarts*, Oxford, Clarendon Press, 1955, p. 259.
20. J. Hammond and B. Hammond, 'Poverty, Crime and Philosophy' in A. Turberville (ed.), *Johnson's England*, Oxford, Clarendon Press, 1933, p. 301.
21. Cf. A. Knapp and W. Baldwing, *The New Newgate Calendar*, London, J. Robins, 1824, vol. I., p. 226.
22. Quoted in P. Pringle, *Hue and Cry*, London, Museum Press, 1955, p. 52.
23. Cf. G. Howson, *Thief-Taker General*, London, Hutchinson, 1970, p. 25.
24. Sir J. Fortescue, 'The Army' in Turberville, *Johnson's England*, pp. 69-70.
25. Cf. C. Hill, *The Century of Revolution*, Edinburgh, Thomas Nelson, 1961, p. 15.
26. Cf. Fortescue, 'The Army', p. 68.
27. ibid., p. 68
28. Cf. J. Western, *The English Militia in the Eighteenth Century*, London, Routledge and Kegan Paul, 1965, p. 3.
29. Cf. C. Barnett, *Britain and her Army*, London, Allen Lane, 1970, pp. 107-10.
30. ibid., p. 107.
31. Cf. Thompson, 'The Moral Economy of the English Crowd in the Eighteenth Century', p. 121.
32. Cf. C. Winslow, 'Sussex Smugglers' in D. Hay *et al.* (eds), *Albion's Fatal Tree: Crime and Society in Eighteenth-Century England*, London, Allen Lane, 1975, p. 144.

33. Thompson 'The Moral Economy of the English Crowd in the Eighteenth Century', p. 121.
34. Cf. Clark, *The Later Stuarts*, p. 259.
35. Cf. J. Plumb, *The Growth of Political Stability in England*, London, Macmillan, 1967, p. 20.
36. Cf. Western, *The English Militia in the Eighteenth Century*, p. 27.
37. ibid., pp. 72-3
38. ibid., p. 72.
39. Cf. Clark, *The Later Stuarts*, p. 259
40. T. De laune, *The Present State of London*, London, George Larkin, 1681, p. 288.
41. Cf. D. Ogg, *England in the Reign of Charles II*, Oxford, Clarendon Press, 1934, vol. 2, p. 493.
42. Cf. L. Pike, *A History of Crime in England*, London, Smith Elder and Co., 1876, vol. II, p. 369.
43. Cf. L. Radzinowicz, *A History of the English Criminal Law and its Administration*, London, Stevens and Sons, 1956, vol. II, p. 27.
44. J. Shaw, *Paris Law*, London, Lintot, 1753, p. 344.
45. Cf. Beloff, *Public Order and Popular Disturbances*, p. 26.
46. Cf. Parkes, *Travel in England in the Seventeenth Century*, p. 45.
47. ibid., p. 152.
48. Cf. Beloff, *Public Order and Popular Disturbances*, p. 24.
49. Cf. ibid., p. 133.
50. Cf. Howson, *Thief-Taker General*, p. 4.
51. Cf. Winslow, 'Sussex Smugglers', p. 128.
52. Cf. L. White, *Medieval Technology and Social Change*, London, Oxford University Press, 1962, p. 38.
53. Cf. Andreski, *Military Organization and Society*, p. 81.
54. Cf. J. Fuller, *Armament and History*, London, Eyre and Spottiswoode, 1946, p. 99.
55. ibid.
56. Cf. E. Thompson, *Whigs and Hunters: The Origins of the Black Act*, London, Allen Lane, 1975, p. 64.
57. Cf. P. Pringle, *Stand and Deliver*, London, Museum Press, 1951, p. 63.
58. Plumb, *The Growth of Political Stability in England*, p. 21.
59. Cf. Scott, *Comparative Political Corruption*, p. 40.
60. Cf. K. Swart, *Sale of Offices in the Seventeenth Century*, The Hague, Martinus Nijhoff, 1949.
61. Cf. Laslett, *The World We Have Lost*, p. 19.
62. Cf. D. Hay, 'Property, Authority and the Criminal Law', in Hay *et al.*, *Albion's Fatal Tree*.
63. Cf. Ogg, *England in the Reigns of James II and William III*, p. 107.
64. Hay, 'Property, Authority and the Criminal Law', p. 52.
65. D. Defoe, *The Poor Man's Plea*, London, no named publisher, 1968, pp. 7-8.
66. J. Fielding, *A Plan for Preventing Robberies Within Twenty Miles of London*, London, A. Millar, 1755, pp. 22-3.
67. Cf. 8 Geo. 2, c. 16, s. 11, 1735.

68. Cf. Pringle, *Hue and Cry*, p. 48.
69. Cf. Sir W. Holdsworth, *A History of English Law*, London, Methuen, 1938, vol. XI, p. 585.
70. Cf. Radzinowicz, *A History of the English Criminal Law and its Administration*, vol. 2, p. 33.
71. ibid.
72. Cf. Howson, *Thief-Taker General*, for an excellent account of thieftaking.
73. For a more recent example, see G. Marx, 'Thoughts on a Neglected Category of Social Movement Participant: The Agent Provocateur and the Informant', in S. Halleck *et al.* (eds), *The Aldine Crime and Justice Annual 1974*, Chicago, Aldine, 1975. See also the report in *The New York Times*, April 1975.
74. Winslow, 'Sussex Smugglers', p. 144.
75. 4 W. and M., c. 8, s. 7.
76. R. Wilson, *A Full and Impartial Account of all the Robberies Committed by John Hawkins, George Sympson . . . and their Companion . . . by Ralph Wilson, later one of their Confederates*, London, J. Peele, 1722, p. 24.
77. E. Thompson, 'The Crime of Anonymity', in Hay *et al.*, *Albion's Fatal Tree*, p. 272.
78. J. Hall, *Theft, Law and Society*, Boston, Little Brown 1935, p. 87.
79. Rogers, *Grub Street*, p. 12.
80. Cf. Pringle, *Honest Thieves*, p. 18.
81. Cf. Plumb, *The Growth of Political Stability in England*, p. 21.
82. Beloff, *Public Order and Popular Disturbances*, p. 95.
83. J. Rule, 'Wrecking and Coastal Plunder', in Hay *et al.*, *Albion's Fatal Tree*, p. 186.
84. Cf. Defoe, *A Tour through the Whole Island . . .*, p. 295.
85. Cf. P. Rock, *Making People Pay*, London, Routledge and Kegan Paul, 1973, ch. 12.
86. Cf. J. Jusserand, *English Wayfaring Life in the Middle Ages*, London, T. Fischer Unwin, no date, p. 165.
87. Cf. Ogg, *England in the Reigns of James II and William III*, p. 66.
88. I. Thornley, 'The Destruction of Sanctuary', in R. Seton-Watson (ed.), *Tudor Studies*, London, Longmans, Green and Co., 1924, p. 184.
89. Pike, *A History of Crime in England*, p. 253.
90. Cf. Thornley, 'The Destruction of Sanctuary', p. 202.
91. In the case of the Sicilian guilds, see H. Hess, *Mafia and Mafiosi*, Farnborough, Hants, Saxon House, 1973, p. 17.
92. Cf. G. Unwin, *The Gilds and Companies of London*, London, Frank Cass, 1908, p. 42.
93. Cf. A. Judges, *The Elizabethan Underworld*, London, George Routledge and Sons, 1930, p. xxvii.
94. See Sutherland's standard definition of professional crime: E. Sutherland, *The Professional Thief*, University of Chicago Press, 1956.
95. Cf. D. Maurer, *Whiz Mob*, New Haven, Conn., Yale University Press, 1964, and D. Maurer, *The Big Con*, New York, Signet, 1962.
96. Cf. Maurer, *Whiz Mob*, p. 52.

97. Unwin, *The Gilds and Companies of London*, p. 98.

98. Cf. Thompson, *Whigs and Hunters*, p. 81.

99. Ogg, *England in the Reigns of James II and William III*, p. 84; emphasis added.

100. Thus, the inhabitants of the Mint in London continued to claim their privileges in 1708. Cf. W. Thornbury, *Old and New London*, London: Cassell, Petter and Galpin, undated, vol. VI, p. 61.

101. E. Ward, *The London-Spy*, London, J. How, 1709, pp. 155, 156.

102. Cf. M. George, 'London and the Life of the Town', in Turberville, *Johnson's England*, p. 163.

103. Cf. Ward, *The London-Spy*, p. 151.

104. Cf. M. George, *London Life in the Eighteenth Century*, London, Kegan Paul, Trubner and Co., 1925, p. 68.

105. Cf. Laslett, *The World We have Lost*, p. 14.

106. Quoted in George, 'London and the Life of the Town', p. 163.

107. Cf. W. Weir, 'St Giles' Past and Present', in C. Knight (ed.), London. *London Born*, 1851, vol. III, p. 262.

108. Howson, *Thief-Taker General*, p. 22.

109. Defoe, *A Tour through the Whole Island* . . ., p. 321

110. G. Rude, *Hanoverian London*, London, Secker and Warburg, 1971, p. 128.

111. 'Alsatia' was named after the disputed frontier region between France and Germany, itself being a disputed territory.

112. George, *London Life in the Eighteenth Century*, p. 82.

113. Cf. Weir, 'St Giles' Past and Present', p. 262.

114. Cf. F. Lyons, *Jonathan Wild: Prince of Robbers*, London, Michael Joseph, 1936, pp. 101-2.

115. Cf. H. Fielding, *An Enquiry into the Causes of the Late Increase of Robbers*, London, 1751.

116. Cf. J. Tobias, 'A Statistical Study of a Nineteenth-Century Criminal Area' in Halleck *et al.*, *Aldine Crime and Justice Annual 1974*.

117. J. Binney, 'Thieves and Swindlers', in H. Mayhew, *London Labour and the London Poor*, London, Griffin, Bohn and Co., 1862, vol. IV, p. 301.

118. T. Beames, *The Rookeries of London*, London, Thomas Bosworth, 1850, p. 41.

119. Ogg, *England in the Reigns of James II and William III*, pp. 56-7.

120. T. Nourse, *Campania Foelix*, London, Bennet, 1700, p. 17.

121. Cf. Ogg, *England in the Reigns of James II and William III*, p. 102.

122. ibid., p. 57.

123. ibid., p. 107.

124. Cf. Pringle, *Stand and Deliver*, p. 28.

125. Cf. Parkes, *Travel in England in the Seventeenth Century*, pp. 162-4.

126. Cf. Swart, *Sale of Offices in the Seventeenth Century*.

127. Cf. Plumb, *The Growth of Political Stability in England*, p. 77.

128. Cf. Howson, *Thief-Taker General*, p. 28.

129. Cf. Pringle, *Hue and Cry*, p. 46.

130. Cf. P. Pringle, *Jolly Roger*, London, Museum Press, 1953, passim.

131. Cf. ibid., p. 47.

132. M. McIntosh, *The Organisation of Crime*, London, Macmillan, 1975, p. 19.

133. Cf. Pringle, *Stand and Deliver*, p. 25.

134. Cf. Pringle, *Jolly Roger*, p. 47.

135. Cf. W. Irwin, *The Making of Jonathan Wild*, New York, Columbia University Press, 1941, p. 3.

136. Thompson, *Whigs and Hunters*, p. 218.

137. Cf. Pringle, *Honest Thieves*, p. 71.

138. Cf. P. Stead, *Vidocq: A Biography*, London, Staples Press, 1953.

139. This was, indeed, part of a larger efflorescence of middlemen discussed by Thompson, 'The Moral Economy of the English Crowd in the Eighteenth Century', and R. Westerfield, *Middlemen in English Business*, Transactions of the Connecticut Academy of Arts and Sciences, New Haven, Yale University, Press, 1915.

140. For a description of an earlier, Elizabethan thieftaker, cf. L. Hutton, *The Black Dogge of Newgate*, London, G. Simson and W. White, 1596.

141. Cf. Howson, *Thief-Taker General*, pp. 37-8.

142. For more recent examples, cf. J. Mack, *The Crime Industry*, Farnborough, Hants, Saxon House, 1975, esp. pp. 126-7.

143. Cf. Marx, 'Thoughts on a Neglected Category of Social Movement Participant'.

144. B. Mandeville, *An Enquiry into the Causes of the Frequent Executions at Tyburn*, London, J. Roberts, 1725, part of unnumbered preface.

145. Howson, *Thief-Taker General*, p. 37.

146. Cf. Pringle, *Hue and Cry*, p. 36.

147. Cf. ibid., p. 35.

148. Cf. Howson, *Thief-Taker General*, p. 5.

149. Cf. Lyons, *Jonathan Wild*.

150. Quoted in A. Hayward, *Lives of the Most Remarkable Criminals . . .*, London, George Routledge and Son, 1927, p. 266.

151. Hall, *Theft, Law and Society*, p. 136.

152. Cf. Howson, *Thief-Taker General*, p. 125.

153. Cf. L. Benson, *The Book of Remarkable Trials and Notorious Characters*, London, Reeves and Turner, undated, p. 89. This charge is also put in a most fanciful form by W. H. Ainsworth, *Jack Sheppard*, London, Richard Bentley, 1839.

154. D. Defoe, *The True and Genuine Account of the Life and Actions of the Late Jonathan Wild*, London, John Applebee, 1725, p. 17.

155. Cf. A. Smith, *Memoirs of the Life and Times of the Famous Jonathan Wild*, London, Sam. Briscoe, 1726, p. x.

156. Cf. F. Ianni, *A Family Business*, London, Routledge and Kegan Paul, 1972, p. 40.

157. B. Mandeville, *The Fable of the Bees*, New York: Capricorn, 1962, p. 31.

9

Eighteenth-century English Society and the Debt Law

PAUL H. HAAGEN

Specially written for this volume

There does not appear to be any more universal concern than the laws between Creditors and Debtors. No man can buy or sell, borrow or lend, but that he may have occasion to appeal to them. They are the laws that belong to every day's business, and equally concern every Rank of the State.

Considerations on the Laws between Debtors and Creditors
(London, 1779), p.3

Lord Mansfield, the greatest of the eighteenth-century common law judges, insisted that 'the most desirable object in *all* judicial determinations especially in *mercantile* ones (which ought to be determined upon natural justice, and not upon the niceties of law), is to do substantial justice.'[1] But however desirable the object, the law that governed the vast majority of credit relationships during the eighteenth century was notable chiefly for its arbitrary application and apparent irrationality. It permitted a creditor to arrest his debtor and keep him in prison until the debt was paid, even if the debtor had been forced into default by circumstances beyond his control and had neither assets nor means of working off his obligations in prison. At the same time, it left much of a debtor's property exempt from actions arising out of the default and allowed wealthy insolvents to live relatively comfortably in prisons which were run like hotels. None the less, throughout the eighteenth century, Parliament staunchly resisted all efforts to reform the debt law. This essay will attempt to outline the massive social costs that resulted and to explain why England tolerated and even protected a system of dealing with default that was superficially so bizarre.

Between 1773 and 1788, the prison reformer John Howard went on a series of tours of all the gaols and houses of correction in England and Wales. He discovered all manner of appalling conditions: prisoners kept in rooms that had earthen floors and no heat, buildings in disrepair, and a serious lack of prison discipline. But most striking of all was his discovery that most of those imprisoned under these conditions were not criminals or suspects awaiting trial – they were debtors. Debtors constituted about half of the entire prison population in England and Wales in the 1770s and 1780s.[2] It is almost certain that they made up an even greater proportion of a larger total inmate population earlier in the century.[3] While the rate of imprisonment is more difficult to estimate, it appears to have remained relatively constant with between 2000 and 4000 debtors imprisoned every year.[4]

Debtors' prisons could be found in most centres of population. Every county had at least one prison where debtors were held; many had several, Yorkshire at least 13.[5] The total number of debtors' prisons fluctuated over the course of the century, as some fell into disuse and disrepair, and others were built or pressed into service, but it never fell below 120.[6] There were also numerous 'sponging houses'. Inns generally run by a tipstaff or his wife, these sponging houses served as places of close confinement for any debtor sufficiently frightened of prison and still sufficiently solvent to be willing and able to pay the exorbitant charge.[7]

In addition to those actually imprisoned, countless others fled from their creditors to other parts of the kingdom, to a debtor sanctuary called the Mint, or abroad. It is impossible, for obvious reasons, to estimate with any degree of confidence the numbers involved. Because Parliament became sufficiently concerned about the threat to public order posed by the Mint, and later about the loss of able-bodied seamen and artisans to foreign sovereigns, that it passed a series of limited amnesty acts, it is possible, however, to get some sense of the numbers involved. The acts did not cover all sanctuary men and fugitives. Insolvent debtors were eligible for relief only if: (1) they surrendered themselves at the Surrey Court of Quarter Sessions, in the case of the Mint Act, or at a debtors' prison in the case of the 15 fugitive debtor acts; (2) their debts were less than a given amount specified in each act; and (3) they agreed to turn over almost all of their property for their creditors. The amnesty did not permit debtors to start their economic lives afresh. It merely protected them from arrest for those debts incurred before the passage of the relevant act. Creditors retained the right to arrest them for failure to pay any debts incurred after the passage of the act, and to sue to recover any debts incurred before the passage of the act out of any property that the debtor managed to acquire in the future. Despite the limited nature of the amnesty, more than 6000 debtors, approximately 4 per cent of the adult male population of London, applied for relief under the Mint Act of 1722.[8] Thousands of fugitive debtors returned from abroad to take advantage of the five amnesty acts passed between 1729 and 1755, and hundreds more after each of the subsequent ten passed between 1761 and 1797.[9]

These debtor prisoners were not distributed randomly in the population. About 95 per cent were males and virtually all were adults.[10] Most had wives and children; a parliamentary study in 1792 showed that two-thirds of the debtors in prison at that time had wives. The study also found that the 2000 debtors had more than 4000 children among them, but fails to indicate what percentage of debtors had children.[11] While some of these wives and children, like Dickens's Little Dorrit, did choose to follow their fathers and husbands to gaol, this practice was never the norm.[12] In the vast majority of cases, the arrest of a debtor meant the break-up of a family.

Very few debtors, unlike most criminals, were from the lowest strata of English society.[13] Most were working poor, either artisans or small shopkeepers.[14] Because such persons suffered from chronic under-employment, it would be difficult to estimate the economic loss that resulted from their imprisonment. But this is not to say that such loss was unimportant. With very few exceptions, imprisonment insured that these workers would be not only unproductive but a burden. Conditions in all but a few gaols were so crowded that debtors could not work and had to subsist on charity.[15]

The most easily measurable cost of imprisonment for debt was the loss of human lives. Samuel Johnson, who had himself been imprisoned for debt, insisted, in an influential article published in *The Idler*, that more Englishmen died in debtors' prisons than in war.[16] He estimated that one-quarter of all imprisoned debtors, 'overborne with sorrow, consumed by famine, or putrified by filth', died every year.[17] In fact, the situation was never that bad, although it was grim enough. Epidemics of lice-borne 'gaol fever', attributed by contemporaries to the appalling stench of the prisons, were common and devastating. When an epidemic of gaol fever broke out at the Marshalsea Prison in 1719, for example, 40 per cent of the inmates died in just three months.[18] Even under normal conditions, the death rate among debtor prisoners was frighteningly high. Ten per cent of all debtors committed to Fleet Prison between 1735 and 1748, a period without an epidemic at that gaol, died before being released.[19] The Fleet, one of the largest debtors prisons in the kingdom, was thought to be unusually healthy.[20]

THE LAW OF DEBTOR AND CREDITOR

These large numbers of persons were in prison or had fled because of the peculiar approach of the English law of debtor and creditor to the problem of default.[21] It gave the creditor his principal legal remedy against his debtor's body rather than his property. Theoretically, imprisonment for debt was not a punishment.[22] Except in the Courts of Requests, which were limited to debts of under £2, there were no determinate sentences.[23] A debtor was released as soon as he paid his debts or his creditors decided to release him. It was instead a form of legalized extortion.[24] The terror of imprisonment, *squalor carceris*, was supposed to frighten a debtor into paying his debts or 'to torture the consciences' of his friends and relatives into paying them for him.[25]

Most creditors faced with the unpleasant fact of a default by one of their debtors never resorted to arrest and imprisonment. They either wrote off the debts or reached some informal, mutually agreed upon composition.[26] Those who decided to take the matter to the courts could also proceed against their debtor's property. Not all this property, however, could be seized in satisfaction of debts. Money, annuities, bonds, choses in action, and stock in the funded companies were all exempt, and wages could not be garnished.[27] Creditors could reach only that property that was attachable under the writ *fieri facias*, *levari facias* and *elegit*. *Fieri facias* ordered the sheriff to seize and sell as much of the debtor's moveable goods and chattels as was necessary to satisfy the debt. The little used *levari facias* permitted the attachment of all rents due to the debtor and of all crops growing on the debtor's land at the time the writ was issued.[28] Neither of these writs precluded a creditor from imprisoning his debtor at some later time if the property seized was insufficient to cover the debt, but a creditor could not proceed against both the person and the property of his debtor at the same time.[29]

Elegit, the only remedy that could be used to attach real property, was a final action. Once a creditor had taken out the writ, he lost the right to proceed against the debtor in any other way.[30] *Elegit* granted the creditor 'tenure in *elegit*', that is, the right to collect rents from one-half of the debtor's freehold property until the debt was paid. It did not extend to leasehold or copyhold property, nor could it compel a debtor to sell his land or convey the full rights of ownership in that land to the creditor.[31]

At the same time that they had strictly limited powers over their borrowers' property, lenders possessed broad, virtually uncontrolled powers of arrest. Every creditor had the right to demand the arrest of almost any of his debtors without warning or proof. In fact, if he could convince a court that there was the slightest reason to fear that his debtor might abscond, a creditor did not need to wait for the debt to fall due.[32] Once arrested, a debtor paid the amount demanded, put up bail equivalent to several times the value of the debt, or remained in prison on *mesne* process until he either became supersedeable or was tried.[33]

The trial was limited to questions of the existence and size of the debt. Neither the cause of the default nor the debtor's ability to pay were treated

as relevant.[34] Once the court determined that a debt was owed, it granted
the creditor the right to sue out a writ of *capias ad satisfaciendum*, which
ordered the imprisonment of the debtor in execution until the debt was
satisfied.[35] Debtors imprisoned in execution in Scotland could obtain their
releases by 'giving up their all', *cessio bonorum*, but their counterparts in
England had no such option.[36] No matter how small the debt, no matter
how futile continued incarceration, creditors could leave their debtors in
gaol indefinitely. In fact, both the debtor and creditor had strong
incentives to be unreasonable. Since a debtor would not be released until he
either paid all his debts or persuaded all of his creditors to agree to his
release, he had little incentive to pay anyone unless he believed he could
satisfy all.[37] Since a *capias ad satisfaciendum*, like an *elegit*, was a final action, a
creditor lost all rights relating to the debt when he released the debtor
from gaol. He had, therefore, a strong incentive to keep his debtor in gaol
as long as he hoped to be paid something by someone at some time.[38]

Debtors in prison on *mesne* process had to bear all the costs of their
imprisonment: lodging, food and fees.[39] As a result, many incurred debts to
their gaolers and were unable to obtain their releases from prison even
after their other creditors had forgiven them.[40] For those who died in gaol
indebted to their keepers, not even death insured their release from prison.
Gaolers frequently refused to allow corpses to be taken from their custody
for burial until they had received some payment from those who came to
retrieve the body.[41]

If the imprisoning creditor failed to proceed to trial within a certain
length of time, usually six months, and if the debtor was not hopelessly in
debt to the gaoler, the debtor could sue for a writ of *supersedeas* which
ordered his immediate release. This legal protection proved to be of only
limited usefulness to the majority of debtors, who did not have the
wherewithal to pay for it. Such persons could and occasionally did languish
in prison for years without trial.[42]

After the passage of the Lords' Act of 1729, debtors imprisoned in
execution could demand a minimum level of support from their creditors,
if they could prove themselves to be destitute. If creditors failed to provide
this support, known as 'groats', for six consecutive weeks, a court could
order the debtor's release.[43] Those destitute enough to be eligible to
receive 'groats' were often too destitute to sue for them. The courts,
moreover, were not always scrupulous in the protection of debtors' rights.
For example, the Mayor's Court of the City of London issued an order on
25 January 1731, directing Peter Francis Olivares and John Philip D'Andrea
to provide a weekly maintenance for their debtor, Samuel St Leger, until
they agreed to his release from prison. After they failed to comply for six
successive weeks, St Leger petitioned the court for his release. On 10

January 1732, the court ordered the two creditors to show cause why it should not release St Leger, and on 10 January 1733 the court was still waiting for a satisfactory reply and the groatless St Leger was still in prison.[44] In the 1770s, the prison reformer John Howard discovered that St Leger's problems were the norm. In most gaols, he reported, no debtor had received groats for years.[45]

The effectiveness of imprisonment for debt was largely dependent on the debtor's fear of incarceration. The prisons were not, however, operated to universalize that terror. While a poor debtor was likely to find himself confined in a crowded, vermin-infested ward, wealthy insolvents could live very comfortably.[46] The reason for the difference was that gaolers ran their prisons like hotels. A debtor received just as many services and privileges as he was prepared to buy. Some of these privileges, like the right not to be shackled to the floor, were quite modest, but others were surprisingly broad. Debtors could, for example, rent suites of rooms in the better section of the gaol known as the masters' side, and purchase the right to go into town during the day.[47] In fact, a debtor could buy the right to live outside gaol altogether. The King's Bench Prison in Southwark and the Fleet Prison in the City of London were each surrounded by an area known as the Rules.[48] A debtor living unguarded and unsupervised in a house or apartment located within that area was legally considered in prison.[49] Any debtor committed to one of those prisons could purchase the permission of the gaoler to live in the Rules of that prison.[50] If the debtor was originally committed to some other prison that had no Rules, he could move to one that did. Every debtor who could pay the cost of suing out a writ of *habeas corpus* could be transferred from any prison in the kingdom to either the Fleet or the King's Bench, and once transferred could purchase the freedom of the Rules.[51] In a letter written to his wife shortly after he had been arrested for debt, Sir William Chaytor made it clear how relatively invulnerable some debtors were:

> There is a good Air in the Fleet and good walks and a booling green and many gentlemen . . . the trouble that any vexatious creditor can bring upon mee, will not signify much; . . . scarce any will be soe mad to be at the Charge of an execution, and run the hazzard of loosing their debt too, by alwaise keeping me in durance.[52]

Imprisonment, moreover, had positive advantages for some wealthy debtors. As soon as any creditor had his debtor arrested, all of that debtor's other creditors lost their rights to proceed against his property. Debtors could, therefore, protect their property and gain leverage in negotiations with their creditors by having themselves arrested on 'friendly' actions.[53]

Since imprisonment put relatively little pressure on the debtor, creditors could be forced to accept very unfavourable terms in order to get anything at all. Ironically, it was only the poor insolvent with no property to protect and no money with which to buy privileges who experienced the full coercive force of the eighteenth-century prison.

Even given the peculiarities of eighteenth-century law, this approach to the problem of default seems bizarre. Based on a series of legal fictions, imprisonment for debt put coercive pressure to pay on those with no ability to pay, while permitting others with the ability to pay to thumb their noses at their creditors.[54] It is tempting, therefore, to treat the law of debtor and creditor as some sort of accident, a wrong turn in the development of the common law that went uncorrected because its victims, both debtors and creditors, were too powerless to bring the problem to the attention of Parliament. Such a dismissive approach would be wrong.[55]

Eighteenth-century Englishmen recognized that imprisonment for debt was a problem of major proportions. In fact, those who had an opinion on the subject believed that it was even worse than it actually was. Most contemporary estimates of the size of the imprisoned debtor population put it at between 20,000 and 60,000, with some writers insisting that the total was closer to 100,000.[56] Ogelthorpe recommended to Parliament that the colony of Georgia be established as a debtors' colony, both to take the pressure off the prisons and to create a place where insolvents could put their lives back together.[57] Towards the end of the century, the Thatched House Society, an organization devoted to releasing 'persons imprisoned for small debts', developed into one of the largest charitable organizations in the kingdom.[58]

This concern did not go unnoticed in Parliament. Parliament conducted several investigations into both debtor sanctuaries and prisons.[59] Almost every year some form of legislation was introduced to modify imprisonment for debt, expand creditors' remedies against their debtors' property, or provide some relief for imprisoned debtors; and most of them were hotly debated.[60] Parliament did, in fact, pass 20 temporary insolvent debtor relief acts.[61] The purpose of these acts was always somewhat ambiguous. In part, they were a simple effort to reduce overcrowding in the prisons. But most of the acts stated that their purpose was also to discharge debtors who had come to their situations 'by losses and other misfortunes' and were thus 'deemed the proper Objects of publick Compassion'.[62] What Parliament adamantly refused to do, however, was make any significant permanent changes in the law of debtor and creditor.[63] With the single exception of the unenforced Lords' Act, the debt law was the same at the end of the century as it was at the beginning. All of the major reforms, *cessio bonorum*, the abolition of arrest on mesne process, and finally the abolition of imprisonment for debt were products of the nineteenth century.[64]

Despite its superficial irrationality, the law of debtor and creditor was well suited to the needs of England's ruling classes. First, imprisonment for debt was a reasonably effective means of protecting the property interests of large segments of the creditor population. In spite of the completely accurate complaints of Defoe (who incidentally had considerably greater difficulty paying his debts than collecting them) that the debt law failed to create a predictable and reliable mechanism for the judicially supervised transfer of property from debtors to creditors, imprisonment for debt in fact proved to be a fairly successful means of protecting the property interests of large segments of the creditor population.[65] The threat of incarceration gave debtors a substantial incentive to meet their obligations. Borrowers who trifled with their creditors were running very serious risks. Second, imprisonment for debt permitted this level of protection to be achieved without seriously endangering the continuity of ownership of real property.

But while these instrumental concerns were necessary, they were not sufficient, causes. Parliament could have reformed the most obnoxious features of the debt law without seriously undermining the efficacy of imprisonment for debt. It did not do so, because the law of debtor and creditor was ideologically important. The debt law was a dramatic statement of the limits of law and of the state. It authorized the use of coercive force and then refused to regulate that force on the theory that the law and the courts were incapable of doing so. Mercy and discretion were the prerogatives of private individuals. This coupling of the right to use imprisonment to coerce and the unhampered power to relieve and release created a situation that reinforced patterns of deference and dependence and greatly buttressed the authority of the English ruling class.

PROTECTION OF CREDIT

The eighteenth-century economy depended on a complex, fragile network of credit. Credit eased the problems caused by the chronic shortage of specie and made possible the relatively rapid development of both production and consumption. Merchants extended credit to each other to facilitate large transactions, and wholesalers expanded their markets by allowing retailers months and even years to pay for goods delivered.[66] Retailers claimed that they could carry on trade only if they provided credit, and there is evidence that, in fact, about half of all retail transactions were made 'on trust'.[67] In many of the putting-out industries, workers depended on credit for their tools and raw materials.[68] Even the very poor were included. Itinerant peddlers and tallymen sold them goods at exorbitant prices on the instalment plan.[69]

This credit network was as precarious as it was pervasive. Because almost all operated on narrow margins and with highly illiquid assets, temporary financial embarrassments were nearly inevitable and real insolvency was common.[70] Sickness, injury or accident, fire, death, the outbreak of war or the simple failure to read changes in the market could, and often did, force debtors into default.[71] In a single year, one Lancashire merchant presided at several bankruptcy proceedings and forgave the debts of 248 poor people.[72] The fledgling insurance industry offered some protection, but only against a limited number of risks, and was unavailable to the vast majority of debtors and creditors. Lenders could not easily act as self-insurers by adjusting the rates at which they loaned. Most lending and borrowing was carried out as an adjunct to some other business, or as part of personal relations.[73] Only a small percentage of credit was provided by institutional lenders capable of making such adjustments.

Edmund Burke argued in Parliament, during debate on the unsuccessful 1791 Insolvent Debtors Relief Bill, that, despite the precariousness of credit 'in cases of commerce, the creditor only wished to secure the *cessio bonorum*'.[74] In fact, creditors made it clear that they much preferred the current system and feared that any other alternative would open up the possibility of massive fraud. That fear had at least some basis in fact. The ineffectiveness of the bankruptcy laws provided eighteenth-century creditors with strong reasons to believe that the courts were incapable of dealing with the problems of concealment of assets and fraudulent conveyance.[75] Nor did they put much faith in the fact that the *cessio bonorum* procedure required debtors to swear an oath that they had made all of their relevant property available to satisfy their debts. Mr Erskine, counsel for the County of Middlesex and the parishes of St John and St Margaret, Westminster, in their successful opposition to the 1780 Insolvent Debtors Relief Bill, argued that such oaths merely 'opened the door to perjury'. Others suggested that requiring the oath was immoral, since it encouraged defaulters to lie and thereby compound their sins.[76]

The concern about fraud extended beyond the fear of fraudulent conveyance and concealment of assets. Opponents of reform used the word 'fraud' to describe a variety of other actions such as the acceptance of loans without a 'reasonable' expectation of being able to repay them, living 'extravagantly' after borrowing someone else's money, failure to anticipate 'avoidable' difficulties, and failure to struggle 'enough' before giving up and defaulting. 'Reasonable', 'extravagant', 'avoidable' and 'enough' proved difficult to define. Even the great Lord Mansfield admitted that he 'knew not how a rule could be laid down for separating the wheat from the chaff'.[77]

The problem that they identified as fraud grew out of the fact that lenders advanced significant quantities of credit to persons who did not have sufficient collateral to cover the loans. If these debtors had a simple, predictable method of clearing their debts, creditors feared that they would lose the ability to compel 'honest' effort. They depended on the fear of the consequences of insolvency to induce debtors to 'struggle with their difficulties' and 'relieve their circumstances' rather than default. Thus lenders believed that they had to retain the right to determine on an individual basis when they should show mercy, and when they should imprison, *pour encourager les autres*.

The existence of remedies against the person of the debtor also greatly reduced the information costs of creditors. As long as a creditor retained the right to arrest defaulters, he was spared the trouble of looking too closely into the affairs of prospective borrowers. It was their business, not his, to determine whether they would be able to repay what they borrowed.[78] If a debtor defaulted, his creditors did not have the responsibility of locating his assets, proving that the property actually belonged to him, and then liquidating the property. These responsibilities were left to the defaulter. Shifting such burdens to the debtor made the cost of recovering a debt much lower for the creditor, whenever the fear of arrest and imprisonment convinced the debtor to co-operate. It also appears, at least in the short run, to have made credit cheaper and more readily available.[79]

PROTECTION OF REAL PROPERTY

The most rustic of Squire Westerns would have acknowledged that eighteenth-century England's extensive network of credit was essential to the economic strength and continued prosperity of the kingdom. But the wide availability of credit was never viewed as an unmitigated blessing.[80] Creditors were held responsible for making it possible for people to buy what they could not afford, and thus for promoting luxury, encouraging speculation and generally corroding morals. These personal vices were believed to threaten the very existence of the social order by threatening the continuity of ownership of real property.

Members of Parliament articulated both this fear of 'excessive' credit and the rationale behind the limited legal protections afforded to creditors during debates on a series of Freehold Estates Bills. These proposals were far from radical. In essence, they would have made it possible for creditors to recover simple contract debts out of the freehold estates of those debtors who died without making sufficient provision for the payment of their debts. In the words of Sir Samuel Romilly, the bills merely cancelled 'a liberty of committing injustice and the power of injuring the lower orders of society, with impunity'.[81] Parliament none the less decisively rejected these measures each time they were introduced between 1772 and 1820. Opponents attacked the bills with hostile, even hysterical, rhetoric, successfully portraying them as a fundamental attack on real property and, hence, on the Constitution itself. Creditors, they argued, would entrap young heirs into frittering away their patrimonies, deprive small landholders of 'the elective franchise', 'one of the most valuable of rights', cause the value of freehold property to tumble, and undermine the aristocracy. Several members insisted that if property rather than persons were liable for debts, there would be increasing prying into borrowers' affairs and possibly even a national register of assets.[82]

These arguments help to clarify the relationship between the desire to insure that maximum possible stability in the ownership of real property and the remedies provided by the law of debtor and creditor. The continuity of ownership of real property was believed to be critical to the maintenance of the social order. As a result, there was great concern in Parliament to guarantee that a landholder not put his property at risk unless he had specifically and consciously used that property as collateral for a mortgage.[83] Such restrictions, it was hoped, would reduce the possibility that landholders would jeopardize their land by incurring debts lightly or irresponsibly, and would discourage unscrupulous lenders from tempting young heirs with easy credit. The maintenance of special privileged status for real property under the debt laws was linked to the existence of a comprehensive alternative remedy in cases of default, summary action against the body of the debtor. Reformers explicitly recognized this connection by pairing their proposals for restrictions on arrest and imprisonment for debt with more complete remedies against real property.[84] The Act that finally abolished arrest on *mesne* process, for example, extended the writ *elegit* to cover all, instead of just half, of a debtor's freehold property.[85] Conservatives in Parliament reasoned that if reform required greater access to a debtor's real property, then to prevent such access it was necessary to prevent reform.

Imprisonment for debt provided a complete and logically consistent remedy for creditors in cases of default. Any change in the law that made that remedy less complete or suggested that creditors should look to the property rather than to the persons of their debtors for security would have created significant secondary pressures to extend remedies against property. This explains why even measures as severely restricted as the

Freehold Estates Bills were viewed with such mistrust. As the Master of the Rolls noted, '[i]f you began with these ideas, there was no end to them'.[86]

SOCIAL CONTROL

[Y]ou will make sure of power and influence by lending privately sums of money to your neighbours, perhaps at small interest, perhaps at no interest, and always having their bonds in your possession.' This is an excellent thought. I am resolved to practice it to a certain extent if it shall ever be in my power; and the scheme of securing influence in the country is so admirably adapted to my high feudal notions that I shall never forget this afternoon when it was suggested to me by the great Mr Samuel Johnson. I am persuaded that in this late age it will supply the place of the old attachment.[87]

As Dr Johnson suggested, the debt law was potentially an exceptionally useful means of influence and control. The threat to use it was certainly credible. So many debtors went to prison that every defaulter must have understood only too well that he was in the power of his creditors. If a creditor decided to arrest, no jury could acquit and no court could intercede. The entire process was in the hands of the creditor. Significant social pressure could, on occasion, be brought to bear on creditors to forbear and forgive, but the moral consensus against imprisoning even those insolvents regarded as 'unfortunate' was never sufficiently well established to make the mobilization of community sentiment likely. Moralists repeatedly warned creditors that they had a responsibility to society to enforce 'the law'.[88]

The system was also remarkably manipulable. Since debts could be bought and sold, a person who wanted, for whatever reason, to gain power over a debtor needed only to buy that debtor's notes from a third party. Conversely, anyone with resources sufficient to meet the obligations could come to the rescue of any debtor.

How frequently the debt law was in fact used for purposes of coercion and control is difficult to know and impossible to quantify. The papers filed in connection with the Insolvent Debtor Relief Acts allow us to discover a considerable amount about the persons who were imprisoned for debt, but seldom tell us more than the names and occasionally an occupational description of those who ordered their imprisonment. It is certainly impossible to say why these creditors took the actions that they did. The difficulties are further compounded by the fact that creditors did not need to carry out the threat to imprison in order to coerce or control. As long as a debtor believed that his creditors might take such action, they did not need to do anything.

There are a significant number of eighteenth-century stories, pamphlets and prints that indicate that the debt law was used for a variety of coercive purposes unrelated to the collection of debts.[89] The largest number of these concern attempts to force women into prostitution or simply to extort sexual favours from them. But there were also claims that the debt law was used more systematically to establish captive retail markets and to control workers.[90] Tallymen, who sold goods on time largely to persons too poor to get credit in the shops, were accused of using that credit relationship to force their customers to accept additional goods or to prevent them from buying from others by threatening to arrest them for non-payment on goods purchased earlier but not yet paid off.[91] Similarly, suppliers in some of the putting-out industries were said to use the debt law to maintain labour discipline.[92] Many of these workers were in a debtor–creditor relationship with their suppliers. Most Norwich weavers, for example, took yarn on credit, weaved it into cloth and sold the finished goods back to their suppliers. They were in a poor position, once in debt, to refuse further work or to dicker over the terms of their employment.[93]

Whether these accusations were reasonably accurate reflections of fact or merely the voicing of disconcerting fears about the debt law is unclear. If the tallymen or clothiers were using the law in the way suggested, it seems likely that their names would appear with some regularity in the prison commitment books as the arresting creditors. They do not. In fact, it was relatively uncommon for any one creditor to arrest two debtors in any given five-year period.[94] It was not until the debt law was reformed in the nineteenth century to limit arrest on *mesne* process and regulate the length of debtor sentences that tallymen clearly made aggressive use of their right to imprison.[95] Whatever the case, Parliament certainly did not defend the unreformed debt law because it offered collateral benefits to tallymen. The gentry had little regard for the interests of such tradesmen, and would have furthered these interests only if they coincided with their own.

In fact, there was such a coincidence of interests. There are suggestions that the debt law was used in subtler ways by landlords to tie their tenants to them with mixed feelings of gratitude and fear. In the play *Wild Oats*, by O'Keefe, Lady Amaranth attempts to repay a passing stranger who has rescued one of her tenants from arrest for debt. '[T]hou hast assumed a right which belongeth alone to me,' she insists, explaining that such rescues were her privilege.[96] After the stranger refused to accept repayment, she immediately orders her bailiff to remit a quarter's rent to all her tenants, to return cattle that had been distrained for rent to the widow who owned them, and to drop the lawsuit against the 'farmer's son, who did shoot the pheasant'.[97] Thwarted in her effort to use her power to prevent the rigorous application of the debt law, Lady Amaranth demonstrates her benevolence by ostentatiously refraining from exercising other legal rights. The juxtaposition of the debt law and those other rights relating to rent, game and the criminal laws clearly suggests that they were all part of a common fund of patronage possibilities.

None of these instrumental concerns can explain the most anomalous features of the debt law: absolute creditor control and 'perpetual' imprisonment. Neither of these was necessary to protect credit, maintain the privileged status of real property or permit leverage with insolvent debtors. Creditors could have functioned quite effectively with some level of judicial review, and debtors would have been just as restrained by the threat of an appropriately long, yet still finite, prison sentence. In fact, the regular passage of the temporary Insolvent Debtor Relief Acts meant that there was considerable judicial interference with creditor prerogatives. Even when these acts were not in effect, most creditors released their debtors after relatively short periods of time. Debtor prison terms decreased steadily from 1730 onwards, and by 1800 the modal debtor prison term was less than six months.[98] There continued to be occasional exceptions. Nicholas Hoskins, for example, was committed to King's Bench at the suit of 'Joseph Taunton, gent.' for £150 on 7 October 1785 and died in gaol more than 38 years later on 13 December 1823.[99] But by the end of the century it was unusual for a debtor to spend two years imprisoned for debt.[100] Parliament's insistence on maintaining the debt law was not so much a balking at radical change as a refusal to make the theoretical possibilities of the debt law correspond to the way in which it was actually used.

The reluctance to tamper with the debt law grew out of the ideological importance of that law to the English ruling class. In many of its essential elements, the law of debtor and creditor closely paralleled the criminal law. This is not to say that the parallel was exact. The criminal law was always more public and its adherence to due process more compelling. But their similarities were more critical than their differences and reflected a common set of attitudes about the role of sanctions and the relationship of law and mercy.

The debt law never functioned as theatre. Robed justices, if they became involved in the process at all, merely committed a debtor to prison until he satisfied his creditors. They did not thunder terrifying sentences, nor attempt to edify the public by expounding on the blackness of the debtor's character. No crowds lined the routes to the Fleet or the King's Bench to watch the bailiffs bring in yet another defaulter. There was neither the opportunity nor the perceived need for public confessions and repentances.

Even the temporary Insolvent Debtor Relief Acts had little dramatic effect. The releases that they authorized were drawn out over years, and the prisons were filled to capacity with new insolvents within weeks of the release of those 'relieved'.[101] Because debt was so pervasive, however, little drama was needed to communicate the message of the debt law. It was a constant force in eighteenth-century English life.

The debt law also failed to evoke the powerful due process images of the criminal law. Eighteenth-century criminal courts, at least on occasion, showed a rigid adherence to legal formalities. Minor errors in pleading could and did lead to the refusal to convict obviously guilty persons. This rigidity greatly contributed to the sense of the law as a force apart from the participants and as blindly evenhanded. The debt law was always much more rough and ready. Its central moment was not the trial, but summary arrest and detention on *mesne* process. The courts issued the crucial writ *capias ad respendendu* without requiring any proof at all, and even permitted creditors to substitute fictitious names in place of the obligatory sureties for prosecution. The division of prisons into common and masters' sides made it clear that the law was not intended to be a levelling force.

But it would be wrong to exaggerate the effect of these differences. While the issuance of the arrest warrant was not regulated, the arrest itself was. Bailiffs and catchpoles who apprehended debtors on Sundays or in illegally entered dwelling places had their quarries released and were themselves often prosecuted.[102] Furthermore, the pieties about the vulnerability of all men to the rigours of the law and of the need to protect property of poor men were voiced about the debt law as often as they were about the criminal law.[103] Like the criminal law, the debt law made little attempt to grade sanctions. The severest penalties could be meted out against the least serious offender. Just as even very minor crimes could be punished capitally, honest debtors could be kept in gaol for ever. The tradesman who borrowed a small sum in reasonable expectation of being able to repay it but was then forced to default because of 'misfortunes and other losses' faced the possibility of incarceration as perpetual as that faced by the most irresponsible spendthrift. Statistically that possibility was very small, but it was never removed, because its retention greatly added to the flexibility of the law. It made it possible for creditors to get very rough, regardless of the situation, and raised the value of their right to forgive.

For the followers of Beccaria and Bentham, the discretion to manipulate the sanctioning power arbitrarily was the most serious defect in the law. It made the resolution of disputes too unpredictable and permitted the introduction of extraneous emotional factors such as the desire for revenge, which prevented defaulters from calculating their options rationally and modifying their behaviour accordingly. The incentives for a debtor to act honestly in the face of impending default were at the least confused, if creditors could treat even blameless insolvents harshly.[104]

Parliament was not moved by such arguments, essentially because it was less interested in creating rational, calculating individuals than it was in reinforcing the attitudes of deference and dependence on which the authority of the propertied classes rested. The unreformed debt law was far better suited to that purpose than was some utilitarian calculus. The uncertainty engendered by the broad discretion to impose or not to impose sanctions and to limit or to extend those imposed encouraged debtors to ingratiate themselves as broadly as possible. William Fleetwood, Bishop of Ely, explained the dynamics of this process in a sermon on preparation for default. Because the uncertainties of the world made insolvency likely, and because the legal consequences of default were so serious, Bishop Fleetwood advised his flock to lead exemplary lives in the hope that their creditors would take pity on them in the future. Like a sinner before God, a defaulter could not justify himself to his creditors. He would be saved by their grace alone. But if he lived circumspectly and knew his place, an insolvent could greatly improve his chances for forgiveness.[105]

Consistent with its theological counterpart, the law of debtor and creditor served only a limited, background role. It declared that a creditor had a property right in his debt and authorized him to send his debtors to prison in order to protect that right. Despite the fact that it was universally recognized that not all such defaulters should be sent to prison, the crucial decisions – whether to prosecute and when to pardon – were all extra-legal.[106] Parliament refused to integrate mercy and the law on the theory that such justice was beyond the competence of the law. No rule could be laid down to separate the wheat from the chaff. In order to realize justice, it was thought necessary to allow creditors the arbitrary authority to deal with each case unhampered.[107]

The creditor's prerogative to show mercy arbitrarily functioned in a way analogous to the pardon power of the criminal law. It softened the harshness of the law and demonstrated that creditors could be trusted to exercise their massive coercive powers with compassion and good sense. It affirmed the right of private persons to protect their property with the aid, but without the interference, of the state. Significantly, even as Parliament found it necessary to chip away at that right by repeatedly passing Insolvent Debtor Relief Acts, it insisted on the fiction that the measures were unusual, extraordinary and not reflective of a need for basic change.[108]

To the extent that debtors followed Bishop Fleetwood's advice and creditors benevolently refrained from arresting them, it is easy to understand how the arbitrary authority permitted by the debt law would have encouraged the attitudes of deference and dependence so crucial to men of property. The justice of imprisoning insolvents was, however, sufficiently problematic, particularly given the large numbers of debtors who were in fact imprisoned, that the law could just as easily have had an opposite, radicalizing effect on the populace. There is evidence that, at least among the New Minters in the 1720s and some debtor prisoners in the 1790s, it did. After the destruction of the Mint in 1722, some of the insolvent debtors who had taken refuge there moved across the river and established another sanctuary in Wapping-Stepney, the New Mint. Walpole's spies reported that these New Minters were Jacobites, possibly because James had left the sanctuaries alone.[109] At the end of the century, unidentified debtors in the Fleet Prison nailed a proclamation to the door of the chapel associating themselves with the French Revolution and demanding the abolition of imprisonment for debt.[110] Much more commonly, however, debtors complained only about their specific creditors and asked for special consideration.[111] Such special consideration was forthcoming, in the form of releases arranged by charities and the Insolvent Debtor Relief Acts, sufficiently frequently to distract debtors from more fundamental attacks.[112]

In May 1772, *The Monthly Review* attacked a recently published treatise on imprisonment for debt for its failure to recognize the need for drastic reform. 'The disease calls for a remedy of more powerful operation. Opiates will furnish only a temporary aid. The medicine to be applied ought to work a radical and perpetual cure.'[113] The medicine that most reformers had in mind was 'rational' law. They believed that law could and should be used, like some Skinnerian device, to alter human behaviour by teaching men to understand that each of their actions would have definite, predictable consequences. Their goal was to proportion punishment to the undesirableness of the conduct in question, considered in the context of the surrounding circumstances. The process had, therefore, to be predictable, and to prevent all extraneous emotional factors, such as an individual victim's desire for revenge, from distorting the calculus.[114]

Parliament, however, was unwilling to administer the medicine. However disquieting the symptoms of the disease, the right to exercise arbitrary authority, and the patterns of deference and dependence that were created by it, were too important to the eighteenth-century English ruling class to be tampered with. The gradual reform of the law of debtor and creditor had to await the declining power of those interested in preserving the 'old attachment', and the development in the nineteenth century of other forms of social and economic control.

NOTES AND REFERENCES

1. John Holliday, *The Life of William Late Earl of Mansfield*, London, 1797, p. 188
2. John Howard, *The State of the Prisons in England and Wales with preliminary observations, and an account of some foreign Prisons and Hospitals*, 3rd ed. London, 1784, appendix, p. 16.
3. These comparisons were calculated by comparing the numbers of persons released from prison pursuant to each of the Insolvent Debtor Relief Acts, the numbers actually in prison at the time of Howard's tours, the number of debtors listed in the scattered censuses of individual prisons, the annual number committed to those prisons for which the commitment books survive, and the mean length of time that debtors remained in those prisons. While these calculations are at best approximations based on reliable, but ambiguous data, the general outlines are clearly correct.
4. ibid.
5. Calculated on the basis of lists of debtor prisoners published in the *London Gazette* following passage of each of the Insolvent Debtor Relief Acts.
6. ibid. See also Howard, *The State of the Prisons*, appendix, p. 16.
7. Corporation of London Record Office, Misc. MSS 87.1 *The Prisoner's Advocate: or Caveat*, London, 1726, pp. 10-15. T. B. Howell, *A Complete Collection of State Trials*, vol. 17, London 1813, p. 432: Daniel Hopkins testified that prisoners preferred sponging houses because 'they have better convenience to transact what business is to be done, than to trouble their friends to go into the gaol'.
8. This total is derived from the lists of debtors published in the *London Gazette* during 1722 and 1723. The Mint Act was 9 Geo I c. 28 (1722).
9. These numbers are derived from the lists of returning fugitives in the *London Gazette* following each of the fugitive debtor relief acts. The fugitive debtor acts were contained in the following Insolvent Debtor Relief Acts: 2 Geo. II c. 20; 10 Geo. II c. 13; 1 Geo. III c. 17; 5 Geo. III c. 41; 9 Geo. III c. 26; 12 Geo. III c. 23; 14 Geo. III, c. 77; 16 Geo. III c. 38; 18 Geo. III c. 52; 21 Geo. III, c. 63; 34 Geo. III c. 69; 37 Geo. III c. 88.
10. See lists filed in connection with the Insolvent Debtors Relief Acts, prison commitment books for the Fleet Prison (Public Record Office, PRIS 1) and King's Bench Prison (Public Record Office, PRIS 5), and sheriff's returns from the City of London, Oxfordshire, Norfolk, and Staffordshire. These proportions were remarkably constant throughout the kingdom and across time.
11. *House of Commons Journals*, 1792, vol. 47 pp. 650-2.
12. *Proposals for Promoting Industry and Advancing Proper Credit*, 1732, p. 9, *The Case of Insolvent Debtors . . .*, 1724, p. 8, *Gentleman's Magazine*, November 1804, p. 992, W. R. Minchin, *Debtor and Creditor Law*, London, 1812, pp. 70-2.
13. *House of Commons Journals*, 1792, vol. 47, pp. 650-2. Common labourers constituted less than 2–3 per cent of persons applying for relief under the Insolvent Debtor Relief Acts. Compare L. L. Robson, *The Convict Settlers of Australia*, New York, 1965.

14. Tradesmen and small shopkeepers constituted 68 per cent of persons applying for relief under the Insolvent Debtor Relief Acts.

15. Oxfordshire Record Office, Quarter Sessions Papers, Trinity Term, 1725, Michaelmas Term, 1731; Howard, *The State of the Prisons*; Peter Southerton, *The Story of a Prison*, Reading, Berkshire, 1975, pp. 14-15; S. A. Peyton, 'Introduction to Minutes of Proceedings in Quarter Sessions held for the Parts of Kesteven in the County of Lincoln, 1674-95'. *Lincoln Record Society*, vol. 25, 1928, pp. xxii–xxiii; Dr J. C. Lettsom, *Hints Respecting the Prison of Newgate*, London, 1794, pp. 15-16; *Gentleman's Magazine*, November 1804, p. 992; John Baptist Grano, *A Journal of My Life while in the Marshalsea, 1728–1729*, Ms. Rawlinson D. 34, Bodleian Library, Oxford, p. 59.

16. *The Idler*, 6 January 1759, no. 38.

17. ibid.

18. *House of Commons Journals*, 1803, vol. 19, p. 63.

19. Public Record Office, PRIS 1 (Fleet Prison Commitment Books)/5-10. Between 28 March 1733 and October 1748, 4273 debtors were committed to the Fleet Prison. At least 387 of them (9.1 per cent) died before being released.

20. John Strype (ed.) *A Survey of the Cities of London and Westminster and the Borough of Southwark* by John Stow, London, 1754, vol. 1, p. 753; The Papers of Sir William Chaytor, N. Yorkshire Record Office, D/CH/ C-507, 5 July 1701.

21. *Vox Dei et Naturae*, 1711, p. 9; *Gentleman's Magazine*, October 1795, vol. 65, pt. 2, p. 852; *James Nield, An Account of the Rise, Progress and Present State . . .*, 1802, pp. 13-14; House of Lords, Sessions Papers, 1820, vol. 117, pp. 8-9; P. J. Coleman, *Debtors and Creditors in America*, Madison, Wisconsin, State Historical Society, 1974, pp. 266-7.

22. Thomas Fowell Buxton, *An Inquiry Whether Crime and Misery are Produced or Prevented, By our Present System of Prison Discipline*, London, 1818, pp. 4-12; William Holdsworth, *A History of the English Law*, 1952, vol. 13, p. 318; 'Rules and Orders for the better Government of the King's Bench Prison', 1729.

23. *The Debtor and Creditor's Guide*, London, 1825, pp. 1-8, 10-17; Corporation of London Record Office, 'Historical Notes on the Court of Requests'; House of Commons, Sessions Papers, 1823, vol. 11, p. 185.

24. Thomas MacDonald, *A Treatise on Civil Imprisonment* London, 1791, pp. 108-11.

25. Daniel Defoe, *A Review of the State of the English Nation*, vol. 4, no. 33, 26 April 1707, p. 131.

26. Parliamentary Debates, *Hansard*, vol. 10, 1812, vols. 1068-71; John Mallory, *Objections humbly offer'd against passing the Bill intitled, A Bill for the More Easy and Speedy Recovery of Small Debts, into a Law*, London, 1730, p. 26.

27. J. S. Carpenter, LLD thesis, University of London, 1918, p. 88; House of Lords, Sessions Papers, 1820, vol. 117, p. 49, 19 May 1820, David Pollack, barrister, witness.

28. Francis John James Cadwallader, *In Pursuit of Merchant Debtor and Bankrupt: 1066-1732*, University of London PhD thesis, 1965, pp. 151-2; William Blackstone, *Commentaries on the Laws of England*, 12th ed. London 1794, vol 3, pp. 417-18.

29. A. W. B. Simpson, *A History of the Common Law of Contract: The Rise of the Action of Assumpsit*, Oxford 1975, p. 393; Cadwallader, *In Pursuit of Merchant Debtor . . .*, p. 334; (anon.), *Tenant's Law: or the Laws concerning Landlords, Tenants and Farmers*, London, 1726, p. 145; House of Lords, Sessions Papers, 1820, vol. 117. pp. 8-9.

30. If nothing at all could be taken on a writ of *elegit*, the courts treated it as if it were merely a *fieri facias*, and thus allowed the debtor to be imprisoned on a subsequent *capias ad satisfaciendum*.

31. Charles Ellis, *A Treatise on the Law of Debtor and Creditor*, London, 1822, pp. 467-8; (anon.), *Considerations on a Commission of Bankruptcy . . .*, London, 1789, p. 89; Theodore F. T. Plucknett, *A Concise History of the Common Law*, 5th ed., London, 1956, pp. 390-1.

32. Wayne Joseph Sheehan, *The London Prison System, 1666-1795*, University of Maryland, PhD thesis, 1975, p. 79; Edward Farley, *Imprisonment for Debt Unconstitutional and Oppressive . . .*, London, 1788, pp. 29-30; (anon.), *A Description of King's Bench Prison*, London, 1824, pp. 23-4.

33. Imprisonment on *mesne* process meant imprisonment prior to the judgment of a court. Imprisonment pursuant to a judgment was referred to as 'in execution'. Ian P. H. Duffy, *Bankruptcy and Insolvency in London in Eighteenth and Early Nineteenth Centuries*, Oxford, DPhil thesis, 1973 pp. 190-210; House of Commons, Sessions Papers, 1833, vol. 22, p. 236; (anon.), *The Debtor and Creditor's Assistant*, London, 1793, p. 77. If a creditor failed to prosecute within two terms of the arrest, the debtor could apply for a writ of *supersedeas* which ordered the jailer to release him; (anon.), *The Debtor and Creditor's Assistant*, London, 1793, pp. 24-6; William Blackstone, *Commentaries*, 12th ed., 1794, vol. 1, p. 353.

34. *Cobbett's Parliamentary History of England*, London, 1814, vol. 22, col. 625.

35. Holdsworth, *History of the English Law*, vol. 8, pp. 232-3.

36. (anon.), 'Some Considerations Humbly offered to the High Court of Parliament for the Benefit of Creditors, and the Relief of honest Insolvents', c. 1719; A Gentleman of the West Riding in the County of York, 'An Essay for a General Regulation of the Law', London, 1727, pp. 156-63; Public Record Office, PRIS 4/10, p. 80 right. King's Bench Prison Commitment Books.

37. *An Humble Representation upon the Perpetual Imprisonment of Insolvent Debtors*, London, 1687, pp. 25-6. The pamphlet, 'A Speech without Doors, In Behalf of an Insolvent Debtor in the Fleet Prison', London, 1729, relates the case of a gentleman who had an estate of 2000 pounds and 40,000 pounds in 'ready money' but fell deeply into debt. He paid all he could, but was five guineas short to the gaoler for fees. The gaoler not only refused to release him, but had him put on the common side of the prison in chains. The tale may be apocryphal; the legal problem was real.

38. Simpson, *History of the Common Law of Contract*, p. 393; Cadwallader, *In Pursuit of Merchant Debtor and Bankrupt*, p. 334; Farley, *Imprisonment for Debt . . .*, pp. 150-1.

39. B. L. of Twickenham, *An Accurate Description of Newgate, with the Rights, Privileges, Allowances, Fees, Dues and Customs thereof . . .*, London, 1724.

40.   *A Report From the Committee to Enquire into the State of the Gaols of this Kingdom*, London, 1729, p. 3; Philanthropos, 1729, pp. 17-18. Releasing debtors confined for their gaol fees only was a common eighteenth-century philanthropic act. See, for example: *Gentleman's Magazine*, vol. 21, November, 1751, p. 520 and vol. 36, May 1766, p. 245. The Thatched House Society, the largest organization for debtor charity, reported that at the end of the eighteenth century about 8 per cent of all debtors were being held for their fees only. *Cobbett's Parliamentary History of England*, 1817, vol. 30, pp. 647-9

41.   For an account of the refusal to release a corpse, see: *A True State of . . . the Fleet*, London, 1727, p. vi:

> His Relations sent in a coffin and Burying Cloaths, in order to take away his Corps, and bury him as they saw fit: But Mr. *Thomas Guybon*, the Deputy Warden, refused them the said Corps, unless they would first pay and discharge what Chamber-Rent and Fees were due and owing from the deceased to said Mr. *Guybon*, which they absolutely refused to do; and as the Corps was carrying through the Gate of the Prison, the Deputy Warden, and his Servants, Stop'd and detained above two Hours (whilst the Hearse and Mourning-Coaches, with his Relations, were all the Time without the Gate) his said Relations were forced, at last to comply with the said Warden's Demands, and to give him Ten Guineas or Ten Pounds, for the purchase of the said dead Body, and to procure the Liberty to bury it themselves . . .

42.   *Report From the Committee to Enquire into the State of the Gaols of this Kingdom*, p. 3.

43.   2 Geo. II c. 22; renewed in 1759 (33 Geo. II c. 28), 1793 (33 Geo. III c. 5) and 1797 (37 Geo. III c. 85). The original 1729 Act set groats at 2s. 4d. a week, raised in 1791 to 3s. 6d. James Bland Burges, *Considerations on the Law of Insolvency with a Proposal for Reform*, London, 1783, pp. 169-70; Charles Ellis, *A Treatise on the Law of Debtor and Creditor*, London, 1822, p. 494.

44.   Corporation of London Record Office, Misc. MSS. 326.13.

45.   *House of Commons Journals*, 1792, vol. 47, pp. 649-50. Sidney and Beatrice Webb, *English Prisons under Local Government*, London, 1922, p. 27.

46.   Peter Southerton, *The Story of a Prison*, London 1975, pp. 14-15; S. A. Peyton, 'Introduction to Minutes of Proceedings in the Quarter Sessions held for the Parts of Kesteven in the County of Lincoln, 1674-1695', *Lincoln Record Society*, vol. 25, 1928, pp. xxii-xxxiii; Lettsom, *Hints Respecting the Prisons of Newgate*, pp. 15-16; *Grano*, p. 59; (anon.), *The Debtor and Creditor's Assistant*, London, 1793, pp. 2-6; Corporation of London Record Office, MSS. 84.21 and Misc. MSS. 173.5; *House of Commons Journals*, 13-14 May 1729, pp. 376-87.

47.   John Strype (ed.), *A Survey of the Cities of London and Westminster . . .*, London, 1754, vol. 2, p. 701.

48.   *The Debtor and Creditor's Assistant*, pp. 2-7

49.   ibid.

50. *House of Commons Journals*, 1792, vol. 47, p. 651.

51. ibid.

52. The Papers of Sir William Chaytor, North Yorkshire Record Office, D/CH/C-507, 5 July 1701.

53. Corporation of London Record Office, Sessions Books, Book 4, 220 F, p. 57.

54. Chaytor, letter no. 474. Chaytor wrote to his wife from prison that he was wholly satisfied with accommodations in the Fleet and in no mood to pay his creditors. 'If a man have mony, he may live here as well as at court.'

55. *Considerations on the Laws between Debtors and Creditors*, London, 1779, p. 3.

56. Daniel Defoe, *Review*, vol. 5, no. 145, 1 March 1709, pp. 579-80; (anon.), 'The Case of Many Thousand Distressed Prisoners', London, 1729; *Norwich Weekly Mercury*, 23 August 1729; *Gentleman's Magazine*, December 1758, vol. 28, p. 609; (anon.), *The Insolvent's Humble Address*, London, 1728, p. 4; *The Idler*, 6 January 1759, no. 38.

57. J. E. Ogelthorpe, *Reasons for Establishing the Colony of Georgia*, London, 1733, pp. 23-4. In a carefully researched article, Albert Berry Saye has demonstrated that few debtors actually went to Georgia. He neglects to point out that apparently they would not go. 'Was Georgia a Debtor Colony?' *Georgia Historical Quarterly*, vol. xxiv, 1940, pp. 323-41.

58. Between 1772, the year it was founded, and 1802, the Thatched House Society arranged for the release of 19,063 debtors at a cost of £49,302 6s. 4¾d. The report indicates that 11,399 (60 per cent) had wives living at the time they were released. The released debtors also had 32,871 children: James Neild, *An Account of the Rise, Progress and Present State of the Society for the Discharge and Relief of Persons Imprisoned for Small Debts Throughout England and Wales*, London, 1802, pp. 353-4.

59. See, e.g., *House of Commons Journals*, 1803, vol. 10, p. 176; *House of Commons Journals*, 1803, vol. 19, p. 35; *A Report from the Committee appointed to enquire into . . . the King's Bench Prison*, 1730.

60. See, e.g., *Cobbett's Parliamentary History of England*, 1814, vols 22-8.

61. I Ann c. 19, 2 and 3 Ann c. 10, 10 Ann c. 29; 6 Geo. I c. 19, II Geo. I c. 21, and the Acts cited in note 9 above.

62. 16 Geo. II c. 17, 1743, Preamble.

63. *Cobbett's Parliamentary History of England*, vol. 22, cols 623-4, Earl Poulet.

64. The first tentative step towards reform was the establishment of the Court for the Relief of Insolvent Debtors in 1813, 'under which any Prisoner for Debt, who should have been in Custody for the Space of Three Months, abandoning to his Creditors, at the Mercy of the Court, all his Property, Real and Personal, in Possession, in Reversion and in Expectancy, became intitled to his personal liberty, his Property subsequently acquired being still liable to be taken, under certain Restrictions, in Satisfaction of his Debts'. House of Lords, Sessions Papers, 1820, vol. 117, p. 3. See also Duffy, *Bankruptcy and Insolvency . . .*, p. 100.

65. House of Commons, Sessions Papers, 1833, vol. 22, p. 36; 'Provisoes and Amendments Humbly Proposed to the Insolvent Debtors Bill . . .', c. 1714; Duffy, *Bankruptcy and Insolvency . . .* , p. 157; Daniel Defoe, 'Some

Objections humbly offered to the Consideration of the Hon. House of Commons . . .', London, 1729; 'The Case of the Merchants and Traders in and about the City of London . . .', c. 1714.

66. David Alexander, *Retailing in England during the Industrial Revolution*, London, 1970, pp. 219-22; Kent County Record Office, Q/C1/438, Account Book of Robert May.

67. T. S. Willan, *The Inland Trade*, Totowa, New Jersey, 1976; J. D. Marshall (ed.), *Autobiography of William Stout*, Manchester, 1967; Kent County Record Office, Q/C1/438; Alexander, *Retailing in England . . .*, pp. 82-4.

68. T. S. Ashton, *An Economic History of England: The 18th Century*, London, 1955, pp. 206-10; T. S. Ashton, *The Industrial Revolution, 1760-1830*, New York, 1964, p. 36; Christopher Hill, *Reformation to Industrial Revolution, 1530-1780*, London, 1967, p. 91.

69. Philopolities, *The Present State of the Prison of Ludgate*, London, 1712, pp. 68-9; House of Commons Sessions Papers, 1835, vol. 11; Lords First Report, pp. 86-7; J. R. McCulloch, *A Dictionary, Practical, Theoretical, and Historical, of Commerce and Commercial Navigation*, London, 1844, pp. 1206-7; Alexander, *Retailing in England . . .*, pp. 82-4.

70. Willan, *The Inland Trade*, p. 97; *Cobbett's Parliamentary History of England*, vol. 13, 1812, cols 1113-23.

71. (anon.), 'A Petition to the Kings most excellent Majestie', London, 1622, pp. 11-12; John Kettlewell, *An Office for Prisoners for Crimes Together with Another for Prisoners for Debt . . .*, London, 1697, pp. 27-9; Daniel Defoe, 'Remarks on the Bill to Prevent Frauds . . .', London, 1706, pp. 2-3; (anon.), 'The Insolvents Humble Address to Her Majesty', London, 1728, p. 4; Henry Fielding, *An Enquiry into the Cause of the Late Increase of Robbers, &c. with some Proposals for Remedying the Growing Evil*, London, 1751; William Eden, *Principles of Penal Law*, 2nd ed., London, 1771, p. 52; Thomas Fowell Buxton, *An Inquiry whether Crime and Misery are Produced or Prevented by our Present System of Prison*, London, 1818, pp. 4-12.

72. Marshall, *Autobiography of William Stout*, p. 7; Willan, *The Inland Trade*, p. 95.

73. Philanthropos, *Letter to Lord S***** . . .*, London, 1729, p. 15; Frederick A. Pottle (ed.), *Boswell's London Journal*, New York, 1950, p. 60; *Cobbett's Parliamentary History of England*, 1813, col. 248; Alexander, *Retailing in England . . .*, p. 222.

74. *Cobbett's Parliamentary History of England*, 1817, vol. 29, 12 May 1791, cols 512-14.

75. ibid., 1814, vol. 20, col. 1399; vol. 22, cols. 629-30. The record of the first few years of the Insolvent Debtors Court did nothing to quiet their fears. Between 1813 and 1816, the Court released debtor prisoners with liabilities totalling £5,597,859. Those same debtors turned over only £1,460 worth of assets – just over one-sixteenth of one pence on the pound. Duffy, *Bankruptcy and Insolvency . . .*, p. 89.

76. *Cobbett's Parliamentary History of England*, 1814, vol. 20, cols. 1396-8.

77. ibid., vol. 22, cols. 629-30; col. 625; House of Commons, Sessions Papers, 1816, vol. 4, pp. 358-9, Samuel Worrall, town clerk of Bristol, witness.

78. *Considerations on a Commission of Bankruptcy* . . ., London, 1789, p. iii.

79. House of Commons, Sessions Papers, 1833, vol. 22, p. 36; 'Provisoes and Amendments Humbly Proposed . . .', c. 1714; 'The Case of the Merchants and Traders in and about the City of London, . . .', c. 1714; Daniel Defoe, 'Some Objections humbly offered to . . . the House of Commons, . . .', London, 1729; Duffy, *Bankruptcy and Insolvency* . . ., p. 157.

80. James Bland Burges, *Considerations on the Law of Insolvency* . . ., London, 1783, pp. 330-1; *A Dissertation on Credit*, c. 1750, p. 1; *Monthly Review*, vol. 65, July 1781, p. 70; *Gentleman's Magazine*, vol. 84, pt 2, December 1814, p. 592; Daniel Defoe, *A Review of the State of the English Nation*, vol. 6, no. 33, p. 130; House of Commons, Sessions Papers, 1835, vol. 11, Lords First Report, pp. 86-7; R. C. G. Fane, *Observations on the Proposed Abolition of Imprisonment for Debt on Mesne Process*, London, 1838, pp. 24n-25n; *A Follower of Bentham, The Prison-House Unmasked:* . . ., London, 1837, p. 21; (A Gentleman), *The Gentleman's Library:* . . ., London, 1744, pp. 163-7; John Prujean, *A Treatise on the Laws of England now in Force for the Recovery of Debt* . . ., London, 1791, pp. 33-6; William Fleetwood, Bishop of Ely, 'The Justice of Paying Debts: A Sermon Preach'd in the City', London, 1718, p. 12.

81. Parliamentary Debates, *Hansard*, vol. 27, 1814, cols 397-9.

82. ibid., vol. 9, 1812, col. 163.

83. ibid., vol. 7, 1812, col. 853.

84. Donald Veall, *The Popular Movement for Law Reform, 1640-1660*, Oxford, 1970, pp. 145-51; Duffy, *Bankruptcy and Insolvency* . . ., pp. 64-5; William Holdsworth, *Charles Dickens as a Legal Historian*, New Haven, Conn., 1928, pp. 142-3; Carpenter, LLD thesis, 1918, p. 88; House of Lords, Sessions Papers, 1820, vol. 117, 31 May 1820, William Ballantine, barrister, witness; Philanthropos, *Proposals for Promoting Industry and Advancing Proper Credit*, London, 1732.

85. 1 and 2 Vict. c. 102.

86. Parliamentary Debates, *Hansard*, vol. 7, 1812, cols 853 and 858.

87. William K. Wimsatt, Jr and Frederick A. Pottle (eds) *Boswell for the Defence, 1769-1774*, New York, 1959, pp. 84-5. I would like to thank Joanna Innes of Cambridge University for this reference.

88. For moral arguments against forgiving debtors see: Thomas Mangey, *Practical Discourses upon the Lord's Prayer* . . , London, 1717, pp. 163-4; Thomas Sherlock, Lord Bishop of Bangor, 'A Sermon preached before the Rt. Hon., The Lord Mayor . . . of the City of London . . .', London, 1728, pp. 12-13; William Dodwell, *Practical Discourses on Moral Subjects*, vol. 2, London, 1749, pp. 234-5. The essential argument in each case is that forgiving debtors undermines the long-term interests of society and of the debtors themselves by leading people to believe that they can get away with not paying their debts.

89. Jonas Hanway, *A Plan for establishing a Charity House* . . ., London, 1758, pp. xxx-xxxii; *The Life and Opinions of Col. George Hangar*, London, 1801, vol. 2, p. 112. *London Magazine*, April 1760, vol. 30, pp. 185-9; John Howard Papers, Bodleian Library, Ms. Eng. Misc. c. 332.

90. John Howard Papers, c. 332; H. E. Rollins, *The Pepys Ballads*, vol. 3, 1930, pp. 265-7.

91. House of Commons, Sessions Papers, 1835, vol. 11, Lords First Report, pp. 86-7; *Philopolities*, 1712, pp. 68-9.

92. T. S. Ashton, *The Industrial Revolution*, New York, 1964, p. 36.

93. *Enquiry into the Causes of the Encrease and Miseries of the Poor in England*, London, 1738, p. 41.

94. Determined by comparing the names of all creditors whose surnames began with six randomly selected letters and whose names appear in prison commitment books. This conclusion should be regarded as somewhat tenuous, because of the small number of surviving commitment books.

95. House of Commons, Sessions Papers, 1835, vol. 11, Lords First Report, pp. 86-7: *Life in a Debtors' Prison*, London, 1880, p. 30. J. R. McCulloch, *A Dictionary: Practical Commerce and Commercial Navigation*, London, 1844, p. 1207.

96. John O'Keefe, *Wild Oats, or the Strolling Gentleman*, 1798, ed. Clifford Williams, London, 1977, Act II, scene ii, p. 18.

97. ibid., Act III, scene i, p. 29.

98. Figures on the basis of returns filed in connection with the Insolvent Debtor Relief Acts and the surviving prison commitment works and sheriff's returns for the counties of Kent, Norfolk, Oxfordshire, and Staffordshire, the Cities of Norwich and London as well as the Fleet and King's Bench prisons.

99. Public Record Office, PRIS 4/10, p. 80 right.

100. See n. 98 above.

101. ibid.

102. *Gentleman's Magazine*, vol. 48, December 1773, p. 616; *The London Journal*, 19 October 1723, n. 221; *Citizen's Law Companion*, London, 1794, pp. 22-4; *The British Journal*, 15 June 1723, no. 39, p. 5.

103. *Philanthropos*, 1729, p. 13.

104. *Imprisonment for Debt Considered* (trans. from Italian), London, 1772.

105. William Fleetwood, 'The Justice of Paying Debts', London, 1718, p. 17.

106. *Cobbett's Parliamentary History of England*, 1814, vol. 22, cols 627-8.

107. ibid., vol. 22, c. 625. On the recognition that creditors had a pardon power analogous to that of the King, see *The Spectator*, vol. 2, p. 22; *The Prisoner's Advocate: or a Caveat*, London, 1726, p. 2.

108. *Cobbett's Parliamentary History of England*, 1814, 1098-1105.

109. Public Record Office, SP, 35 (55) 3.

110. Public Record Office, TS 11/943: '!!*This House to be Let*!! Peaceable possession will be given by the present tenants, on or before the 1st day of January 1793 – being the commencement of the 1st year of *Liberty in Great Britain* !!! The *Republic* of *France* having rooted out *Despotism* their *glorious example* and *complete success* against *Tyrants* render such infamous *Bastiles* no longer necessary in Europe.'

111. See e.g. Corporation of London Record Office, Misc. MSS. 87.1, Debtor Petitions, 319.8, Debtor Petitions; Kent County Record Office, U 1515, OQ/B1 bundle 2, Oxford County Record Office, Sessions Minute Book II,

QSM I/2/iii, p. 53; 'The Case of the poor confined Debtors,' (undated); *House of Commons Journals*, 1803, vol. 22, p. 739.

112. James Stephens, *Considerations on Imprisonment for Debt*, London, 1770, p. 15.
113. *Monthly Review*, vol. 46, May 1772, p. 540.
114. *Cobbett's Parliamentary History of England*, 1816, vol. 26, col. 1200; (anon.), *Multum in parvo* . . ., London, 1653, pp. 13-14; A Gentleman of the Middle Temple, *Some Abuses of the Law Detected* . . ., London, c. 1687; (anon.), *Vox Dei et Naturae:* . . ., London, 1711, pp. 1-15; a Gentleman of the West Riding in the County of York, *An Essay for a General Regulation of the Law* . . ., London, 1727, pp. 31-3; Philanthropos, *Proposals for Promoting Industry and Advancing Proper Credit*, London, 1732, p. 19; *Gentleman's Magazine*, vol. 20, April 1750, p. 175; James Bland Burges, *Considerations* . . ., London, 1783, pp. 344-56; (anon.), 'More Reasons for a Reform in Parliament', London, 1793; James Neild, *An Account of the Rise, Progress and Present State* . . ., London, 1802, p. 27 n; John Prince Smith, *A Practical Summary and Review* . . ., London, 1814, pp. vii-x.

10

Moral Treatment: Mental Therapy and Social Control in the Nineteenth Century

ROBERT CASTEL*

That all memory is composed of recollections illuminated against a background of an oblivion is doubtless a verifiable proposition, for the history of a collective practice just as much as for that of an individual. Thus it is one of the commonplaces of the history of mental medicine to inscribe the majority of therapeutic initiatives that have appeared since the end of the Second World War under the heading of a 'third psychiatric revolution'. This 'revolutionary' quality is attributed both to the transformation of the internal environment of the hospital (the reorganization of hospital life in full conformity with the requirements of treatment, in contrast to the quasi-exclusive custodial concern of the traditional asylum) and the modification of the relation between the hospital and the outside world (the new methods strive to be simultaneously therapeutic and 'resocializing', preparing the patient to reassume the roles of everyday life).

Under this idealized genealogical schema, each 'revolution' marks the end of its own Middle Age, from which only its negative characteristics are recollected: the barbarity of an authoritarian mode of social control which did not even trouble itself to identify mental illness medically before Pinel; the classificatory mania of nineteenth-century psychiatrists supported by the illusions of a mechanistic organicism before Freud; and finally the obscurantist decay of the asylum tradition that preceded the intervention of the current reformers of psychiatric assistance.[1]

It would be easy to show the part that retrospective illusion plays in such reconstructions. But if the selectivity of a discipline's memory is comparable in this respect to that of an individual, this is perhaps because in both cases the functions of forgetfulness and memory filters are

*Translated by Peter Miller
Source: 'Le Traitement Moral', Topique, no. 2, pp. 119-29, Paris, Presses Universitaire de France.

homologous. If, by analysing 'moral treatment' as it was practised and justified in the nineteenth century, we are proposing here a critique of a myth that the history of psychiatry has lived off, this is not, accordingly, undertaken in the vain hope of showing that the golden age of medical assistance is behind us; it is not even primarily to exhume 'influences'. We shall indeed show that moral treatment installed a complex system of intervention, certain of whose provisions have been retained by modern psychiatry. But everything takes place as though modern psychiatry *did not wish to know this*, and it is here in particular that the current implication of the problem lies. We will try to show that the principles of moral treatment strikingly exemplify the deep complicity that existed in the nineteenth century between psychiatric practices and very precise techniques of social control, and if it is true that one is dealing here with something more than a simple conjunctural alliance, we will perhaps be able to understand not only why the official genealogy of psychiatry finds good reasons for censoring such a compromising collusion, but also why the most daring innovators only reluctantly take account of this hidden, and somewhat shameful, aspect of their practice.

Moral treatment constitutes the principal component of the strategy elaborated in the nineteenth century to neutralize and manipulate mental illness.[2] As the deployment of an ensemble of therapeutic procedures, it is supposed to transpose to the level of a *practice* a certain theoretical conception of the nature and aetiology of mental illness. To the extent that it has as its common element the task of gathering together all the means of intervention on the psyche of the patient, it distinguishes itself from *physical* treatment, an ensemble of means of acting on the patient's body,[3] and this opposition comes down in the last analysis to the dualism of two systems of explanation of mental illness whose conflict forms one of the principal themes of the history of mental medicine:

> Two rival schools divide, and will long continue to divide, alienist doctors: the somatic school and the psychological school. The one maintains that, madness being a physical illness, it is absurd to seek to cure it by means other than medications, and that moral means can at the very most have value as consolation or as a temporary palliative. The other school, seeing in madness only an affection of the mind, considers as effective only moral means of the kind used for example by Reil and Leuret, means analogous to those which can be brought to bear against an error or a passion in a normal person; they denounce the absurdity of prescribing a purging or bleeding (*un purgatif ou un vesicatoire*) to drive out an error of the mind, rather than employing against it the only really effective remedy: *objections*.[4]

The reasons that justify the eminent place accorded at the time to moral treatment seem to have to do with the nineteenth-century speculations aimed at elucidating the nature of mental illness by investigating its 'causes', and in particular the attempts to establish a psychological aetiology for psychic disturbances; inversely, and logically, the 'somatist thinkers' (organicists *avant la lettre*) like Calmeil, Bayle and Georget were also those who accorded least respect to moral treatment.[5]

This interpretation appears to be confirmed by an important distinction introduced by Falret within moral treatment itself, and which explicitly links two kinds of moral treatment to two different moments of the development of medical knowledge:

> Moral treatment can be divided into general or collective treatment, and individual treatment. If science were more advanced, individual treatment could occupy the first place. It would indeed seem natural to proceed in mental as in ordinary medicine, to take account, in the treatment of an insane person, of the special form of his illness, of the particular indications resulting from his morbid individuality, in a word to vary the means employed according to the thousand nuances of individual examination.
>
> Such must indeed be the goal of the efforts of science: to arrive one day at a more accurate specification of the indications resulting from the special condition of each patient, and to discover physical and moral remedies appropriate to the variety of these conditions to obtain this result will certainly be an advance that we should not in the least wish to contest, but we should nevertheless be wary of exaggerating this direction of science; by celebrating to excess the benefits of a purely individual treatment, we would be in danger of neglecting the unquestionable advantages of the treatment that we call general and which, in the current state of mental medicine, is our most precious resource. . . .
>
> . . . General treatment, instead of applying itself to a single insane person in particular, is directed toward a large number of patients at the same time. It rests on general principles, applicable to almost all insane persons, and put into practice in the establishments devoted to them.[6]

Thus it would seem that it is the backward state of theory – the empty site of a knowledge which would be no less than a science of mental illness capable of deducing a therapeutics from exact knowledge of 'the special condition of each patient' – that forces the doctor to organize his practice around more or less provisional expedients, treating collectively those

individuals presenting general characteristics as defined by a crude
semiology. One can equally relate to the same theoretical uncertainty the
hesitation of practitioners between the procedures proposed by moral
treatment and those of physical treatment, and their propensity to
amalgamate them in a 'therapeutic eclecticism' (the expression comes
from Falret himself[7]). The doctor is indeed obliged to mobilize the
ensemble of means of intervention technically available at a given
moment, without being able to wait until they can be deduced from a
coherent set of principles. Besides, does not experience in the most
empirical sense of the term prove to him that 'every means which is called
moral acts at the same time on the physical system, just as every means
called physical, whether directed upon the nervous system or even on other
organs, can and must act on the moral system'?[8]

In short, the situation of moral treatment in the context of nineteenth-
century psychiatry seems to accord in a satisfactory manner with the
classical problematic of the lag of theory behind practice: a psychiatric
knowledge that is still uncertain of its bases resigns itself with modesty and
– at least where Falret is concerned – with lucidity to a provisional
empiricism in the choice of its methods. Indeed, one might be tempted to
wonder whether the subsequent progress of medicine in the sense of a
better scientific knowledge of the case – does psychoanalysis not offer the
possibility of reconstituting the specific, differentiated aetiology of a
morbid syndrome? – does not justify an interpretation of the moral
treatment of madness, and especially of 'general treatment', as an early
stage in the continuing process of development of medical knowledge
towards its adulthood. This seems to be the conclusion that Falret himself
suggests in the peroration of his lecture:

> We hoped that you will take away with you the reassuring conviction
> that, if the special science that we are cultivating is unfortunately still
> little developed, we possess at least some beneficial principles of
> general treatment, applied with success in the best run asylums of any
> country, and that if much still remains to be carried out along the path
> so gloriously opened by our illustrious masters, an immense progress
> has however been gained under their powerful impetus, allowing us
> to hope for more in the future from subsequent advances of mental
> medicine.[9]

No doubt such an interpretation is not radically false, but it is a one-sided
and partial one. Independently of theoretical reasons – or of the absence of
such reasons – there exists another basis for medical practice which
dictates the supremacy of moral treatment. For it would be a mistake to

interpret 'therapeutic eclecticism' exclusively in terms of what it *lacks* in order to fulfil the requirements of scientific rationality; it would be equally mistaken if, by taking note only of the alienists' confessions of their inability to establish solid scientific foundations for the 'general treatment' of madness, one were to represent its supporters as pure empiricists, justified in their humility by the impossibility of constituting a general theory of mental illness. In many respects the case is quite the reverse: this 'eclecticism' is at the same time a totalitarianism, at the level of the ends that it poses as well as of the means that it employs; this 'empiricism' establishes itself on 'principles', affirmed dogmatically and from which one can *deduce* a global and coherent strategy of therapeutic intervention. Through an instructive paradox, it is precisely the authors who are most conscious of the gaps in their knowledge – Leuret, Falret – who are most systematic in the statement of a therapeutic method whose value is at no time called into question. To say that nineteenth-century psychiatric knowledge is uncertain of its foundations signifies that it possesses only a weak autonomy in relation to other systems of interpretation, and hence that it is *permeable to non-medical norms*, and ready to reinterpret within the framework of an extra-medical synthesis representations which have no theoretical relation with medically founded knowledge. These representations are the dominant social values, the guiding ideas of the politico-moral ideology of the time: order, discipline, sanctification of family ties, the cult of work as source of all moralization, respect for hierarchies, acceptance of one's allotted place in the social system. It is adherence to this system of social beliefs, much more than allegiance to scientific theories, which in any case were unsure of themselves and contradicted each other, that accounts for the *consensus* achieved in the nineteenth century around moral treatment. F. Voisin admits this almost explicitly:

> Everywhere, today, one seeks to cure the insane, everywhere one seeks to modify, enlighten and reform criminals, and everywhere the necessary scientific elements are lacking. . . . Our knowledge has not attained the same level as our sentiments.[10]

Voisin omits only to formulate the corollary: if the 'knowledge' is not adequate to the 'sentiments', the sentiments can make up for the knowledge, and this is the entire secret of moral treatment. What still needs to be made clear, however, is the fact that this system of representations is not so much an external point of reference for mental medicine, present also in other sectors of social practice, but rather an integral component of the structure of medical discourse.

One can use the word 'structure' here without abusing language too much, since moral treatment is at the centre of a coherent practical system whose principal elements – social sensibility to mental illness, conception of the therapeutic act according to the model of an authoritarian pedagogic relation, medico-administrative organization centred on the asylum – are intrinsically and functionally connected.

Social perception of mental illness first. Whereas mental illness is almost impossible to characterize medically on the basis of an aetiology, it is perceived socially in accordance with a very simple set of criteria, and this perception *directly* entails a particular therapy. In fact, the whole ideological context in which mental illness inscribes itself in the mid-nineteenth century is contained in a phrase of one of the most authoritative alienists of the age, H. Girard:

> The most salient feature of madness being physical and moral disorder, since it is through this that it manifests itself, the most uniform therapeutic tendency must be the re-establishment of order in the exercise of the functions and in that of the faculties.[11]

Note that Girard speaks of the 'most salient feature' through which madness 'manifests' itself: it is not a coincidence if he leaves in suspense the question of its underlying 'nature' in order to situate himself on the terrain of a sort of social phenomenology, where a consensus exists on the acceptance of the obviousness of what *signals* madness. Independently of its organic or psychic aetiology, there is a moral symptomatology of mental illness, an ensemble of *signs*, which enables it to be recognized with certainty.[12] In other words, there exists less a medical theory of illness than a *social perception of health*, against which the pathological stands out as that which is *lacking* in relation to this normality characterized by orderliness of conduct, equilibrium between affectivity and intelligence, the capacity to adopt social roles without fail. Thus, the set of characteristics that identify the insane person are purely negative; they declare the absence of qualities that make the normal man; but they define by this very fact the only possible type of conduct towards the patient:

> He is egoistic and unsociable; he is carried away by his unhealthy ideas and sentiments beyond the real world, and exercises only a weak control over his own ideas; without a hold over himself, he reacts only very weakly against his unhealthy tendencies or dispositions, which he allows to manifest themselves unchecked and thus reinforce themselves through their own operation. These very general characteristics, which are displayed by almost all insane

persons, are the true basis of the fundamental principles of general treatment; general treatment thus proves applicable to all these patients, since it attacks the predispositions common to them all.[13]

That there is no specifically medical content to this moral discourse should not be cause for surprise since, as Falret says in another text, 'Whether one is dealing with errors, incipient vices, or prodromes of mental illness, are not these all still disorders which need to be controlled and prevented?'[14]

This is precisely what accounts for the importance of moral treatment: it achieves a synthesis of medicine and morality. For mental medicine is a moral medicine, an enterprise to safeguard public hygiene and restore social health. This is so much the case that it is not absolutely necessary to be insane in order to benefit from its regime: it can do no harm to anyone, given the abundantly evident truth that individuals who are even slightly marginal, unstable or extravagant in their behaviour will always benefit from being firmly maintained within the norms:

> But, it will be said, in view of our ignorance and uncertainty of the final outcome of the strange phenomena that one observes, should one treat as a sick person someone who displays only transitory oddities of temperament and character? Any why not? Since this treatment consists principally of hygienic precautions, moral influences of the same order as those employed by the judicious man in matters of education, what disadvantage can there be in employing it?[15]

As T. J. Scheff has shown – and the proposition is well established as far as the current era is concerned – when confronted with the uncertainty of a difficult diagnosis, and although it may mean making a mistake, a doctor considers it less serious to decide that a person who is not sick requires treatment than to leave a 'genuinely' sick person untreated.[16] But in the question of mental medicine, this attitude entails adherence to a system of values that is not only an act of faith in the technical resources of the speciality; it rests on a usually implicit theory of the relations between the normal and the pathological assimilated to the opposition between good and evil, with all that this implies – and all the implications that require spelling out – in the way of moral, philosophical and political connotations.

Moral treatment is thus immediately caught within the framework of a pedagogic analogy. The task that it sets itself – to annul the disorder of mental illness through a restructuring of the personality of the insane – does not differ substantially, with respect to the inegalitarian relation that it entails, from any educational enterprise:

If you wish to reduce the number of lunatics, to supply them if need be with arms against their blind instincts, pay attention to the formation of their morals, the tempering of their characters. Wise institutions, manly and intelligent education, that is the whole problem.[17]

The analogy between the child and the lunatic is constant in the psychiatric literature of the time (and beyond, where the constellation enriches itself with the theme of the 'savage'). 'It is the same with this new environment in which one places an insane person,' Falret again remarks (referring to the asylum) 'as with the one which plays so influential a part in the education of the child, or of man in general.'[18] Elsewhere he justifies the unified administration of the asylum under the medical director by the need to guarantee a coherent control over the inmates: 'This precept, like many others, is common to the education of the insane and that of children.'[19] Elsewhere again, he recommends this same doctor to act as 'the zealous and intelligent guardian of the unfortunate minors entrusted to his solicitude as a man'.[20]

This general pedagogic analogy does not, however, exclude an essential difference which gives moral treatment its originality among educational techniques. Compared with the majority of learning situations (in the family, at school, in the professions, through influences experienced in everyday life, etc.), the therapeutic relation defines itself by the fact that the patient is not immediately disposed to interiorize the norm that it is sought to instill in him. The way madness is experienced in the nineteenth century is perhaps determined precisely as a relationship to law that it is impossible to give a positive character, but which is distinguished at any rate by its irreducibility to the dimensions of a mere distance, such as could be overcome by a rational learning process: the insane person is not only in a position of retarded socialization, he is in a state of profound anomic crisis:

Experience demonstrates that it is quite mistaken to treat mental illness as simple aberrations of sentiment or errors of the understanding. Reasoning only has a very limited power over unhealthy disturbances of the understanding.[21]

If then the aim is common to all socializing enterprises – to exert a normalizing influence over individuals who have not yet interiorized the norm or who have rejected it – the seriousness of the disturbance by which madness manifests itself demands the employment of new and obviously more radical means:

The more the insane person is hostile to all regularity, the more it is necessary that a methodical order should envelop him from all sides and shape him to a normal existence which sooner or later ends by becoming a need for him.[22]

Moral treatment is precisely this authoritarian pedagogy whose socialization procedures are original in part because they are adapted to the degree of disorder of mental illness. Such means can, from the technical point of view, often fail (there are incurable cases, escapes, suicides, crimes); nevertheless, the dogmatism of moral treatment is not challenged by these contingent mishaps, because the end that it pursues can never be called in question: it rests entirely on confidence in a system of dominant ideas whose authority suffices by itself to demarcate madness from normality. One can thus speak of the 'principles' of such a treatment even though one may know nothing, in terms of scientific medical certainty, about the 'nature' or 'causes' of mental illness.

The fundamental corollary – the first principle – that follows from the depth of the 'desocialization' of the insane person is the necessity to break totally with his accustomed milieu, establishing him in a new environment, arranged wholly for the purpose of enabling re-educative action to deploy itself there with maximum efficacy. The principle of assistance for the mentally ill in the nineteenth century, which means to make a *tabula rasa* as far as possible of all previous influences – a personal past, a family, an occupation, a neighbourhood – rests in the last analysis on an immense constructivist Utopia organized around the connected themes of isolation, complete manipulation of individuals, complete restructuring of their personality and enlightened medical despotism. This is the 'principle of isolation', or, in its more medical translation, the 'principle of diversion of delirium';[23] the 'principle of occupation or of work in all its forms',[24] reinstating exactly *the same norms* as those that reign in society – work, discipline, strict organization of the use of time; the 'principle of communal living',[25] which means taking full advantage of the possibilities offered by a completely regulated environment in order to regroup and redistribute individuals purely as a function of the decisions of the administrators of the Utopia, resulting in the 'favourable effects of the classification of the insane and the reaction of patients on each other';[26] finally, the principle of 'substituting a foreign authority for the sick will',[27] which uses the situation of juridical and psychological minority in which the patient finds himself as an excuse to deprive him of all initiative and, through a veritable transplantation of consciousness, to replace his will by that of the doctor.

Such, according to Falret, are the four 'principles' of moral treatment. One can hence understand 'how the asylums, as they are organized today, represent the realization of these principles'.[28]

> What, in fact, does one see in our asylums today? One sees a strictly observed, positive ordering, which determines the use of time for every hour of the day and forces each patient to react against the irregularities of his tendencies by submitting himself to the general law.[29]

It seems to me that too much stress has been laid exclusively on the internment function of the asylum. Of course, this is a space that excludes. But, at least in the medical ideology of the mid-nineteenth century, the transformative aspiration of total tutelage of the patient almost always precedes the intention of drawing a sanitary cordon around madness. It is rather the failure of this medical Utopia that reduces it to that which doubtless constitutes its most objective social meaning, namely to condemn the mad person to institutionalize his rejection. The guardianship function of the asylum can accordingly be understood as the inert residuum of this transformative passion, but also, and at the same time, as its negative shadow. Nevertheless, the principle of isolation entails a more ambitious, more totalitarian project than the one that is fulfilled simply by the act of banishment. Its failure becomes evident only after the exhaustion of all the efforts to neutralize the totality of influences liable to interfere with this enterprise of complete restructuring of the personality through exercise over it of continuous internal and external control. The goal that is pursued, as the *Report of the Inspectors of Mental Health* still formulates it in 1874, is that even 'the most stubborn, disorderly, refractory patient will end by unknowingly submitting to the influence of the new environment in which he has been placed and by becoming governable'.[30] It is thus in order to enable reason to triumph over chaos, discipline over anarchy, that the patient is first uprooted from his familiar environment, the source of disruptive influences; then placed in a special environment whose external organization and internal economy embody the order whose interiorization is the condition for cure. Falret says:

> Everything in a well organized asylum, the layout, the rules, the staff, becoming as it were impregnated with this general spirit of order and submission, thus cooperates, without the knowledge of those who are its object or instrument, in the realization of the general aim, the cure, or at least the amelioration of the insane.[31]

Or again in another text: one needs to realize of course that it is the person of the doctor, one whose omnipotence does not at all need to be founded on an omniscience, nor even on a science in the proper sense of the word, who stands at the centre of this web and holds all its threads: 'It is a human network within which the doctor surrounds his patients in order to coordinate their movements, regulate their thoughts, moderate their sentiments and preside over all their actions.'[32]

Thus one finds achieved as in an experimental situation – and it is indeed a question of a veritable human laboratory, isolated, sterilized, all of whose elements have been pre-constructed and pre-articulated in the experimenter's programme, from which all nature, all intrusion of history or spontaneity has to be excluded – all the conditions for social reconditioning in which moral treatment consists:

> The asylum, correctly organized, constitutes for them [the patients] a genuine medical atmosphere; its incessant action is almost imperceptible, but they absorb it through all their pores, and it modifies them, in the long run, much more profoundly than one would first be inclined to believe, in so far at least as they are amenable to change and the illness has not yet set on them a mark so decisive that no modifying force can exert the least influence upon them.[33]

The images of the 'general spirit', of the 'network' that encloses the patients 'without their knowing it', of the 'atmosphere' that impregnates them 'through all their pores', merit particular attention. In the best tradition of repressive socialization, it is the bonds that liberate, and the process offers the greatest chance of success when those who undergo it are unaware of its workings. Thus the medical organization of the asylum can equally be read as an image of the global social structure from which this milieu is so carefully cut off; it is the closed space constructed by the technocrats of the soul – doctors aided by administrators – where one breathes only the pure oxygen of bourgeois morality, alone capable of resuscitating for the social order those subjects who have failed in it, at least those who have not yet lapsed irretrievably. Moral treatment is the manipulative technique that deduces this institution as the necessary and sufficient condition of its implementation. Its 'principles' are clearly legible in the architecture of the buildings and the arrangement of the furniture in the rooms, in the organization of groups for work and leisure, in the rigid accounting for time and the strict separation of activities, in the objective and subjective relations of subordination of patients to the medical personnel. Everything is organized there in order that reason, as complete conditioning by rules, shall annul the disorder of the spirit and morals that is madness:

> How true it is to say that the habit of conformity to order in one's acts greatly helps to put order into one's ideas, and that, conversely, constant irregularity in even the most ordinary events of life, the incessant lack of uniformity in the mode of employing one's time, can induce profound disturbances and defects of method in thoughts and will.[34]

Let us try to draw some implications from this analysis pertinent to the present psychiatric conjuncture.

1. First, concerning the meaning of medical philanthropy, one can see that it would be a mistake to assimilate moral treatment to a set of philanthropic procedures (benevolence, care directed towards the patient, attempts to avoid the traumatizing effects of the therapeutic relation; and so on), unless the explanation of the content of this notion is of use in helping to characterize the exact meaning and limits of medical philanthropy. Moralism does not in fact necessarily go together with sentimentality. Moral treatment always establishes a fundamental inequality between patient and therapist and gathers together in the latter's hands all the positive attributes of the relation (knowledge, power, respectability, etc.). The ideal patient, or the ideal for the patient, consists in the pure malleability whose utmost active capacity is that of espousing the form of regeneration offered by the doctor.

This relation, defined from the outset as non-reciprocal, can be formulated at will in a language more or less tinged with humanism. We know of the polemic that opposed Leuret to the majority of his colleagues shocked by the explicitly repressive techniques employed in the second section of Bicetre. Against this 'veritable reign of terror'[35] they insisted on the necessity of retaining the confidence of the patient by treating him/her with maximum kindness, by trying always to persuade rather than constrain. Thus Falret, to restrict ourselves again to him, recalls in these terms the meaning of the work of Pinel and Esquirol, or rather the reconstructed image of this work in psychiatric memory:

> These benefactors of humanity were not mistaken in the direction they chose to follow and impressed on their successors; they began to neutralize the evil which, above all others, called out for their tutelary succour; they avenged outraged human dignity; they raised man up in the eyes of man; they paid homage to our moral nature;

they rediscovered and claimed our unrecognized rights; they
surrounded the person afflicted by mental alienation with the
concern required by sufferings and hygienic conditions previously
shamefully neglected.[36]

With Leuret the tone is very different:

> To be just towards the insane, to seek to inspire confidence in them,
> not to make fun of the false ideas which torment them – all that can be
> valid in certain circumstances, but not in all. If, to divert the attention
> of a monomaniac who has fallen prey to ideas which constantly
> preoccupy him, techniques of kindness and patience are useless, is it
> necessary to continue to use them, rather than to have recourse to
> irony and even to injustices and disputes? What should it matter to me
> then whether an insane person likes or detests me, desires or fears me,
> believes me to be his friend or persecutor, provided that I can break
> the chain of his depraved ideas, that I inspire in him passions capable
> of diverting his own ones? My aim is to cure not through a specific
> means, but through all possible means; and if, in order to stir him, it is
> necessary to appear hard and even unfair, why should I shrink from
> such means? Strange pity! Let us then tie the hands of a surgeon about
> to undertake an essential operation, since this operation will not take
> place without pain. If a man has a gallstone, drug him with *eau de
> guimauve*, cover him in leeches, rather than remove from him by a
> painful operation the cause of all his ills. Offering consolations to
> certain kinds of monomaniacs is like giving *eau de guimauve* and leeches
> to gallstone cases.[37]

There is certainly more than a difference of nuance between these two
attitudes, and they can lead to very different therapeutic effects. They
stand none the less at the two extremes of a single field, that of moral
treatment characterized by the omnipotence of medical authority, and the
omnipresence of the constraints that it enforces. The very most one could
say is that Leuret dispenses with the soft-heartedness of humanist
phraseology to push the logic of repressive manipulation to its limits.
Without doubt, the realism of his formulation clarifies one of the constant
operative forces of medical conduct. The myth of the surgeon as a
paradigm of therapeutic efficacy is a familiar denizen of the psychiatric
unconscious; with the practice of lobotomy it finds a means of incarnating
itself in an even more coherent manner. In any case, with regard to moral
treatment, paternalist or cynical, benevolent or ruthless in its mode of
application, it is still of its essence to impose on a patient defined as

dispossessed of the attributes of the species the dominant norms in which a society recognizes human accomplishment.

2. If the endeavour to reconstruct this historic context provides a certain interest today, it is because this past of mental medicine is not yet dead. It is merely expunged from its contemporary memory, something that is rather different. It has to be asked why the contemporary representation of the tradition in which psychiatric practice inscribes itself becomes selectively slanted precisely in proportion with therapeutic claims of innovation, while those who are often called, with a pejorative nuance, 'classical psychiatrists' are at least aware of the heritage that still partially determines this practice. Thus it is the affected originality of the majority of contemporary currents, grouped by the Anglo-Saxons under the label of 'social psychiatry', that is largely responsible for the denial of the past, replacing it with a memory filter whose entirely fabricated character is manifest in the way it represents the past as exactly the opposite of what the new promoters claim to be doing today. We have already emphasized how false it is to see the asylum only as a place of confinement; it is just as false to believe that the nineteenth-century alienists were possessed by a classificatory mania and exhausted all their energy in elaborating abstract nosographies. This imagery of inverse edification might apply rather less imperfectly to French psychiatry during the period 1875–1940, during which – for complex reasons which it is impossible to enter into here – the previous synthesis progressively disintegrates. On the other hand, most of the leading ideas of the mid-nineteenth century, as I have tried to chart them here, are precisely the ones that come to be rediscovered around the mid-twentieth century. The resocializing techniques of *occupational therapy*, *egotherapy*, *administrative psychiatry*, and so on, rest on the same principles as moral treatment. The analogy is particularly striking in the case of the 'therapeutic communities' movement. If it is true that a therapeutic community aims to be an environment where 'everything is therapeutic', and whose principal originality consists in utilizing as part of a medically calculated *rehabilitation* of the patient the 'other twenty-three hours' that are not devoted to explicitly medical treatment,[38] one can see that what is involved is precisely a renewal of the basic project that inspired the organization of the classic asylum.

Of course, it would be an inverse error here if one were merely to assimilate the present to the past. There exists at least a genuinely original aspect of the 'therapeutic communities', as of the majority of modern psychiatric initiatives; namely, the importance given to the ideology of permissiveness in so far as this is supposed to preside over the implementation of the new set of practices. The distorted representation of psychiatry's heritage correspondingly assumes here a precise meaning: it obscures the problem posed by the observation that similar normalizing strategies can exist in conjunction with contrary justifying ideologies. Awareness of the profound analogies between the most traditional practices and what claim to be the most 'revolutionary' initiatives risks calling into question the postulate on which most of the 'new methods' depend: that what remain extremely manipulative practices are capable of being reconciled, subject to certain strains yet without contradiction, within a liberal or even a 'progressive' ideology.

3. It would however certainly be profoundly unjust to see, between the nineteenth and twentieth century, only a difference of ideology, a difference in ways of rationalizing identical practices. The change is also one of knowledge. One of the fundamental reasons for the permeability of nineteenth-century psychiatry to the social and political norms of the time resides in the impossibility for practitioners at that time of grounding their intervention on the basis of a corpus of theoretically articulated knowledge. A number of the changes that have ensued since the nineteenth century in forms of assistance to the mentally ill can be linked with a progression towards a greater specific autonomization of medical knowledge. Thus it is surely not unduly far-fetched to see psychoanalysis as the discovery that comes to occupy the place outlined by Falret when he voiced the requirement for a science enabling one to 'specify more clearly the diagnostic traits resulting from the special condition of each person'. One might suppose that, once it is in a position to base itself on a *sui generis* body of knowledge, mental medicine henceforth finds itself capable of breaking with dominant ideology and even of developing, if its own analyses happened to lead in that direction, a theory that was subversive of that ideology.

To a certain extent this does indeed happen. It would require a further study to illustrate the displacement effected in the course of a century of the *relation* of psychiatric ideologies to dominant ideologies. Schematically, there has been a movement from a situation – that of the nineteenth century – in which the ensemble of psychiatrists as a social body explicitly assumes the role of a representative of accepted values charged with defending them and seeing that they are accepted by certain marginal populations either willingly or through force, to a general attitude of contemporary psychiatrists composed of a feeling of underlying solidarity with the patient, of suspicion of a conformist definition of normality, and often of political critique of the role played by a repressive social structure in the aetiology of mental illnesses.

Can one say that the problematic of therapeutic intervention is thereby

completely overturned; that the system of reasons, which were in the last
instance moral and political, on which moral treatment was based has been
replaced by a pure system of theoretical reasons? If, restricting ourselves to
the case of the 'new communities', one can maintain that in them
everything is therapeutic, does that not mean that rather few of their
practices are therapeutic in the sense of being an application of a medically
grounded knowledge, a large number of the procedures called therapeutic
limiting themselves to reinterpreting in medical language interventions of
the same type as those that constituted moral treatment? Certainly, in
relation to the nineteenth century, even a crude lexicographical analysis
would show an increasing medicalization of the vocabulary of therapeutic
intervention. Few psychiatrists or psychoanalysts today speak explicitly of
order, of discipline, of correct morals, of the necessity for submission and
so forth; but rather of the control of aggressiveness, of reinvestment of
reality, of the maturation of feelings, of institutional transference and the
like.

But that does not necessarily mean that the two series of concepts may
not have comparable normalizing effects. The situation today is much
more complex than in the nineteenth century because the progress of
medical knowledge has made the *immediate* transposition of interests of
social control into a medical synthesis much more difficult; all the same, it
is not an absolutely different one, because the progressive autonomization
of medical knowledge goes hand in hand with their diffusion and
reinterpretation as a function of these same interests. It belongs to another
study, for which this historical sketch might serve as introduction, to
attempt to assess the impact of each of these two logics on the unstable
conjuncture of contemporary mental medicine.

POSTSCRIPT

The necessarily limited scope of these remarks risks giving the impression
that I am confusing, at least in their effects, the practical impact of opposed
theoretical positions. One should certainly distinguish carefully, not only
between the different contexts of practical therapeutic activity, from the
dual relationship of private therapy to the hospital situation, but also, and
especially, between the different systems for legitimating these
interventions, from the naive ideology of 'adjustment' to the forms of
psychoanalytic theory that have been most rigorously purified of any claim
to normalize. On the other hand, and this is why I have put most of the
emphasis on the analogies, the natural tendency for a number of psychoanalysts to posit an absolute dichotomy between the normalizing role of

the psychiatrist and the position of innocence assured the analyst by the neutrality of his attitude during the time of the cure constitutes the kind of epistemological obstacle that makes it impossible even to formulate the central problem I wish to pose: that of the normativizing function of medical discourse *as such*.

NOTES AND REFERENCES

1. Robert N. Rapoport, *Community as Doctor*, London, Tavistock Publications, 1959, in particular p. 9. Cf. also Rudolf Dreikurs, 'Group psychotherapy and the third revolution in psychiatry', *International Journal of Social Psychiatry* (London), I, 1955.

2. It is not possible to recount here the full story of the notion, but one can note that, by 1840, F. Leuret can make an assessment of all of his professional colleagues in terms of the amount of space they give to this type of therapy (*Du traitement moral de la folie*, Paris, J.-B. Baillière, 1840), and that almost all the nineteenth-century alienists found it necessary to define their own positions relative to his. Within the limits of this article it is not possible to enter further into the methodological problems of the exterior demarcation and inner homogeneity of the nineteenth-century psychiatric corpus. Schematically, one can identify, in relation to the problem that concerns us here, a relatively homogeneous period covering the elaboration and implementation of the 1838 law, approximately between 1830 and 1870, the first fissures in this synthesis becoming perceptible a little after 1860 with the outbreak over the custodial provisions of the 1838 law. A fuller justification of this periodization – as well as an attempt to follow through the system of transformations of this synthesis down to the contemporary organization of mental health – will be found in a work in preparation [*L'Ordre Psychiatrique*, Paris, Éditions de Minuit, 1976. For a summary of this book see Peter Miller, 'The territory of the psychiatrist', *I&C*, no. 7, 1980 (translator's note)]. To avoid these methodological problems as far as is possible I will focus my current remarks, without denying myself other references, on the analysis of a lecture given at the Salpêtrière Hospital in 1854 by J.-P. Falret (published under the title of 'Du traitement général des aliénés' in *Des maladies mentales et des asiles d'aliénés*, Paris, J.-B. Baillière & fils, 1864). To my knowledge this is the most systematic exposition of the principles of moral treatment, synthesizing all the themes that one finds dispersed elsewhere in the writings of the period.

3. The methods of moral treatment include not only all the obvious techniques of psychological intervention, but also 'moral' reinterpretations of mechanical procedures such as the *douche*. Certain authors distinguish between direct means (the psychological interview, the immediate relation with the therapist) and indirect means (work, recreation, varied activities). Cf. H. Laforgue, 'Observations sur le traitement de la folie par les moyens moraux', *Archives générales de Médecine*, août 1841. Cf. below for a systematic statement of

these means, as well as a more complete account of what is to be understood here by 'moral'.

4. Falret, 'Du traitement général des aliénés', p. 678.

5. Cf. on this point the criticisms of Leuret, *Du traitement moral de la folie*, part one.

6. Falret, 'Du traitement général des aliénés', pp. 682-3.

7. ibid., p. 680.

8. ibid., p. 679.

9. ibid., p. 699.

10. F. Voisin, *Du traitement intelligent de la folie*, followed by *Application de quelques-uns de ces principes à la réforme des criminels*, Paris, 1847, p. 10.

11. H. Girard, 'De l'organisation et de l'administration des établissements d'aliénés', *Annales médico-psychologiques*, II, 1843, p. 231.

12. One could show that this difference between two types of approach to mental illness – an aetiology and a social semiology – is frequently formulated in the nineteenth century in a very ambiguous manner through the distinction between two types of causes, 'organic' and 'moral'. This ambiguity, which one encounters already with Esquirol, is particularly clear with Falret, who, with regard to the organic aetiology, maintains that 'there is here, as with all illnesses, an entirely unknown initial modification which, by its nature, is probably inaccessible to all investigation', a proposition that ought to make it difficult for him to employ the vocabulary of causality; but he adds that 'a completely established fact is that madness is more often engendered by moral causes than by physical causes' (cf. 'Considérations générales sur les maladies mentales' in *Des maladies mentales et des asiles d'aliénés*, pp. 60-4). This subtle dialectic of 'physical causes' and 'moral causes', which can be traced running throughout the nineteenth century, has to do with both a theoretical opposition ('somatists' against 'psychologists') and a practical compromise between a scientific theory of illness and a spontaneous perception of madness in terms of disorder. This is why the theoretical dichotomy does not exclude a practical consensus ('therapeutic eclecticism'), treatment being more immediately tied up with the attitude towards madness than with the knowledge of illness.

13. Falret, 'Du traitement général des aliénés', p. 686.

14. Falret, 'Considérations générales sur les maladies mentales', p. 72.

15. ibid.

16. Thomas J. Scheff, *Being Mentally Ill, a Sociological Theory*, London, Weidenfeld and Nicolson, 1966.

17. L. J. F. Delasiauve, 'De la folie transitoire homicide', *Journal de médecine mentale*, II, 1862, p. 170.

18. Falret, 'Du traitement général des aliénés', p. 684.

19. Falret, 'Considérations générales sur les maladies mentales', p. 93.

20. J.-P. Falret, 'Visite à l'établissement d'aliénés d'Illenau', in *Des maladies mentales et des asiles d'aliénés*, Paris, J.-B. Baillière & fils, 1864, p. 667.

21. Falret, 'Considérations générales sur les maladies mentales', p. 73.

22. Dr Renaudin, 'L'asile d'Auxerre et les aliénés de l'Yonne', *Annales médico-psychologiques*, 5, 1845, p. 242.

23. Falret, 'Du traitement général des aliénés', p. 687.
24. ibid., p. 693.
25. ibid., p. 694.
26. ibid., p. 695.
27. ibid., p. 687
28. ibid., p. 688.
29. ibid., p. 690.
30. *Rapport général à M. le Ministre de l'Intérieur sur le Service des aliénés en 1874*, par MM. les Drs Contans, Lunier et Dumesnil, Paris, Imprimerie Nationale, 1878, p. 121.
31. Falret, 'Du traitement général des aliénés', p. 698.
32. Falret, 'Considérations générales sur les'asiles d'aliénés', p. 659.
33. Falret, 'Du traitement général des aliénés', p. 685.
34. Dr Teilleux, *Rapport sur la situation morale, administrative et médicale pendant l'année 1861*, département de Gers, asile public d'aliénés, p. 116.
35. Dr Billod, *Lettre en réponse aux articles de M. Lisle sur le régime moral auquel sont soumis les aliénés de l'hôpital de Bicêtre*, Paris, Imprimerie Malteste, c. 1845, p. 14.
36. Falret, 'Discours prononcé sur la tombe d'Esquirol le 14 decembre 1840', in *Des maladies mentales et des asiles d'aliénés*, Paris, J.-B. Baillière & fils, 1864, p. 778.
37. Leuret, *Du traitement moral de la folie*, pp. 120-1.
38. Cf. Rapoport, *Community as Doctor*, especially the chapter 'Treatment and Rehabilitation', pp. 9-34.

11

Psychiatrists and the State in Tsarist Russia

JULIE VAIL BROWN

Specially written for this volume

Russia participated in the transformation of the social response to the insane that occurred throughout the Western world during the late eighteenth and nineteenth centuries. As in the West, many of Russia's madmen were institutionalized under the supervision of a new breed of physician, the psychiatrist, who claimed to possess a singular expertise in the diagnosis and treatment of 'mental diseases'. The central government in Russia was the moving force behind asylum reform in the mid-nineteenth century, and by its own direct actions spawned a group of domestic medical specialists in the treatment of insanity. The government very early championed the notion that insane asylums should be humanitarian medical institutions, the purpose of which was to help those within their walls. It continued to pay lip service to that idea until the end of the last century. However, in the long run the government proved unwilling either to commit the resources necessary to sustain those institutions in the capacity for which they were presumably designed or to grant to the new experts that measure of control they demanded for the free exercise of their 'healing' techniques. As the cost of humanitarianism increased dramatically, *and* as internal threats to the autocracy mounted, the government instead promulgated laws that rested upon the assumption that asylums were 'police' institutions, that is, that they existed for the protection of those who remained on the outside. This made irrelevant the psychiatrist's claim to special expertise by virtue of his medical training and reduced his role from that of 'free professional' to little more than that of an adjunct to the tsarist police.

Russian psychiatrists consistently struggled to attain those status prerogatives that they perceived their Western colleagues to possess. Their efforts to professionalize centred on the acquisition of control over both the terms and the technical content of their work. They were largely unsuccessful in influencing the former, the socio-economic, conditions of their work. In this respect they differed little from other Russian physicians, the vast majority of whom were governmental employees with minimal control over their work lives. 'One cannot exaggerate the extent of the state's control over Russian-trained physicians beginning with their education and then encompassing their professional lives.'[1]

Most physicians, however, managed to retain control over the *technical content* of their work, the diagnosis and treatment of disease. In sociological terms this is of considerable significance.

> So long as a profession is free of the technical evaluation and control of other occupations in the division of labor, its lack of ultimate freedom from the state, and even its lack of control over the socio-economic terms of work do not significantly change its essential character as a profession.[2]

Psychiatrists did not fare so well in that regard. As governmental policies were clarified towards the end of the nineteenth century, the ability of psychiatric physicians to control both conditions within their institutions and access to those institutions was severely curtailed. Given that the asylum itself was regarded by psychiatrists as the central weapon in their therapeutic arsenal, these were serious infringements upon their self-proclaimed right to autonomous conduct. Increasingly denied control over the technical content of their work, many Russian psychiatrists joined the ranks of those advocating the overthrow of the tsarist regime. Their outspoken opposition to the government was in no small measure a product of their realization that they could never achieve the status of 'free professionals' given the existing structure of their society and the assumptions of its rulers as to the function of mental institutions.

Prior to the reign of Catherine II (1762–1796), such formalized care as was available to the insane in Russia was provided by the Russian Orthodox Church. This was in conformity with tradition as old as pre-Mongol Kievan Rus'. The first secular institutions for madmen were established under the auspices of the provincial Departments of Public Welfare (Prikazy Obshchestvennago Prizreniia), organized in 1775 as part of large-scale reforms intended to decentralize certain aspects of an often unwieldy empire. A central function of these madhouses was the protection of society from potentially dangerous individuals, as is evident from the government's instructions to those who would manage them: 'It is incumbent upon the Department of Public Welfare to insure that the building chosen is sufficiently large and sturdy in all respects, so that escape from it will be impossible . . .'[3] Popularly termed 'yellow houses' (*zheltye doma*) after the colour of the inexpensive paint that was often used on governmental buildings, the *prikaz* madhouses were regarded by the populace with fear and dread as places of horror to be avoided if at all possible. Noblemen were rumoured to have sent their unruly serfs to work in the madhouses as punishment for misbehaving, and many of the institutions remained half-empty.[4]

The origins of psychiatric reform in Russia are to be found during the reign of Nicholas I (1825–1855). Much of the impetus for reform appears to have come from the Emperor himself, a man generally regarded as a staunch conservative. The same Nicholas, tsar of 'autocracy, orthodoxy and nationality' who once declared the philosopher Chaadaev insane because of certain of his writings, had an abiding interest in madhouse reform.[5] During the 1840s the government decided to supplement the existing provincial *prikaz* madhouses with a network of regional asylums (*okruzhnye lechebnitsy*) under the auspices of the Medical Department of the Ministry of Internal Affairs. Each of these facilities was intended to serve several provinces. By design they were to be therapeutic institutions. They were to care for those with acute forms of insanity (believed to be the most amenable to treatment), and the patients were to be under the supervision of medically trained specialists in insanity.[6]

Having set lofty goals for themselves, the governmental reformers soon discovered that there were few psychiatric specialists to be found on Russian soil. The existing madhouses were staffed by physicians only rarely, and the function of those doctors was to minister to the somatic ailments of the inmates. The only psychiatrists in Russia were directors of a few progressive asylums which had recently been established in the capital cities of Moscow and St Petersburg. Having thus legislated into existence a system of institutions to treat the insane, the government set about to create a cadre of specialists with which to staff them. Kazan was chosen as the locale for the first regional asylum, in large part because of the presence there of a university which could cooperate in the training of psychiatrists. The government's concern with the dearth of specialists was also a primary consideration in the decision to establish a department (*kafedra*) of psychiatry at the prestigious St Petersburg medical school, the Medical Surgical Academy, in 1857. Thus it was that in Russia – unlike many other countries – the government was among the first to endorse the principles of scientific psychiatry and was itself largely responsible for the growth of an indigenous psychiatric profession.[7]

The interval between the conception of the regional asylum project and the opening of the first such institution in Kazan in 1869 was a period of great social upheaval for Russia. In 1861 serfdom was abolished, and during the next several years significant changes were effected in educational, judicial, military and administrative institutions. One of those reforms directly affected the provision of care to the insane: the establishment of the *zemstvo* system of local self-government in January 1864. The *zemstvos*, organized at both the provincial and smaller district (*uezd*) levels, were given responsibility for the provision of a variety of services to their areas: education, public health, insurance, roads and famine relief, among others.

Considering the enormity of the tasks facing them and their limited sources of revenue, it is perhaps not surprising that some *zemstvo* officials should have suggested that fiscal responsibility for the insane properly belonged in the hands of the central government.[8] The proponents of that position pointed to the fact that in 1852 the administration had added a special psychiatric wing to the central St Petersburg correctional institution, and on 14 November 1864 had ordered that *each* correctional facility throughout the empire construct such a facility. The current construction of the regional asylum at Kazan and the planned construction of seven others – all initiated by the central government and designed to treat recent and 'curable' cases – were also taken as clear indication that the tsarist government had intended to assume primary responsibility for the care of the insane.

The *prikaz* madhouses had been transferred to the *zemstvos* along with hospitals and schools. However, many of Russia's madmen were incarcerated in prisons and workhouses (*smiritel'nye doma*), which remained subject to control by the central government. Furthermore, a significant proportion of the madhouse population consisted of convicted criminals and individuals incarcerated temporarily by government representatives for the purpose of evaluating their mental competence. There certainly were conflicting signals from the central government. This ambiguity, as well as the hope of many *zemstvos* that they could avoid the burden of caring for the insane, was no doubt largely responsible for the fact that little was accomplished in the way of provincial madhouse reform during the first decade of *zemstvo* operation.[9]

The *prikaz* madhouses inherited by the *zemstvos* were almost without exception frightfully inadequate. A contemporary described one of their number (in Poltava) in the following fashion:

> The appearance of the facility is indescribably dismal. The sight of the high fences, the iron bars on the windows, the heavy bolts on the doors, and the stern figures of the guards lead one to the conclusion that prisoners are held here. But the unprecedented crowding and the chaotic noises persuade one that this is none other than a lunatic asylum. . . . All of the patients are combined into one un-differentiated mass. . . . The laughing, crying, singing, swearing, and brawling result in an unbearable racket which continues without pause both night and day.[10]

Similar descriptions exist for many of the *prikaz* madhouses. With each passing year the facilities became more decrepit and increasingly overcrowded. Many institutions that had remained half-empty during the pre-reform era could now scarcely contain the flow of peasant admissions.

A number of *zemstvos* responded by restricting admissions to their madhouses. In 1870 in Novgorod the provincial *zemstvo* assembly voted 'to make it clear to the Executive Board that it is under no obligation to accept lunatics over and above the authorized number of beds'. Two years later the *zemstvo* assembly of Riazan decreed that all harmless insane were to be denied admission to the madhouse. Others followed suit.[11] The central government either remained uninformed of these actions or chose to ignore them. However, a similar move by the provincial *zemstvo* assembly of Vladimir touched off a controversy that lasted into the twentieth century, ultimately clarifying the government's perception of the problem represented by the insane and in the process contributing significantly to the disaffection of psychiatrists.

By the early 1870s the number of inmates in the Vladimir provincial madhouse had increased dramatically, and the inadequacy of the facility was obvious to the local *zemstvo* officials. Unwilling or unable to part with the large sum of money required to construct a new facility, the assembly decided 'to permit the provincial Executive Board to limit admissions to the madhouse . . . as the admission of more than 30 individuals is not obligatory for the *zemstvo*'.[12]

The assembly's decision was soon brought to the attention of the provincial governor, who insisted that the establishment of a quota was inappropriate and demanded that the order be revoked. When the *zemstvo* assembly refused to yield to the will of the governor, the matter was referred to the Senate in St Petersburg for resolution. On 15 June 1875 the Senate announced its decision. Relying upon the statutes that had established the Departments of Public Welfare a century before, it insisted that:

> the number of patients supported in madhouses is not to be limited to any specific number. In the event that the existing facilities are insufficient to meet the demand, the *zemstvo* is obligated . . . to acquire additional space as needed. . . . The Senate regards the decision of the provincial assembly to limit admissions to the madhouse to a maximum established by that assembly as lacking legal justification.[13]

The Senate argued that the 1775 decree had not given the *prikazy* the power to restrict admissions. As heirs to those institutions and their financial resources, the *zemstvos* were bound by the earlier regulations. While the *prikazy* had not been specifically forbidden from establishing madhouse population quotas, neither were they explicitly given the right to do so. The assumption of the Senate clearly was that, unless such authority was unambiguously granted by the government, it could not be presumed to exist.

In 1878 the Senate went one step further. In response to a complaint from the governor of Tula that the provincial *zemstvo* continued to restrict admissions to the local madhouse, it issued a new ruling which stressed that the *zemstvo* responsibility towards the insane was an obligatory (*obiazatel'noi*) one.[14]

Zemstvo reaction to the Senate rulings was to unleash a torrent of vehement protests in the direction of St Petersburg. Faced with the need for large capital outlays for basic improvements in a number of areas, the *zemstvos* argued that, by requiring them to provide facilities for *all* insane persons in their geographical areas, the government was placing upon their shoulders an intolerable burden. The demand that *zemstvo* madhouses accept all comers was unreasonable, they insisted, unless the government was willing to offer significant financial assistance.

During this same period the central government had become increasingly disenchanted with the regional asylum concept. The cost of the Kazan facility had far exceeded the expectations of all involved, and it had soon become apparent that the asylum was incapable of meeting the needs of such a large area. Inadequate transport proved a major obstacle. Moreover, the fact that care was not free placed it beyond the means of much of the population. As a result, many beds remained empty, and operating costs were enormous.[15] Thus, at the same time that the *zemstvos* were arguing that the central government should take over more of the responsibility of caring for the insane, the latter was itself eager to terminate its venture into the asylum construction business.

In 1879 the Ministry of Internal Affairs responded to the pleas of the *zemstvos* for assistance. While undoubtedly motivated by a desire to improve a situation which by its own admission was deplorable, the government's offer to help served its own purposes as well. In addition to pacifing the noisy protesters, the ministry's decision enabled it to withdraw gracefully from the 'madhouse business' and to turn over to the provincial self-governments primary responsibility for the care of the insane. The method by which this was accomplished was to order a halt to the unwieldy regional asylums and to make available to the *zemstvos* much of the money that had previously been designated for that project.

The ministry's decision was announced in a circular addressed to all governors which was published on 11 November 1879. The document specifically rejected the notion that institutions for the insane were places of detention ('police' institutions), while acknowledging that the *prikaz* madhouses had generally been run in that fashion. Rather, as the minister placed the full weight of the burden of providing for the insane on the shoulders of the local self-governments, he argued eloquently for a more enlightened and humanitarian interpretation of the function of psychiatric care:

> . . . our first step should consist of the improvement of those physical facilities for the insane which were constructed in an earlier era characterized by a different set of assumptions about the insane with the result that they bear a greater resemblence to places of imprisonment than to institutions for care. I cannot help but be especially mindful of the fact that the construction of facilities for the insane in accordance with psychiatric demands requires significant one-time expenditures – something difficult for individual *zemstvos* to manage under current circumstances.

The minister concluded by announcing the government's intention to offer the *zemstvos* 50 per cent subsidies for the construction of new institutions for the insane.[16]

The 1879 announcement marks what is generally regarded as a turning point in the history of the care of Russia's insane. The initial reaction of many *zemstvo* assemblies to the promise of aid from the Ministry of Internal Affairs was to begin to plan seriously how they could best meet the demands placed upon them. To that end a number of *zemstvos* either sought out specialists in the care of the insane from among those being produced in St Petersburg or sent their own local medical personnel to the capital or abroad for additional training in the new specialty of psychiatry. Thus, the vacillation and confrontation that characterized the 1870s was followed by a brief period of optimism and growth.

During the 1880s there appeared, on the one hand, the first systematic efforts on the part of the provincial *zemstvos* to expand their facilities for the insane, and, on the other hand, a significant increase in the number of physicians with special training in psychiatry. These new psychiatrists soon began to conceive of themselves as members of a distinctive group with common aims and unique problems. Early on they became active propagandists for the institutionalization of the insane. However, there was a curious duality to their arguments. Their journals were rife with accounts of dangerous acts committed by madmen, and they advocated the removal of all of the insane from society for the protection of the latter. On the other hand, they cited examples of cruel treatment of madmen by their families and communities and insisted that institutionalization was in the best interests of the insane; they would be protected and provided with medical care. Implicit in both of these arguments was the notion that *only* psychiatrists were equipped to diagnose and treat dangerousness and/or insanity. Therefore, they alone should determine which individuals would be admitted to mental institutions.[17]

During that optimistic decade many psychiatrists achieved a measure of control not only over the medical operations of their asylums but over their administrative and financial affairs as well. They fought long and hard for those rights, arguing that 'success in both the treatment of the insane and the administration of an asylum depends upon acquaintance with the science of insanity and practical experience acquired through study in a psychiatric clinic or asylum'.[18] Every aspect of the functioning of a mental institution was said to have direct implications for the medical treatment of its inmates. Hence, all aspects of its operations should be under the autonomous control of psychiatrists.

The initial enthusiasm of the *zemstvos* for asylum construction began to fade as it became increasingly apparent, towards the end of the 1880s, that the promised governmental assistance was not so easily acquired. Many provincial *zemstvo* assemblies developed plans, purchased land and even began construction based upon the assumption that the 50 per cent subsidies would be immediately forthcoming. Such was not the case. Rather, the procedures involved proved to be complex and frustrating; progress was slow, and receipt of funds by no means assured. In Riazan, for example, a new asylum was constructed in strict accordance with ministry instructions at a cost of 258,000 rubles. After a lengthy delay and much pressure from local officials, the ministry finally granted the *zemstvo* a subsidy of 35,000 rubles – much less than the promised 50 per cent and made available only some years after the construction was completed.[19] By the early 1890s the amount of money granted as subsidies for asylum construction totalled 1.5 million rubles – a negligible amount considering the number of *zemstvos* (34) and the high costs of construction.[20] Moreover, as the original circular had stipulated, the Ministry of Internal Affairs provided funds for new construction only. Operating costs were the burden of the *zemstvos*, and they continued to escalate rapidly as asylum populations steadily increased.

In the 1890s the problem reached crisis proportions. Bound by the 1875 ruling to provide asylum space for all comers, the *zemstvos* began to face difficulties in funding other endeavours. Consequently, they insisted upon maintaining stricter control over their psychiatric institutions. The result was a rash of conflicts between the local self-governments and their psychiatric employees. As psychiatric physicians found their newly acquired autonomy being eaten away by money-conscious *zemstvos*, they protested, believing that the shortage of trained psychiatric experts would strengthen their position.[21] Many found themselves instead dismissed from their posts. Financial solvency was clearly more highly valued than psychiatric expertise.

Zemstvo action was not limited to efforts to increase control over the purse strings of psychiatric facilities. As subsidy money became less available, the *zemstvos* insisted that the 1875 ruling be changed. Psychiatrists had originally supported the ruling on the grounds that it implied that all of the insane were entitled to medical care. The local self-governments had consistently opposed it. The braver among them had blatantly violated the law by continuing to establish quotas. Others had quietly ignored it at home while continuing to protest the ruling in the capital. Now the *zemstvos* began to demand in addition that the central government directly assume more of the burden of financing care for the insane.

In the 1880s the tsarist government had on several occasions reaffirmed its initial ruling. During the following decade it issued clarifications that were designed to reduce the burden on the *zemstvo* institutions. Whether they did in fact do so is debatable; however, they not only failed in the long run to satisfy the *zemstvos*, but they simultaneously alienated the psychiatric profession.

The rulings were issued in 1891, 1895 and 1899. While they differed in specifics, the essence of each was to limit obligatory admissions to psychiatric institutions to those individuals deemed to be 'dangerous' to society. The initial rulings merely implied that the *zemstvos* had the *right* to deny admission to certain categories of 'harmless' insane. The 1891 ruling was directed at the provincial self-government of Riazan, which had established an admissions quota for its asylum. The Senate directed that the quota be abolished, because it 'deprived the provincial administration of the ability to remove quickly from society those individuals with dangerous forms of insanity'. The 1895 ruling (Medical Department to Kursk) went one step further by acknowledging that *zemstvo* provision of accommodation for all those who could conceivably live in society (that is, idiots, the feebleminded and the able-bodied harmless insane) would be an 'unattainable luxury'. However, it was not until 1899 that the government's position was clarified to the satisfaction of anyone involved. On August 20 of that year the following edict was issued:

> The ruling by the governing Senate of 15 July 1875 should be understood as referring only to those insane the hospitalization of whom is deemed necessary because of either the nature of their illness or their family situation, i.e., those whose admission is ordered by the administration and the courts. . . .[22]

Ironically, the government appeared to agree with psychiatrists' concern about the danger of madmen. However, it insisted upon retaining for its own representatives the right to determine which individuals were dangerous and should be incarcerated.

For psychiatrists, the implications of the rulings for their role were clear: given the cramped condition of most provincial asylums, control over admission to mental institutions would henceforth be largely in the hands of the courts and the police. While psychiatrists had long protested their insignificant role in legal proceedings regarding the insane, they were particularly apprehensive about the effect of these rulings upon their relationship with the police. In the past, physician and policeman had conflicted over the need to institutionalize individuals, with psychiatrists turning away borderline cases in an effort to minimize inmate populations and policemen insisting upon the admission of individuals who were troublesome for them. The populace learned early on that if a resident physician refused to admit someone to an asylum, he could be taken to the police. The latter in turn would take that individual to the asylum and insist upon his admission. A psychiatrist in the Crimean city of Simferopol reported that local people routinely went first to the police in the effort to gain admission for their charges to the local asylum. In 1886, he asserted, almost half (46.4 per cent) of all admissions had occurred through the police. Towards the end of the century only 9 out of 75 patients confined to the same madhouse had been admitted by the staff psychiatrist. The remainder had been institutionalized in response to the demands of 'official' persons.[23]

Prior to the 1899 ruling it had been difficult for psychiatrists to refuse to accept individuals brought to their portals by representatives of the central administration. Thereafter it was well-nigh impossible. A few psychiatrists insisted that they were able to resist the pressures brought to bear on them, but such audacious individuals were a small minority. The remainder of the profession angrily reported that the police regarded mental institutions as dumping grounds for individuals whom they preferred not to handle. In the wake of the new order, psychiatrists throughout the empire complained that they were being forced to accept large numbers of sane alcoholics and derelicts.[24]

By the end of the century, Russia's physicians for the insane faced a distressing predicament. They were losing control over the internal administration of their institutions because of the *zemstvos'* desire to minimize costs. The failure of their remonstrances had served only to demonstrate the extent to which the *zemstvos* regarded psychiatric expertise as a superfluous commodity. They were also being forced to surrender their role as gatekeepers of those institutions. Given the psychiatric definition of residence in an asylum as the treatment of choice for virtually all types of insanity, this development was particularly significant. To deny psychiatrists the prerogative of determining who should be treated in mental institutions was tantamount to appointing the police as diagnosticians of insanity.

One must question whether psychiatrists ever in actual fact exercised significant control over access to the madhouses. Certainly they had consistently shared that responsibility with other parties – *zemstvo* physicians and executive boards as well as the courts and the tsarist police. The importance of the government's new rulings lay more with their symbolic value than in any demonstrable effect upon madhouse admission procedures. Heretofore, psychiatrists had been able to interpret those instances of interference as improper and exceptional – their relative frequency notwithstanding. Once that 'interference' was given official sanction (and at the highest levels of government), their efforts at self-delusion were rendered much less effective.

Another dimension of the psychiatrist's role as gatekeeper of the asylum was compromised as well. There were two statutes in the criminal code in the latter part of the nineteenth century that restricted psychiatrists' freedom to release certain types of patients. These statutes (Articles no. 95 and 96) required that individuals found guilty of certain crimes – murder, arson or attempted suicide – and judged mentally incompetent to stand trial be committed until such time as they had been fully recovered for two years. If psychiatrists released such an individual prematurely (that is, if he subsequently committed another crime), the physicians were subject to criminal prosecution. As it was virtually impossible to guarantee against recidivism, psychiatrists were understandably reluctant to release such patients. In fact, many even assumed that they lacked the legal authority to release so-called 'Article 95' patients (*stateinye bol'nye*).[25]

Towards the end of the century events conspired to make them particularly sensitive to the issue. Madhouses were extremely overcrowded, and, for reasons already outlined, there was little psychiatrists could do to stem the ever-rising tide. Thus, their inability to rid themselves of large groups of patients was a major annoyance. In addition, the popular press began to report cases of 'Article 95' patients who had deduced that their incarceration was to be life-long and in desperation had resorted to suicide or violent escape attempts. Psychiatrists were held responsible and were publicly chastised for the hopeless plight of those miserable beings.[26]

Psychiatrists faced substantial popular opposition on other fronts as well. They were accused of wrongly admitting healthy individuals, they were held responsible for the abominable conditions within asylums, and they were denounced for employing harsh and sadistic methods of 'treatment'.[27] In short, they found themselves blamed by the public for the results of the very governmental policies by which *they* felt victimized. Ever sensitive to popular criticism, psychiatrists found themselves trapped in the middle between a hostile public and an unmoving government.

One of psychiatrists' harshest critics was himself a member of the psychiatric profession, P. Iakobii. Born and raised in Russia, Iakobii spent most of his adult life in Western Europe. He returned to his homeland in 1890 at the invitation of the Moscow *zemstvo*, which was then planning its first psychiatric hospital. Iakobii soon came into conflict with that city's psychiatric community and was forced to move on to a position in the provincial city of Orel. It was there in 1900 that he published his *magnum opus*, a 700-page treatise entitled *The Principles of Administrative Psychiatry* (*Osnovy administrativnoi psikhiatrii*). Despite its sober and rather innocuous title, the work was in reality a polemic against what Iakobii termed 'police' psychiatry, particularly as it manifested itself in Russia. Starting from the premise that, 'of all human institutions, the most logical is the madhouse',[28] Iakobii produced a wealth of cross-cultural and historical data in an effort to demonstrate a correlation between the social, economic and political structure of a society and its response to its insane. Of Russia, he said that the appearance of capitalism and the rise in importance of a bourgeoisie with its high valuation of personal property had resulted in the predominance of a view of the insane as representing a direct threat to society. The outcome of this view was the construction of madhouses the purpose of which was to protect the rest of society from the insane rather than to help those unfortunates. Given such a state of affairs, he argued, it should surprise no one that conditions within the institutions were abominable. Those conditions were a logical consequence of the function that the institutions were designed to fulfil. Built in the interest of those on the outside, Russia's madhouses were hardly likely to reflect the needs of the individuals within their walls.

Iakobii reserved his harshest criticism for members of his own profession, whom he decried as 'the most typical representatives of the bourgeoisie in Russia'.[29] Russian psychiatrists, he argued, were foremost among that society's proponents of 'police' psychiatry. While purporting to have their patients' best interests at heart, they helped to perpetuate a system of grossly inadequate facilities for the insane by insisting upon the dangerousness of mentally disturbed individuals.

In sum, Iakobii argued that the two roles that Russian psychiatrists attempted to occupy simultaneously were incompatible. They could function either in the interests of their patients (as physicians) or as agents of the state (as policemen). By choosing to emphasize their function as defenders of society against the peril of the insane, they had effectively eliminated the possibility that they might help their ailing patients.

> Once the issue has been formulated in terms of the defense of society from attack by the insane, two belligerents are distinguishable: society and the insane. We psychiatrists constitute the advanced detachment of society, the vanguard, trackers of the enemy, skirmishers. We psychiatrists open fire against the insane. We search them out like medieval lepers and instruct the administration that it take steps, but not to help them. Oh no! We ask that it protect us from them, and preferably that it 'lock them up'. Like medieval Dominicans we track down the heresy of intellectual processes and without delay we turn the heretic–criminals *au bras seculier* over the authorities.[30]

Already troubled deeply by the serious threat to their professional autonomy and by their inability to change conditions at the local level (the frequent firings had demonstrated the futility of protest), Russia's psychiatric profession was stung to the quick by Iakobii's accusations. The initial response was an attempt to discredit both the author and his work.[31] None the less, within a short space of time many of Iakobii's conceptualizations had found widespread acceptance among his colleagues. Subject to criticism and manipulation by the central government, the *zemstvos*, the educated public and the peasantry, the psychiatric profession finally began a major offensive of its own in the early years of the twentieth century. Many of psychiatrists' arguments were based upon those of Iakobii; however, they modified his interpretations in an attempt to exonerate themselves and lay the blame instead upon the tsarist government. They acknowledged the predominance of the 'police' psychiatry perspective in Russia and its detrimental effects on the insane. Yet, rather than blaming themselves, psychiatrists faulted the government.

According to psychiatrists, the central government chose to use psychiatric institutions as 'police' institutions and was responsible for the abominable state in which they were to be found. Choosing to use the institutions to suit its own purposes, the government was oblivious to their inadequacies and refused to make available the funds that were needed to correct the situation. Psychiatrists also underscored their own powerlessness to effect change – addressing in particular the problems that devolved from their lack of control over admissions to and discharges from mental institutions.

Psychiatrists' discussion of these problems reflects a major ideological about-face in their attitudes on a number of issues – most noticeably the dangerousness of the insane. On the one hand, psychiatrists became active opponents of the 1875 *ukase* and its later reinterpretations. The evil of that ruling, they now argued, lay in the fact that, as a result of it, decisions concerning admissions to mental institutions were made not on the basis of a medical criterion – that is, on whether psychiatrists could cure the patient – but on the basis of a non-medical criterion – an untrained official's perception of how troublesome or dangerous that person was.

> If the task of a hospital consists of the removal from society of madmen who are considered for whatever reason to be inconvenient or dangerous, it follows that those who end up in it are those whose insanity (curable or not) is expressed in a manner unpleasant for those around him. If we add to this the fact that the individuals making decisions as to the danger posed by a patient are in most cases not medical specialists but persons with power and with no connection whatsoever to medicine, it is not surprising that most admissions to hospitals are of chronic and incurable madmen.[32]

In an earlier, more optimistic, era psychiatrists had awarded dangerousness a prominent niche among other rationalizations for institutionalization, and have even by implication accorded it the status of a 'medical' phenomenon by asserting that only experts could diagnose it. Now they sought instead to disassociate themselves from the issue. The decision to incarcerate a madman, they maintained, should be made solely on the basis of his physical and mental condition – in practical terms, on the treatability of his disease. 'Not the degree of dangerousness of any given individual but only the extent to which he needs the hospital can serve here as a criterion.'[33] While acknowledging that society must be protected from persons prone to violence, they insisted that such was the responsibility of the state, not of physicians. If the state was more concerned that the 'dangerous insane' be restrained than treated, then it should do so in institutions of its own devising and leave other psychiatric institutions to continue their medical and humanitarian works in peace.

Psychiatrists stressed that they had very little say as to who was admitted to any mental institution because of their inability to veto the decisions of governmental representatives. In some areas they could even be brought to trial for refusing to admit individuals brought by official persons.[34] In an obvious response to Iakobii, one psychiatrist went so far as to claim:

Our psychiatrists play *no* role whatsoever in the admissions process. The psychiatric hospital and its physicians are merely passive participants. The way in which admissions decisions are made is not affected in the least by the orientation of the hospital's psychiatrist – 'police' or 'civilized'.[35]

In the first few years of the twentieth century, psychiatrists also intensified their attacks upon Articles 95 and 96. Ironically, their arguments as to the injustice of these laws now frequently cited cases of 'harmless', feeble-minded individuals initially incarcerated because they had accidentally set fires – 'a completely harmless imbecile, superb worker and breadwinner of his family, was sentenced in accordance with Article 95 for burning a straw hut having no value at all.'[36] Such statements are in striking contrast to psychiatrists' earlier views regarding the propensity of the insane to arson. What they had once represented as serious threats to the Russian countryside, necessitating active preventive intervention, they now discounted as meaningless and trivial chance occurrences. That an individual had started a fire – or even committed a murder – was not *ipso facto* grounds for his removal from society, and it was certainly no justification for lifelong preventive detention. Psychiatrists angrily charged the government with gross violations of the civil rights of the insane.

A mentally disturbed person accused of a crime is treated much more harshly by the law than a sane person accused of the same crime. . . . If the individual is charged with murder, arson, or an attempt on his own life, the court is not content to declare him not responsible for his actions. The court is not satisfied with its punitive function but takes upon itself a prophylactic role as the guardian of public safety.[37]

Over the course of the next several years psychiatrists became progressively more angered by and alienated from the Russian government. The revolution of 1905 served to widen still further the gap between the government and psychiatrists. Psychiatrists were outraged by the government's incarceration of so-called 'political' patients in their institutions. Prison officials maintained that many such individuals feigned insanity in order to be placed in psychiatric institutions from which it was relatively easy to escape, and they insisted that the prisoners remain shackled.[38] Because of the presence of such inmates in asylums, the administration frequently equipped them with military sentinels, a practice that had been outlawed more than a half-century earlier by Nicholas I, and one that infuriated psychiatrists.[39]

Increasingly, psychiatrists' public remarks were expressions of outrage at the situation in which they found themselves. 'Do not transform the hospital into a public safety institution and psychiatric physicians into judicial officials,' warned a speaker at a meeting of psychiatrists in 1905.[40] The same refrain was repeated in 1909: 'Do not turn the physician into a prison warden. He will always protest against that with all of his might. . . . Demand from the physician only that he help the physically and mentally crippled.'[41]

In 1911 the first meeting of the Russian Union of Psychiatrists and Neuropathologists was held in Moscow. So harsh was the criticism of the government in the opening speeches that the meeting was closed by the police after its first session. Psychiatrists were later allowed to reconvene the meeting with the proviso that no further 'unlawful' actions would be permitted, and its proceedings were carefully monitored.[42] Although the effect was to subdue the rhetoric somewhat, the conference participants still managed to convey their displeasure with the current state of both psychiatry and the administration of the Russian Empire as a whole.

The proceedings of the conference provide a particularly apt summarization of the events of previous decades. Pessimistic about the future, psychiatrists reflected on the past. As they surveyed the history of the administration's response to the insane, they were struck by the hollowness of its expressions of humanitarian concern. No one disputed the fact that Russia's first madhouses had been 'police' institutions. However, the 'enlightened' opinions expressed by the government in the immediate post-reform era were associated with its transfer of responsibility to the *zemstvos* – a move that decreased rather than increased its obligations. Only when the local self-governments proved unable to shoulder the entire burden did the tsarist government reveal clearly its attitude toward mental institutions – as places of detention for certain categories of individuals deemed *by it* to be dangerous:

> [Since the time of Nicholas I] all governmental statutes, *ukases*, and circulars dealing with the insane have been dominated by an 'administrative–police' perspective, i.e., by a concern with the protection of society from any possible harm which might be caused by the insane.[43]

Psychiatrists could only conclude that the government regarded madhouses as humanitarian medical institutions only in so far as it was spared the expense of building and operating them and to the extent that it was otherwise provided with institutions for the removal of dangerous individuals from society. In other words, its humanitarian pleas had little practical meaning whatsoever.

A number of speakers at the 1911 meeting pointed to the lack of improvement in asylum conditions in the quarter-century since psychiatrists had first met together in 1887. Of the major issues raised at the earlier meeting, none had since been resolved to the satisfaction of the conference participants. Rather, matters had worsened. Their working conditions had become nearly unbearable. Psychiatrists had little control over either admissions to or discharges from their institutions, which remained underfunded, understaffed, overcrowded and manned by military guards. Most of them saw little reason to expect improvement without fundamental changes to the socio-economic structure of the country.

It seems clear that Russian psychiatrists had concluded that they could not hope to function as self-determining 'free professionals' under the existing regime, which consistently denied them control over both the terms of their work *and* its technical content. The latter was of particular significance, as it is the source of 'the wherewithal by which to be a "free" profession'.[44] Moreover, unless the government was willing to support the notion that psychiatric care was a humanitarian *medical* endeavour, any claim they might make to special expertise was meaningless. Given popular scepticism of psychiatry and the predominant official view of psychiatric facilities as 'police' institutions, at best they would be allowed to function as an auxiliary and subordinate police force; at worst they would be unemployed. With this realization, doubtless came the awareness that both they and their clients might be better served by a different regime.

On the eve of the First World War much of the profession was openly hostile to the tsarist government. Many psychiatric hospitals had become centres of underground left-wing political activity. Psychiatrists in ever-increasing numbers were fired, imprisoned, exiled or resigned in protest against governmental policies. Of the major spokesmen for the profession, there were only a very few who had managed to retain their institutional posts without interruption throughout the post-1905 period of political reaction.[45]

Every profession is dependent upon the state 'in establishing and maintaining the profession's pre-eminence'.[46] Under the circumstances one would not normally expect to find great numbers of professionals among the ranks of those advocating its overthrow. Yet Russian psychiatrists clearly had nothing to lose from the downfall of the tsarist government. That they were in some measure aware of their dependence upon the authority of the state is suggested by the fact that psychiatrists were one of the first professional groups to offer their services to the regime that replaced it.[47]

The traditional explanation for the changed social response to insanity that occurred in the last century credits the advance of science and humanitarianism. Scientific progress resulted in the 'inevitable' discovery that insanity was a disease of the body which would respond to medical intervention, and humanitarian concern for the welfare of such unfortunates was responsible for the willingness of governments to make available the large sums of money necessary for the construction and maintenance of institutions for the insane.

Recent scholarship has brought this interpretation into question.[48] Focusing on events as they transpired in a few Western societies under relatively similar socio-economic and political conditions, several studies have attempted to demonstrate the fallacy of the notion that advances in medical knowledge accounted for the new approach to insanity. Furthermore, it has been argued that the humanitarian zeal of governments was often little more than a veneer masking less altruistic motivations for the removal of troublesome individuals from society. The Russian case would appear to lend support to that argument. In fact, the blatant terms in which the latent functions of madhouses were discussed in tsarist Russia suggests that additional studies of the state's response to deviance in 'backward' autocratic states might generate a number of hypotheses that could be fruitfully examined in the more 'modern' democratic societies of the West.

NOTES AND REFERENCES

1. Nancy Frieden, 'The Russian Cholera Epidemic, 1892–93 and Medical Professionalization', *Journal of Social History*, vol. 10, 1977, p. 539.
2. Elliot Freidson, *Profession of Medicine*, New York, Dodd, Mead and Co., 1973, p. 25.
3. Cited in A. Shul'ts, 'Prizrenie pomeshannykh v Rossii', *Arkhiv sudebnoi meditsiny i obshchestvennoi gigieny*, vol. 1, no. 1, 1865, p. 10.
4. B. Veselovskii, *Istoriia zemstva za sorok let*, vol. 1, St Petersburg, 1909, p. 292.
5. Nicholas I's interest in asylum reform is usually explained as the result of a visit he made during his youth to the York Retreat. William Tuke is said to have so impressed the young Grand Duke that the encounter remained with him throughout his life. N. N. Bazhenov, *Psikhiatricheskiia besedy na literaturnyia i obshchestvennyia temy*, Moscow, 1903, p. 83. As for Nicholas I's treatment of Chaadaev, see S. Monas, *The Third Section: Police and Society under Nicholas I*, Cambridge, Harvard University Press, 1961.
6. A. D. Kotsovskii, 'Ocherk prizreniia dushevno-bol'nykh v Rossii', *Voprosy nervno-psikhicheskoi meditsiny*, vol. 7, 1902, pp. 238-303, 357-425, 537-674. See also A. M. Shereshevskii, 'Istoriia sozdaniia okruzhnykh psikhiatricheskikh

bol'nits v Rossii', *Zhurnal nevropatologii i psikhiatrii im. S. S. Korsakova*, vol. 78, 1978, pp. 432-6.

7. These events are analysed in some detail in Julie V. Brown, 'The Professionalization of Russian Psychiatry: 1857-1911', PhD dissertation, University of Pennsylvania, 1981, chapter 2.

8. The *zemstvos'* main sources of income were land taxes and taxes on non-agricultural immovable property. Many historians argue that the revenue that resulted from these taxes was inadequate to their needs. See, for example, Hugh Seton-Watson, *The Russian Empire 1801-1917*, Oxford, Clarendon Press, 1967, p. 470.

9. N. M. Frieden, *Russian Physicians in an Era of Reform and Revolution*, Princeton University Press, 1981, discusses the general lack of *zemstvo* enthusiasm for public health reform during these early years.

10. T. I. Iudin, *Ocherki istorii otechestvennoi psikhiatrii*, Moscow, 1951, pp. 213-14.

11. V. I. Iakovenko, *Otmena ukaza senata ot 15 iiulia 1875g za No. 29937 zhelatel'na i neobkhodima v interesakh pravil'nago razvitiia zemskago popecheniia o dushevno-bol'nykh*, St Petersburg, 1897, p. 10. By 'authorized' number of beds, the assembly referred to the number in the madhouse at the time of its transfer to the *zemstvo*.

12. V. I. Iakovenko, *O merakh uporiadocheniia prizreniia dushevno-bol'nykh i o neobkhodimosti deiatel'nago uchastiia v etom dele vsei zemsko-meditsinskoi organizatsii*, Moscow, 1896, p. 4.

13. Cited in N. N. Bazhenov, 'Proekt zakonodatel'stva o dushevno-bol'nykh i ob'iasnital'naia zapiska k nemu', *Trudy pervago s'ezda russkago soiuza psikhiatrov i nevropatologov sozvannago v Moskve v pamiat' S. S. Korsakova*, Moscow, 1914, pp. 142-364.

14. N. Kamenev, 'Meditsinskii otchet po psikhiatricheskomu otdeleniiu bol'nitsy Tul'skago gubernskago zemstva s 1-go ianvaria 1896g po 1-e ianvaria 1897 goda'. *Voprosy nervno-psikhicheskoi meditsiny*, vol. 2, 1897, pp. 538-92.

15. A. Iu. Freze, *Kotkrytiiu kazanskago okruzhnago doma umalishennykh*, Kazan, 1869, p. 22. P. Ostankov, 'Vinnitskaia okruzhnaia lechebnitsa', *Obozrenie psikhiatrii nevrologii i eksperimental'noi psikhologii*, vol. I, 1896, pp. 439-46. Many *zemstvos* had eliminated fees for the poor. This helps to explain the fact that the *zemstvo* madhouses were crowded while the Kazan asylum had difficulty filling its beds.

16. *Pravitel'stvennyi vestnik*, no. 263, 24 November 1879.

17. For a detailed discussion of psychiatric attitudes toward the dangerousness of the insane, see Brown, op. cit., chapter 5.

18. *Trudy pervago s'ezda otechestvennykh psikhiatrov*, St Petersburg, 1887, pp. 333-4.

19. P. O. Arkhangel'skii, *Otchet po osmotru russkikh psikhiatricheskikh zavedenii*, Moscow, 1887, p. 293.

20. Veselovskii, op. cit., p. 298.

21. Psychiatrists contended that their extraordinarily difficult working conditions dissuaded young physicians from entering the profession. See, for example, V. F. Chizh, 'O vnutrennei organizatsii zavedenii dlia

dushevnobol'nykh', *Vestnik klinicheskoi i sudebnoi psikhiatrii i nevropatologii*, vol. 9, no. 1, 1891, pp. 1–45.

22. Iakovenko, 'O merakh', p. 7; Bazhenov, 'Proekt', p. 218.
23. P. Iakobii, *Osnovy administrativnoi psikhiatrii*, Orel, 1900, p. 543.
24. See, for example, Kotsovskii, op. cit., p. 600, and B. S. Greidenberg, *Otchet po psikhiatricheskim otdeleniiam Khar'kovskoi gubernskoi zemskoi bol'nitsy za 1900g*, Kharkov, 1901, p. 21. During this period psychiatrists became quite active in the anti-drink movement. Insisting that mental institutions were not designed to serve as 'sobering-up stations' for drunks, they urged the establishment of separate treatment facilities for alcoholics.
25. See Iakobii, op. cit., p. 58.
26. See *Trudy vtorogo s'ezda otechestvennyky psikhiatrov*, Kiev, 1905.
27. See, for example, A. M., 'K psikhiatricheskomu voprosu', *Russkaia mysl'*, no. 4, p. 130. This particular incident involved the famous writer Leo Tolstoy.
28. Iakobii, op. cit., p. 123.
29. ibid., p. 518.
30. ibid., p. 300.
31. He was accused of ignorance of the 'realities' of Russian life and of engaging in a personal vendetta against those individuals who had been responsible for his departure from Moscow.
32. A. A. Govseev, *Stariyia i novyia techeniia v voprose o dushevno-bol'nykh*, Ekaterinoslav, 1902, pp. 6–7.
33. V. M. Gakkebush, 'Krepkiia otdeleniia v russkikh psikhiatricheskikh bol'nitsakh', *Sovremennaia psikhiatriia*, vol. 5, 1911, pp. 255–60.
34. O. A. Chechott, *K razvitiiu prizreniia dushevno-bol'nykh s-peterburgskim gorodskim obshchestvennym upravleniem 1884–1912*, St Petersburg, 1914, p. 44.
35. Kotsovkii, op. cit., p. 618.
36. V. P. Serbskii, 'Zakonodatel'stvo o dushevno-bol'nykh', *Trudy vtorogo s'ezda otechestvennykh psikhiatrov*, Kiev, 1907, p. 387.
37. Govseev, op. cit., pp. 6–7.
38. See *Trudy tret'iago s'ezda otechestvennykh psikhiatrov*, St Petersburg, 1911, p. 545.
39. See Bazhenov, 'Proekt', p. 216.
40. P. P. Tutyshkin, 'K voprosu o zakonodatel'stve o dushevno-bol'nykh i psikhiatricheskikh uchrezdeniiakh', *Trudy vtorogo s'ezda otechestvennykh psikhiatrov*, Kiev, 1907, pp. 397–406.
41. V. M. Bekhterev and P. A. Ostankov, 'O kandalakh i ispytuemykh i dushevno-bol'nykh arestantov', *Trudy tret'iago s'ezda otechestvennykh psikhiatrov*, St Petersburg, 1911, pp. 532–41.
42. *Trudy pervago s'ezda russkago soiuza psikhiatrov i nevropatologov*, Moscow, 1914.
43. Bazhenov, 'Proekt', p. 217.
44. Freidson, op. cit., pp. 45–6.
45. See, for example, *Zhurnal nevropatologii i psikhiatrii, 1907–11*; *Sovremennaia psikhiatrii, 1907–11*; S. I. Mitskevich, *Zapiski vracha-obshchestvennika (1888–1917)*, Moscow, 1969; and Brown, op. cit., chapter 5.
46. Freidson, op. cit., p. 23.
47. P. E. Zabludovskii, *Istoriia otechestvennoi meditsiny*, Moscow, 1960, lists many

psychiatrists who worked with the Bolsheviks. See also Mitskevich, op. cit., and Iudin, op. cit.

48. See, for example, Michel Foucault, *Madness and Civilization*, New York, Mentor Books, 1965; Gerald Grob, *Mental Institutions in American Social Policy to 1875*, New York, Science House, 1969; David Rothman, *The Discovery of the Asylum*, Boston: Little Brown, 1971; Andrew Scull, *Museums of Madness: the Social Organization of Insanity in Nineteenth Century England*, New York, St Martin's Press, 1979; Thomas Szasz: *The Manufacture of Madness*, New York, Dell, 1970.

12

Chastizing the Unchaste: Social Control Functions of a Women's Reformatory, 1894–1931

NICOLE HAHN RAFTER*

Specially written for this volume

The social control of women *as women* takes many forms. As Carol Smart has recently pointed out, punishments of deviations from prescribed gender roles can be formal or informal, external or internal, so subtle as to go unnoticed in everyday communication or overtly coercive. But all are directed towards correcting women who stray from the prescribed roles of their times. Smart argues that 'the primary sources' of such control are informal and of low visibility; they

> rest within, or arise from prevailing material conditions, cultural values, customs and social practices, such as the differential social-isation of male and female children within the family, schooling, forms of speech and language, media propagated stereotypes and numerous other seemingly innocuous social processes.[1]

This study deals with a more formal type of female social control.

The purpose of the study is to analyse how a particular prison – the Western House of Refuge operated at Albion, New York, from 1894 to 1931 – formalized and intensified the punishment of women who refused to conform to certain standards of female propriety. With establishment of this reformatory, New York extended the power of state control over a population of young, working-class women guilty mainly of 'offences' such as promiscuity, vagrancy and saloon-visiting. It created a new arm of

*For their comments on earlier drafts of this paper I thank Mary Bularzik, Laura Frader, John Laub, Gary Marx and Andrew Scull. I am also grateful to Ronald A. Farrell, Peggy Hobcroft, Laurie Mulcahy, Roberta Tarkin and (especially) Nicolette Parisi for help with aspects of the research.

Funding for the larger study of which this is a part was provided by Grant no. 79-NI-AX-0039 from the National Institute of Justice, US Department of Justice. Points of view or opinions stated in this paper are those of the author and do not necessarily represent the official position or policies of the US Department of Justice. Nor are they entirely shared by those whose help is acknowledged above.

the criminal justice system with authority to incarcerate such women for a period of years, during which the reformatory tried to retrain them to become chaste, proper and domestic. The Albion reformatory, like other women's prisons founded in the late nineteenth and early twentieth centuries, became a means of increasing and legitimating sexual and class inequality. And, like other institutions of its type, it was founded and operated entirely by women.

This study is based on three types of records. Official reports, mainly those published annually by the institution itself, constitute one source. The second consists of prisoner registries, volumes in which clerks recorded, often in immense detail, each inmate's background and personal characteristics, her institutional history and her degree of success on parole and in 'after life'. Third is a series of inmate case files which contain commitment and other court papers, institutional records and intercepted letters to and from family members, suitors and friends. The latter two sources, because they include information that official reports screen out, make possible a more complete study of social control processes than one based on published records alone.[2]

THE WOMEN'S REFORMATORY MOVEMENT

The women's reformatory movement began about 1870 with the founding of, first, a House of Shelter for women operated briefly at the Detroit House of Correction and, second, the first completely separate, independent and female-run prison for women, in Indianapolis. Two other reformatories, one in Framingham, Massachusetts, the other in Hudson, New York, opened before Albion was established near the turn of the century. Each of these forerunners took another step towards defining what eventually became regarded as the ideal women's reformatory: an independent institution, operated exclusively by women and dedicated to rehabilitating young misdemeanants through a programme of domestic, educational and moral training. The model reformatory was to be located in the country, far from the demoralizing city's influences, and architecturally it should consist of a central administrative building around which clustered 'cottages' for 30 or so inmates. Each cottage was to operate as a family unit, headed by a mature, respectable matron; its activities were to centre around food preparation and service in the cottage's kitchen and dining room. As even these few details suggest, conceptualization of the ideal women's reformatory was a major development in prison history, for the new model broke radically with male-oriented prison traditions, creating a set of feminized penal practices. The first institution to realize all aspects of the new model, Albion culminated the successive approximations of its predecessors. Its historical importance has not generally been recognized because other institutions with more prominent superintendents captured national attention. Yet Albion's plant, programme and sentencing practices established the ideal that the many reformatories established in the early twentieth century tried to emulate.[3]

Throughout the country, the campaigns that persuaded legislatures to fund reformatories for women were spearheaded by upper-middle-class women. (In Albion's case, the founder was Josephine Shaw Lowell.) Their activities formed part of the social feminist and social purity movements which in the late nineteenth and early twentieth centuries, led many middle-class women into the public arena. According to reformatory advocates themselves, their purpose was twofold: to rescue and to reform. Those they proposed to rescue were usually not the female felons held along with men in state penitentiaries but rather misdemeanants, a population of minor offenders not hitherto subject to state punishment (or 'care', to use the reformers' term). Before establishment of reformatories, female misdemeanants were punished, at most, with brief gaol terms. Gaols, reformatory advocates argued, did nothing but corrupt. Hannah Chickering, a founder of the Massachusetts reformatory, reported that, after release from gaol, women 'are soon again arrested, re-committed, and this mournful round is trodden again and again, till a wretched death closes the scene for these victims of misfortune, neglect, and sin'. Gaols should be replaced by institutions run by 'refined and virtuous' women who would provide good examples and feminine sympathy to the fallen and wayward. Moreover (the reformers' argument continued), women's prisons should be empowered to retain their inmates for long terms, for it might take years 'for the sundering of old and evil associations, the breaking of pernicious habits, [and] the formation of new. . . .'[4]

Albion's commitment law initially permitted it to hold inmates for up to five years. An amendment of 1899 lowered the maximum to three years, but this was still a long term for the minor public order offenders who constituted the majority of its inmates.[5] (Other women's reformatories also concentrated on youthful public order offenders – those who appeared both tractable and worthy of salvation – and most of them followed Albion by adopting an indeterminate sentence of up to three years.) No comparable intensification of punishment occurred in the case of men sent to state prisons, even those men's institutions that were also called 'reformatories'.[6] If arrested at all for the petty offences that led women to reformatories, men were fined or sentenced to short terms in gaol, just as women had been before reformatories were established. Thus, founding of institutions like Albion legitimated the double standard. It extended the mantle of state control over a new segment of the female population and made it possible to punish (or 'help', as the reformers put it) such women more extensively than men who had committed the same acts. Men simply were not sentenced to state prisons for promiscuity and saloon-visiting.

SOCIAL CONTROL FUNCTIONS OF THE ALBION REFORMATORY

Records of the Albion reformatory indicate that the institution served two primary functions: sexual control and vocational control. It attempted the first, control of inmates' sexuality, by training 'loose' young women to accept middle-class standards of propriety, especially that which dictated chastity until marriage and fidelity thereafter. It tried to achieve the second, control of inmates' work lives, by training charges in home-making, a competency they were to utilize either as dutiful daughters or wives within their own families or as servants in the homes of others. Operationally, techniques used to achieve these ends were usually indistinguishable. In what follows, they are separated for analytical purposes, but in fact means used to realize the dual functions of sexual and vocational control worked together, coalescing and mutually reinforcing one another.

From Premarital Pregnancy to Propriety: Preparation for the
'True Good Womanly Life'[7]

To control women's bodies, especially those of 'promiscuous' women, the Albion reformatory used three approaches. One was the initial act of incarcerating women who had violated middle-class standards for the way 'true women' ought to conduct themselves.[8] Second was parole revocation if a prisoner showed signs of lapsing back into impropriety while out on conditional release. Third was transfer of intractables to a custodial asylum for 'feeble-minded' women at Rome, New York, where they could be held indefinitely.

   Let us begin by looking at the type of women on whom the reformatory concentrated its efforts and the types of offences for which they were committed. Over the 37 years of its operation as a reformatory,[9] Albion received about 3150 prisoners. Three-quarters of them were between 15 and 21 years old, all the rest under 30. Racially, the vast majority – over 95 per cent – were white. Most had been born in New York State (particularly in the rural western area, where the institution was located) of native-born parents; most were Protestant; and most were single. The composition of the population reflected the desire of its officials to work with cases who appeared malleable and deserving. Albion's commitment law authorized it to receive women between the ages of 15 (later raised to 16) and 30 convicted of petty larceny, habitual drunkenness, common prostitution, frequenting a disorderly house or any other misdemeanour.[10] Table 1, based on a sample of inmates drawn from the prisoner registries, shows that only 1.2 per cent had been convicted of violent crimes (and these were mainly second- or third-degree assault) and but another 13.7 per cent of property offences (mainly petty larceny). The great majority (81.4 per cent) and been sentenced for public order offences – victimless crimes.

TABLE 1

NEW YORK STATE WESTERN HOUSE OF REFUGE, CONVICTION OFFENCES,
*1894–1931**

Offence category	No. of cases	Per cent
Public order crimes	1288	81.4
Property crimes	217	13.7
Violent crimes	19	1.2
Other	51	3.2
No information	8	0.5
Totals	1583	100

*The table is based on a sample drawn from the Inmate Admission Ledgers; every odd-numbered case was used. The property offences were mainly petty larceny.

Closer examination of the public order offence category reveals that more than two-thirds of women sent to Albion had been convicted of four particular public order crimes: intoxication (about 6 per cent of the total), waywardness (7 per cent), prostitution (8.5 per cent) and vagrancy (46.5 per cent). These are not offences for which men were sent to state prison and held for years; they clearly indicate operation of a double standard for the sexes.

Further scrutiny of offences in the public order category indicates, moreover, that a large proportion of women sent to Albion for public order crimes had in fact been found guilty of sexual misconduct. According to the registries, half of those sentenced for vagrancy, or about one-fourth of the total reformatory population, were convicted of violating Section 887, Sub-division 4 of the Code of Criminal Procedure, a combined vagrancy–prostitution charge. At first glance, this suggests that at least a quarter of Albion's inmates had been prostitutes. Offence details given in the registries and case files, however, show that women arrested for the 887 violation, instead of being professional prostitutes, were often openly sexual young women who cared little for conventional notions of female propriety.

The 887 charge might be used to punish a premarital pregnancy, for example – or a series of them, as with no. 1451, who had just borne her third illegitimate baby when county officials decided to send her to Albion. Sometimes an 887 charge was brought on complaint of a member of the woman's family, such as an exasperated mother or embarrassed husband. According to a newspaper clipping attached to the registry entry for Rosetta B., for instance, one month prior to her commitment this 18-year-old's husband had had her arrested for truancy, and the judge had put her on probation. When, a month later, she ran away for an entire weekend, only to be discovered on Monday morning by the police 'in a resort on Elm Street', the husband complained again to the judge, who committed Rosetta to Albion under the vagrancy–prostitution statute. Similarly, 19-year-old Sarah M., married for one month, was committed on the 887 charge. 'Sarah did not know it,' reads a note on her record, 'but it was her husband who had her sent here.' In yet other cases the 887 charge was used to arrest women who were in poor health or poor company. A woman found to have syphilis could be sent to the reformatory under this charge, as might an inebriate like Hattie, who led a 'life of shame and drunkenness. When arrested, she was found in an unconscious condition on an ash heap' and sent to Albion for a second time. Mary N., sent to Albion on the same charge, had been caught with two Italian chicken thieves; she 'admitted she was keeping bad company, seemed very willing to be sent to Albion'. The vagrancy–prostitution charge, then, could cover a multitude of peccadilloes from cuckolding to keeping bad company; but women convicted under it were not professional prostitutes.[11]

Others among Albion's inmates doubtless *were* professional prostitutes – the 8.5 per cent sentenced for prostitution, for example, and the additional 0.5 per cent convicted of keeping a house of ill fame. There were also women who had engaged casually in acts of sex for money, such as one who had frequented 'Jimmy Joe's place on Railroad Ave. where she received men'. But the majority were, like Jennie B., merely sexually active: Jennie was sent to Albion for having 'had unlawful sexual intercourse with young men and remain[ing] at hotels with young men all night particularly on July 4, 1893'. In fact, reformatories like Albion had little interest in the professional prostitute; instead, they aimed at susceptible women who might respond positively to their programmes.[12]

Some women committed to Albion for sexual misconduct had in fact been sexually victimized. Such was the case with Anna B., who at the age of 14 had been charged with ungovernability and sent to the Salvation Army Home in Buffalo, where she bore her first child. Not long after she returned home with her baby, her father was sent to prison for rape. Anna's case file strongly suggests (without positively confirming) that she was the victim. While her father was still on trial, Anna was sent to live with her grandmother in Pennsylvania. 'The grandmother was housekeeper for Emanual G———, 60 years of age, who, Anna said, is the father of her second child,' born at Albion in 1922. Convicted of 'running around', Anna seems in fact to have been exploited twice by much older men.[13]

Although a handful of cases were, like Anna B., 'led astray', most of Albion's inmates appear to have been rebels of some sort – against the double-standard of sexual morality; against their birth families or husbands; or against public regulations such as that prohibiting drunk and disorderly conduct. Perhaps 'rebels' is not the best description, however; instead of defying conventional norms, many of these young women may have been acting in accordance with other norms which they themselves considered legitimate. Despite their youthfulness, the majority were independent at the point when police officers plucked them from saloons, hotel rooms and street corners to be sent to the reformatory. Nearly 80 per cent held jobs – this in contrast to only 27 per cent of all New York State women employed in 1910.[14] Although 70 per cent of them had not yet married, they had moved beyond regulation by their parents. Whether reacting defiantly against conventional notions of propriety or simply behaving in ways they regarded as acceptable, most clearly had not internalized a view of themselves as docile, dependent and proper. It was this situation that the reformatory, with its goal of imposing and teaching sexual control, sought to remedy.

If incarceration and training within the institution did not teach the prisoner to conform, the reformatory employed another means: parole revocation. Nearly all of Albion's inmates were released on parole before their sentences expired. While on parole, their activities were scrutinized by a variety of agents – Albion's parole officers, who paid regular visits; clergymen, community nurses and police officers who had been asked to keep an eye on specific women; and the employers in whose homes some parolees were placed as domestics. When parole was revoked, as it was in about 16 per cent of the cases, the violation was frequently sexual in nature.

Some women had parole revoked for overt returns to vice. Such was the case with Isabel W., paroled to an aunt in Buffalo, where she began 'going out with a disreputable married man and on several occasions [remained out] all night'. Similarly, women who became pregnant while on parole were returned to the institution – unless they quickly married a 'respectable' man. At other times revocation was triggered not by blatant signs of immorality but rather by indications that a lapse was imminent. One woman was returned to the reformatory because she 'became infatuated with a married man named Ludwig. Mrs Ludwig wrote us' and, after investigating, the institution decided to recall her. Another parolee was revoked for associating with the father of her child ('they were not married and Washington is a most disreputable character'), and no. 1313 barely escaped revocation when 'Two former inmates report[ed] seeing her frequently at night with different conductors on the Genessee St. line.'[15]

In cases that appeared hopeless to Albion administrators, a third step was sometimes taken to insure against relapse: transfer to the State School at Rome or another of New York's institutions for the feeble-minded. Such transfers carried an automatic extension of sentence up-to-life, the theory being that the feeble-minded never improve. At the turn of the century, the feeble-minded were considered innately promiscuous, so Albion's authorities easily assumed that women who would not reform were feeble-minded.[16] Because intelligence testing was still in a primitive stage, it was not difficult to 'scientifically' confirm a suspicion of feeble-mindedness and thus establish the basis for a transfer. These transfers, which occurred in cases of women who were disciplinary problems within the institution as well as in instances of overt sexuality while on parole, constituted the final disposition for 48 of the sampled cases, or 3 per cent of all first releases. In addition, 13 women returned to the reformatory for parole violation, or 5.2 per cent of those released a second time, were transferred to institutions for the feeble-minded, as were two women or 5.6 per cent of the 36 cases returned twice to the reformatory and then released a third time. Case file documents such as letters written by these allegedly feeble-minded women indicate that they were not in fact mentally weak. They were, however, non-compliant. The lesson of their transfer to civil institutions was probably not lost on those left behind at the reformatory.

From Sauciness to Subservience: Preparation for Domestic Service

The second central social control function of the Albion reformatory was to train inmates to become competent housekeepers either in their own homes or in those where they were placed as domestics. To understand how Albion went about achieving this end, it is necessary to look first at its programme.

The institution aimed, in the words of its managers, at 'the reformation and proper education of . . . unfortunate and wayward girls . . .; to give such moral and religious training . . ., and such training in domestic work as will eventually enable them to find employment, secure good homes and be self-supporting'. To the achievement of these ends, the managers viewed the cottage system, with its 'plan of ordinary domestic life', as crucial. The cottages, as noted earlier, created a familial environment in which inmates were taught homemaking skills under supervision of matrons.[17]

Gentility pervaded most aspects of Albion's programme. Exercise, for example, was referred to as 'physical culture training'. Easter 1895 was celebrated with 'an evening of music, song and recitation by Miss Cousins, teacher of elocution in the Albion High School', and later that year a Mr Irving M. Thompson helped inmates celebrate Arbor Day 'with an appropriate address on the uses of trees, their beauty and value'. Such details indicate how closely the institution's administrators associated middle-class mannerisms with reform. They did not expect their girls to *become* ladies, but rather sought to inculcate respect for the values associated with the lady – refinement, propriety, decorum.[18]

Within this general context of induced gentility, inmates received two types of training, academic and domestic, with by far the heavier emphasis on the latter. Albion usually did not educate inmates beyond the sixth-grade level, but it provided abundant opportunities for perfection of domestic skills, instructing prisoners in dressmaking, plain and fancy sewing, knitting, crocheting, 'cookery', cleaning and ventilation, and laundering. A steam-operated washing machine was purchased for the institution's laundry, but the sight of it made visiting prison commissioner Sarah L. Davenport 'sorry', for its use was 'not educating the women or the girls for the homes they will go to, when they leave Albion'. Thereafter, the laundry was washed by hand.[19] A 'finely equipped domestic science department', outfitted with dining room furniture, coal and gas burners and kitchen utensils, was added in 1912, and from that time on inmates received instruction in:

> manufacture and source of food supplies, relative cost, and nutritive values; the care of the kitchen, pantry, and dining room; construction and care of the sinks, stoves, (both gas and coal) and refrigerators; table etiquette; the planning and serving of meals; and waitress' duties.[20]

When the board of managers met at the reformatory, inmates practised for future employment by waiting on the managers' table.

To middle-class women who lived in its vicinity, Albion provided trained, inexpensive household help. It was the institution's policy 'to place our girls in the home of a woman who will take a motherly interest in them'.[21] One-quarter of the prisoners were paroled directly to live-in domestic positions. Of the 50 per cent paroled to members of their own families, another sizeable proportion also took jobs as domestics. Albion was not the first prison to train female inmates in domestic work; incarcerated women have always been required to sew and launder, and institutions for women and girls established earlier in the nineteenth century also placed parolees as domestics. Nor was domestic work necessarily new to its inmates, one-third of whom reported their previous occupation as 'domestic' or 'houseworker'. But the reformatory records suggest that some, at least, had been less than satisfactory servants, given to carelessness, impudence and running off with young men. The institution attempted to turn these and other inmates into competent, submissive domestics.[22]

Nearly 20 per cent of Albion's prisoners, before arrest, had worked in mills or factories. In light of this fact, the reformatory's refusal to provide training in skills that might 'unfit' women for domestic service is especially significant. 'No industries are maintained,' one report pointed out, 'but every inmate is taught to cook and care for a home. This is the most important thing in the work of the institution. Most of the girls when paroled go into homes where this knowledge is necessary.' Thus Albion not only provided rigorous training in housekeeping but also discouraged any hopes that inmates might have had of moving beyond the home. It reinforced its point by paroling most women to family situations where they were needed as paid or unpaid domestic help.[23]

Over the discipline of women paroled as servants, employers and the institution formed a symbiotic alliance of mutual aid. The reformatory required women released to domestic positions to sign a form agreeing to:

> accept the wages agreed upon between the Superintendent . . . and her employer, . . . her wages to be retained by employer, excepting such amount as the latter thinks necessary for [the] girl. . . .
>
> . . . consult employer as to her amusements, recreation, and social diversions. To form no friendships, not to visit or receive visits from members of her own family unless approved by the Superintendent. Is not to go out nights excepting when accompanied by a responsible person, and to go very seldom at night. To have one afternoon a week. . . .[24]

Parolees were also required to send monthly reports to the reformatory, and they were further supervised through visits from a parole officer. If despite these controls a domestic became difficult, the reformatory could revoke parole, a threat that no doubt helped employers maintain discipline. According to the prisoner registries, revocations were occasioned by 'sauciness' and 'obscenity', failure to work hard enough, and other demonstrations of independence. Case no. 13, for example,

> Went to Rochester to work for Mrs . . . Johnson and for a time did very nicely, but finding some girls of her acquaintance she began to visit them too often and to neglect her work. She came back to institution in Aug. 1897 and there remained till [sentence] expiration.

Case no. 2585 was originally paroled to a Mrs Foulds of Rochester. But 'Jane was a slow worker and very untidy and shiftless. She was very fond of reading. Returned [to the reformatory] for a change of place. . . .' Next Jane was sent to a Mrs Sticklin of Buffalo. This time, 'On Oct. 11 went to a movie and did not return until eleven o'clock when she was expected at nine.' When Mrs Sticklin threatened to return her to Albion, Jane ran away. She was not recaptured, but others like her frequently had parole revoked for laziness, disobedience and running-away.

In return for the institution's aid in disciplining difficult domestics, employers supervised prisoners in its stead. They were 'authorized and requested to open and read all mail sent and received by girl' and further charged 'to guard her morals, language and actions, and aid her as much as possible by advice as to her present and future conduct. . . .' In the course of aiding fallen women, employers were also aiding themselves, by maintaining the quality of the services they received. The entire arrangement, in fact, seems to have been one from which employers benefited greatly, receiving trained and supervised servants who promised to consult them in all matters and work six-and-one-half days a week. If the servant became shiftless or impudent, the criminal justice system would step in to do the necessary disciplining.[25]

TECHNIQUES OF SOCIAL CONTROL

Albion developed a variety of techniques to encourage reform. Some have already been identified: the initial act of incarcerating women for sexual misconduct and other minor violations; intensive training in gentility and domesticity; a policy of parole to domestic positions; community surveillance; parole revocation; and transfer of the most uncooperative to civil institutions where they could be held indefinitely. Implicit in many of the techniques just listed was another: infantilization. From the moment of arrest, Albion's inmates were reduced to the status of children. Like juvenile delinquents, many were detained for status offences – immorality, waywardness, keeping bad company – for which adults (that is, men and older women) were not arrested. At the reformatory they were supervised by matron-mothers, and at parole they were usually released to family situations in which they had a dependent status. Indeed, the very concept of an institution dedicated to the rescue and reform of women under the age of 30, and operated with an extremely high level of discretionary authority, was rooted in a view of such women as childlike creatures. Appropriately, like institutions for juvenile delinquents, Albion was titled a 'refuge'.

Disruption of inmates' ties with their families was another mechanism used by the reformatory to encourage inmates to rely on it and adopt its values. Familial disruption was a technique to which women were especially susceptible, their roles being so intimately involved with family life. Disconnected from their own families, Albion inmates were more likely to identify with the surrogate 'families' of their cottages and, on parole, with those to which they were sent as servants.

Disruption of family life is an inevitable by-product of incarceration, but Albion developed policies relating to mail and visitors that intensified the break. Once in its custody, inmates had immense difficulty contacting families and friends. For example, they were allowed to write letters only once every two months, and these were censored. If the superintendent decided that either the contents or the designated recipient was unsuitable, she would file the letter in the inmate's folder – quite probably without notifying the writer and certainly without notifying the intended recipient, both of whom might therefore wait in vain anticipation. Incoming mail was also censored and frequently filed away, undelivered. Visits were permitted only four times a year. Further restrictions limited the pool of potential visitors to close relatives, and even these might be banned if deemed bad influences. Moreover, some approved visitors were probably discouraged from actually visiting by the institution's geographical isolation. For all these reasons, commitment to the reformatory resulted in near-total severance of ties to former support systems. Isolated in this fashion, prisoners were more likely to become dependent on the institution's staff and receptive to their instruction.[26]

Separation from children, which continues to pose special difficulties for female prisoners, was probably more traumatic at the turn of the century: even when women had husbands living at home, their children were often sent to orphanages or placed out for adoption when they were committed. Thus not only were young mothers separated from their children; many also had to suffer the pain of knowing that their family had been dissolved. In such cases, moreover, the children were now being cared for by strangers. (There is no indication in the records that women at Albion were informed of the welfare of institutionalized or adopted children.)

Sometimes ultimate disposition of children would be left undecided and used to induce the mother to conform. Of a woman committed for vagrancy, for example, the registry tells us that 'Edna made a splendid record while on parole. Mr Angel, Humane Officer of Courtland County, was so well pleased with her that he returned her children to her.'[27] Not to please Mr Angel, it seems, would have resulted in loss of her children. Another example is provided by the case of Martha, a mother of four sentenced to Albion for public intoxication. Threat of removal of her children kept Martha sober even in times of great stress:

> Martha returned [on parole] to her husband who had promised every [thing] in the way of reform but who is the veriest hypocrit [sic]. She continued leading a true good womanly life hoping to be worthy of her children, as the authorities had promised to restore them when they were satisfied she would hold out.[28]

In instances like these, there was the initial familial disruption occasioned by commitment and then a threat of further disruption – loss of children – if the prisoner did not comply with the institution's requirements.

Similar methods of control involved babies who stayed with mothers at the institution. If a woman was nursing at commitment, she was allowed to bring the child with her, and she could keep an infant born while she was imprisoned; but reformatory policy decreed that all babies had to leave when they reached the age of two. Sometimes the institution decided not to parole a woman until after the baby had been sent away. Mary P., for example, had a baby a few days after her arrival at Albion in 1922, and in September 1924, its two years having expired, it was sent to the Delaware County Superintendent of the Poor. Mary was paroled just a month later to work in her father's cigar factory. Mary's parents may have refused to let her bring home an illegitimate child. Whatever the reason, the effect of holding her slightly beyond the mandatory release date for the baby was to cut Mary off from the only family she had had for two years. She was, moreover, returned to a situation in which she herself was the child.[29]

Some babies brought into or born at the prison were sent to adoption agencies or other institutions before they reached the age of two. How long their mothers might keep them was a matter of administrative discretion, and like all such matters, liable to be used as a mechanism of control. The only documentation I have found for the practice of using children to coerce institutionalized mothers relates not to Albion but another reformatory. I quote it here, however, as this form of social control, though of very low visibility (and thus seldom documentable) was probably widespread in institutions which permitted women to keep infants. The practice is described in a letter from the superintendent of Maine's State Reformatory for Women to a journalist who had requested information on babies in prison. 'The conduct of the mothers,' the superintendent informed him,

> decides in a measure the time they are allowed to spend with their babies. . . . They dress and undress and feed their own babies after the baby is six months old. They always have the privilege to kiss them good night and to spend an hour in the afternoon with them, unless their conduct precludes the loss [*sic*] of this privilege.[30]

Restricting access to children – threatening family disruption – was probably used as a social control device at Albion as well.

Despite its heavy emphasis on the home as woman's place, Albion developed parole policies that further disrupted some inmates' ties to their former homes. Women who before incarceration lived in stable family situations were frequently paroled not to their own families but to domestic positions in the homes of others. In some instances, the institution deemed the original family unsuitable and wanted to keep the woman away from it as long as possible. In others, the officials simply seem to have decided that for a woman to work and save money was the best way for her to pass parole. Often the domestic jobs were in towns distant from the prisoners' families. Women could sometimes take infants with them to domestic positions, but at others they had to separate from their babies in order to accept a live-in job.

Many of these dislocational factors are present in the case of Marjorie M., a 20-year-old German woman who, before commitment, lived with her parents and seven siblings in Batavia, where she was employed as a domestic. The mother of a three-year-old and again pregnant, Marjorie was convicted of disorderly conduct in 1917 and sent to Albion. There she gave birth to her second daughter, Helen. Paroled to a domestic position in Rochester, Marjorie sent $5 of her $8 weekly salary to the home where Helen was boarded. After parole, she found employment as assistant housekeeper at the Rochester Orphans' Asylum, where Helen was now living. In the winter of 1920 Helen died of diphtheria. At this point Marjorie, who at the time of arrest had been living with ten members of her immediate family, was left entirely alone.[31]

The reformatory's policies also perpetuated familial disruption in the case of Henrietta S., a Binghampton woman with two children who had been sentenced to Albion for intoxication. Henrietta was paroled to a domestic position in Lyndonville, where she earned $4 a week. When her term was up, she returned to her family with $154 she had managed to save from her wages. The institution interpreted the large sum as a sign of success, but Henrietta and her family paid a high psychological price in return: their family life had been disrupted for three years, and while Mrs K. Fraser of Lyndonville had had cheap use of her services, Henrietta's own children had gone without them.[32]

The reformatory's policies were certainly not disruptive of family life in all cases, and, arguably, some women would have profited by *not* being returned to their parents or husbands. The point is that the institution exercised tremendous control over inmates' social contacts (probably more than any contemporary prison for men cared to exercise), and that it used this control to induce conformity. Denying inmates access to mail and visitors; institutionalizing their children or threatening to do so; blocking their access to infants; developing parole policies that frequently prevented contact with former families – through such means the prison often disrupted the continuity of whatever family life had existed. The effect, as observed previously, was to encourage dependency upon the institution and increase the likelihood that inmates would respond with openness and gratitude when its personnel offered them help and moral advice. They became, in short, more likely to internalize the reformatory's teachings about how women like themselves should behave.

'THE BEST PLACE TO CONQUER GIRLS': AN EVALUATION OF ALBION'S SUCCESS

Many women incarcerated at Albion went on to lead lives that met the institution's criteria for success, marrying and maintaining homes of their own or remaining for long terms in domestic placements. No doubt many former inmates would have quietened down in their mid-twenties or early thirties even without the moral influence of the prison, just as more serious offenders often 'mature out' of crime. But the reformatory does seem to have set some formerly wayward women on the path to becoming ladylike; to have served, in the words of one inmate's sister, as 'the only and best place to conquer girls'. Albion appears, that is, to have achieved its goals in some, perhaps even a majority, of cases.[33]

If we ask how it managed to do so, the answer seems to lie with its use of both carrots and sticks. So far, I have mainly identified the sticks, ways in which Albion negatively reinforced disapproved behaviours. However, the reformatory worked through kindness as well as coercion. Had it merely punished, it would have antagonized; but it also performed extensive nurturing functions. It alleviated some of the harsher aspects of poverty. It served as a hospital where the diseased could receive treatment, the malnourished food, the pregnant decent care at delivery. It also functioned as a shelter to which women could turn from incestuous fathers, brutal husbands and oppressive employers. The superintendent and other staff offered counselling in marriage and child-rearing, and the institution as a whole provided the kind of training that many working-class women might have considered valuable: refined and genteel behaviour was, after all, accepted as a sign of female superiority, particularly by people with status.

Clearly, the reformatory did not bring every case to a successful conclusion. Its records are dotted with cases in which officials simply gave up on a bad job:

Julia was a great care throughout her parole . . . deceitful and deceptive. [No. 1581]

March 10th 1916. Visited by Parole Officer. Found that Grace had left her place of employment. Could not be found. [No. 1335]

She was arrested while on parole and sentenced again to the W.H. of R. But we refused to take her again. 1915. [No. 1355]

Minnie gave entire satisfaction [on domestic parole] for several months saved her mon~y was quiet and unobtrusive. . . . The spirit of unrest [then] took possession of her and she absconded, and no trace of her has been found. [No. 89]

While reformatory officials often went after parole violators, in many instances they let the matter drop, sometimes because the inmate had fled beyond their reach, at other times because she had been re-arrested, at still others because they decided the woman was not worth more effort. When no. 61 sold her discharge clothes, 'bought a telescope' and ran away from the Wayfarers' Lodge in Buffalo, they resigned themselves with the observation that 'a perverse nature and bad blood [had] proved too strong for human endeavor'.

On the other hand, Albion's records also provide evidence that numerous inmates were grateful for its help. Some, especially those who were very young, alone in the world or in poor health, seem not to have found incarceration onerous. A few, for example, requested to stay for their full terms, without parole, and some ran back to the institution from unpleasant parole situations. One woman, after having been paroled twice, returned 'and asked to be admitted. She was a wreck, physically and morally – her clothing torn and soiled, and evidently [she] had no place to go for the night nor money to pay her way'. The reformatory gave her medical attention and sheltered her for another six months. After marrying, some ex-inmates brought their husbands to visit the reformatory and meet its superintendent. A woman who had escaped later wrote from a distant state to announce that she was happily married; her resentment at being confined, in other words, was not incompatible with a desire to demonstrate she could achieve the institution's ideals.[34] Many women wrote back after release. 'My dear Mrs Boyed', began a letter received by the superintendent in 1907,

> have [you] entirely forgotten Nellie that one time lived in your pleasant Home for Homeless Girls [*sic*].
>   I have been thinking for some time that I would write to you. . . . Of course you have heard from Mrs Green that I am married and have a good Husband. . . . Are any of the Ladies [officers] with you now that were in the year of 1894 or 95 . . . how I would like to see them as well as your self. Perhaps none of them are there now. Do you see dear Mrs Green often. How I should love to see her dear face once more. . . . If you see Mrs Parmaly will you say how I would like to hear from her. . . . I have a very pleasant home and appreciate it I think as I ought to. Yours in haste and with love.
>   Nellie (I am Ever) L——[35]

Some of the needs to which the reformatory responded were in fact exacerbated by it (separation from friends and family, for instance, and a sense of disgrace), while others were more circumstantial; but in any event, women like Nellie frequently found Albion's care satisfactory and in turn responded positively to its training.

It seems probable that the reformatory's values influenced not only those sentenced to it but also women in the broader community. Albion's records show that some inmates knew each other before commitment and continued to associate after release: the brother of no. 69, for example, was the husband of no. 81; inmates nos 84 and 85 were sisters; and at the time of commitment no. 2133 was living with the husband of another inmate. If such acquaintanceship networks existed among inmates, they must have been even more extensive between prisoners and women never incarcerated. Through such interconnections, Albion no doubt came to play a role in the consciousness of working-class women in its area.

Women who never set foot inside it would have been aware, through word of mouth, that there existed a state institution prepared to punish them for sexual and other transgressions.

Informal as well as formal police actions provided a back-up to the social values endorsed by the Albion, reminding women in the community of the institution's potential for punishment. This kind of informal social control is almost invisible today, since it was seldom noted in official records. Yet we can catch glimpses of it through reformatory documents. One hint appears in the registry record of inmate no. 2441, a woman confined in 1922 for vagrancy. She had had no previous arrests, we are told, but had been 'taken to the Police Station twice and talked to for being out late, attending dances'. Whereas this particular woman was evidently not influenced by police efforts to get her to behave properly (she did, after all, end up at the reformatory), others so treated may have been. Of no. 1775, paroled in 1919, we are told that

> Edna was very erratic and unreliable during her parole. She was reported [to the reformatory] by the Binghamton police as being on the streets at a late hour very frequently with different men. Chief Cronin was asked several times [by reformatory officials] to arrest her and instructed his men to that effect. Parole Ofcr [*sic*] went after her but could not find her.

Chiefs other than Chief Cronin probably also instructed their men to keep women like Edna in line. Thus, through informal procedures as well as formal arrests, the police helped to uphold the reformatory's values; they too gave women incentives to submit and behave.

CONCLUSION

The women's reformatory movement developed in the context of a variety of nineteenth- and early twentieth-century social changes to which it contributed and from which it drew sustenance. It began as part of a much broader nineteenth-century movement to establish institutions for members of 'the dependent, defective, and delinquent classes' – institutions for the insane, the mentally retarded ('feeble-minded'), the aged and chronically ill, orphans and so on. This trend in turn was fed by changes that have been attributed to immigration, urbanization and the development of capitalism. Within the prison system, pressure for reform came to a head at an historic meeting in 1870 at which leading penologists drew up a plan for prisons which would treat rather than punish. This articulation of the ideology of rehabilitation helped set the stage for the nascent women's reformatory movement. As Rothman demonstrates in his most recent history of 'asylums', when proto-Progressives and Progressives focused their reformist energies on criminals, they not only expanded the range of state control but also raised levels of discretionary power and instituted individualized treatment through casework; all three developments spilled over into the establishment and operation of women's reformatories. Of special relevance to the evolution of the women's prison system were changes in methods of handling juvenile delinquents. Just before the women's reformatory began, as Schlossman has shown, institutions for juvenile delinquents inaugurated new policies, replacing the huge congregate buildings of the past with the cottage plan and generally domesticating treatment. From models provided by the juvenile system (especially by the Lancaster, Massachusetts, school for delinquent girls, which pioneered in both the cottage plan and domestic parole), leaders in women's prison reform drew inspiration as they laboured to design the reformatory type of prison for adult women.[36]

Just as influential as institutional developments on the evolution of women's reformatories were growth of the so-called social feminist and social purity movements. After the Civil War, middle-class women increasingly involved themselves in public affairs, mainly those relating to children, other women (including female prisoners), and public morality. Some of these social feminists specialized in social purity work, concentrating on issues like temperance and prostitution. That alcohol consumption and sexuality became topics of widespread concern at the turn of the century helps account for the type of offender on whom the reformatories focused. Moreover, as Connelly points out in his recent social history of prostitution in the Progressive era, those who devoted their energies to eradication of white slavery and other facets of sexual vice defined 'prostitution' broadly, to include 'any form of sexual behavior that violated the moral imperatives of civilized morality'. The looseness of this definition also explains why reformatories reached out for the promiscuous and wayward.[37]

Among the many factors that encouraged the founding of institutions like Albion, two were of particular importance; the solidification of gender roles in nineteenth-century America, and the hardening of divisions between social classes. As production came to be located outside the family, women were increasingly isolated within the home. Their labour was devalued and a premium came to be placed on feminine characteristics such as domesticity, demureness, purity and piety. But the ideal of 'true womanhood' was more easily approximated by women of the middle than the working class. The former were likely to have servants and other aids to gentility, and if they became restless they could take up respectable causes like temperance and prison reform. Intensification of gender roles had different implications for working-class women, however: for them, 'true womanhood' was more difficult to achieve and less rewarding.

Convinced of innate temperamental differences between the sexes, the reformers naturally set about establishing separate, women-run prisons for women; and believing that woman's mission included rescue of the unfortunate, they naturally focused on fallen women – not serious felons or confirmed prostitutes, but wayward 'girls' who might be saved. Those among them active in social purity campaigns argued against the double standard of sexual morality for men and women. Yet all the reformers worked to found prisons that in fact institutionalized the double standard, prisons that punished women for behaviour often overlooked in the case of men; held women for terms longer than those to which men were liable; and deliberately feminized penal practices, thus legitimating differential treatment of the sexes. Their understanding of 'woman's nature' led logically to advocacy of special help for the frailer sex.

Two groups of women – the working-class offenders and the middle-class reformers – met, so to speak, at the gate of the women's reformatory. The struggle between them was economically functional in some ways to the reformers: it helped maintain a pool of cheap domestic labour for women like themselves, and, by keeping women in the surplus labour force, it undergirded the economic system to which they owed their privileged positions. But such purely economic explanations do not account adequately for the dedication with which the reformers went about their tasks of rescue and reform. The struggle also involved the definition of gender. Reformers hoped to recast offenders in their own image, to have them embrace the values (though not assume the social station) of the lady. And through reformatories like Albion, some working-class women were taught to accept a new concept of gender which entailed restriction of their sexual and vocational choices. They were, in fact, reformed.

NOTES AND REFERENCES

1. Carol Smart and Barry Smart (eds), *Women, Sexuality and Social Control*, Boston, Routledge & Kegan Paul, 1978, pp. 1-2.
2. The registries and case files are held by the New York State Archives in Albany. In using the registries, I sampled every other case from 1894, when the first prisoner arrived, through the institution's close in 1931, for a total of 1583

cases. (In the material that follows, I identify cases by the numbers used in the prison registries.)

3. On the history of the women's reformatory movement, see Estelle B. Freedman, *Their Sisters' Keepers: Women's Prison Reform in America, 1830–1930*, Ann Arbor, University of Michigan Press, 1981; Eugenia Cornelia Lekkerkerker, *Reformatories for Women in the United States*, The Hague, Bij J. B. Wolters' Uitgevers-Maatschappij, 1931; and Nicole Hahn Rafter, *The Punishment of Women: State Prisons and Their Inmates, 1790–1935*, Boston, Northeastern University Press, 1984.

4. Dedham Temporary Asylum for Discharged Female Prisoners, *Annual Report 1864*, p. 6, as quoted in Mary Bularzik, 'The Dedham Temporary Asylum for Discharged Female Prisoners: The Interaction of Female Charity and the Criminal Justice System', paper delivered at the November 1980 meeting of the Social Science History Association, Rochester, NY, p. 3 (Chickering quotation); Detroit House of Correction, *Annual Report 1868*, p. 7 ('refined and virtuous'); New York State House of Refuge of Women, Hudson, *Annual Report 1899*, p. 10. On Lowell's work, see William Rhinelander Stewart, *The Philanthropic Work of Josephine Shaw Lowell*, New York, Macmillan, 1911. On social feminism, see Lois W. Banner, *Women in Modern America: A Brief History*, New York, Harcourt Brace Jovanovich, 1974; Jill Conway, 'Women Reformers and American Culture, 1870–1930', *Journal of Social History*, vol. 5, winter 1971–72, pp. 164–77; and William L. O'Neill, *Everyone Was Brave: The Rise and Fall of Feminism in America*, Chicago, Quadrangle Books, 1969. On the social purity movement, see David J. Pivar, *Purity Crusade: Sexual Morality and Social Control, 1868–1900*, Westport, Conn., Greenwood Press, 1973.

5. The establishing legislation, New York *Laws of 1890*, Ch. 238, was amended by *Laws of 1899*, Ch. 632, dropping the maximum term of commitment to three years.

6. In New York, the men's prison most comparable to the Albion reformatory was the State Reformatory at Elmira. According to Elmira's *Annual Report for 1900* (pp. 50-3), reporting conviction offences on 9933 inmates received since the institution's opening in 1876, these offences broke down as follows:

	Number	Per cent
Offences against property	9076	91.4
Offences against the person	808	8.1
Offences against the peace	49	0.5
Totals	9933	100.0

Of the sample of inmates received at Albion 1894–1931 (see table 1, below), 1.2 per cent were convicted of violent crimes, 13.7 per cent of property crimes and 81.4 per cent of public order crimes (equivalent to the Elmira category of offences against the peace). That most Elmira prisoners were convicted of more serious offences than Albion inmates is further confirmed by taking the conviction offences of prisoners admitted to the Elmira Reformatory in a later year, 1920, and coding them into the categories used for the Albion data:

Comparison of Conviction Offences of Men Received, 1920, at the New York State
Reformatory for Men at Elmira and of Sample of Women Received 1923–25 at the
Western House of Refuge at Albion, New York.

| | Elmira | | Albion | |
	Number	Per cent	Number	Per cent
Violent	135	19.7	4	3.2
Property	535	78.0	17	13.4
Public order	7	1.0	93	73.2
Other	9	1.3	13	10.2
Totals	686	100.0	127	100

Sources: New York State Reformatory, Annual Report for 1920, p. 461: New
York State Archives, Western House of Refuge for Women, Inmate
Admission Ledgers (sample based on every odd-numbered case received).

7. The phrase is taken from a registry entry for case no. 107; see note 28 below
and accompanying text.
8. On 'true women', see Barbara Welter, 'The Cult of True Womanhood, 1820–
1860', American Quarterly, vol. 18, summer 1966, pp. 150-74.
9. In 1931 Albion was closed as a reformatory and turned into an institution for
mentally defective female prisoners. At about the same time, most other
women's reformatories that had restricted their populations mainly or
entirely to misdemeanants began to receive felons. Increasing numbers of
felons eventually pushed female misdemeanants out of state prisons entirely.
10. New York Laws of 1890, Ch. 238, sec. 8.
11. Inmates nos 1246 (Rosetta B.), 1331 (Sarah M.), 1585 (Hattie) and 1431 (Mary
N.).
12. Inmates nos 2185 and 4.
13. Inmate no. 2183.
14. US Department of Commerce, Bureau of the Census, Thirteenth Census of the
United States Taken in the Year 1910. Vol. IV. Population 1910. Occupation Statistics,
Washington, US Government Printing Office, 1914, p. 37.
15. Inmate nos 1713 (Isabel), 1791 (in love with Mr Ludwig) and 1829 (associating
with Washington).
16. See Mark H. Haller, Eugenics: Hereditarian Attitudes in American Thought, New
Brunswick, Rutgers University Press, 1963, esp. chapter VII, and Peter L.
Tyor, '"Denied the Power to Choose the Good": Sexuality and Mental
Defect in American Medical Practice, 1850–1920', Journal of Social History, vol.
10, no. 2, summer 1977, pp. 472-89.
17. New York State Western House of Refuge (hereafter NYSWHR), Annual
Report 1894, pp. 10, 12.
18. NYSWHR, Annual Report 1895, pp. 15-17.

19. New York State Commission of Prisons, *Annual Report 1897*, p. 106; NYSWHR, *Annual Report 1896*, p. 21.
20. NYSWHR, *Annual Report 1912*, p. 13; *Annual Report 1917*, p. 18.
21. NYSWHR, *Annual Report 1917*, p. 14.
22. No doubt some had been satisfactory servants before arrest. However the institution – having no other programme – put them through the full course anyway. For an analysis of domestic service at the time Albion was in operation, see David M. Katzman, *Seven Days a Week: Women and Domestic Service in Industrializing America*, New York, Oxford University Press, 1978.
23. New York State Commission of Correction, *Annual Report 1927*, p. 87.
24. NYSWHR, *Information and Regulations*, Albion, NY, n.d.
25. ibid.
26. Nearly every case file that I examined contained intercepted mail. Female state prisoners today are often nearly as isolated, geographically, as their earlier counterparts – a direct effect of the women's reformatory movement, which deliberately located institutions in the country to isolate their inmates from pernicious influences.
27. Inmate no. 2051.
28. Inmate no. 107.
29. Inmate no. 2233. According to Mary, the father of the child was a state trooper.
30. Mary W. Libby to Clement J. Wyle, 24 October 1941 (letter located by Linda Dwelley, Media Resources, Maine Criminal Justice Academy in Waterville, who planned to send the original to the state archives).
31. Inmate no. 1699.
32. Inmate no. 1701.
33. Mrs J. A. H—— to Mrs Flora Daniels, 28 February 1924, in file of Virginia S., Inmate no. 2157.
34. Inmates nos 79 (the 'wreck') and 1917 (escapee writes to report marriage).
35. Nellie L. to Mrs M. K. Boyd, 8 April 1907, in case file of Inmate no. 18.
36. 'Dependent, defective, and delinquent classes' was common parlance in the later nineteenth and early twentieth centuries; see, for example, US Department of Commerce, Bureau of the Census, *Statistical Directory of State Institutions for the Defective, Dependent, and Delinquent Classes*, Washington, US Government Printing Office, 1919. For explanations of the trend toward institutionalization, see Gerald M. Grob, *Mental Institutions in America: Social Policy to 1875*, New York, Free Press, 1973; Michael B. Katz, 'Origins of the Institutional State', *Marxist Perspectives*, vol. 1, no. 4, winter 1978, pp. 6–22; Anthony M. Platt, *The Child Savers: The Invention of Delinquency*, 2d enlr. ed., University of Chicago Press, 1977; and Andrew T. Scull, *Decarceration: Community Treatment and the Deviant – A Radical View*, Englewood Cliffs, NJ, Prentice-Hall, 1977. The key document of the prison reform movement, which began about 1870, is National Congress on Penitentiary and Reformatory Discipline, *Transactions*, ed. E. C. Wines, Albany, Weed, Parsons and Company, 1871. David J. Rothman discusses turn-of-the-century penal developments in *Conscience and Convenience: The Asylum and its Alternatives*

in Progressive America, Boston, Little, Brown, 1980; and Steven L. Schlossman analyses developments in the treatment of juvenile delinquents in *Love and the American Delinquent: The Theory and Practice of 'Progressive' Juvenile Justice 1825–1920*, University of Chicago Press, 1977. On Lancaster, see Barbara Brenzel, 'Domestication as Reform: A Study of the Socialization of Wayward Girls, 1856–1905', *Harvard Educational Review*, vol. 50, no. 2, May 1980, pp. 196-213.

37. Mark Thomas Connelly: *The Response to Prostitution in the Progressive Era*, Chapel Hill, University of North Carolina Press, 1980, p. 18.

13

The Rationalization of Crime Control in Capitalist Society

STEVEN SPITZER*

> If the economic take-off of the West began with the techniques that made possible the accumulation of capital, it might perhaps be said that the methods of administering the accumulation of men made possible a political take-off in relation to the traditional, ritual, costly, violent forms of power, which soon fell into disuse and were superseded by a subtle, calculated technology of subjection.
>
> *Michel Foucault* Discipline and Punishment

The regulation of social life under capitalism obviously requires the use of force to secure public order and intimidate the working class, as well as protect the assets, profits and all concrete forms of capital itself. It is this feature of crime control, with its emphasis on the overt and repressive control of labour by capital, which has received the majority of the 'new criminology's' attention.[1] However, if we are successfully to situate the study of crime control within the entire political economy of capitalist society, we must recognize that legally based coercion emerged as part of a far more general historical process. We will describe this process as the *rationalization of social relations*, and argue in the discussion that follows that it has significantly shaped and provided the framework for changes in the social organization of crime control under capitalism. More specifically, we will suggest that historically specific forms of legally based coercion which have emerged over the last two centuries represent both a reflection of and a basis for the progressive rationalization of social life in capitalist societies.

Source: Contemporary Crises, vol. 3, 1979, pp. 187–206.

*Portions of this analysis are based on work which was discussed at the New York University Institute in Radical Criminology, July 1977, and The Second National Conference on Critical Legal Studies, November 1978.

For purposes of our analysis it will be useful to sketch some of the most salient features of the 'tendency towards rationalization' in capitalist society. In examining this tendency it is essential that we recognize it as part of a dialectical process. Viewed dialectically, the rationalization of crime control can be seen as part of the necessary, yet contradictory, relationship between specific forms of social regulation and the transformation of capitalist society. Moreover, since a dialectical perspective posits 'the simultaneous existence of stabilizing and disruptive elements',[2] we can investigate continuities and directions in the historical development of crime control without either missing the pattern exhibited in general historical tendencies (e.g. the decomposition of feudal structures, the centralization of control, bureaucratization, etc.), or turning those tendencies into ineluctable laws. Marx provides an excellent illustration of how one type of dialectical process operates in his analysis of the 'tendency' of the rate of profit to fall:

> We have thus seen in a general way that the same influences which produce a tendency in the general rate of profit to fall, also call forth counter-effects, which hamper, retard, and partly paralyze this fall. The latter do not do away with the law, but impair its effect. Otherwise, it would not be the fall of the general rate of profit, but rather its relative slowness, that would be incomprehensible. Thus, the law acts only as a tendency. And it is only under certain circumstances and only after long periods that its effects become strikingly pronounced.[3]

If we take Marx's method seriously, then we must keep in mind that the 'tendency towards rationalization' in capitalist societies not only characterizes the movement of social formations in a single direction, but also tends to 'call forth counter-effects, which hamper, retard, and partly paralyze' this movement.

As capitalism has become the dominant mode of production in the world economy, it has progressively eliminated qualitative, human and individual attributes from the productive system. This process of *depersonalization* has not only transformed the relationship of the working class to the means of production, the product of their labour, and each other;[4] it has also come to govern the mechanisms through which more and more social behaviour is regulated, coordinated and managed. The traditional social institutions which depended on 'personal' forms of domination, i.e. the family, church, community, patrimonial authority, etc., have given way in favour of 'rational–legal' forms. While

the organic unities of pre-capitalist societies organized their
metabolism largely in independence of each other, the 'natural laws'
of capitalist production have been extended to cover every
manifestation of life in society – for the first time in history – the
whole of society is subjected, or tends to be subjected, to a unified
economic process, and . . . the fate of every member of society is
determined by unified laws.[5]

The rise of the capitalist market economy, 'which demands that the official
business of the administration be discharged precisely, unambiguously,
continuously, and with as much speed as possible',[6] thus has not only
transformed production relations in particular, it has reorganized social
life in general. In order to pave the way for its development, capital has
continuously turned traditional social relationships into matters of
exchange between isolated social atoms, thereby promoting a progressive
decomposition of social relations which are not founded upon *calculable
rules*. In this sense, all structures of authority and methods of social control
(both formal and informal) have been transmuted as both a precondition
for and a consequence of capitalist expansion. On the one hand, this pattern
of change has involved the destruction of 'private' prerogatives and
traditional claims to status and privilege in favour of 'public' (rational-
legal) forms of authority. On the other hand, this process has encouraged
the separation of the subjects of administration and exploitation (the
masses) from the pre-bureaucratic institutions, practices and loyalties
which bound them to the old order. In Marx's formulation, 'the formation
of the political state and the dissolution of civil society into independent
individuals, who are related by law just as the estate and corporation men
were related by privilege, is completed in one and the same act'.[7] In
Weber's terms, 'mass democracy makes a clean sweep of feudal,
patrimonial, and – at least in intent – the plutocratic privileges in
administration. Unavoidably it puts paid professional labour in place of the
historically inherited avocational administration of notables.'[8]
    Viewed from the perspective of changes in systems of coercive control,
the rationalization of social relationships has promoted the development of
what Foucault calls 'the disciplinary society'.[9] In general, such a society
seeks continuously to 'insert the power to punish more deeply into the
social body'. The distinctive feature of this power is that, in contrast to
earlier pre-capitalist forms, it is *impersonal*. Unlike the highly symbolic,
personalized and often savage punishments of pre-capitalist societies and
pristine states,[10] a rationalized system seeks 'to substitute for a power that
is manifested through the brilliance of those who exercise it, a power that
insidiously objectifies those on whom it is applied; to form a body of

knowledge about these individuals, rather than to deploy the ostentatious signs of sovereignty'.[11] When understood in these terms, the emergence of public policing, bureaucratized court systems, modern prisons and, indeed, even criminology itself was part of a more 'preventive', 'calculable' and 'professional' approach to social regulation and surveillance. The external trappings of this process are most easily recognized as capitalist inventions to legitimate and tighten the hold of the ruling class over the working and 'redundant' classes.[12] But at their core these developments were much more than simple by-products of class conflict: they were part of a comprehensive rationalization process – a significant step in establishing what Foucault calls the modern 'technology of subjection'.

One of the most important aspects of the rationalization of social life associated with the triumph of the capitalist mode of production has been the *intensification* of regulatory controls. Proceeding on both the economic and the political levels, this intensification has brought about a revolution in the management of domestic populations. Just as Foucault speaks of the deeper insertion of punishment into the social body, we may argue that capitalism has made possible and stimulated the development of a whole new range of devices and strategies which are far more effective in harnessing the labour power and productive potential of the labouring classes, regimenting and synchronizing the behaviour of the masses and insuring their continued compliance. With the expansion of public authority and public law,[13] the greater centralization and hierarchicalization of the political order, as well as the extension of managerial controls over the entire production process,[14] it has become possible to treat the working and dependent classes in a unique way. While slavery-based, feudal and monarchic structures of domination were dependent on *extensive, indirect* and *ceremonial* forms of coercive regulation, capitalism was able to transform relations of production and domination in such a way that controls could become far more *intensive, direct* and *banal*.

Under feudal and patrimonial forms of domination, it was only possible to rule 'at-a-distance'. One reason for this was the political incapacity of ruling elites. The limited technical ability and superintending resources of the pre-capitalist state made it difficult to penetrate the day-to-day lives of subject populations. In consequence, techniques of managing social conduct tended to be indirect, crude and sluggish, and in many cases *ad hoc*. For example, at an early level of political development it was necessary for certain patrimonial and feudal rulers to establish a system of *collective liability* to effect even nominal control over social behaviour. This arrangement, typified in the English system of the frankpledge,[15] provided a mechanism for enforcing compliance by holding entire local populations responsible for the conduct of their members. Lee describes how this system of collective responsibility operated under the early Anglo-Saxon Kings:

> the Hundred . . . was a group of ten tythings, under a responsible head. Hundreds as well as tythings had definite police functions to perform: when a crime was committed, information had to be at once given to the hundred-men and tything-men of the district, and it was their duty to pursue, arrest, and bring to justice all peace-breakers. In the event of non-appearance of a culprit at the court of justice to which he was summoned, his nine fellow pledges were allowed one month in which to produce him, when, if he was not forthcoming, a fine was exacted, the liability falling, in the first place, on any property of the fugitive that might be available, in the second place, on the tything, and – should both these sources prove insufficient to satisfy the claim – on the Hundred. Furthermore, the headboroughs were required to purge themselves on oath, that they were not privy to the flight of the offender, and swear that they would bring him to justice if possible.[16]

A structurally similar, although far more sophisticated and hierarchicalized, system was organized in China under the Ch'ing dynasty during the seventeenth and eighteenth centuries. This system, known as the *pao-chia* is described by Hsiao.

> Each inhabitant was required to report to his *pao-chia* head the presence of criminals and the commission of criminal or culpable acts; the *pao-chia* heads were responsible for reporting them to the local authorities. The failure of anyone to perform the required duty would bring punishment not only upon himself but upon all his neighbors who belong to his ten-household group. Since obviously the police duties of the *pao-chia* could be carried out only if records of the inhabitant were available, the imperial government imposed penalties on any person who failed to register. . . . Under this system the people became potential informers against wrongdoers or lawbreakers among their own neighbors – in other words, they were made to spy upon themselves. Such mutual fear and suspicion were instilled in their minds that few of them dared to venture into seditious schemes with their fellow villagers. Thus, even if individual criminals could not be completely eliminated, the opportunity for instigating concerted uprisings was greatly reduced.[17]

At least in principle, systems such as the frankpledge and *pao-chia* would seem to permit a reasonable degree of control over the manners, morals and rebellious tendencies of local communities. In practice, however, their efficacy as modalities of fine-grained rule were frequently compromised. As Lee points out,

> it [the frankpledge] can only be applied with success to an agricultural community that is content to live always in the same spot, or whose migratory instincts the authorities are prepared to suppress; and . . . such a system puts a premium both on the concealment of crime, and on the commission of perjury, since a tything had every inducement to forswear itself in order to escape the infliction of a fine or to save one of its members.[18]

In China, as well, compliance became a problem, 'since landowners had a stronger motive than other inhabitants to evade registration'. Not surprisingly, 'the law provided heavier punishment for such delinquency among them'.[19] But even these penalties eventually proved inadequate, and 'as time went on, disturbances occurred, and the authorities had to raise bands of militia to deal with them, thus acknowledging the inadequacy of the *pao-chia* machinery'.[20] In other words,

> it appears that the *pao-chia* proved an effective deterrent only in times of relative tranquility when few of the rural inhabitants were driven by desperation to 'tread the dangerous path'; but in a period of general unrest the *pao-chia* was no more able than any other instrument of imperial control to operate with peace-time efficiency . . . [21]

In sum, the absence of direct information about miscreants, the centrifugal pressures of local power centres, as well as the structural incentives to avoid collective penalties, militated against the use of 'integral systems' such as the frankpledge and *pao-chia* as systematic and reliable methods of crime control. Although the effectiveness of these systems could be increased by more aggressive administration,[22] their basic incompatibility with pre-capitalist forms of social, economic and political organization limited their overall utility as mechanisms of social control.

In other instances of pre-capitalist social organization, political control was achieved by a combination of bribery, the use of paid informants and the judicious cultivation and/or intimidation of local leaders. In these cases, ruling-at-a-distance required the articulation of elite and sub-elite interests in such a way that general patterns of exploitation and domination could be superimposed on existing relations of production and dependence. Under conditions of this sort, most commonly found in certain redistributive economics and hydraulic civilizations,[23] political and economic objectives were frequently achieved by co-opting and monitoring local power centres. In order for the co-optation to prove effective, however, a chain of legal liability had to be forged between the masses, their immediate overlords, and the dominant elite.[24] An interesting example of these relationships is found in Tokugawa Japan, where:

> In order to maintain the Shogunate and warrior supremacy, the primary concern of the new positive law was to enforce compliance with the status law by a harsh law of crimes. The technique was to give the representatives of groups both unfettered authority and complete responsibility for the performance and conduct of the group members based on principles of vicarious liability. Individuals were subordinated summarily to the authority of their chief, who was responsible to the Shogunate for their conduct; against their chief they had no legal rights, only the duty to obey. Within this authoritarian framework the whole area of 'private law' was left largely to the customary practice of the locale, to be enforced by the local authorities.[25]

The fact that local elites had to be kept in place and manipulated under Tokugawa law, rather than totally destroyed, is one indication of the political and ideological weaknesses characteristic of certain types of pre-capitalist states. Moore describes the operation of another such arrangement under the Inca empire:

> another important consideration is the jealous guarding of power and sumptuary symbols on the part of central government. While local rulers were not removed when conquered, and while they were not stripped of their property, neither did they enjoy their previous governing powers. They could not exploit the local population for their own ends beyond a fixed point. But it is unnecessary to assume that this was entirely a question of central government benevolence. . . . Far more probably, there was a great concern lest there be rebellion against the central government or competition with it for resources. Even the Inca governors, who must have formed a relatively trusted inner circle, were spied on, checked on, and limited by law to dependence on the Inca for some sumptuary articles. This fear of local strength suggests that a good deal of local power and loyalty remained in the conquered kingdoms.[26]

But the reliance on indirect controls was not limited to early empires and 'despotic' societies. Even in late eighteenth- and early nineteenth-century England we can find evidence of social controls which were established and improvised in the absence of effective means of direct surveillance and punitive certainty. In this case, the techniques used seemed to reflect the relative underdevelopment of a fiscal base,[27] resistance to political centralization,[28] and the lingering hegemony of the squirarchy and their preference for ceremony, paternalism and private rule.[29] Crime control in eighteenth-century England was based on the theory that fear and greed could be harnessed as a single force to orchestrate a type of popular-based discipline of the 'criminal classes'. Without an effective public police system or other mechanisms to 'penetrate the social body', domestic pacification could only be attempted by expanding the number of offences punishable by death,[30] on the one hand, and broadening the network of rewards and pardons to stimulate 'community responsibility'[31] on the other. Unable to rely upon either direct supervision or bribed sub-elites to achieve regulation of refractory urban populations, the strategy of crime control came to be based on suspicion, betrayal and appeals to the self-interest of the criminal and respectable classes alike. In Pringle's words, the architects of legal controls came to ask 'private individuals for no higher motive than self-interest, and were confident that they could, by a system of incentive and deterrents – rewards and punishments, bribes and threats – so exploit human greed and fear that there would be no need to look for anything so nebulous and unrealistic as public spirit'.[32]

In contrast to the Inca and Tokugawa patterns, evil-doers in eighteenth-century England could not be managed 'by proxy' through manipulation of traditional sub-elites. The social organization of crime control in this instance was thus *emergent* rather than imposed. The peculiar relationship between weak government and disorganized community life, on the one hand, and the widespread use of rewards to encourage co-operation, on the other, led to the appearance of at least one type of relatively specialized group mediating between the errant masses and the ruling elite – the 'thief-takers'. As middle-men between thieves and victims, and as operatives on both sides of the law, thief-takers were in a strategic position to establish an *imperium in imperio*: a concentration of local power over criminal classes which had to be acknowledged, if not condoned, by the state.[33] Although thief-takers were typically receivers of stolen property themselves, they were regularly called upon to regulate and provide official access to the 'nether world of crime',

Perhaps the most notorious and powerful of the thief-takers who operated at this time was Jonathan Wild. By the 1720s Wild was able to establish a virtual monopoly over thief-catching, receiving and thieving in southern England. As the 'Thief-taker General', Wild organized a lucrative enterprise as a broker in stolen goods and became a quasi-legitimate precursor to the modern English police.[34] The paradoxical position that he occupied as a 'subcontractor' in both crime and its control is perhaps best illustrated by the fact that, before his career was cut short by public execution in 1725, he was called upon by the Privy Council to supply advice 'about ways and means to check the growing number of highway robberies'.[35] By straddling the ill-defined boundary between crime and law enforcement, Wild became the personification of a system which could neither separate the thief-taker from the thief, nor penetrate the local milieu within which crime had become a way of life. It should be clear from this example how 'second-hand' methods of the sort established in eighteenth-century England not only fail to achieve the regulation of the underclass, but may actually encourage the very behaviours they were created to suppress.[36]

One further technique which was common under pre-capitalist forms of political organization was the use of mercenaries to govern and/or suppress local populations. In situations where indigenous leaders and local functionaries could not be trusted, patrimonial or feudal elites frequently brought in paid agents to administer, tax or coerce local groups. The objective in these instances was to insure loyalty by 'the use of officials who did not come from socially privileged strata, or even were foreigners, and who therefore did not possess any social power and honor of their own but were entirely dependent for these on the lord'.[37] As long as these mercenaries were alien (*stammfremd*) to the subjects, they were less likely to sympathize with or support those over whom they were expected to rule.

The advantages of mercenary-based control thus derived from its ability to: (1) insulate the immediate administrators and regulators from community ties, and (2) insure that supervision was organized in the direct interest of the sovereign. But these relational characteristics of the mercenary system were also its fatal flaw. Since mercenaries were necessarily 'private' representatives of those who could afford their services, it was virtually impossible for them to legitimate their actions in the eyes of those they ruled. Although they might claim that they were acting to restore 'public' order and protecting 'public' interests, it was highly unlikely that mercenaries could convince the subject population that they were enforcing anything other than the sovereign's personal rules. The absence of a legitimate foundation for mercenary power, at least in their role as managers of domestic populations, meant that this form of social regulation frequently proved unstable. The politically transparent and personal character of this sort of coercion for profit, as well as the fiscal limitations of pre-capitalist states,[38] restricted its use to situations where rebellion was imminent or traditional forms of 'self-policing' had completely broken down.

But in spite of its origins in pre-capitalist systems of domination, it is interesting to note that, under a limited set of circumstances, mercenary-based policing could provide the basis for establishing a capitalist order. In the 'company towns', which grew rapidly in America during the post-bellum period,[39] a variety of factors combined to stimulate the development of mercenary-based controls.[40] Despite their contribution to rapid industrialization and the 'take-off' of the capitalist mode of production, these company towns were frequently modelled after the feudal manors of an earlier era. At least initially, relations between workers and the 'captains of industry' were paternalistic, combining the immigrant labourer's willingness to judge 'the economic and social behavior of local industrialists by . . . older and more humane values'[41] with the proclivities of these industrialists towards a personal style of rule. However, under the pressure of working-class militancy in the last quarter of the nineteenth century and the unreliable and sometimes hostile reactions of local enforcement officials,[42] industrialists began to look outside the local community to obtain more effective repressive controls. The hiring of private police during this period thus represented an effort on the part of industrial elites to preserve their hegemony and economic superiority within 'closed towns'. Strike-breaking and labour espionage were among the most important services provided by agencies like the Pinkerton's,[43] who were quite willing to provide 'private police' under conditions where local enforcement was either inadequate or antagonistic to the interests of the capitalist class.

The demise of this 'big stick' system in America was related to: (1) the decline of company towns, (2) the 'socialization' of the costs of labour control, (3) the increased power of organized labour, and (4) major changes in the economic infrastructure itself.[44] But no matter what its proximate causes, it is clear that the use of mercenaries to divide and coerce an industrial proletariat was only possible under a peculiar combination of historical circumstances associated with primary capital accumulation and rapid industrial growth. As closed towns were gradually engulfed by and absorbed into the increasingly atomized and impersonal society of twentieth-century corporate America, the structural supports for the mercenary system were swept away along with the patrimonial relationships upon which it was built. Moreover, once it was no longer possible to achieve a 'monopoly by exclusion' in company towns, it became evident that the private authority under which mercenaries operated had to give way in favour of 'publicly' legitimated (rational–legal) forms of coercive control.

Another example of the transitional character of mercenary-based control is found in the use of 'collaborators' in the Rhodesian mining industry at the beginning of the twentieth century.[45] In this instance of colonially imposed primary industry, indigenous groups were utilized to perform policing functions, but only after their social distance from the majority of African workers had been insured. Demonstrating Weber's assertion that mercenaries must be alien to those they control, Van Onselen points out that, 'in many cases, collaborators were selected because of their social distance from the majority of Africans amongst whom they would work. The social remoteness of the collaborators would ensure that they held loyalties distinct from those of the majority of the group and this fact in turn could be utilized by the settlers for political control.'[46] In fact, the decision to select a particular tribe (the Ngoni) for policing service was based on the judgment that they 'would have little in common with the local Shona communities and thus were unlikely to be allied with them in any future revolt. Further, being isolated from local pressures and sympathies, the Ngoni police could more readily assist in the collection of taxes which would in turn facilitate the flow of labour to the mines.'[47] In this case, as in the instance of American company towns, it is clear that a mercenary system could only flourish as long as a 'monopoly by exclusion' could be maintained. Moreover, the inherently unstable character of these arrangements forced them to serve as temporary, rather than long-standing, solutions to the problems of imposing political and economic controls.[48]

Up to this point, we have been examining the ways in which the political shortcomings of pre-capitalist social formations provided fertile ground for the development of control arrangements which formed part of a system of 'indirect rule'.[49] But if we are to understand how crime control has become part of a far more direct and intensive system of social regulation, we must also consider the economic forces which have supported and shaped these political arrangements. Prior to the emergence of full-blown capitalist economies, most state systems treated their populations as economic resources in a very limited sense. For the most part, domestic populations under slavery-based, feudal, 'Asiatic' and mercantile productive systems were regarded as a relatively inexhaustible reservoir of wealth and labour. The orientation of pre-capitalist elites towards the labouring and dependent classes and their efforts to regulate these classes were thus both *extractive* and *extensive*. These economies were socially extractive in the sense that the economic value of the masses was defined almost completely in terms of the level of surplus-product that could be pumped out of the working class under existing conditions of social and economic organization. The system thus 'proceeded essentially by levying'; and, at least in its European form, it was based on 'levying on money or products by royal, seigniorial, ecclesiastical taxation, levying on men or time by *corvées* or press-ganging, by locking up or banishing vagabonds'.[50] Because the productive capacities of domestic populations were assumed to be finite – limited by the physical and mental capacities which were brought to the work setting – there was little, if any, attention to qualitative improvement of or investment in the workforce. Accordingly, methods of controlling and exploiting domestic populations were primarily *extensive*, treating both labour power and material wealth as fixed quantities which could only be increased by expanding the *extent* of exploitable resources (land, labour, raw materials, etc.) available to the governing elite.

In a word, what was of paramount importance to pre-capitalist elites was the *number* of labourers who could be employed and the *proportion* of their absolute wealth (surplus-product) which could be appropriated by them. Because economic relationships were cast in these terms, the rulers limited their interest in the masses to: (1) establishing the amount of deployable surplus and labour (including military labour) that could be plundered, taxed, tythed and otherwise transferred from the working classes to the elite, and (2) insuring the willingness of domestic populations to acquiesce in these arrangements. Under these conditions,

> the majority of the population was affected less by what the state did to them than by what it did not do to them in order to preserve their taxpaying capacity. The peasant, that is, was exploited for taxes, he was occasionally impressed into the army, he was compelled to perform various kinds of (mostly locally inspired) forced labour on roads, buildings or manor; but he was otherwise hardly touched by central policies. In his habits of work and leisure, in his beliefs and values, he was barely affected by interests of state or by any rationalizing pressure.[51]

As long as the minimum conditions of domination and exploitation could be met, that is, as long as sufficient levels of tribute and obedience were forthcoming, there was little reason for patrimonial, feudal, and other pre-capitalist elites to establish direct control over and supervision of the habits, motives, and private lives of their subjects. Since pre-capitalist regimes were far more interested in the *results* than the *methods* of exploitation, the details of social administration could be 'farmed out',[52] 'subcontracted' or otherwise delegated to representatives, agents, intermediaries or existing local elites without doing violence to either the foundations or the mechanisms of class rule. The forms of mediated and decentralized rule that were discussed above, despite their many contradictions and chronic flaws, were thus reflective of economic as well as political priorities in many pre-capitalist states.

The decisive break with the extractive and extensive approach to economic organization and social control came as the result of two major forces: (1) the progressive rationalization of productive and social relationships, and (2) the revolutionizing of administrative practices and principles under the modern capitalist state. The increasing pressure for the rationalization of production and all spheres of social existence on which production was based can be traced to the growing demands for capital accumulation and its prerequisite productive efficiency. The efficiency of production, it was learned, could be increased not only by promoting the division of labour, but also by two additional innovations: first, by taking into account and gaining control over the social environment within which production takes place, and, second, by taking into account and gaining control over human labour as a 'factor of production', i.e., treating living labourers more and more as 'instruments of production'. Capitalist development thus came to be predicated upon economic rationalization, which came to depend in turn on both the regularization of the social context which surrounds and conditions all economic activity on the one hand, and the cultivation and investment in *human capital* on the other. These developments created enormous pressure on traditional institutions and policies of social regulation. And despite its claims to be based on principles of *laissez-faire*, as capitalism sought to free itself from the fetters and limitations of feudal society it was forced to tighten rather than loosen its grip on the everyday lives of domestic populations. If capitalism was to triumph it was no longer possible to: (1) ignore the background, training and social development of the workforce, (2) allow discretionary control over populations by self-interested intermediaries or local elites, or (3) permit social relationships outside of the productive sphere to either evolve at random or be governed by traditional (pre-capitalist) priorities or sources of authority.

These developments signalled a significant shift in the long-standing theory and practice of exploitation in class societies. Instead of viewing domestic populations as 'finished products', available for simple and direct exploitation, these populations came increasingly to be seen as potential sources of investment. From the point of view of the new (capitalist) logic, these investments should be made for the same reason all other prudent investments were made – to yield profit and provide a further basis for capital accumulation. The management of domestic populations could thus no longer be extensive and extractive; it had to become *intensive* and based on the concept of sound investment. The need to distinguish between 'good' and 'bad' investments in human capital stimulated a further development: the emergence of screening, sorting and classifying institutions for people processing, e.g. schools, welfare systems, therapeutic facilities, prisons, etc. And as capitalism continued to dissolve the traditional institutions of socialization, integration and social regulation, i.e. the family, church, community, etc., bureaucratic institutions became more and more important as mechanisms to differentiate and supervise categories of 'worthy' and 'unworthy' human material.[53]

At the same time that these pressures for the penetration of the individual developed, there was a concomitant push for the penetration of the external (social) world. This push, which was based on the same imperatives of capitalist growth, has taken the form of *internalization*: the effort to identify, take into account and manipulate what were previously unpredictable, disruptive and potentially costly 'externalities' through a single, centralized and highly rationalized system of administration.[54] At the very minimum, the regulation of external relations required the maintenance of social order: the preservation of predictable, stable patterns of social intercourse. Accordingly, it became more and more important to eliminate outbreaks of discontent and disorder.[55] In contrast to the pre-capitalist era, where collective disorder had served as a form of communication between the classes,[56] the new order required that social relationships remain pacific, if only to guarantee that production and exchange were not impaired. But domestic tranquillity was only the first step in the penetration of social life. As profits under capitalism have come to depend less on price competition and costs of production[57] and more on maintaining monopolistic control over markets and elevating levels of demand, the cultivation of consumer habits, the creation of 'consumption communities'[58] and the shaping of consciousness itself[59] have become the *sine qua non* of capitalist growth. It was in this sense that rationalization has meant not only the extension of control and supervision over individual (private) existence, but the increasing management and regulation of social existence as well.

In order to pervade more thoroughly the depths of private and public existence and overcome the 'irrationalities' of pre-capitalist rule, it was necessary to establish a mechanism to articulate, coordinate and direct the rationalization process. This mechanism was the modern capitalist state. In the first stages of its development, capitalism's reliance upon the state was limited to its role in creating the *infrastructure* for capital accumulation. The development of infrastructure took two forms: physical and social. The physical infrastructure includes such 'social overhead capital' as harbours, roads, bridges, canals and railways that 'require much greater outlays of capital than the individual entrepreneur can normally be expected to get access to', and that 'take a long time to construct and even longer to yield a substantial profit'.[60] The social infrastructure, on the other hand, comprises all those institutions, habits, casts of mind and patterns of social intercourse which promote the development of the capitalist economic order. In establishing the social infrastructure the state is called upon to guarantee public order, regulate conditions of production, distribution and exchange, and provide the structural supports necessary for the emergence of a mature market system. It was the provision of social infrastructure that led, among other things, to the initial socialization of crime controls in England and America during the nineteenth century.[61]

But as capitalism evolved, the state was called upon to take a more and more active role in the solution of its chronic problems. In addition to establishing the *minimum* conditions for capital accumulation, the state was forced to become more *affirmative* in character: to take a more active and direct role in the guidance, coordination, planning and support of economic activity. This shift from *reactive* to *promotive* involvement has become more and more pronounced as the problems confronting capitalist societies have changed in both degree and kind. And because of the relationship between economic development and social control outlined above, the state has become increasingly involved in the habituation, supervision, training and pacification of domestic populations. Under the spur of the rationalization process, proprietary, hereditary and other pre-bureaucratic forms of indirect rule were gradually replaced by hierarchically organized 'public' organizations. These organizations, which came to include what we know today as the criminal justice system, were specially designed to achieve a more thorough and effective penetration of subject populations and to remain more responsive to the dictates of central authority. The pre-capitalist state had to depend on the cooperation of intermediaries to achieve its relatively modest goals, but with the bureaucratization of state administration it became possible to transform the cumbersome process of indirect and personal rule into an impersonal and 'objective' system of centralized command.[62] Just as the economic development of capitalism required the supplanting of the early capitalist's personal authority with that of the impersonal corporation,[63] and the unification of independent production and distribution units within a unitary economic complex (the vertically integrated corporation), its political development required the substitution of centralized state bureaucracies for the decentralized pockets of personal rule and the unification of previously autonomous arenas of power. Bureaucratization attacked all forms of local discretion by removing managerial authority from direct overseers to bureaus which were directly accountable to the executive, suppressing special privileges attached to hereditary or proprietary offices, and removing 'unauthorized opportunity for profit in the office' including bribery, graft and embezzlement, 'which had earlier constituted the normal sources of remuneration for officials'.[64] In each of these ways an attempt was made to 'reform' the administration of local populations and more effectively concentrate authority in the political apparatus of the state. The history of the development and reform of crime control agencies can quite easily be read as one tendency within this more general process.

THE CONTRADICTIONS OF RATIONALIZED CONTROL

Thus far we have been concerned only with the general tendency towards the rationalization of social control in capitalist societies. It will be useful to remind ourselves, however, that rationalization is only a tendency, not a law, and to remain aware of some of the major contradictions in the rationalization process. Even though the streamlining, regimentation and synchronization of social life can be understood as part of the movement towards a 'totally administered society',[65] it is quite obvious that the rationalization imperative has also called forth forces which have impeded, undermined and come into conflict with this trend.

Some of the most obvious counter-effects include: (1) the enormous social costs and political problems created by the corrosive effects of capitalist development on traditional social institutions and modalities of informal control (the family, church, community, etc.) – effects which were a necessary consequence of the destruction of 'pockets of resistance' and other impediments to the levelling and atomization of subject populations for both economic and political purposes; (2) the growing problems associated with the management of superfluous populations – populations rendered 'socially useless' by the progressive increase in the organic composition of capital[66] and the movement of capitalism from its accumulation to its disaccumulation phase;[67] (3) the conflicts associated with the continued legitimation of the increasingly differentiated and hierarchicalized social order – differentiation and ordering which is essential to rational population management and the new forms of economic organization, but which none the less comes into conflict with the levelling ideology of equality and democratic participation in capitalist societies;[68] (4) the creation of new 'pockets of resistance' to the rationalization process: special interest groups, e.g., professionals,[69] civil servants, bureaucratic functionaries, unionized workers, who were themselves formed as mechanisms to destroy structures of privilege and to facilitate rationalized people-processing in an earlier age; and (5) the fact that, while the arena for the development of capitalism's productive forces has been increasingly narrowed to the sphere of 'human services', i.e. health, education, welfare, crime control,[70] these are the very areas which are most likely to be contracted or eliminated as capitalism faces the fiscal crisis of the state.[71] While it is still too early to tell whether these contradictions can provide strategic levers for social change and the creation of a viable alternative to the capitalist order, it is clear that the rationalization process that we have described is neither 'functional' in a narrow sense, nor one of capitalism's inexorable laws.

As it moves along its twisted course, capitalism requires an ever-changing ensemble of strategies to meet new crises. In the current period the 'remedy' is clearly based upon the 'privatization of profit' and the 'socialization of costs'. But this strategy can only be carried to a certain point because of the deepening contradictions upon which it is based. While the expansion of productive forces requires a policy of investment in human capital, these same forces are removing more and more human labour from the productive process.[72] As the social costs of capitalist growth continue to increase it becomes more and more important to divert both human and non-human resources from social expenses to social investment. While the privatization of public services has permitted advanced capitalism to turn some social expenses into forms of social investment – mainly by encouraging the growth of certain profit-making human service industries, i.e. foster care, remedial education, home health care, franchised day care centres and old age homes,[73] it is clear that many coercive 'public' functions (law enforcement, imprisonment, etc.) cannot be carried out under private auspices without eroding the rational–legal legitimations upon which the broader structure of hegemonic control must be built. Finally, even though many of the damaging effects of 'ordinary crime' can be directly 'socialized' by forcing certain segments of capitalist societies to bear the brunt of their costs[74] as both victims (through property loss, physical and mental injuries and death) and consumers (through the costs of security devices, private police patrols, personal armaments, etc.), it is clear that there are finite political, economic and ideological limits beyond which the destructive consequences of capitalist growth cannot be heaped upon its labouring and dependent classes.

Through an understanding of these and other contradictions in capitalist development it will be possible to locate the study of crime control within a materialistic, historical and dialectical perspective. And, if we take the complexity and variability of these relationships seriously, it will also be possible to construct a framework within which the political economy of crime control can begin to take on a far more systematic and empirically grounded form.

NOTES AND REFERENCES

1. Good examples of this approach to the study of crime control may be found in R. Quinney (1974), *Critique of Legal Order: Crime Control in Capitalist Society*, Boston: Little, Brown; Center for Research on Criminal Justice (1975), *The Iron Fist and Velvet Glove: An Analysis of the U.S. Police*, Berkeley: Center for Research on Criminal Justice; and S. Harring and L. M. McMullen (1975), 'The Buffalo Police 1872–1900: Labor Unrest, Political Power and the Creation of the Police Institution', *Crime and Social Justice*, 4, 5-15.
2. B. Johnson (1976), 'Taking Care of Labor: The Police in American Politics', *Theory and Society*, 3, 90.
3. K. Marx (1974), *Capital: A Critique of Political Economy*, vol. 3, London: Lawrence and Wishart, p. 239.
4. K. Marx (1964), *The Economic and Philosophic Manuscripts of 1844*, ed. Dirk J. Struik, New York: International Publishers.
5. G. Lukacs (1971), *History and Class Consciousness*, Cambridge, Mass.: M. I. T. Press, pp. 91-2.
6. M. Weber (1946), *From Max Weber: Essays in Sociology*, ed. H. H. Gerth and C. Wright Mills, New York: Oxford University Press, p. 215.
7. K. Marx (1977) 'On the Jewish Question,' in D. McLellan (ed), *Karl Marx: Selected Writings*, London: Oxford University Press, p. 56.
8. Weber (1946), pp. 224–5.
9. M. Foucault (1977), *Discipline and Punish: The Birth of the Prison*, New York: Pantheon Books.
10. See D. Hay (1975), 'Property, Authority and the Criminal Law', in D. Hay, P. Linebaugh, J. G. Rule, E. P. Thompson, and C. Winslow (eds) *Albion's Fatal Tree: Crime and Society in Eighteenth-Century England*, New York: Pantheon Books, pp. 17-63; and also S. Spitzer (1975a), 'Punishment and Social Organization: A Study of Durkheim's Theory of Penal Evolution', *Law and Society Review*, 9, 613-37.
11. Foucault (1977), p. 220.
12. See S. Spitzer (1975b), 'Toward a Marxian Theory of Deviance', *Social Problems*, 22, 638-51.
13. The emergence of public law under capitalism permits the unprecedented juxtaposition of the 'subjective' individual and the 'objective' law. As Weber (1946), p. 239 notes, 'only with the bureaucratization of the state and of law in general can one see a definite possibility of separating sharply and conceptually an "objective" legal order from the "subjective rights" of the individual which it guarantees: of separating "public" law from "private" law. Public law regulates the interrelationships of public authorities and their relationships with the "subjects"; private law regulates the relationships of the governed individuals among themselves. This conceptual separation

presupposes the conceptual separation of the "state", as an abstract bearer of sovereign prerogatives and the creator of "legal norms", from all personal "authorizations" of individuals. These conceptual forms are necessarily remote from the nature of pre-bureaucratic, and especially from patrimonial and feudal, structures of authority.'

14. See H. Braverman (1974), *Labor and Monopoly Capital*, New York: Monthly Review Press.
15. W. L. M. Lee (1901), *A History of Police in England*, London: Methuen and Co., Chapter 1.
16. ibid., pp. 4-5.
17. K. C. Hsiao (1960), *Rural China: Imperial Control in the Nineteenth Century*, Seattle: University of Washington Press, pp. 45-6.
18. Lee (1901), p. 13.
19. Hsiao (1960), p. 45.
20. S. Van Der Sprenkel (1962), *Legal Institutions in Manchu China*, London: Athlone Press, p. 47.
21. Hsiao (1960), p. 55.
22. Ching-Chih Chen (1975), 'The Japanese Adaptation of the *Pao-Chia* System in Taiwan, 1895–1945', *Journal of Asian Studies*, 34, 406, argues that 'In contrast to their Ch'ing predecessors, the Japanese authorities pursued an aggressive approach in the administration of Taiwan, regardless of the exploitative nature of their colonial policy. To fulfil their goals, the Japanese set up a strong and efficient government. As a result, they were able to control the *pao-chia* system and keep it under close, well-organized bureaucrative surveillance from the moment the system was legalized. And it was their efficient police system that determined, in large part, the success of the *pao-chia*.' Nevertheless, Chen also notes that there were instances of militia units revolting against the Japanese authorities and *pao-chia* headmen failing to report plots as was their duty.
23. K. Wittfogel (1957), *Oriental Despotism: A Comparative Study of Total Power*, New Haven: Yale University Press.
24. On the implications of this type of control system in Japan see E. D. Genovese (1974), *Roll, Jordan, Roll: The World the Slaves Made*, New York: Pantheon Books.
25. D. F. Henderson (1964), *Conciliation and Japanese Law: Tokugawa and Modern*, vol. 1, Seattle: University of Washington Press, p. 61.
26. S. F. Moore (1958), *Power and Property in Inca Peru*, New York: Columbia University Press.
27. G. Ardant (1975), 'Financial Policy and Economic Infrastructure of Modern States and Nations', in C. Tilly (ed.), *The Formation of National States in Western Europe*, Princeton, NJ: Princeton University Press, pp. 164-242.
28. E. Barker (1944), *The Development of Public Services in Western Europe, 1660–1930*, London: Oxford University Press.
29. Hay (1975).
30. L. Radzinowicz (1948), *A History of English Criminal Law and Its Administration from 1750*, vol. 1, London: Stevens and Sons Ltd.
31. P. Pringle (1958), *The Thief-Takers*, London: Museum Press.

32. ibid., p. 212.
33. P. Rock, 'Law, Order and Power in Late Seventeenth and Early Eighteenth Century England', Chapter 8 above.
34. F. Howson (1970), *Thief-Taker General: The Rise and Fall of Jonathan Wild*, London: Hutchinson.
35. ibid., p. 125.
36. See S. Spitzer and A. T. Scull (1977a), 'Social Control in Historical Perspective: From Private to Public Responses to Crime', in David F. Greenberg (ed.), *Corrections and Punishment*, Beverly Hills: Sage, pp. 281-302.
37. M. Weber (1968), *Economy and Society*, vol. 3, in, eds Guenther Roth and Claus Wittick, New York: Bedminster Press, p. 1043.
38. See Weber (1968) and Ardant (1975).
39. S. Brandes (1976), *American Welfare Capitalism*, Chicago: University of Chicago Press.
40. S. Spitzer and A. T. Scull (1977b), 'Privatization and Capitalist Development: The Case of the Private Police', *Social Problems*, 25, 18-29.
41. H. Gutman (1963), 'The Worker's Search for Power'. In H. W. Morgan (ed.), *The Gilded Age: A Reappraisal*, Syracuse: Syracuse University Press, p. 43.
42. Johnson (1976).
43. J. D. Horan (1967), *The Pinkertons*, New York: Crown Publishers.
44. See Spitzer and Scull (1977b).
45. C. Van Onselen (1973), 'The Role of Collaborators in the Rhodesian Mining Industry 1900–1935', *African Affairs*, October, 401-18.
46. ibid., p. 403.
47. ibid., p. 404.
48. In the Rhodesian case some of the precariousness and inefficiency of the system was associated with the fact that the colonials depended on a spoils system to bond the collaborators to their coercive roles. As Van Onselen (1973, p. 408) observes, 'These opportunities for acquiring spoils must have made the role of collaborator more attractive for some Africans, but they also draw attention to another aspect of the collaborators – their notorious unreliability in the eyes of their settler masters. All the collaborators – police, recruiters, compound police and messengers alike – were considered unreliable and likely to abuse their authority unless under close personal supervision of settlers. The nature, frequency and similarity of these abuses, however, leave little doubt that they should be attributed not so much to personal weakness of the Africans concerned but rather to the nature of the roles which collaborators were called on to fill.'
49. For a discussion of 'indirect rule' in colonial Africa see C. K. Meek (1970), *Law and Authority in a Nigerian Tribe: A Study in Indirect Rule*, New York: Barnes and Noble: and H. F. Morris and J. S. Read (1972), *Indirect Rule and the Search for Justice*, Oxford: Clarendon Press. While the term 'indirect rule' has been developed in these studies to describe the dynamics of British colonial rule, it can easily be broadened to encompass all those forms of political administration which, in the transition from stateless to state societies, depend upon the cultivation of existing forms of decentralized authority.

50. Foucault (1977), p. 219.
51. J. T. Moffett (1971), 'Bureaucracy and Social Control: A Study of the Progressive Regimentation of the Western Social Order', unpublished PhD dissertation, Columbia University.
52. The practice of 'farming out' was in no sense restricted to the organization of political control over domestic populations. It became, for example, an important economic prop for the expansionist monarchies of Europe who could find no other mechanism to increase their fiscal base. As Moffett (1971, pp. 112-13) notes, 'under . . . circumstances of irregular budgets, uncertain revenues, and erratic financial practices, the crown could typically . . . raise money only by mortgaging the patrimony of the crown. Tax farming led the way among these practices. Tax-farming was perpetuated largely as the crown was forced to sell monopoly rights over the collection of various state revenues to creditors as security on state borrowing. . . . But tax-farming was only one of the large number of fiscal expedients devised and perpetuated due to the financial position of the king in the nation, practices which included the mortgaging of royal mines (or mining rights), tolls, estates, commercial rights, and other remunerative prerogatives, and the sometimes wholesale marketing of offices in the army, the church, the courts and in other areas of state administration. The practice of farming out state fiscal, legal and military administration to private individuals or corporations merges imperceptibly with the outright sale of administrative office; that is, essentially the sale or rental of monopoly rights over some lucrative source of income, which together with the mortgaging of the patrimony of the state, places an indelible stamp on pre-19th century state administration.' Also in this connection see our (Spitzer and Scull, 1977a) discussion of 'deviant farming' in England.
53. See G. V. Rimlinger (1966), 'Welfare Policy and Economic Development: A Comparative Historical Perspective,' *Journal of Economic History*, 26, 556-71; and Foucault (1977).
54. Spitzer and Scull (1977b).
55. See A. Silver (1967), 'The Demand for Order in Civil Society: A Review of Some Themes in the History of Urban Crime, Police and Riot', in D. Bordua (ed.), *The Police*, New York: John Wiley; and K. Polyani (1944), *The Great Transformation*, Boston: Beacon.
56. See E. P. Thompson (1971), 'The Moral Economy of the English Crowd in the Eighteenth Century', *Past and Present*, 50, 76-136.
57. See P. Baran and P. Sweezy (1966), *Monopoly Capital*, New York: Monthly Review Press; and J. O'Connor (1974), *The Corporations and the State*, New York: Harper and Row.
58. D. J. Boorstin (1973), *The Americans: The Democratic Experience*, New York: Vintage Books, pp. 89-174.
59. S. Ewen (1976), *Captains of Consciousness*, New York: McGraw-Hill.
60. P. Dean (1969), *The First Industrial Revolution*, Cambridge: Cambridge University Press, p. 69.
61. See Spitzer and Scull (1977a).

62. See Weber (1968).
63. On the process of depersonalization in the economic development of capitalism see A. D. Chandler (1962), *Strategy and Structure: Chapters in the History of the American Industrial Enterprise*, Cambridge, Mass.: M.I.T. Press; and Braverman (1974).
64. Moffett (1971), pp. 126–7.
65. H. Marcuse (1964), *One Dimensional Man*, Boston: Beacon Press.
66. Spitzer (1975b).
67. M. J. Sklare (1969), 'On the Proletarian Revolution and the End of Political-Economic Society', *Radical America*, 3, 1–41.
68. Weber (1946, chapter 8) was well aware of this contradiction in capitalist development, which he summarized in the observation that the levelling which accompanies the advance of political democracy makes possible an unprecedented subjugation of the masses to central authority. R. Jacoby (1975), *Social Amnesia: A Critique of Contemporary Psychology from Adler to Laing*, Boston: Beacon Press, pp. 108–12, has also examined this process in his discussion of 'repressive equality' which is 'progressive in its democratic content against feudal privilege, and regressive in that it is ultimately grounded in the market of "equal" exchange and works to further the domain of the market'. See also F. Neumann (1957), *The Democratic and the Authoritarian State*, New York: Free Press, chapter 2.
69. On the resistance to rationalization by lawyers' guilds in England see Weber (1946, p. 21); and on the relationship between bureaucracy and professionalization see M. S. Larson (1977), *The Rise of Professionalism*, Berkeley: University of California Press.
70. One measure of this development is the percentage of the labour force involved in the provision of social services. A recent analysis of labour force transformations (J. Singlemann, 1978, 'The Sectoral Transformation of the Labor Force in Seven Industrialized Countries, 1920–1970', *American Journal of Sociology*, 73, 1224-34) disclosed that social service workers had increased as a percentage of the total labour force in the United States from 8.7 per cent in 1920 to 21.5 per cent in 1970. This more than twofold increase over the last 50 years also occurred in such capitalist nations as Germany (2.9 times), France (2.8 times), Canada (2.8 times), England (2.2 times) and Japan (2.1 times).
71. See J. O'Connor, *The Fiscal Crisis of the State*, New York: St Martin's Press; and L. Hirschhorn (1978), 'The Political Economy of Social Service Rationalization: A Developmental View', *Contemporary Crises*, 2, 63-81.
72. See Sklare (1969) and Spitzer (1975b).
73. See S. Spitzer and A. T. Scull (1977c), 'The Privatization of Public Services: The Case of the Private Police', paper presented at the 72nd Annual Meeting of the American Sociological Association.
74. See my discussion (Spitzer, 1975b) of 'containment' and 'selective victimization' in connection with this form of 'socializing' the costs of crime.

Author Index

Subject Index